Youth and Dissent

Books by Kenneth Keniston

THE UNCOMMITTED

YOUNG RADICALS

Youth and Dissent

The Rise of a New Opposition

by KENNETH KENISTON

NEW YORK

HARCOURT BRACE JOVANOVICH, INC.

For Ann and Sarah

"The Sources of Student Dissent," *The Journal of Social Issues,* July, 1967, 23:108–37; copyright © 1967 by The Society for the Psychological Study of Social Issues.

"Dropouts: Development through Discontinuity" (as "Psychosocial Issues in Talented College Dropouts"), *Psychiatry,* with Stephen J. Hirsch, February, 1970, 33:1, 1–20; copyright, The William Alanson White Psychiatric Foundation, Inc.; reprinted by permission.

"Idealists: The Perils of Principle" (as "Student Activism, Moral Development and Morality"), *American Journal of Orthopsychiatry,* July, 1970, 40:4, 577–92; copyright, the American Orthopsychiatric Association, Inc.; reproduced by permission.

"The Speed-up of Change" (as "Social Change and Youth in America") and "Faces in the Lecture Room" are reprinted by permission of *Daedalus.*

ISBN 0–15–199890–6

Library of Congress Catalog Card Number: 71–160404

Printed in the United States of America

B C D E

Contents

Introduction   *vii*

Prologue: Youth as a Stage of Life   *3*

I. *The Roots of Youthful Dissent*

The Decline of Utopia   *27*
The Speed-up of Change   *58*
The Political Revival   *81*
Faces in the Lecture Room   *99*
The University as Critic   *127*
The Sources of Student Dissent   *143*

II. *Faces of Dissent*

The Alienated: Rejection of Conventional Adulthood   *173*
Dropouts: Development through Discontinuity
(with Stephen J. Hirsch)   *189*
Radicals: Renewal of the Tradition   *213*
Drug Users: Heads and Seekers   *230*
Idealists: The Perils of Principle   *253*
Radicals Revisited: Some Second Thoughts   *269*

III. *The Two Revolutions*

Youth, Change, and Violence   *287*
You Have to Grow Up in Scarsdale   *303*
What's Bugging the Students?   *318*
Vulnerabilities of the Counterculture   *339*
Scenarios of Confrontation   *344*
The Unholy Alliance (with Michael Lerner)   *352*

Epilogue: Revolution or Counterrevolution?   *369*

Acknowledgments   *401*

Introduction

THE essays in this volume span a decade of dissent that began with American students slumbering in the doldrums of the Eisenhower Administration and ended with the murders at Kent State, Jackson State, and the University of Wisconsin. In 1960, the age of ideology was allegedly over, consensus politics reigned, and class warfare had been brought to its knees at the collective-bargaining table. By 1970, ideology was again rampant, the consensus of the previous decade had splintered, and one social analyst was describing student unrest as the emerging "class warfare" of postindustrial society. Future historians will doubtless attribute this change, dramatically sudden by any standard, to a variety of factors: to the deeply divisive effects of American involvement in Vietnam, to the revolution of rising but unfulfilled expectations of American blacks, to the apparent thaw in the Cold War.

But no event in this decade was more significant than the rise of a youthful opposition—a dissenting order of the young, a counterculture of the educated, privileged children of the American dream, who found the society they were to inherit failing and flawed. The emergence of this opposition was totally unexpected. In 1960, the "silence" of youth during the previous decade was taken even by the most revolutionary social critics as evidence that advanced industrial societies had effectively "socialized" the young to their purposes. The intellectual apparatus of sociology, political science, and psychology had organized itself to explain why this was inevitable. Powerful "systems of social control," it was argued, suppressed "deviants" and guaranteed "social equilibrium" and "incremental change" without conflict. Even the "beat generation," the much-publicized rebels of the late 1950's, seemed to confirm the theory of the acculturating power of American society. For the beats were largely ineffective in their actions, privatistic in their social criticism, cultural and aesthetic in their orientation, and essentially apolitical. Moreover, the speed with which they were engulfed by the mass media—transformed from rebels into celebrities—seemed to demonstrate the impossibility of rebellion in a highly industrialized society.

To be sure, even in 1960, there were premonitions and rumblings. But they went unheeded, for they rarely took political form. In the late 1950's, at the elite colleges and universities, one sensed an undercurrent of skepticism, disaffection, and alienation. A few courageous black students had, in early 1960, inaugurated the first sit-ins, which would expand into the Civil Rights Movement, then the Black Power Movement, the Black Muslims and Black Panthers, and the powerful militancy of blacks in the last few years of the decade. In the late fifties, on one or two campuses, like Chicago and Wisconsin, lonely groups of radical graduate students began the effort—still woefully incomplete in 1970—to define a "New" Left. But for all of these premonitions the overwhelming majority of American students and young people in 1960 were politically apathetic, accepting, and inert.

By 1970, the situation had changed profoundly. As one index of this change, the percentage of students agreeing with the statement "America is a sick society" rose steadily after 1960, until in 1970 a solid majority agreed. In the apocalyptic mood of May, 1970, three-quarters of American college students believed that "basic changes" were necessary to improve the quality of life in American society, while only 19 per cent believed that basically the system was "on the right track." Almost half believed that these changes were most likely to come from "radical pressures from outside the system" instead of from traditional institutions, like government, politics, and business. The events of the spring of 1970—Cambodia, Kent State, Jackson State—brought out 1.5 million students in demonstrations throughout the country, a number and a proportion never before seen in American history. A few weeks later Americans deemed "campus unrest" the nation's number-one problem. And in the Congressional-election campaign of November, 1970, the Republican Party, led by Vice President Agnew and President Nixon, made the issue of campus violence a prime campaign issue and held their losses to a minimum. By 1970, the youthful opposition in all of its forms was in the center of the political arena.

There is no need to overstate the extent of youthful disaffection in order to stress its significance. Polls and statistics are subject to multiple interpretations; for example, even in May, 1970, half of the students polled still believed that the traditional institutions of social change were capable of producing the needed "basic changes" in American society. And when we include nonstudents among the youthful population, their voices are overwhelmingly in support of the *status quo*. Even now the youthful opposition—the counterculture—comprises a minority of the young, and by conventional political standards it is a fractured, tattered, and ineffectual movement. Those who stress the complexity and variety of American youth therefore continue to be correct, while the assertion that most young Americans "believe in" American society was as true in 1970 as it was in 1960.

But what is significant is how much less true it is today than it was a decade ago. The emergence of several million oppositional young Americans, largely concentrated at the most selective and prestigious colleges, is much weightier historically and politically than is the persistence of a majority who do not dissent. These dissenters are selectively drawn from among those who have benefited most from American society: they are usually the products of its most favored families; they have been the best educated; and they are, by traditional standards, those most likely to assume the national leadership in the future. Opposition among today's young, far from springing from deprivation, poverty, or discrimination, springs from affluence, wealth, and privilege. Never before have so many who had so much been so deeply disenchanted with their inheritance.

The essays that follow are a chronicle, a description, and an effort to explain the emergence of an oppositional culture of youth. Apart from their focus on dissenting students during the 1960's, they share several other themes. For one, I believe that the emergence of a youthful counterculture is an event that can be understood only psychohistorically. It involves the interaction of individual personalities in all of their complexity, depth, and changeability with new social, cultural, and educational conditions. Merely psychological accounts neglect all of those determinants of human conviction and action that profoundly affect the psyche but do not originate within it. But accounts that consider changes only in the social, political, and historical environment equally neglect the capacity of individual personalities to transform, organize, and distort historical reality in unique and often unpredictable ways. Thus on the one hand I have been critical of those who saw in youthful dissent "nothing but" Oedipal rebellion or "adolescent acting-out"; but on the other hand I have also argued against those who see the youthful opposition as but a simple "reflection" of the real economic, social, and cultural forces that allegedly motor history.

The validity of a psychohistorical approach is constantly brought home to me by my daily research, which consists of extended conversations with individual students, often prolonged over a period of years. These conversations, or "research interviews," differ from psychotherapy in that it is *I* who ask the help of my research subjects (though, at times, they claim they gain something as well). Were the contract to be reversed so that my primary obligation was to help *them* accommodate themselves to the world as it is, I would perhaps be more impressed than I am with the primary and decisive power of intrapsychic forces. But the experience of interviewing a great many young men and women, each of whom differs in countless ways from the others, and hearing them all voice similar sentiments, anxieties, or fears impresses upon the listener (or at least upon this listener) how much young men and women share with each other, even in their most intimate lives. This fact in turn demands explanation: is the community of the educated young a product of their stage in life, of their youth? And if so, what does their shared "youthfulness" consist of? Or is their community a result of their shared social situation as students, as privileged members of American society, as citizens of the twentieth century? And if so, what does it mean humanly to be young, educated, American, and to live in the last third of the twentieth century?

My answer, spelled out in the pages that follow, is that what the contemporary young share is a product of both their psychological youth and their historical condition—an interaction between a peculiar stage of development, postadolescent yet preadult, that is emerging on a mass scale in our own time *and* an historical situation that contains new contradictions and ambiguities with which all of the young and old must cope in some way. And to me, the most challenging questions concern the relation of these psychological and historical forces. How, for example, has accelerating historical change altered the nature of psychological experience and the extent and form of human development? And how do young men and women with a new psychological orientation affect the history of their time?

The essays here collected try to deal with such questions. These essays fall into three groups. First are a series of pieces, largely written in the early 1960's, that set the stage on which youthful dissent was to emerge at Berkeley and thereafter. These essays consider the absence of utopian thinking in American life, the impact of accelerating social change, and the changed role of the university. They go on to examine the "political revival" in the early sixties, and on to a more general consideration of the sources of student dissent. Together, these essays set a backdrop for what has happened since.

The second group of essays consists of studies of particular types of students, mostly dissenters, with whom I have concerned myself over the last ten years. I have studied alienated students, dropouts, radicals, drug users, idealists, and once again radicals. These essays are, as it were, close-ups of very small groups I have studied intensively. Some of what I wrote is no longer true. For example, the radicals of Vietnam Summer, 1967, are today older and wearier, and the Movement from which they drew their strength has since splintered and grown despairing and sometimes ugly or violent. The estimates of drug use I gave only three years ago now seem very low: on dozens of campuses it is the student who has *not* smoked marijuana who is unusual. Even single events can outdate a portrait. The murders of six students at Kent State and Jackson State by civil authorities, like the murder of a graduate student by a group of terrorist bombers at the University of Wisconsin, made clear that neither "repression" nor "terrorism" was simply a paranoid specter conjured up by the extremists of Left and Right. But here I have chosen to leave these portraits untouched, for I believe they were largely accurate in their time.

The third theme in these essays is more broadly interpretative—an attempt to understand youthful dissent in the context of psychohistorical changes that are affecting America and all of the industrialized nations of the world. These essays are united by my conviction that the youthful opposition is not merely an interesting sociological phenomenon, but a political and historical force to be reckoned with. And even more, they are informed by the belief that much of what is happening today in the affluent nations of the world has no historical precedent and therefore cannot be understood in terms of analogies with the past. It was, I think, as unprecedented as it was unexpected for American students, the most privileged group in the most privileged nation in the world, to rise up in arms against the society that had made them.

Rereading these essays has been a chastening experience, since I often failed to anticipate what was to happen, erred in my predictions, or now disagree with the political tone of what I wrote. Students are fond of reminding me, for example, that I wrote in 1963 that I saw little likelihood of American students ever playing a political role, much less a radical role, in our society. On rereading my comments in "The University as Critic," I am today tempted to supplement them with a less euphoric account of the university, stressing the extent to which it has also been an *un*critical agent of the surrounding society. Yet in the end, to update, correct, and emend what I wrote five or ten years ago would be to pretend to an omniscience or a definitively formed position that I did not have. I have therefore made no changes in these essays, only occasionally altering a phrase so as to make what I meant clearer.*

I have no final judgment of the youthful opposition, except that I believe it will continue, in some form, into the foreseeable future. These essays generally reflect my sympathy, and at times my identification, with that opposition. I continue to see youthful dissent as an effort to fulfill the old promises of American society, while identifying and defining the new promises inherent in the affluence and power given man by his modern technology. But I am not certain, or even optimistic, that either set of promises will be fulfilled.

The historical fate of the youthful opposition depends, I believe, not only upon youth, but upon all of us who are not so young. Above all, it depends upon the capacity of our society to respond to the sometimes inarticulate and often strident demands and discontents of the young, and to do so in a way that honors both their intensity and our own experience.

But the fate of the youthful opposition also depends upon those who

* In the interests of readability, I have eliminated most footnotes, references, and other scholarly apparatus. Readers interested in such matters should consult the essays in their original published form, as listed at the end of the Acknowledgments.

are a part of that opposition. The last decade has shown that once the demands of the young become serious and fundamental, and once their tactics become militant, the response of the wider society is often harsh and repressive. A small band of a few million youths have not been able to persuade a nation of 200 million people that their world views and life styles constitute an adequate basis for national policy. The youthful opposition is immensely vulnerable—not only to co-optation and repression, but equally to its own despair and its own potential for self-righteousness. It is indeed asking a lot today to ask the dissenting young to remain true as they grow older to their own principles of love, peace, justice, and the celebration of human life. But ask we must, both of ourselves and of them.

I am not confident that we can respond to the youthful opposition with understanding and change, or that it can respond with humanity and peace. But if together we fail, we may have lost what could have turned out to be the last bright chance to transform—and, by renewing, to preserve—our civilization.

Youth and Dissent

Prologue: Youth as a Stage of Life

*More than a decade's work with college and graduate students has
convinced me that we have no psychology, apart from the work of Erik
Erikson, adequate to understand the feelings and behavior of today's
American youth. Millions of young people today are neither psychological
adolescents nor sociological adults; they fall into a psychological no man's
land, a stage of life that lacks any clear definition. Yet those who occupy
this limbo between adolescence and adulthood today form the core of
the youthful opposition in America as in a dozen other nations of the
world.*

*The very fact that so many millions of young people are in a stage of
life that lacks even a name seems to me one of the most important
psychohistorical facts about modern societies. In this essay I argue that
the unprecedented prolongation of education has opened up opportunities
for an extension of psychological development, which in turn is creating
a "new" stage of life. In a preliminary way I sketch some of the
characteristics of this stage; and I suggest that its central characteristic—
the tension between selfhood and the existing social order—underlies
many of the attitudes and behaviors of contemporary youth.*

*The opening up of youth as a stage of life to millions of young people
seems to me a human advance, whatever its perils and dangers. A
prolonged development can make possible a more autonomous, more
individuated position vis-à-vis the existing society and can permit the
individual to achieve a degree of inner complexity, differentiation, and
integration not vouchsafed those whose development is foreshortened
or foreclosed. Furthermore, the extension of human development means
that we are creating—on a mass scale—a "new" breed of people whose
psychological development not only inclines them to be critics of our own
society, but might even make them potential members or architects of a
better one than ours. Be this as it may, the emergence of a youthful
opposition in the industrialized nations reflects not only changed social,*

economic, political, and moral conditions, but a profound change in the
nature and extent of human development. One reason I remain optimistic
about the potentials of the youthful opposition is because I believe that
among the members of this opposition, there are those whose own
development could begin to provide the psychological basis for a more
truly liberated society.

BEFORE the twentieth century adolescence was rarely included as a
stage in the life cycle. Early life began with infancy and was followed by a
period of childhood that lasted until around puberty, which occurred
several years later than it does today. After puberty, most young men and
women simply entered some form of apprenticeship for the adult world.
Not until 1904, when G. Stanley Hall published his monumental work
Adolescence: Its Psychology and Its Relations to Physiology, Anthropol-
ogy, Sociology, Sex, Crime, Religion, and Education, was this further preadult stage widely recognized. Hall's work went through many editions
and was much popularized; "adolescence" became a household word.
Hall's classic description of the *Sturm und Drang,* turbulence, ambivalence, dangers, and possibilities of adolescence has since been echoed in
almost every discussion of this stage of life.

But it would be incorrect to say that Hall "discovered" adolescence. On
the contrary, from the start of the nineteenth century, there was increasing
discussion of the "problem" of those past puberty but not yet adult. They
were the street-gang members and delinquents who made up what one
nineteenth-century writer termed the new "dangerous class"; they were
also the recruits to the new public secondary schools being opened by the
thousands in the late nineteenth century. And once Hall had clearly defined adolescence, it was possible to look back in history to discover men
and women who had shown the hallmarks of this stage long before it was
identified and named.

Nonetheless, Hall was clearly reflecting a gradual change in the nature
of human development, brought about by the massive transformations of
American society in the decades after the Civil War. During these decades
the "working family," where children labored alongside parents in fields
and factories, began to disappear; rising industrial productivity created
new economic surpluses that allowed millions of teen-agers to remain outside the labor force. America changed from a rural agrarian society to an
urban industrial society, and this new industrial society demanded on a
mass scale not only the rudimentary literacy taught in elementary schools,
but higher skills that could be guaranteed only through secondary education. What Hall's concept of adolescence reflected, then, was a real change
in the human experience, a change intimately tied to the new kind of
industrial society that was emerging in America and Europe.

Today, Hall's concept of adolescence is unshakably enshrined in our view of human life. To be sure, the precise nature of adolescence still remains controversial. Some observers believe that Hall, like most psychoanalytic observers, vastly overestimated the inevitability of turbulence, rebellion, and upheaval in this stage of life. But whatever the exact definition of adolescence, no one today doubts its existence. A stage of life that barely existed a century ago is now universally accepted as an inherent part of the human condition.

In the seven decades since Hall made adolescence a household word, American society has once again transformed itself. From the industrial era of the turn of the century, we have moved into a new era without an agreed-upon name—it has been called postindustrial, technological, postmodern, the age of mass consumption, the technetronic age. And a new generation, the first born in this new era of postwar affluence, television, and the bomb, raised in the cities and suburbs of America, socially and economically secure, is now coming to maturity. Since 1900, the average amount of education received by children has increased by more than six years. In 1900, only 6.4 per cent of young Americans completed high school, while today almost 80 per cent do, and more than half of them begin college. In 1900, there were only 238,000 college students; in 1970, there were more than 7 million, with 10 million projected for 1980.

These social transformations are reflected in new public anxieties. The "problem of youth," "the now generation," "troubled youth," "student dissent," and "the youth revolt" are topics of extraordinary concern to most Americans. No longer is our anxiety focused primarily upon the teen-ager, upon the adolescent of Hall's day. Today we are nervous about new "dangerous classes"—those young men and women of college- and graduate-school age who can't seem to "settle down" the way their parents did, who refuse to consider themselves adult, and who often vehemently challenge the existing social order. "Campus unrest," according to a June, 1970, Gallup Poll, was considered the nation's *main* problem.

The factors that have brought this new group into existence parallel in many ways the factors that produced adolescence: rising prosperity, the further prolongation of education, the enormously high educational demands of a postindustrial society. And behind these measurable changes lie other trends less quantitative but even more important: a rate of social change so rapid that it threatens to make obsolete all institutions, values, methodologies, and technologies within the lifetime of each generation; a technology that has created not only prosperity and longevity, but power to destroy the planet, whether through warfare or violation of nature's balance; a world of extraordinarily complex social organization, instantaneous communication, and constant revolution. The "new" young men and young women emerging today both reflect and react against these trends.

But if we search among the concepts of psychology for a word to describe these young men and women, we find none that is adequate. Characteristically, they are referred to as "late adolescents and young adults" —a phrase whose very mouth-filling awkwardness attests to its inadequacy. Those who see in youthful behavior the remnants of childhood immaturity naturally incline toward the concept of "adolescence" in describing the unsettled twenty-four-year-old, for this word makes it easier to interpret his objections to war, racism, pollution, or imperialism as "nothing but" delayed adolescent rebellion. To those who are more hopeful about today's youth, "young adulthood" seems a more flattering phrase, for it suggests that maturity, responsibility, and rationality lie behind the unease and unrest of many contemporary youths.

But in the end, neither label seems fully adequate. The twenty-four-year-old seeker, political activist, or graduate student often turns out to have been *through* a period of adolescent rebellion ten years before, to be all too formed in his views, to have a stable sense of himself, and to be much further along in his psychological development than his fourteen-year-old high school brother. Yet he differs just as sharply from "young adults" of age twenty-four whose place in society is settled, who are married and perhaps parents, and who are fully committed to an occupation. What characterizes a growing minority of postadolescents today is that they have not settled the questions whose answers once defined adulthood: questions of relationship to the existing society; questions of vocation; questions of social role and life style.

Faced with this dilemma, some writers have fallen back on the concept of "protracted" or "stretched" adolescence—a concept with psychoanalytic origins that suggests that those who find it hard to "settle down" have "failed" the adolescent developmental task of abandoning narcissistic fantasies and juvenile dreams of glory. Thus, one remedy for "protracted adolescence" might be some form of therapy that would enable the young to reconcile themselves to abilities and a world that are rather less than they had hoped. Another interpretation of youthful unease blames society, not the individual, for the "prolongation of adolescence." It argues that youthful unrest springs from the unwillingness of contemporary society to allow young men and women, especially students, to exercise the adult powers of which they are biologically and intellectually capable. According to this view, the solution would be to allow young people to "enter adulthood" and do "real work in the real world" at an earlier age.

Yet neither of these interpretations seems quite to the point. For, while some young men and women are indeed victims of the psychological malady of "stretched adolescence," many others are less impelled by juvenile grandiosity than by a rather accurate analysis of the perils and injustices of the world in which they live. And plunging youth into the "adult world" at an earlier age would run directly counter to the wishes of most youths, who view adulthood with all of the enthusiasm of a condemned man for the guillotine. Far from seeking the adult prerogatives of their parents, they vehemently demand a virtually indefinite prolongation of their nonadult state.

If neither "adolescence" nor "early adulthood" quite describes the young men and women who so disturb American society today, what can we call them? My answer is to propose that *we are witnessing today the emergence on a mass scale of a previously unrecognized stage of life,* a stage that intervenes between adolescence and adulthood. I propose to call this stage of life the stage of *youth,* assigning to this venerable but vague term a new and specific meaning. Like Hall's "adolescence," "youth" is in no absolute sense new: indeed, once having defined this stage of life, we can study its historical emergence, locating individuals and groups who have had a "youth" in the past. But what is "new" is that this stage of life is today being entered not by tiny minorities of unusually creative or unusually disturbed young men and women, but by millions of young people in the advanced nations of the world.

To explain how it is possible for "new" stages of life to emerge under changed historical conditions would require a lengthy excursion into the theory of psychological development. It should suffice here to emphasize that the direction and extent of human development—indeed the entire nature of the human life cycle—is by no means predetermined by man's biological constitution. Instead, psychological development results from a complex interplay of constitutional givens (including the rates and phases of biological maturation) and the changing familial, social, educational, economic, and political conditions that constitute the matrix in which children develop. Human development can be obstructed by the absence of the necessary matrix, just as it can be stimulated by other kinds of environments. Some social and historical conditions demonstrably slow, retard, or block development, while others stimulate, speed, and encourage it. A prolongation and extension of development, then, including the emergence of "new" stages of life, can result from altered social, economic, and historical conditions.

Like all stages, youth is a stage of transition rather than of completion or accomplishment. To begin to define youth involves three related tasks. First, we need to describe the major *themes* or issues that dominate consciousness, development, and behavior during this stage. But human development rarely if ever proceeds on all fronts simultaneously: instead, we must think of development as consisting of a series of sectors, or "developmental lines," each of which may be in or out of phase with the others. Thus we must also describe the more specific *transformations* or changes in thought and behavior that can be observed in each of several "lines" of development (moral, sexual, intellectual, interpersonal, and so on) during youth. Finally, we can try to make clear what youth is *not*. What follows is a preliminary sketch of some of the themes and transformations that seem crucial to defining youth as a stage of life.

Major Themes in Youth

Perhaps the central conscious issue during youth is the *tension between self and society*. In adolescence, young men and women tend to accept their society's definitions of them as rebels, truants, conformists, athletes, or achievers. But in youth, the relationship between socially assigned labels and the "real self" becomes more problematic and constitutes a focus of central concern. The awareness of actual or potential conflict, disparity, lack of congruence between what one is (one's identity, values, integrity) and the resources and demands of the existing society increases. The adolescent is struggling to define who he is; the youth begins to sense who he is and thus to recognize the possibility of conflict and disparity between his emerging selfhood and his social order.

In youth, *pervasive ambivalence* toward both self and society is the rule: the question of how the two can be made more congruent is often experienced as a central problem of youth. This ambivalence is not the same as definitive rejection of society, nor does it necessarily lead to political activism. For ambivalence may also entail intense self-rejection, including major efforts at self-transformation employing the methodologies of personal transformation that are culturally available in any historical era: monasticism, meditation, psychoanalysis, prayer, hallucinogenic drugs, hard work, religious conversion, introspection, and so forth. In youth, then, the potential and ambivalent conflicts between autonomous selfhood and social involvement—between the maintenance of personal integrity and the achievement of effectiveness in society—are fully experienced for the first time.

The effort to reconcile and accommodate these two poles involves a characteristic stance vis-à-vis both self and world, perhaps best described by the concept of the *wary probe*. For the youthful relationship to the social order consists not merely in the experimentation more characteristic of adolescence, but with now more serious forays into the adult world, through which its vulnerability, strength, integrity, and possibilities are assayed. Adolescent experimentation is more concerned with self-definition than are the probes of youth, which may lead to more lasting commitments. This testing, exacting, challenging attitude may be applied to all representatives and aspects of the existing social order, sometimes in anger and expectation of disappointment, sometimes in the urgent hope of finding honor, fidelity, and decency in society, and often in both anger and hope. With regard to the self, too, there is constant self-probing in search of strength, weakness, vulnerability, and resiliency, constant self-scrutiny designed to test the individual's capacity to withstand or use what his society would make of him, ask of him, and allow him.

Phenomenologically, youth is a time of alternating *estrangement* and *omnipotentiality*. The estrangement of youth entails feelings of isolation, unreality, absurdity, and disconnectedness from the interpersonal, social, and phenomenological world. Such feelings are probably more intense during youth than in any other period of life. In part they spring from the actual disengagement of youth from society; in part they grow out of the psychological sense of incongruence between self and world. Much of the psychopathology of youth involves such feelings, experienced as the depersonalization of the self or the derealization of the world.

Omnipotentiality is the opposite but secretly related pole of estrangement. It is the feeling of absolute freedom, of living in a world of pure possibilities, of being able to change or achieve anything. There may be times when complete self-transformation seems possible, when the self is experienced as putty in one's own hands. At other times, or for other youths, it is the nonself that becomes totally malleable; then one feels capable of totally transforming another's life; or creating a new society with no roots whatsoever in the mire of the past. Omnipotentiality and estrangement are obviously related: the same sense of freedom and possibility that may come from casting off old inhibitions, values, and constraints may also lead directly to a feeling of absurdity, disconnectedness, and estrangement.

Another characteristic of youth is the *refusal of socialization* and acculturation. In keeping with the intense and wary probing of youth, the individual characteristically begins to become aware of the deep effects upon his personality of his society and his culture. At times he may attempt to break out of his prescribed roles, out of his culture, out of history, and even out of his own skin. Youth is a time, then, when earlier socialization and acculturation is self-critically analyzed, and massive efforts may be made to uproot the now alien traces of historicity, social membership, and culture. Needless to say, these efforts are invariably accomplished within a social, cultural, and historical context, using historically available methods. Youth's relationship to history is therefore paradoxical. Although it may try to reject history altogether, youth does so in a way defined by its historical era, and these rejections may even come to define that era.

In youth we also observe the emergence of *youth-specific identities* and roles. These contrast both with the more ephemeral enthusiasms of the adolescent and with the more established commitments of the adult. They may last for months, years, or a decade, and they inspire deep commitment in those who adopt them. Yet they are inherently temporary and specific to youth: today's youthful hippies, radicals, and seekers recognize full well that, however reluctantly, they will eventually become older; and that aging itself will change their status. Some such youth-specific identities may provide the foundation for later commitments; but others must be viewed in retrospect as experiments that failed or as probes of the existing society that achieved their purpose, which was to permit the individual to move on in other directions.

Another special issue during youth is the enormous value placed upon change, transformation, and *movement,* and the consequent abhorrence of *stasis.* To change, to stay on the road, to retain a sense of inner development and/or outer momentum is essential to many youths' sense of active vitality. The psychological problems of youth are experienced as most overwhelming when they seem to block change: thus, youth grows panicky when confronted with the feeling of "getting nowhere," of "being stuck in a rut," or of "not moving."

At times the focus of change may be upon the self, and the goal is then to *be moved.* Thus, during youth we see the most strenuous, self-conscious, and even frenzied efforts at self-transformation, using whatever religious, cultural, therapeutic, or chemical means are available. At other times, the goal may be to create movement in the outer world, to *move others:* then we may see efforts at social and political change that in other stages of life rarely possess the same single-minded determination. And on other occasions, the goal is to *move through* the world, and we witness a frantic geographic restlessness, wild swings of upward or downward social mobility, or a compelling psychological need to identify with the highest and the lowest, the most distant and apparently alien.

The need for movement and terror of stasis are often a part of a heightened *valuation of development* itself, however development may be defined by the individual and his culture. In all stages of life, of course, all individuals often wish to change in specific ways: to become more witty, more attractive, more sociable, or more wealthy. But in youth, specific changes are often subsumed in the devotion to change itself—to "keep putting myself through the changes," "not to bail out," "to keep moving." This valuation of change need not be fully conscious. Indeed it often surfaces only in its inverse form, as the panic or depression that accompanies a sense of "being caught in a rut," "getting nowhere," "not being able to change." But for other youths, change becomes a conscious goal in itself, and elaborate ideologies of the techniques of transformation and the *telos* of human life may be developed.

In youth, as in all other stages of life, *the fear of death* takes a special form. For the infant, to be deprived of maternal support, responsiveness, and care is not to exist; for the four-year-old, nonbeing means loss of body intactness (dismemberment, mutilation, castration); for the adolescent, to

cease to be is to fall apart, to fragment, splinter, or diffuse into nothing-
ness. For the youth, however, to lose one's essential vitality is merely *to
stop*. For some, even self-inflicted death or psychosis may seem preferable
to loss of movement; and suicidal attempts in youth often spring from the
failure of efforts to change and the resulting sense of being forever
trapped in an unmoving present.

The youthful *view of adulthood* is strongly affected by these feelings.
Compared to youth, adulthood has traditionally been a stage of slower
transformation, when, as Erik H. Erikson has noted, the relative developmental stability of parents enables them to nurture the rapid growth of their
children. This adult deceleration of personal change is often seen from a
youthful vantage point as concretely embodied in apparently unchanging
parents. It leads frequently to the conscious identification of adulthood
with stasis, and to its unconscious equation with death or nonbeing. Although greatly magnified today by the specific political disillusionments of
many youths with the "older generation," the adulthood = stasis
(= death) equation is inherent in the youthful situation itself. The desire
to prolong youth indefinitely springs not only from an accurate perception
of the real disadvantages of adult status in any historical era, but from the
less conscious and less accurate assumption that to "grow up" is in some
ultimate sense to cease to be really alive.

Finally, youths tend to band together with other youths in *youthful
countercultures*, characterized by their deliberate cultural distance from
the existing social order, but *not* always by active political or other opposition to it. It is a mistake to identify youth as a developmental stage with
any one social group, role, or organization. But youth *is* a time when solidarity with other youths is especially important, whether the solidarity be
achieved in pairs, small groups, or formal organizations. And the groups
dominated by those in this stage of life reflect not only the special config-
urations of each historical era, but also the shared developmental positions
and problems of youth. Much of what has traditionally been referred to as
"youth culture" is, in the terms here used, adolescent culture; but there are
also groups, societies, and associations that are truly youthful. In our own
time, with the enormous increase in the number of those who are entering
youth as a stage of life, the variety and importance of these youthful countercultures is steadily growing.

This compressed summary of themes in youth is schematic and interpretive. It omits many of the qualifications necessary to a fuller discussion,
and it neglects the enormous complexity of development in any one person in favor of a highly schematic account. Specifically, for example, I do
not discuss the ways the infantile, the childish, the adolescent, and the
truly youthful interact in all real lives. And perhaps most important, my
account is highly interpretive, in that it points to themes that underlie

diverse acts and feelings, to issues and tensions that unite the often scattered experiences of real individuals. The themes, issues, and conflicts here
discussed are rarely conscious as such; indeed, if they all were fully con-
cious, there would probably be something seriously awry. Different youths
experience each of the issues here considered with different intensity.
What is a central conflict for one may be peripheral or unimportant for
another. These remarks, then, should be taken as a first effort to summarize some of the underlying issues that characterize youth as an ideal type.

Transformations of Youth

A second way of describing youth is by attempting to trace out the
various psychological and interpersonal transformations that may occur
during this stage. Once again, only the most preliminary sketch of youthful development can be attempted here. Somewhat arbitrarily, I will distinguish between development in several sectors or areas of life, here
noting only that, in fact, changes in one sector invariably interact with
those in other sectors.

In pointing to the *self-society relationship* as a central issue in youth, I
also mean to suggest its importance as an area of potential change. The
late adolescent is only beginning to challenge his society's definition of
him, only starting to compare his emerging sense of himself with his culture's possibilities and with the temptations and opportunities offered by
his environment. Adolescent struggles for emancipation from external
familial control and internal dependency on the family take a variety of
forms, including displacement of the conflict onto other "authority figures." But in adolescence itself, the "real" focus of conflict is on the family
and all of its internal psychic residues. In youth, however, the "real" focus
begins to shift: increasingly, the family becomes more paradigmatic of
society than vice versa. As relatively greater emancipation from the family
is achieved, the tension between self and society, with ambivalent probing
of both, comes to constitute a major area of developmental "work" and
change. Through this work, young people can sometimes arrive at a synthesis whereby both self and society are affirmed, in the sense that the
autonomous reality, relatedness, yet separateness of both is firmly established.

There is no adequate term to describe this "resolution" or the tension
between self and society, but C. G. Jung's concept of *"individuation"*
comes close. For Jung, the individuated man is a man who acknowledges
and can cope with social reality, whether accepting it or opposing it with
revolutionary fervor. But he can do this without feeling his central selfhood overwhelmed. Even when most fully engaged in social role and societal action, he can preserve a sense of himself as intact, whole, and distinct

from society. Thus the "resolution" of the self-society tension in no way necessarily entails "adjusting" to the society, much less "selling out"—although many youths see it this way. On the contrary, individuation refers partly to a psychological process whereby self and society are differentiated internally. But the actual conflicts between men and women and their societies remain, and indeed may become even more intense.

The meaning of individuation may be clarified by considering the special dangers of youth, which can be defined as extremes of *alienation, whether from self or from society.* At one extreme is that total alienation from self that involves abject submission to society, "joining the rat race," "selling out." Here society is affirmed but selfhood denied. The other extreme is a total alienation from society that leads not so much to the rejection of society, as to its existence being ignored, denied, and blocked out. The result is a kind of self-absorption, an enforced interiority and subjectivity, in which only the self and its extensions are granted live reality, while all the rest is relegated to a limbo of insignificance. Here the integrity of the self is purchased at the price of a determined denial of social reality and the loss of social effectiveness. In youth both forms of alienation are often assayed, sometimes for lengthy periods. And for some whose further development is blocked, they become the basis for lifelong adaptations—the self-alienation of the marketing personality, the social alienation of the perpetual dropout. In terms of the polarities of Erikson, we can define the central developmental possibilities of youth as individuation vs. alienation.

Sexual development continues in important ways during youth. In modern Western societies, as in many others, the commencement of actual sexual relationships is generally deferred by middle-class adolescents until their late teens or early twenties: the modal age of first intercourse for American college males today is around twenty, for females about twenty-one. Thus, despite the enormous importance of adolescent sexuality and sexual development, actual sexual intercourse often awaits youth. In youth, there may occur a major shift from masturbation and sexual fantasy to interpersonal sexual behavior, including the gradual integration of sexual feelings with intimacy with a real person. And as sexual behavior with real people commences, one sees a further working-through, now in behavior, of vestigial fears and prohibitions whose origin lies in earlier childhood—specifically, of Oedipal feelings of sexual inferiority and of Oedipal prohibitions against sex with one's closest intimates. During youth, when these fears and prohibitions can be gradually worked through, they yield a capacity for genitality, that is, for mutually satisfying sexual relationships with another whom one loves.

The transition to genitality is closely related to a more general pattern of *interpersonal development.* I will term this the shift from *identicality* to mutuality. This development begins with adolescence* and continues through youth: it involves a progressive expansion of the early-adolescent assumption that the interpersonal world is divided into only two categories: first, me-and-those-who-are-identical-to-me (potential soulmates, doubles, and hypothetical people who "automatically understand everything"); and second, all others. This conceptualization gradually yields to a capacity for close relationships with those on an approximate level of *parity* or similarity with the individual.

The phase of parity in turn gives way to a phase of *complementarity*, in which the individual can relate warmly to others who are different from him, valuing them for their dissimilarities from himself. Finally, the phase of complementarity may yield in youth to a phase of *mutuality*, in which issues of identicality, parity, and complementarity are subsumed in an overriding concern with the other *as other*. Mutuality entails a simultaneous awareness of the ways in which others are identical to oneself, the ways in which they are similar and dissimilar, and the ways in which they are absolutely unique. Only in the stage of mutuality can the individual begin to conceive of others as separate and unique selves and relate to them as such. And only with this stage can the concept of mankind assume a concrete significance as pointing to a human universe of unique and irreplaceable selves.

Relationships with elders may also undergo characteristic youthful changes. By the end of adolescence, the hero worship or demonology of the middle adolescent has generally given way to an attitude of more selective emulation and rejection of admired or disliked older persons. In youth, new kinds of relationships with elders become possible: psychological apprenticeships, then a more complex relationship of mentorship, then sponsorship, and eventually peership. Without attempting to describe each of these substages in detail, the overall transition can be described as one in which the older person becomes progressively more real and three-dimensional to the younger one, whose individuality is appreciated, validated, and confirmed by the elder. The sponsor, for example, is one who supports and confirms in the youth that which is best in the youth, without exacting an excessive price in terms of submission, imitation, emulation, or even gratitude.

Comparable changes continue to occur during youth with regard to

---

* Obviously, interpersonal development, and specifically the development of relationships with peers, begins long before adolescence, starting with the "parallel play" observed at ages two to four and continuing through many stages to the preadolescent same-sex "chumship" described by Harry Stack Sullivan. But puberty in middle-class Western societies is accompanied by major cognitive changes that permit the early adolescent for the first time to develop hypothetical ideals of the possibilities of friendship and intimacy. The "search for a soulmate" of early adolescence is the first interpersonal stage built upon these new cognitive abilities.

parents. Adolescents commonly discover that their parents have feet of clay and recognize their flaws with great acuity. Childish hero worship of parents gives way to a more complex and often negative view of them. But it is generally not until youth that the individual discovers his parents as themselves complex, three-dimensional historical personages whose destinies are partly formed by their own wishes, conscious and unconscious, and by their historical situations. Similarly, it is only during youth that the questions of family tradition, family destiny, family fate, family culture, and family curse arise with full force. In youth, the question of whether to live one's parents' life, or to what extent to do so, becomes a real and active question. In youth, one often sees what Ernst Prelinger has called a "telescoped re-enactment" of the life of a parent—a compulsive need to live out for oneself the destiny of a parent, as if to test its possibilities and limits, experience it from the inside, and (perhaps) free oneself of it. In the end, the youth may learn to see himself and his parents as multidimensional persons, to view them with compassion and understanding, to feel less threatened by their fate and failings, and to be able, if he chooses, to move beyond them.

In beginning by discussing affective and interpersonal changes in youth, I begin where our accounts of development are least precise and most tentative. Turning to more cognitive matters, we stand on somewhat firmer ground. Lawrence Kohlberg's work on *moral development,* especially on the attainment of the highest levels of moral reasoning, provides a paradigmatic description of developments that occur only in youth, if they occur at all. (For a discussion of Kohlberg's three stages of moral development, see "Idealists: The Perils of Principle," pp. 255–56.)

Kohlberg's research suggests that most contemporary Americans, young or old, do not pass beyond the conventional stage of moral reasoning. But some do, and they are most likely to be found today among those who are young and educated. Such young men and women may develop moral principles that can lead them to challenge the existing moral order and the existing society. And Kohlberg finds that the achievement of his highest level, the stage of personal principles, occurs in the twenties, if it occurs at all. Moral development of this type can thus be identified with youth, as can the special moral "regressions" that Kohlberg finds a frequent concomitant of moral development. Here the arbitrariness of distinguishing between sectors of development becomes clear, for the individual can begin to experience the tension between self and society only as he begins to question the absolutism of conventional moral judgments. Unless he has begun such questioning, it is doubtful whether we can correctly term him "a youth."

In no other sector of development do we have so complete, accurate, and convincing a description of a "development line" that demonstrably characterizes youth. But in the area of *intellectual development*, William Perry has provided an invaluable description of the stages through which college students may pass. Perry's work emphasizes the complex transition from epistemological dualism to an awareness of multiplicity and to the realization of relativism. Relativism in turn gives way to a more "existential" sense of truth, culminating in what Perry terms "commitment within relativism." Thus, in youth we expect to see a passage beyond simple views of right and wrong, truth and falsehood, good and evil, to a more complex and relativistic view; and as youth proceeds, we look for the development of commitments within a universe that remains epistemologically relativistic. Once again, intellectual development is only analytically separable from a variety of other sectors—moral, self-society, and interpersonal, to mention only three.

In his work on *cognitive development*, Jean Piaget has emphasized the importance of the transition from concrete to formal operations, which in middle-class Western children usually occurs at about the age of puberty. For Piaget the attainment of formal operations (whereby the concrete world of the real becomes a subset of the hypothetical world of the possible) is the highest cognitive stage possible. But in some youths, there seem to occur further stages of cognitive development that are not understandable with the concept of formal operations. Jerome Bruner has suggested that beyond the formal stage of thought there lies a further stage of "thinking about thinking." This ability to think about thinking involves a new level of consciousness—consciousness of consciousness, awareness of awareness, and a breaking-away of the phenomenological "I" from the contents of consciousness. This breaking-away of the phenomenological ego during youth permits phenomenological games, intellectual tricks, and kinds of creativity that are rarely possible in adolescence itself. It provides the cognitive underpinning for many of the characteristics and special disturbances of youth, for example, youth's hyperawareness of inner processes, the focus upon states of consciousness as objects to be controlled and altered, and the frightening disappearance of the phenomenological ego in an endless regress of awarenesses of awarenesses.

Having emphasized that these analytically separated "lines" of development are in fact linked in the individual's experience, it is equally important to add that they are never linked in perfect synchronicity. If we could precisely label one specific level within each developmental line as distinctively youthful, we would find that few people were "youthful" in all lines at the same time. In general, human development proceeds unevenly, with lags in some areas and precocities in others. One young woman may be at a truly adolescent level in her relationship with her parents, but at a much later level in moral development; a young man may be capable of extraordinary mutuality with his peers, but still be struggling intellectually with the dim awareness of relativism. Analysis of any one person in terms of specific sectors of development will generally show a simultaneous mixture of adolescent, youthful, and adult features. The point, once again, is that the concept of youth here proposed is an ideal type, a model that may help understand real experience but can never fully describe or capture it.

What Youth Is Not

A final way to clarify the meaning of youth as a stage of life is to make clear what it is not. For one thing, youth is not the end of development. I have described the belief that it is—the conviction that beyond youth lie only stasis, decline, foreclosure, and death—as a characteristically youthful way of viewing development, consistent with the observation that it is impossible truly to understand stages of development beyond one's own. On the contrary, youth is but a preface for further transformations that may (or may not) occur in later life. Many of these center around such issues as the relationship to work and to the next generation. In youth, the question of vocation is crucial, but the issue of work—of productivity, creativity, and the more general sense of fruitfulness that Erikson calls generativity—awaits adulthood. The youthful attainment of mutuality with peers and of peerhood with elders can lead on to further adult interpersonal developments by which one comes to be able to accept the dependency of others, as in parenthood. In later life, too, the relations between the generations are reversed, with the younger now assuming responsibility for the elder. Like all stages of life, youth is transitional. And although some lines of development, such as moral development, may be "completed" during youth, many others continue throughout adulthood.

It is also a mistake to identify youth with any one social group, role, class, organization, or position in society. Youth is a *psychological* stage; and those who are in this stage do not necessarily join together in identifiable groups, nor do they share a common social position. Not all college students, for example, are in this stage of life: some students are psychological adolescents, while others are young adults—essentially apprentices to the existing society. Nor can the experience of youth as a stage of life be identified with any one class, nation, or other social grouping. Affluence and education can provide a freedom from economic need and an intellectual stimulation that may underlie and promote the transformations of youth. But there are poor and uneducated young men and women, from Abraham Lincoln to Malcolm X, who have had a youth, and rich, educated ones who have moved straightaway from adolescence to adulthood. And although the experience of youth is probably more likely to occur in the economically advanced nations, some of the factors that facilitate youth also exist in the less advanced nations, where comparable youthful issues and transformations are expressed in different cultural idioms.

Nor should youth be identified with the rejection of the *status quo* or specifically with student radicalism. Indeed, anyone who has more or less definitively defined himself as a misanthrope or a revolutionary has moved beyond youthful probing into an "adult" commitment to a position vis-à-vis society. To repeat: what characterizes youth is not a definitive rejection of the existing "system," but an ambivalent tension over the relationship between self and society. This tension may take the form of avid efforts at self-reform that spring from acceptance of the *status quo,* coupled with a sense of one's own inadequacy vis-à-vis it. In youth the relationship between self and society is indeed problematical, but rejection of the existing society is not a necessary characteristic of youth.

Youth obviously cannot be equated with any particular age-range. In practice, most young Americans who enter this stage of life tend to be between the ages of eighteen and thirty. But they constitute a minority of the whole age-grade. Youth as a developmental stage is emergent; it is an "optional" stage, not a universal one. If we take Kohlberg's studies of the development of postconventional moral reasoning as a rough index of the "incidence" of youth, less than 40 per cent of middle-class (college-educated) men and a smaller proportion of working-class men have developed beyond the conventional level by the age of twenty-four. Thus, "youths" constitute but a minority of their age group. But those who are in this stage of life today largely determine the public image of their generation.

Admirers and romanticizers of youth tend to identify youth with virtue, morality, and mental health. But to do so is to overlook the special youthful possibilities for viciousness, immorality, and psychopathology. Every time of human life, each level of development, has its characteristic vices and weaknesses, and youth is no exception. Youth is a stage, for example, when the potentials for zealotry and fanaticism, for reckless action in the name of the highest principles, for self-absorption, and for special arrogance are all at a peak. Furthermore, the fact that youth is a time of psychological change also inevitably means that it is a stage of constant recapitulation, re-enactment, and reworking of the past. This reworking can rarely occur without real regression, whereby the buried past is re-experienced as present and, one hopes, incorporated into it. Most youthful transformation occurs *through* brief or prolonged regression, which, however benignly it may eventually be resolved, constitutes part of the psychopathology of youth. And the special compulsions and inner states of youth—the euphoria of omnipotentiality and the dysphoria of estrangement, the hyperconsciousness of consciousness, the need for constant motion, and the terror of stasis—may generate youthful pathologies with a

special virulence and obstinacy. In one sense those who have the luxury of a youth may be said to be "more developed" than those who do not have (or do not take) this opportunity. But no level of development and no stage of life should be identified either with virtue or with health.

Finally, youth is not the same as the adoption of youthful causes, fashions, rhetoric, or postures. Especially in a time like our own, when youthful behavior is watched with ambivalent fascination by adults, the positions of youth become part of the cultural stock-in-trade. There thus develops the phenomenon of *pseudo youth*—preadolescents, adolescents, and frustrated adults masquerade as youths, adopt youthful manners, and disguise (even to themselves) their real concerns by the use of youthful rhetoric. Many a contemporary adolescent, whether of college or high school age, finds it convenient to displace and express his battles with his parents in a pseudo-youthful railing at the injustices, oppression, and hypocrisy of the Establishment. And many an adult, unable to accept his years, may adopt pseudo-youthful postures to express the despairs of his adulthood.

To differentiate between "real" and pseudo youth is a tricky, subtle, and unrewarding enterprise. For, as I have earlier emphasized, the concept of youth as here defined is an ideal type, an abstraction from the concrete experience of many different individuals. Furthermore, given the unevenness of human development and the persistence throughout life of active remnants of earlier developmental levels, conflicts, and stages, no one can ever be said to be completely "in" one stage of life in all areas of behavior and at all times. No issue can ever be said to be finally "resolved"; no earlier conflict is completely "overcome." Any real person, even though on balance we may consider him a "youth," will also contain some persistent childishness, some not-outgrown adolescence, and some precocious adulthood in his makeup. All we can say is that, for some, adolescent themes and levels of development are *relatively* outgrown, while adult concerns have not yet assumed full prominence. It is such people whom one might term "youths."

The Implications of Youth

I have sketched with broad and careless strokes the rough outlines of a stage of life I believe to characterize a growing, although still small, set of young men and women. This sketch, although presented dogmatically, is clearly preliminary; it will doubtless require revision and correction after further study. Yet let us for the moment assume that, whatever the limitations of this outline, the concept of a postadolescent stage of life has some merit. What might be the implications of the emergence of youth?

To most Americans, the chief anxieties raised by youth are over social stability and historical continuity. In every past and present society, including our own, the great majority of men and women seem to be, in Kohlberg's terms, "conventional" in moral judgment and, in Perry's terms, "dualistic" in their intellectual outlook. Such men and women accept with little question the existing moral codes of the community, just as they endorse their culture's traditional view of the world. It is arguable that both cultural continuity and social stability have traditionally rested on the moral and epistemological conventionality of most men and women, and on the secure transmission of these conventional views to the next generation.

What, then, would it mean if our particular era were producing millions of postconventional, nondualistic, postrelativistic youth? What would happen if millions of young men and women developed to the point that they "made up their own minds" about most value, ideological, social, and philosophical questions, often rejecting the conventional and traditional answers? Would they not threaten the stability of their societies?

Today it seems clear that most youths are considered nuisances or worse by the established order, to which they have not finally pledged their allegiance. Indeed, many of the major stresses in contemporary American society spring from or are aggravated by those in this stage of life. One aspect of the deep polarization in our society may be characterized psychologically as a struggle between conventionals and postconventionals, between those who have not had a youth and those who have. The answer of the majority of the public seems clear: we already have too many "youths" in our society; youth as a developmental stage should be stamped out.

A more moderate answer to the questions I am raising is also possible. We might recognize the importance of having a *few* postconventional individuals (an occasional Socrates, Christ, Luther, or Gandhi to provide society with new ideas and moral inspiration) but nonetheless establish a firm top limit on the proportion of postconventional, youth-scarred adults our society could tolerate. If social stability requires human inertia—that is, unreflective acceptance of most social, cultural, and political norms—perhaps we should discourage "youth as a stage of life" in any but a select minority.

A third response, toward which I incline, seems to me more radical. To the argument of social stability and cultural continuity, one might reply by pointing to the enormous *in*stabilities and gross cultural *dis*continuities that characterize the modern world. Older forms of stability and continuity have *already* been lost in the postindustrial era. Today it is simply impossible to return to a bygone age when massive inertia guaranteed social stability (if there really was such an age). The cake of custom crumbled long ago. The only hope is to learn to live without it.

In searching for a way to do this, we might harken back to certain strands in socialist thought that see new forms of social organization possible for men and women who are more "evolved." I do not wish to equate my views on development with revolutionary socialism or anarchism, much less with a Rousseauistic faith in the goodness of the essential man. But if there is anything to the hypothesis that different historical conditions alter the nature of the life cycle, then men with different kinds of development may require or be capable of living in different kinds of social institutions. On the one hand, this means that merely throwing off institutional shackles, as envisioned by some socialist and anarchist thinkers, would not automatically change the nature of men, although it may be desirable on other grounds. "New men" cannot be created by institutional transformations alone, although institutional changes may, over the very long run, affect the possibilities for continuing development by changing the matrix in which development occurs.

But on the other hand, men and women who have attained higher developmental levels may be capable of different kinds of association and cooperation from those at lower levels. Relativism, for example, brings not only skepticism but also tolerance of the viewpoints of others and a probable reduction in moralistic self-righteousness. Attaining the stage of personal principles in moral development in no way prevents the individual from conforming to a just social order or even, for that matter, from obeying unreasonable traffic laws. Men and women who are capable of interpersonal mutuality are not for that reason worse citizens; on the contrary, their capacity to be concerned with others as unique individuals might even make them better citizens. Examples could be multiplied, but the general point is obvious: higher levels of development, including the emergence on a mass scale of "new" stages of life, may permit new forms of human cooperation and social organization.

It may be true that all past societies have been built upon the unquestioning inertia of the vast majority of their citizens. And this inertia may have provided the psychological ballast that prevented most revolutions from doing more than reinstating the *ancien régime* in new guise. But it does not follow that this need always continue to be true. If new developmental stages are emerging that lead growing minorities to more autonomous positions vis-à-vis their societies, the result need not be anarchy or social chaos. The result might instead be the possibility of new forms of social organization based less upon unreflective acceptance of the *status quo* than upon thoughtful and self-conscious loyalty and cooperation. But whether or not these new forms can emerge depends not only upon the psychological factors I have discussed here, but even more upon political, social, economic, and international conditions.

I. The Roots of Youthful Dissent

WRITERS on the youthful opposition often attempt to single out one factor as *the* cause for the emergence of an adversary culture of the young. But in my view, any answers to the questions of "Why now?" and "Why in this form?" must be complex ones. As I see it, the roots of the youthful opposition are many, and they have in common only their shared connection to the unprecedented kind of society appearing in the industrialized nations in the last third of the twentieth century.

Starting in 1960, I wrote a series of essays which, taken together, point to some of the intertwined roots of the youthful opposition. The essays examine a series of drastically changed social and historical conditions, which together contribute to an understanding of youthful dissent. I begin by examining the impact of the much-touted "end of ideology," and the reductionist attack on utopian, synthetic, and generous conceptions of the human future. I next turn to the accelerating rate of social, political, and cultural change, seeing in the contemporary speedup of history a major source of the restlessness of youth. In considering the "political revival," I deal more specifically with historic American images of the student, arguing that traditional conceptions of the student-as-apprentice until recently prevented the appearance of a politically oriented youth movement like that found in other industrializing countries. And in "Faces in the Lecture Room," I suggest that it is largely from the newest historical stratum of students—those whom I here call "professionalists"—that visible and vocal dissent is emerging.

"The University as Critic" looks at how the functions of the university have changed, and defines and justifies a concept of a "critical university." And finally, in "The Sources of Student Dissent," I try to show how the trends I have earlier discussed—an altered cultural climate, a new historical situation, changed institutions, and new types of students—interact to produce growing dissent on campus.

None of this constitutes a finished theory of the youthful opposition. But these essays underline the complexity of the factors behind the new youth culture and the resulting inadequacy of any theory that attempts to single out some one factor—generational revolt, war in Southeast Asia, permissiveness, bureaucracy, racism, the impersonal university, etc.—as *the* cause of youthful unrest. Most important, they reflect my continuing conviction that the revolt of many of the ablest of American youth is not simply a repetition of history, but a unique response to a kind of society that has no historical precedent.

The Decline of Utopia

*Between 1956 and 1960, I worked closely with a small group of
undergraduate research subjects at Harvard. In studying their lives and
their attitudes toward the wider society, I was struck by their lack of
enthusiasm about the adulthood American society offered them. This lack
of enthusiasm especially characterized a group of highly "alienated"
students, but it also extended, in less extreme form, to most of their
classmates. Even in 1960, then, American society seemed to me to have
lost much of its capacity to enlist the deepest commitments of its youth.*

*In this essay I attempt to describe and explain the lack of enthusiasm
I observed among so many of these talented and privileged students. My
account places greatest emphasis on broadly ideological factors and, in
particular, on the erosion of utopian and "ideological" thinking during
the Cold War decade that had gone before. Today, with the benefit of
ten years' hindsight, I would place at least equal emphasis upon social,
economic, and political changes—seeing the "end of ideology" school as
a reflection of a particular stage in the history of highly industrialized
societies. Today, furthermore, one need no longer call for the
reinstatement of ideological and utopian thought; on the contrary, one
must also caution against the oversimplification and self-righteousness of
some of the prevalent ideologies.*

*Of one point made in this essay I am even more convinced than when
I wrote it in 1960—namely, that the concepts with which we attempt to
understand our present situation are largely inadequate to the task, and
that we have not yet been able to make that radical reanalysis of the
present that would enable us really to understand ourselves and our
society. In that respect the New Left today remains a largely unfulfilled
promise; but a promise urgently worth working to fullfill.*

THIS is an age that inspires little enthusiasm. In the industrial West,
and increasingly now in the uncommitted nations of the East, ardor is
lacking; instead men talk of their growing distance from one another, from
their social order, from their work and play, and even from the values that
in a perhaps romanticized past seem to have given their lives cohesiveness

and direction. Horatio Alger is replaced by Timon, Napoleon by Ishmael, and even Lincoln now seems pallid before the defiant images of "hoods" and "beats." The vocabulary of social commentary is dominated by terms that characterize this distance: alienation, estrangement, separation, withdrawal, indifference, disaffection, apathy, noninvolvement, neutralism—all these words describe the increasing distance between men and their former objects of love, commitment, loyalty, devotion, and reverence. Alienation, once seen as the consequence of a cruel (but changeable) economic order, has become for many the central fact of human existence, characterizing man's "thrownness" into a world in which he has no inherent place. Formerly imposed *upon* men by the world around them, estrangement increasingly is chosen *by* them as their dominant reaction to the world.

These tendencies can of course be exaggerated in individual cases. As many or probably more men and women lead individually decent and human lives as ever did. There are pockets of enthusiasm in every nation. Old values are clung to the more tenaciously by some as they are disregarded by others. But other facts are equally incontrovertible: that there has seldom been as great confusion about what is valid and good as there is now; that more and more men and women are fundamentally alienated from what their culture offers them; that hopeful visions of the future, idealisms, and utopias become increasingly rare and difficult. In short, the *direction* of cultural change is from commitment and enthusiasm to alienation and apathy.

In the comments to follow I shall take it for granted that this change is taking place and will explore two questions which seem to me important to its understanding: Why are young people increasingly unwilling to accept what their culture offers them? And, closely related to this, why do we lack positive visions of the future?

But before turning to these questions, I should like to consider briefly one possible explanation of alienation—if only to exclude it from consideration here. Several years of research into the psychology of alienation have shown that, as might be expected, unhappy home lives, disillusionments, and unresolved breaks in personal relationships predispose young men to spurn their cultures. But such psychological explanations, however relevant in individual cases, explain both too much and too little. On the one hand, the accidents of an individual's past life are all too often used to "explain away" his present views, as if these could be nothing but a reflection of his own psychic conflicts. A man's views of the world are in fact much more than this; furthermore, an unhappy life can make him perceptive of actual inequities that remain unperceived by his more fortunate fellows. On the other hand, psychological accounts alone are seldom adequate to explain attitudes and stances that characterize large numbers of people simultaneously. To understand these as social phenomena, we must trace the complicated interplay of cultural and historical forces which, by their influence on individual families and the other agencies of "socialization," produce individuals who are unusually sensitized to special aspects of their environment. A more complete account of alienation would seek to detail these influences. Here, however, I will concentrate on only one aspect of the problem—namely, on the cultural context in which and to which predisposed individuals react with alienation.

Coming of Age in America

Growing up is always a problem, whether in Samoa, Nigeria or Yonkers. It entails abandoning those special prerogatives, world views, insights, and pleasures that are defined by the culture as specifically "childish" and substituting for them the rights, responsibilities, outlooks, and satisfactions that are suitable for the culturally defined "adult." Although the concepts of "childish" and "adult" differ from one culture to another, every culture requires *some* change in the child's habitual ways of thinking, feeling, and acting—a change which involves psychic dislocation and therefore constitutes a "problem" for the individual and the culture. The transition may be relatively painless, especially when the adult's role is viewed as the more attractive and children are therefore eager to grow up; it may be eased or hastened by elaborate ceremonials and rites of passage, whose wan vestiges we see in today's graduation-day exercises; or it may be delayed by a socially sanctioned "moratorium" that permits young men and women to experiment with adult identities until they find one that suits them. In societies where the transition to adulthood is unusually painful, young people often form their own "youth culture" with a special set of antiadult values and institutions, in which they can at least temporarily negate the feared life of the adult. But somehow children must be induced to accept their roles as adults if the society is to continue.

Youth culture as we know it in America is a characteristic American transition from childhood to adulthood, a kind of socially ambivalent and indefinitely prolongable moratorium. Central to all forms of youth culture is the absence of a straight and smooth transition to what the culture defines as "adult roles." Instead, the American version of youth culture offers a hiatus—an eddy, a whirlpool, a waiting period, or even a final resting point—in which young men and women adopt a way of life that constitutes a protest against the adult world. It may take the form of being a "hood," being "beat," being "Joe College," being a Bohemian, intellectually rejecting the whole trapping and tradition of American culture or—less obviously—simply being utterly indifferent to the many voices and beckonings of the wider society.

It is important to define "youth culture" broadly enough to include not only those who protest through word or deed, but those who reject through inaction. Overt rebellion, in the sense of programmatic and revolutionary activity, is extremely rare in our society; and even overtly antisocial behavior, despite our fascination with deviance, is relatively rare. Much more common is that covert rejection of society that David Riesman has called "inner emigration," a term broad enough to include not only those who consciously absent themselves from what they see as the "American way of life," but those who remain inwardly silent, apathetic, bored, and uncommitted, even while outwardly going through the motions of participation. To be bored or indifferent to something is in many ways the supreme rejection of it. Even opposition and antagonism constitute recognition of the object; boredom simply denies that its existence is significant. "Silent generations" and "angry young men" share a common rejection of their culture: the first rejecting through lack of response, the other through open opposition.

We would idealize the past if we thought that these problems were unique to individuals of our time: thousands of young men have found it difficult to accept the adulthood which their worlds offered them, many have left accounts of their perplexities, and a few have made significant changes in their cultures as a result of their dissatisfactions. Furthermore, "adolescent rebellion" has always been a special feature of melting-pot America, with its lack of clear traditions and clear definitions of the good life. But in the past those who rejected their cultures were generally the brilliant or tragic exceptions to their age, the Kierkegaardian "individuals" who could not accept the solutions embraced by their fellows. Now, however, it is increasingly the youth who *does* accept adult roles with enthusiasm and without hesitation who is the exception. In the past "adolescent rebellion" has been almost by definition a transient phase, which one "grew out of" later by a genuine acceptance of what the culture offered; what we deal with today is not always so happily resolved.

If, then, "youth culture" is characterized by a rejection of the "adult world" through hostility or indifference, and if this rejection is both more widespread and more enduring than in previous generations, how can we account for the change? In the United States, a number of specific historical factors conspire to augment the importance and possibility of youthful deviance and indifference: the absence of any clear tradition except the rejection of tradition; the relative comfort and ease of life, which gives young men time and implements to express their disaffection; the instability of American families, which provides a reservoir of young people prepared to generalize their private hurts to public plaints, and so on. But I doubt that these factors, important as they are in explaining the particular forms and recruiting policies of American youth culture, suffice to explain its existence—nor are they adequate to explain the Teddy Boys of England, Italy, or Greece, the quickly suppressed hooligans of Moscow, or the rebellious "dry" youth of Japan. A more general explanation of youth culture (and of the present extent of alienation) seems to me to lie in the social and cultural situation created by a highly successful industrial society—a society that asks for more from an adult, offers less in return, and yet encourages higher aspirations than any before it.

Three closely related social trends help to explain the increasing distastefulness of our culture to its potential recruits. One of these is what we might call the gap between the cultural images of the child and of the adult—the first (apperceived as) integral, concrete, immediate, and spontaneous; the other (as) dissociated, abstract, specialized, and conformist. Second, even when the youth is willing to "choose" the adult world as he sees it, it is difficult for him to know *what* to choose; adult roles in our society are ambiguously defined and subject to unpredictable and drastic changes. Finally, the vast increase in our material wealth and power has made us less willing to acquiesce to the nonmaterial deprivations that adulthood seems to involve. Although we are seldom able to articulate our ideals clearly and forcefully, our level of aspiration has increased and the number of conditions we are willing to accept as "inevitable tragedies of life" has correspondingly decreased.

Childhood vs. adulthood. It is by now a sociological commonplace that the high standard of living in industrial societies has been partly the result of an increasing division of labor. Division of labor demands that men do highly specialized jobs in the preparation of the final product; the assembly line, our mythology has it, is more efficient than Henry Ford in his garage. "Efficiency" has historically meant that men were trained to do ever more specific and detailed work with an increasing degree of expertise—sometimes even in traditional occupations like teaching, where efficiency was once considered irrelevant at best. The routine and mechanical nature of work on an assembly line is the classic illustration of this trend toward specialization. But even in highly skilled jobs, "automated jobs," or work in service industries, routine and specialization are almost as marked: watching the controls of a self-regulating machine, feeding cards into a computer, or running a cash register in a supermarket do not differ markedly in this respect from screwing bolts into an incipient refrigerator motor. These jobs have in common that they require highly compartmentalized, specialized work which is monotonous and repetitive, and which, above all, enlists a very small proportion of the worker's total talent and understanding.

They are also alike in their distance from the final use of the work—from the man who sits in the chair made by the automated machine, from the actual receipt of the payments calculated by the computer, or from eating the food bought in the supermarket. Furthermore, the operations required of the worker are themselves highly abstract, in that they select a small number of the total features of the environment as relevant to the task. The total environment of the cash register operator includes the personalities of her customers; the "job-relevant" features of that environment include only the price of the groceries. In other words, most work is not only *specialized* in terms of the worker's total talents, but it bears a highly *abstract* and distant relation to the final use of the product.

The specialization and abstractness of work is increasingly characteristic of professional roles as well. One is not merely a lawyer, but a corporation lawyer specializing in problems of investment; one does not simply teach literature, but French literature (Late Middle Ages and Early Renaissance); one is rarely now simply a doctor, but rather a gastroenterologist. Even relatively intact fields like architecture are being divided into subdivisions of city planning, industrial design, etc. Between the lawyer and the client stands the law firm; between the teacher and the student stands the field, the dean, the grader, the reader, and the section man; even the doctor seldom deals with the entire patient. The professional man is forced to develop one skill to the neglect of others; his relation to the subject of his work becomes increasingly distant, partial, and abstract.

These features of work extend into a number of other areas of life in our society: they can be seen in the increasing distance between work roles, family roles, and play; they are manifest in the formalization of on-the-job and off-the-job personal relationships; they are reflected even in the advertisements of job opportunities which seek to counter the fear that work will be overly specialized ("varied, *interesting* work"). But they are above all apparent in the relationship between fantasy and work.

Imagination is at its best when it is related to, but not tied to, the problems that confront the imaginer in his everyday life. When this is not the case, we can speak of the *dissociation of fantasy:* fantasy then not only has a life of its own, but this life bears little relationship and has little relevance to everyday life except as an escape. It is perhaps unreasonable to expect that every act of an individual be garlanded with rich imaginative and symbolic meaning; yet acts that are so enriched assume significance far beyond their immediate consequences. When imagination and life are separated, imagination continues to operate but becomes sterile and escapist, no longer deepening life but impoverishing it at the expense of another dream world that contains all that real life lacks.

The dissociation of fantasy is increasingly a characteristic of our social order. Never before have such quantities of "packaged fantasy" been so available and so eagerly consumed. In *Raw* magazine the IBM operator reads of cannibalism on the Amazon while the computer relentlessly writes checks; the benign image of Arthur Godfrey lulls the housewife through her routine housework; the fearless exploits of Batman counter the dull afternoon monotony of P.S. No. 117; and the tired and friendly businessman relaxes in the evening to the sadism of Mickey Spillane. The point about these packaged forms of imagination is not that they are in themselves new, but that their prevalence, availability, and acceptance are new.

To be sure, insofar as private fantasies are projected onto a television screen or into a comic book where they can be shared with others, this may, under the right circumstances, tie society together more cohesively. But the price of cohesion is high. For one thing, our shared fantasies are almost entirely contrasts or oppositions to daily life: they contrast with the lack of violence or intense passion in the average man's life, and with the specialization and abstraction of his work. Thus, they seldom serve to enrich life but rather to vitiate its imaginative vitalities. The "self-alienation" of which Fromm and others have written is an alienation of man from his own creative potentialities, imbedded in his fantasy life. When a man's primary contact with his own imagination is through the negative visions of the comic book or the television screen, these potentialities remain unexpressed. Social cohesion, if thus gained, is not cohesion of shared goals but of shared escapes and dreads. Fantasy that deepens the meaning of work, love, or play becomes less and less potent.

Finally, we should mention the much-discussed theme of "conformity," "loss of individuality," "massification," etc. Without attempting to judge whether "individuality" is in fact on the wane, we can state with certainty that most observers *believe* that it is; and that most intellectuals are continually on guard against conformity in any form. Perhaps this belief is more important to our questions than the actual facts, whatever they be. For the fear of conformity is closely related to the topics we have discussed: specialization, abstraction, and the dissociation of fantasy. Lacking symbolically meaningful work and relationships, men have almost no alternative but to see instances where they act like their fellows as acts of conformity.* Were adult roles viewed as exciting and fulfilling, there could be little problem for most men and women, even the most discriminating, about conforming to the adult world. What makes conformity appear as a danger is that what one conforms to seems so humanly unappealing. Whatever the actual nature of society, if a significant portion of those who are asked to constitute the community in the

---

* No one argues against conformity with others in a good cause; what is opposed and seen as universal is conformity for the sake of conformity—"keeping up with the Joneses," "not standing out." The problem of conformity is coextensive with the lack of good causes. Were such causes readily apparent, we could perhaps discuss specific instances of conformity more concretely in terms of whether conformity to this or that pattern was justified in terms of our ends.

next generation view it as unattractive, they will be reluctant to accept their task. In the case of American youth, this reluctance is heightened by the sharply contrasting image (and to a lesser extent, facts) of childhood in our society.

Childhood in America is defined as a time for the development of the total personality and the cultivation of a fresh immediate perception of the world; as a time when fantasy and life are still inextricably connected through the rituals of work and play, and when there is still room for spontaneity and hooky-playing nonconformity. These definitions are important not only because we view our childhoods in their terms, but because they correspond in fact with important aspects of our own (and all men's) childhoods. Childhood is a time for experimentation and the use of diverse talents; the child is not yet expected to limit himself to any one area of endeavor or accomplishment. And children—although certainly members of their cultures—have not yet assimilated its norms so as to develop that capacity for selective inattention and special emphasis which marks the "successfully socialized" adult in any society. (Wisdom comes from the mouths of babes because they have yet to learn the cultural taboos about what can be noticed and said without fear of reprisal.) The experience of the child, furthermore, tends to be less abstract and conceptualized than that of the adult: where the meteorologist sees signs of rain, the child sees fluffy clouds; the engineer who now contemplates the design of the Brooklyn Bridge may have once seen a graceful structure in mid-air. For many adults, the immediacy and aesthetic depth of childhood experiences are never equaled in later life.

Another characteristic of childhood in most societies, including our own, is what we can call "integral fantasy." The child's imagination operates on the objects of his daily environment, which become mythologized —first invested with supernatural attributes and later loaded with a cargo of associations and mental images that add to the meaning of the "realistically perceived" object. What we usually call "immediacy of perception" is, above all, perception in close touch with imagination, in which the stimulus—the cloud or person or bridge—is allowed to act not only on the higher cortex but on the entire psyche, so that the resulting experience is in some sense more "whole" than the pre-eminently adult experience of the physicist watching his laboratory dials. The games of children—played with utter seriousness—illustrate the same closeness of fantasy and reality: the child can work through the problems of growing up and the difficulties of associating with other people, and can learn to master his environment in a setting not at all detached from the other activities of his life. Work, play, love, and fantasy are closely intertwined; and the resulting connection is not only useful for the child's development, but independently and inherently satisfying.

The nonconformity of children can be easily exaggerated, especially in an age of "peer-group morality." Here again, perhaps the most important fact is that we tend to *think of* children as noncomformist, as saying the true but inconvenient thing, as not yet knowing how to behave according to adult standards. Most parents smile indulgently on hooky-playing in all but their own children; and even our impoverished mythology is rich with tales of children who unmask the phoniness of the adult world, expose the bombast of the pedant, and delightfully violate the conformities of the adult. Even allowing for the truthful exaggerations of myth, childhood *is* a time when conformity (to adult standards) is not yet fully required, and when spontaneous and impetuous reactions are far more likely. More than most societies, we allow children a long period of freedom before demanding that they assume adult responsibilities; if children conform, they conform to their own and not the adult's rules.

That we tend to romanticize our childhoods is probably the best evidence of the contrast between the world of the child and that of the adult. Psychologists know all too much of the sufferings of children, and many of us recall the unhappiness of our own childhood. Nonetheless we tend to idealize the first years of our lives, reserving "youthful" as the highest term of praise, and viewing the "innocent" games of children with nostalgia.*
We see children in the image of Huck Finn, the Catcher in the Rye, and freckle-faced boys on the covers of our family magazines. Such idealization of one period of life, coupled with a denigration of another, usually has a firm basis in fact (although not always in the facts that are *cited* in evidence for the judgments). Here I think the facts are relatively clear: the values and images we have about a given period of life shape this period and are shaped by it, too: underneath the absolute stereotype lies a real tendency in the same direction.

Childhood emerges well from this comparison with adulthood. The adult abandons a world of directness, immediacy, diversity, wholeness, integral fantasy, and spontaneity. He gains abstraction, distance, specialization, monotony, dissociated fantasy, and conformity. Faced with a transition into an adult world that he sees as denying these very human qualities of childhood, the youth can only hesitate on its threshold. Like the child who is told to go to bed, he falters, drags his feet, becomes angry, creates diversions, byplays, and distractions, changes the subject, seeks so to fascinate the "grownups" by his charm, wit, or violence that the initial pressures are forgotten—anything to avoid the sensed extinction of bedtime. And even if he is eventually tucked in, the temptation not

---

* "Innocence" in this context connotes, I think, not only relative ignorance af adult responsibilities and sexuality, but a kind of epistemological naïveté and directness, the same immediacy and aesthetic quality which is to some extent a characteristic of the outlooks of children.

really to sleep remains very great. The more marked the felt contrast between the bliss one leaves and the emptiness one enters, the greater the
foot-dragging, diversion, and anger. A vicious circle begins: the world of
childhood is romanticized, and the prospect of "settling down," "growing
up," and "assuming responsibilities" is seen in an even blacker light. The
Holden Caulfields of this country love children because they love themselves best as children; it is the "phony" grownups who are the objects of
anger and pity.

One explanation of youth culture, then, is the felt contrast between
what is expected of a child and what is expected of a man or woman. The
real contrast between the two states has, historically, increased with industrialization. Children's play is more and more separate from adults' work:
children no longer work in the fields or factories; instead they go to school,
developing their own culture and styles of life appropriate to their age.
And adults no longer retain the element of play, total involvement, and
immediate contact with their work or with the people near them that appear to characterize less industrial societies. Small wonder, then, that there
are symptoms of reluctance to enter adulthood. The humanization of
childhood has been accompanied by a dehumanization of adulthood:
youth culture is one consequence.

The ambiguities of adulthood. Although some separation of the
worlds of the child and the adult is a biologically rooted requirement of
every society, in ours this separation is probably more complete, more
sharply defined, and far more evaluatively laden than in most. But this
fact alone will not suffice to explain the widespread and diverse alienation
of youth today. Anthropologists have studied other societies with similar
contrasts between childhood and adulthood in which no youth culture
exists. Adults in these societies may always preserve a nostalgia and envy
for youth, they may create myths of a golden age in the distant past, and
they may individually find the transition into the adult world painful—but
the transition is made. To explain why a protracted, sometimes unending,
period of delay, rebellion, or indifference characterizes adolescence in our
society, we must examine adult roles in greater detail.

I have so far spoken of the "adult world" as if Americans had a clear
and univocal view of what it is to be an adult. Actually, of course, this is
far from true, and the felt characteristics of adult life—specialization, abstraction, dissociated fantasy, and conformity—are informal *qualities* of
most adult roles rather than formal definitions of what the adult is to do,
how he is to behave, what he is to say—how, concretely, he is to run his
life. The very absence of, and in some ways the impossibility of, such clear
definitions is another factor that makes our social order unattractive. On
the one hand, the *variety* of roles now open to young people might seem

to make their choice of adulthood less difficult; for given this variety, it should be possible to find some role that "fits" the needs and individuality of the adolescent.

Yet, without a criterion for choice, variety itself can be confusing, as when we stand with a small plate before a groaning smorgasbord. Choice becomes even more difficult when variety appears to be chaos, or when variety itself varies kaleidoscopically. And if, finally, we cherish the suspicion that none of what is offered us is as good as that which we are asked to renounce, the temptation to dally, walk away, or only nibble often becomes overpowering. The variety of adult roles is so great, and the boundaries of each role so imprecise, that for any but the most resolute or unimaginative, a period of inaction is almost mandatory when faced with choosing between them. And the accelerating pace of technological and social change seems to teach us that a definition of adulthood to which we commit ourselves in one decade may prove obsolete in the next. Apart from the shared and unattractive informal qualities we see in adult roles in general, we can seldom be sure precisely what is required to be an adult.

Even such universal adult roles as those of mother and father are variously defined, amorphous, and changeable. We lack any but the most minimal legal definitions of these functions in society: physical maintenance and lack of physical cruelty are mandatory. Beyond these legal requirements, however, few universally accepted precepts can be found. A parent should love his or her children, but "love is not enough." Children should be brought up democratically, but they also need the strong hand of authority and parents whom they can admire. Government manuals provide parental advice, but it is the opposite of the advice of twenty years ago. Do parents become anxious about how to raise their children? Then they learn that the worst fault of all is anxiety. Or take another equally basic definition, that of maleness, of what it is to be a man. Here the adolescent boy is confronted with a welter of conflicting pressures: images of violence, tenderness, ambition, renunciation, hardness, and sensitivity— all of which actively compete for his attention. If, as is increasingly the case, he is unable or unwilling to accept the models his own parents offer him, the prospect of manhood must be disturbing as well as intriguing.

In the occupational sphere, work roles are somewhat more rigorously defined. But even here there are wide areas of uncertainty as to precisely what being a lawyer, mechanic, doctor, or truck driver will involve. The problem is not so much that the individual is unaware of the operations he would perform as a mechanic or lawyer, but rather that these specific occupational efforts have no associated styles of life and, in addition, may change under the role-occupier without any warning. Having decided to become a plumber, a young man still has to make all the other decisions about how, where, and with whom he will live; an advertising man can live in Greenwich Village, Upper Manhattan, a suburb, or an exurb. Vocational commitment is only a preface to a series of other decisions that are relatively independent of it: close association between vocation and style of life is a thing of the past. Everyone must in some ways choose an idiosyncratic arrangement of selections from the vast repertory of life styles available in our cultural juke box.

The increasing rate of social change also makes the stability of adult commitments equivocal. In the past fifty years our society has changed at a devastating and accelerating pace. Today's world was inconceivable fifty years ago; the world of twenty-five years from today is probably equally unimagined. Generations, formerly measured by a man's life span, now span a decade at most. One of the great problems of an industrial society is to ease the effects of these changes on the members of the society. Technological changes produce job obsolescence and skill obsolescence: painfully learned work techniques may be unwanted in an age of automation. But even deeper stresses result from social changes that replace one ethic and ethos with another, making obsolete not only a man's skills, but often the entire structure of his character and outlook. Partly to cope with these stresses, new types of social character are developing, producing men whose commitment is to the shifting pressures of the environment, to adaptability, and to change itself. Yet the very nature of this "otherdirected" character is that it cannot be pinned down or specified in terms of values and life goals. "Other-directedness" offers little to a youth who seeks some stable or constant core of adult identity. "Choose to be changed" may be feasible as a once- or twice-in-a-lifetime imperative, but it is seldom viable as a way of life.

In short, many of our current models of adult character and identity are by their very nature vague and amorphous, emphasizing the ability to adapt, to accommodate oneself, and to change with shifting circumstances. Even in the occupational sphere, it is more difficult for a young man to bring himself to learn the techniques of the engineer when he believes that these may be outmoded in fifteen years. More general adult roles are even more fluid, with a kind of built-in principle of change. The perceptive youth may consciously or unconsciously sense in all of these roles are even more fluid, with a kind of built-in principle of change. The ciated fantasy; at the same time he is unable to find in our social order roles or definitions of selfhood that promise to outlive the next technological, moral, or social revolution. Thus, the choice of adulthood becomes even more difficult, and the probability of alienation increases.

The change in aspirations.   Youth culture and alienation have been characterized as a silent rebellion against the prevailing order, what it asks, and what it seems to offer. Yet one of the lessons of the study of rebellions is that they come about not because of any absolute level of misery, but because of a gap, a *felt* discrepancy, between what is and what is believed to be important, desirable, and possible. Revolutions usually occur in times of increasing prosperity and well-being and thus cannot be explained on grounds of absolute poverty or deprivation. Rather it is the *conviction, the belief,* that the present order is inadequate that produces discontent.

If we distinguish between revolution, with an active and articulate program of change and reform, and rebellion, which is more random, unfocused on goals, amorphous, and inarticulate, then ours is an age—in the industrial democracies of the West—of rebellion but not of revolution. The lack of program among the alienated makes true revolution unlikely. But this is, nonetheless, a time of silent rebellion, of nay-saying of a thousand kinds. And rebellions differ from revolutions not in their origins but in their articulateness. Even in explaining a phenomenon like youth culture, we must therefore consider the *gap between aspirations and actualities* as one of the chief sources of alienation.

Many of the outward facts of our culture are happy ones: as we are continually reminded by the defenders of our culture, we live in the greatest plenty the world has ever known. Our society has exceeded the material dreams of our forefathers; yet, the conditions they yearned for having been attained, their dreams have ceased to excite us. To foreigners—indeed to many American parents—dissatisfaction with today's security and prosperity seems gross petulance or rank ingratitude. And it is undoubtedly true that judged by the standards of fifty or a hundred years ago, our contemporary society gives grounds only for delectation and rejoicing. That such rejoicing is uncommon, and that alienation is so prevalent, therefore indicates different standards of judgment, a new and narrower definition of "what must be endured without protest"—and beneath this, an implicit change in what men feel they are entitled to ask of life.

It is easy to be misled here. Young people often seem to justify their elders' criticisms of their irresponsibility or ingratitude when they protest that there is "no longer anything to protest against." This complaint at first seems absurd and childish: nothing to protest against implies a perfect world and is clearly no grounds for protest. But in fact there are many things people do protest against—many of them the things we have earlier discussed. On closer examination, "nothing to protest against" seems rather to mean "no articulate principles upon which to ground one's intuitive dislikes and rejections" and is thus joined to another common complaint, "nothing left to believe in." The lack of any positive morality upon which to ground criticism of the existing world helps explain the absence of reform and revolutionary spirit today, and I will return to this point later. But for now we need to remind ourselves that absence of articulate expression does not demonstrate the absence of feeling, passion, and belief. That a man cannot fully articulate his aspirations does not mean that he may not still rebel against the discrepancy between what is and what he dimly, almost unconsciously, senses might be. Men may feel that they have a right to "something better than this," without being able to define the "something."

Given the proverbial silence of this generation about its objects of devotion, any attempt to investigate the "real aspirations" of those who react to their culture with apathy or alienation must necessarily remain speculations. But one clue to these aspirations can be found in what young people find it difficult to accept about the lives they are asked to lead. To dislike abstraction, specialization, or the dissociation of fantasy presupposes that one cherishes direct experience, a more total employment of talents, and the integration of fantasy into everyday life. And in the prevalent rejection of conformity, routinization, "massification," and the submersion of the individual in the group, there often appear to be implicit aspirations toward individuation, autonomy, integrity, "authenticity," and uniqueness. These values have long been imbedded in our culture but were never before considered adequate grounds for rejecting it. Why should they now become more compelling and urgent?

One obvious reason is that the values one stresses are to some extent a reflection of the defects of the current situation. In sunny regions, shade is treasured; northern climates prize the sun. Insofar as modern society has characteristic weaknesses, we should expect their opposites to be emphasized as values. Our industrial society, however great its virtues, has brought attendant evils; and it is unrealistic to expect that each generation will merely continue to be grateful for the victories won by its predecessors. More understandable and more desirable is that it should turn to attack the problems that follow these triumphs. The aspirations of a generation should counter its own most painful realities, not those of its parents.

This change—in many ways an extremely basic change—in our social and cultural facts of life suffices to account for the apparent ingratitude of this generation. But it is not adequate to explain what seems not only a change in aspirations but a heightened, if still largely mute, sense of what can be demanded of life. To understand this we must consider the psychological effects of our vast extension of physical power in the past century. As Galbraith has pointed out, we live on the brink of an age of affluence whose full significance for our thinking remains to be comprehended. Many nations can foresee the total abolition of scarcity in the next generation; that traditionally most fantastic of all unreal imaginings, a trip to the moon, seems possible within the next decade. When the conquest of poverty and space are almost within our grasp, we naturally—although perhaps unconsciously—tend to view. all frontiers as within our reach, whether they be physical, economic, social, or psychological. Given our immense physical powers, we are less willing to accept a social and personal milieu that leaves us unfulfilled.

The current situation is therefore paradoxical; and in this paradox lies a key to understanding the peculiar quality of modern alienation. For it is important to recall that very few modern men are actively possessed of the belief that they can control their own destinies or the shape of society with the same assurance that they can manage the forces of nature. Quite the opposite is true, in fact; rarely before have men experienced such mass resignation before the forces of society, such a sense of distance from the sources of power, such defeatism in the face of an explosive world situation.

The paradox is therefore this: the natural logic of our immense technological and material progress is, by generalization, to convince us that we should be able to determine our fates as human beings in our social and cultural settings just as we begin to control the physical world; yet consciously we lack any such conviction. The cultural correlate of material progress is therefore not, as we would expect, reform or revolution, but what we might call "unprogrammatic alienation"—rejection of society without any explicit program of objectives or techniques for improving it, and without even an articulate set of principles from which to criticize it. Our discontent necessarily remains at the level of a "feeling," a dumb unrest, a vague sense that something is wrong, an unwillingness to put up with a life that seems in some undefined way less than we might demand.

In other words, the extension of some of our powers reinforces our dissatisfaction with how little we seem able to ask for in our own lives. Even though our aspirations are seldom explicit in our complaints and inertias, our implicit definition of "psychological subsistence" has changed. In an enormously successful age such as this, young men are more likely to refuse to pay too high a price for membership in society. Since we already live in the material utopia dreamt of by the nineteenth century, why settle for anything less than the best in any other area?

Myths and Unconscious Utopias

This account of the roots of alienation has so far been incomplete in two ways. To be sure, in many areas of life, our culture demands a higher degree of abstraction, specialization, and dissociation than any before it, while at the same time offering few stable incentives for abandoning the integrities of childhood. And it is doubtless true that our material power has lessened our willingness to accept nonmaterial deprivations. But these considerations alone will not suffice to explain our increasing disaffection. For one, they give inadequate weight to those real social and material advances that in themselves should make alienation less likely. Scientific and technological progress has removed many of the former targets of protest, reform, rebellion, and revolution. In many Western countries— precisely those in which alienation now seems most widespread—the senseless sufferings of physical illness, the vast disparities of extreme affluence and extreme poverty, and the injustices of tyrannical rule seem on the way to being eliminated. Never before have there been so many alternatives open to man, such varied experiences available, so much real freedom to choose between beliefs, work, styles of life, and domiciles. These new social realities might well have outweighted the disadvantages of adulthood of which we have spoken; the fact is, however, that they have not; their net effect has, if anything, been the opposite.

But all of these proffered explanations of alienation are also incomplete in a more fundamental sense. Like individual behavior, social phenomena can be viewed from two points of view: in terms of the *presence* of forces that co-operate to produce them, or in terms of the *absence* of factors that might prevent them. An individual neurosis can be "explained" in terms of the factors that predispose the individual to the illness and immediately occasion its symptoms; but it can also be understood by studying the forces deterrent to illness that are absent. The more we study "normal" individuals, the more we see that they often share common backgrounds with neurotics; the determining difference may lie in the "normal's" experience of a single admired teacher who filled him with an abiding love of knowledge and wisdom, in the influence of an understanding aunt who early gave him a kernel of self-esteem on which he could later build, in an early acquired and tenaciously held conception of what he might become —in short, in constructive, integrative forces that enabled him to overcome or profit from the same conflicts that have incapacitated the neurotic. I have so far considered only the present, active determinants of alienation; the missing countervailing forces remain to be discussed.

Men will happily tolerate great discomfort, discontinuity, and frustration if—and only if—they are working for some purpose, toward some end, which they consider wise, true, exciting, and meaningful. It is a tragic fact that during wars or revolutions that coalesce societies around a central purpose, the symptoms of internal social pathology decline: mental illness, despondency, and suicide decrease. The ambivalent nostalgia with which Englishmen recall the glorious-tragic days of the Blitz, the significance of the Resistance to the average Frenchman fifteen years after the war—these attest to the importance of a common purpose and a common enemy. For the war was a time of intense frustration and daily suffering, when society asked much and offered little but a distant hope of victory, and when the gap between the contest in which men struggled and the peace to which they aspired was greatest. It is precisely the absence of any such positive vision which would make frustration worth while that most explains our contemporary alienation.

The transvaluation of utopia. The decline of cultural morale—of co-operation based on the acceptance of some common vision of the desired future—is perhaps most obvious in the decline and devaluation of utopias. There was a time when "utopian" was, for at least some men, a term of praise, and when utopias were defined as tangible and desired possibilities that men might write about and actually set out to realize. The Brook Farms and Nauvoos of America, the Proudhons, Saint-Simons, Owens and Fouriers of Europe—all expressed the conviction that there *were* certain values which should be implemented concretely through new forms of social organization, and that such implementation was well within the practical immediate possibilities of ordinary human beings.

Perhaps it is significant that Brook Farm, initially the most American of the utopian communities, perished in a holocaust and was never fully rebuilt. A parallel destiny pursued all of the other implementations of utopia in this country; and throughout the Western world concrete images of the desired future have met with the same fate. Marx's classless society, the greatest of all nineteenth-century utopias, has as surely died as an object of aspiration to most Westerners. We can or dare no longer visualize a future better than the present about which we complain.

But if we define a utopia as any attempt to make the possibilities of the future imaginatively concrete, utopias have not in our day ceased to exist; they merely have been transvalued. The contrast between nineteenth- and twentieth-century utopias is drastic. Our visions of the future have shifted from images of hope to vistas of despair; utopias have become warnings, not beacons. Huxley's *Brave New World,* Orwell's *1984* and *Animal Farm,* Young's *The Rise of the Meritocracy,* and, ironically, even Skinner's *Walden Two*—the vast majority of our visions of the future are negative visions, extensions of the most pernicious trends of the present. They are deterrents, cautionary tales: utopia has become counterutopia. The connotations of "utopian" have similarly changed: the term is now unequivocally associated with "unrealistic," with "self-defeating," and, for some, with man's deepest and most prideful sins.

The reasons for this shift are complex, and to consider them fully would take us far afield. Most fundamentally, this shift is part and symptom of a more general "loss of faith" in the West, seen in the movement from "positive values" (ends which men should seek) to a "negative morality" (which elucidates the evils and terrors men should avoid), and in our widespread doubt as to whether there are *any* values that can be legitimately and passionately held. This transition has often been discussed: it begins with the breakdown of medieval certainty, progresses through centuries of increasing rational skepticism and "demythologizing" of religion, and culminates in the cynicism and sense of ideological defeat that have followed our two world wars. Nietzsche's "transvaluation of values" has taken place. But the old creeds have not been replaced, as he hoped, by values more adequate to what man might become, but by the value nihilism against which he explicitly warned. The hammer has been retained, but not the concept of a transcendent man above all men so far envisaged.

A more immediate cause of the transvaluation of utopia is our unhappy experience with attempts to make real the visions of the past century—above all the vision of Marx. Whatever the reasons for the failure of Marxism in Russia to achieve its high moral and spiritual aims, the repercussions of this failure have been disastrous. Not only has the world been divided into two hostile camps, each with the power to destroy the other at an instant's notice, but—if possible even more important—the failure of this utopia has further crushed interest in visualizing and hope of attaining a better world. Communism in Russia involved far more than a parochial national revolution that failed. It was an attempt, like that of the French Revolution, to create a world in which men would be free not only from the tyrannies of want and power, but from the oppressions of their social and economic order—an attempt to make concrete the spiritual promises of Christianity. Its failure has been a tragedy for the entire West, one that has materially undermined our declining faith in our capacity to improve our world.

But I doubt that the failure of Marxism is really adequate grounds for the far-reaching, if implicit, conclusions that many seem to have drawn from it. The collapse of one enterprise, however mammoth, does not necessarily show that all such enterprises are inevitably doomed. Perhaps the most general lesson that can validly be drawn from such collapses is that means and ends are inextricably related. It is difficult to attain peace through violence or mass happiness through genocide: it is impossible to change radically an entire society at a single stroke. (Characteristically, many modern Communists deny this integral relationship between what is to be accomplished and how it is to be attained.)

We have, however, already overlearned even this lesson. Spengler speaks of "technicism"—an exclusive concentration on the techniques, instruments, and means for attaining once-desired ends—as the mark of the declining civilization. Other writers have commented on the replacement of "substantive" reason, which can judge the validity of ends and goals, by "instrumental" reason, which can judge only the efficacy of techniques in attaining preordained ends. This technicism is more and more pervasive: in every area methodology replaces substance; technical proficiency is

valued over final excellence; the analysis of philosophical questions substi-
tutes for their resolution; "know-how" supplants wisdom; "Whither?" has
become archaic, but "How?" is on every man's lips. It is small wonder that
men should feel powerless before a social order in whose day-to-day workings they are technically enmeshed but whose direction they feel unable to
judge.

Even in ethics, apparently the field most concerned with the proper
ends of conduct and life, technicism reigns virtually unchallenged. Academic ethics has concentrated more and more on what was once only a
prelude to substantive ethics: the formal logical and linguistic analysis of
ethical propositions and their characteristic justifications. Philosophers
now seldom try to define the good life but rather consider the several
senses in which the term "good" can be used. Popular philosophy is of
equally little help. Our most characteristic tracts on popular ethics have a
certain "how-to-do-it" quality; how to think positively (about doing in
your neighbor?); how to get along with people (what if they are not
worth getting along with?); how to cope with guilts and anxieties (but
suppose you *have* sinned?).

Even the nonacademic philosophers offer few noninstrumental suggestions. Perhaps the most appealing moral terms of our time are words like
"spontaneity," "individuality," "authenticity," "identity," and "autonomy,"
terms usually most fully developed by psychoanalytic or existential writers. Yet one can "spontaneously" commit murder and "authentically"—
God forbid—press a guided-missile button. These terms give us criteria
for judging *how* a thing is done, but only indirectly if at all for evaluating
what is done. To recur to an old philosophical distinction, the manner in
which an act is performed may be a necessary condition but is not a sufficient condition for its virtuousness. To suffice, a virtuous act or goal is also
needed.

The transvaluation of utopia is thus part of a wider transvaluation of
values, a long-term decline of positive morality, which has not only left
men unable to visualize a better future, but has deprived them of articulate bases on which to judge the present. The rise of the counterutopia is
one aspect of this more general historical trend, which reaches its acme in
the negative visions of the twentieth century.

The submersion of positive myth.   Every age has its characteristic
myths, its imagined or real events, laden with associations, symbols, and
marginal meanings, which express that time's deepest interpretation of the
visible world and of the world of good and evil. These myths vary in time,
among individuals, and among nations. So it is only as an abstraction that
we can speak of the "myth of an age" or of the general characteristics of
myth in any time and place. Nonetheless, even as abstraction such dis-

course is useful, for the deepest vitalities of rational belief and discourse lie in its mythic substructure. The myth of an age must be sought in the concrete representations of that age: in the stories, the folk tales, the philosophical visions, the entertainments, the questions that are taken for granted and those that are in issue in the age's exhortations and cautions.

Every age, too, has its characteristic balance between *positive*, eductive, hortatory, constructive, imperative, visionary, utopian myths, and *negative*, deterrent, cautionary, warning, direful, destructive, and counterutopian myths. In some periods of Western history, images of violence, demonism, destructiveness, sorcery, and witchcraft have prevailed; in others, myths of blessedness, justice, co-operation, and universal concordance with divine order have dominated. Other times, perhaps the happiest, have been able to include visions of both light and darkness in one mythic embrace. Only in such times do we find a clear public articulation of the existence of and the links between the divine and the demonic.

But despite the great differences between the dominantly positive myths of one age and the predominantly negative myths of another, a more subtle equilibrium also prevails. The sweet reasonableness of the Enlightenment is the backdrop for De Sade's most demonic of all envisioned republics. When the devil is denied, he manifests himself nonetheless—in some ways the more because his existence is no longer recognized and thus cannot be combatted. Similarly, the divine reasserts itself most powerfully in individuals when the collective myths ignore the good: saints live in times of the devil. Without denying that there are real contrasts between different ages in their ratio of positive and negative myths, we should also be aware that both types of myth are always present, sometimes on the surface, sometimes submerged deep below the dominant consciousness of the time.

Few would disagree that our own time is one of predominantly negative, deterrent, or even satanic myths. Our dissociated fantasy is fantasy of violence, cruelty, and crime, presented ostensibly as a warning, but often acting as a stimulant. More fundamentally, the highest literary and intellectual attainments of contemporary culture present us not with images of integration, co-operation, and reality, but with myths of decay, chaos, warfare, and illusion. Analysis everywhere replaces synthesis; fission, fusion; asymmetry, symmetry; regression, growth. Even in immediate world politics, the myth of the bomb and of inevitable war has greater cogency than any belief in peace or concord.

This shift, which we have seen clearly only in the past fifty years, has been long in the making. Our specific disillusionments and tragic experiences of recent history only partly account for it; for the very willingness to be disillusioned and to consider history's lessons tragic is itself a part of the more general submersion of positive myth. Historically, the change in the type of myth seems to consist of two related processes: one the *intellectualization of positive myth,* the other the *debunking of ideology.* I obviously cannot hope to chronicle adequately the stages through which these processes have taken place but can only suggest them in general terms.

Rationalism, as it emerged subsequent to the Renaissance, attempted to dissociate reason and faith, extirpating superstition and basing belief on the sounder tenets of "self-evident reason." The Cartesian critique of religion, although it finally arrived at religious truths almost identical with those from which it had started, nonetheless founded these truths on a primarily cognitive and intellectual basis. Faith was not really necessary; reason alone could arrive at truth in matters of value just as in matters of science. The primary effect of this new faith in reason was to separate the emotional and the cognitive sources of myth, abetting the rationalistic critique of the affective, imaginal components of the medieval myth, and producing a new myth which, on the surface at least, was far more rooted in reason and less attached to fantasy and the nonrational. "Demythologizing" religion did not, however, result in the disappearance of myth (as we here use the term), but merely in a new kind of myth, which we might call an "ideology" to indicate its primarily intellectual content, and to distinguish it from other myths more directly rooted in passion, faith, imagination, and poetic experience. This ideology, carrying a vision of a new society, was expressed above all by the French philosophers of the eighteenth century, and its utopian aspects culminated in the French Revolution. The excesses of this revolution might well have taught that the optimistic rationalism of the Enlightenment had ignored important aspects of human experience, for it had been unable to anticipate or even to comprehend the eagerness with which men rejected reason and in its name chose first terror and then Napoleon.

But in fact, of course, this lesson was not learned. Instead of a deepening of what had become a primarily ideological myth, this myth persisted in the same form and merely proved itself more vulnerable to attack. Purely cerebral values are usually the most vulnerable; those that are rooted in personal experience are more passionately held. Without a sanctioned basis in feeling, tradition, or fantasy, the values of the Enlightenment were difficult to defend. Just as it was easy to show that the rationalists' natural laws had no basis in physical fact but were rooted in faith (now disreputable), so it proved simple to demonstrate that intellect standing alone was impotent to arrive at valid conclusions about ultimate questions. Concepts like "progress," "reason," and "perfectibility" could readily be shown to be principles of interpretation, not facts: bereft of their nonintellectual foundations, they too have collapsed. Since history continually refuted the rationalists' claims, and since they had voluntarily deprived themselves of any appeals but those to the intellect, they could do little to defend their causes.

Openness to such debunking is a necessary characteristic of any system of beliefs that attempts to separate itself completely from the nonrational and the negative. With a fury that seems born of deprivation and frustration, modern thought has systematized the techniques of intellectual subversion. Whatever their positive content, psychoanalysis, existentialism, Marxism, and even modern philosophical analysis start from a systematized debunking of existing belief. The techniques for this destruction vary, but they have certain features in common. All consist in demonstrating the impotence of intellect before more powerful nonintellectual forces, which "truly" determine the beliefs men hold and profess to justify by reason. Whether these beliefs are held because of the denial of irrational impulses in man, refusal to face the true conditions of existence and death, economic interest, or simple "misunderstandings" about the use of language, the result is the same: conviction is undermined by associating beliefs with undesirable interests, fears, or errors.

Through this intellectualization of positive myth and the debunking of the ensuing ideologies, little remains of our former faiths. What started as an attack on specific beliefs and types of illusion has become a general attack on all positive myths. Reason and the good have been firmly associated since Plato, and the attack on the one has in effect resulted in subverting the other. Our positive myth has been shorn of its strength, separated more and more from the nonrational, the imagination, and from its roots in fantasy, desiccated from substantive to instrumental reason. The vitalities that it once possessed have passed to the negative myth. What fascinates, horrifies, enchants, and seduces us now is not any positive vision, but the disparate images of chaos, destructiveness, and cruelty.

To be sure, we rationalize our fascination with these images by appealing to their deterrent effects. Two hours of violence and cruelty is a morality play if the culprit is punished in the last scene of the last act. But Satan dominates the play and secretly triumphs, as he is wont to do in our day. And not without reason, for by accepting the affective desiccation of positive myth, we almost guarantee that emotion should be on the side of the negative, whatever intelligence may dictate. Evil always has its seductiveness; but when good has been deprived of adventure, poetry, and excitement, the fascination of the demonic becomes almost overwhelming, even when we believe that we observe it merely to learn its negative lessons.

The unconsciousness of contemporary utopias. The dominance of deterrent and destructive myths should not lead us to conclude that utopias and eductive myths have simply vanished without vestige. I have argued that the positive and negative components of myth are related much as the constructive and destructive sides of an individual's fantasy life: if one dominates it usually indicates that the other has been driven underground, where it continues to exist until it can be reintegrated into consciousness and given coherent form. There is much indirect evidence that such is the case with eductive myths at the present time. As Camus points out, every act of rebellion presupposes an implicit affirmation of that in the name of which one rebels; so, too, inasmuch as alienation constitutes a refusal to participate, it indicates that some interest stands above participation. It need hardly be said that disaffection has its purely destructive components and, by itself, can be sheer nihilism. But it may also contain, especially when articulate, the seeds of potential commitment. Indeed, the very fact of widespread alienation from a society dominated by vestigial ideologies or destructive and deterrent myths itself suggests that more positive values, however inarticulate or unconscious, still exist.

At first it may seem paradoxical to speak of an unconscious myth. For we usually associate myths with their spoken, written, pictorial, or filmed expressions. And yet none of these is the myth itself, which may be expressed variously and thus cannot be identified with any one of its concrete articulations. A myth resides above all in the deepest places in men's minds and may utterly lack expression without therefore ceasing to exist. To speak of an unconscious or implicit myth, as of an unconscious fantasy, merely requires an inference, based on evidence that cannot be readily explained without such an inference. Much of the evidence for the unconsciousness—as opposed to the nonexistence—of positive myths in our time has already been discussed in considering alienation and youth culture. The rather surprising contrast between our sense of physical power and the clarity of our material aims on the one hand and our sense of spiritual impotence and purposelessness on the other should lead us to the inference that for some reason men are *prevented* from expressing their aspirations, which exist nonetheless, although not in communicable form. Second, I have mentioned the unprogrammatic—sometimes nihilistic—nature of modern alienation, which only occasionally reaches the form of articulate protest and almost never leads to an impulse toward reform. Yet if to refuse to take part in something presupposes some superordinate value on which the rejection is at least implicitly based, we again have indirect evidence that men feel some attachment to values which, although unexpressed, they nonetheless serve.

But perhaps the most cogent evidence of implicit positive myths is to be had simply by conversing with people about what they desire from life. There is normally a signal incongruity between the superficiality, the banality, and remoteness of their expressed aims and purpose, and the depth and "feltness" of their implicit goals, which we must usually infer from what they *dis*like and seek to avoid. Young men and women today

feel great uneasiness and discomfort at expressing any ambition or conception of life that has not been long since sapped of any real vitality for
them or their fellows. Were such unease, embarrassment, and incongruity
between overt and covert values evident in a discussion of sex or hostility,
we would know what conclusion to draw: beneath the expressed views lie
less conscious, contrasting, and perhaps opposite values and attitudes.

Another obstacle to accepting the conclusion that men have unconscious constructive fantasies and unconscious eductive myths is our current notion of "the contents of the unconscious." We are accustomed to
think of unconscious processes in terms of Freudian repression, which
consists primarily in rejecting unacceptable aggressive and sexual fantasies. According to this principle, only the destructive or libidinal fantasies
on which a myth might be based could be repressed, and it would be
virtually impossible not to be aware of "good" fantasies.

But there is increasing reason to believe that Freud's definition of the
contents of the unconscious is an historical one, relevant primarily to the
Victorian world in which he lived. Psychoanalysts comment on the increasing rarity of the hysterical and compulsive symptoms upon which
Freud based his views of repression; the newer type of patient arrives at
the analyst's office more fully aware of his aggression and sexuality, but
seeking to find some purpose for his life. Perhaps a more general statement of the determinants of repression is this: whatever would, if it were
conscious, cause the individual trouble (discomfort, pain, guilt, ridicule,
shame, etc.) tends to remain unconscious. This formulation would suggest
that "good" impulses, drives, fantasies, and aspirations might be those
most unconscious in the patient without a purpose in life. We might even
speculate that in the mid-twentieth century, the "contents of the unconscious" have changed to counterbalance our inverted myths: what is most
unconscious today is the constructive, prospective, and affirmative part of
man.

A number of psychoanalysts have developed terms that permit us to
speak of unconscious "good" fantasies. Erikson's "positive identities,"
Horney's "real self," Sullivan's "personifications of the good me," Fromm's
"creative potentialities"—all of these aspects of the self admit of repression, and the analyst sees one of his tasks as making the patient aware of
them. But although such components of personality are increasingly discussed, we know little about the reasons why therapeutic assistance is so
often required to make them conscious. And more important to the understanding of alienation, we do not understand why, despite the widely expressed desire for a more positive and cogent myth, and despite the signs
that the seeds of such a myth are present in many of us, such a myth does
not find more ready cultural expression. What prevents us from articulating our now-dumb aspirations?

I have already mentioned our contemporary disillusionment with utopias, a disenchantment born partly of the spiritual failure of so many attempts to translate utopia into practice. Western civilization has come to
bear a deep and ultimately destructive conviction that not only utopias,
but every systematic attempt to translate ideals into practice, especially in
the social and political spheres, is similarly doomed to defeat, or worse, to
that reinstallation of the evils of the old regime that has attended most
major revolutions. Given a widespread conviction that deliberate attempts
at reform lead to excesses worse than those they seek to correct, the easiest
solution for the individual or the culture is never to voice the principles by
which reform might be guided. Disillusion of overly high hopes has
produced cynicism—not the cynicism of the native opportunist, but the
more corrosive cynicism of the man or the culture that has seen its hopes
dashed.

Beneath this cynicism, which usually expresses itself in lack of interest
in idealism or in boredom at high aspirations, lie more concrete fears. If
one articulates a set of principles, constructs a utopia or other eductive
myth—whether for himself or for his culture or for both—he automatically becomes in some way *responsible* to this vision. Most men consider
the cynicism of not acting to promote one's avowed purposes a worse
offense than the cynicism of not having any purposes at all. But to act to
promote or make real a positive vision of the future is—in our current
world view—to condemn oneself to certain frustration and probable failure. The thought that it may make matters worse is even more paralyzing
for men of good faith. Thus, a welter of good intentions, desire not to do
harm, doubt as to whether there are *any* means to promote worthy ends,
and fear of frustration or failure conspire to make it far easier not to articulate any positive morality in the first place.

But even if a man overcomes these obstacles himself, he must next
overcome the neglect, skepticism, or even active hostility of most of his
fellows. Any attempt, however tentative, to enunciate some principle of
positive action or enthusiasm must thus face attacks on two fronts. First,
the motives of the proponent will be thoroughly and hostilely investigated,
with the intent of showing that the proposals conceal "irrational," "ulte-
rior," or other undesirable motives, interests, or errors. And second, the
proposals themselves will be attacked as merely leading to further evils,
usually by extending some already undesirable trend. To take only one
example, the World Federalist must answer charges that he himself is up-
rooted and without sound national ties, and furthermore that his proposed
One World would merely lead to further extremes of homogenization, uniformity, legalism, bureaucratization, or whatever the dominant present
evils are seen to be.

Many an advocate of a worthy cause, however, would be grateful for criticism, which at least acknowledges the existence of his proposals. His more common fate is neglect. As we have argued before, indifference is as great a rejection as attack: as Dostoevsky knew, the ultimate reduction of a man is to stare through him without seeing him. Whether neglect or criticism is or is not valid is not at issue here: the point is that the complete predictability of such reactions makes even the most affirmative hesitate before affirming in public.

Little subtlety is needed to unearth the reasons for these responses. In some cases, they may be justified. Some purportedly good causes are what all are usually said to be: "crackpot," "harebrained," "naïve," and "unrealistic." But the response to any proposal for reform is so invariant that this explanation will not suffice. He who proposes innovation must always face opposition grounded in the universal inertial unwillingness to move from the familiar to the unknown. Even more important, as a man of virtue is a reproach to those without virtue, so a man of vision shames those who lack vision, implicitly finds them wanting, and calls for them to change. When change involves making explicit what for good reasons is kept unstated, indifference and (if this fails) angry rejection can surely be foreseen.

But probably the most potent deterrent to the enunciation or even the search for any more positive myth is the genuine humility of those who are most conscious of our cultural problems. If a fear must be found here to parallel the fear of responsibility and failure or the fear of criticism and neglect, it is the simple fear of being wrong. To those who lack agreed principles for the interpretation of reality, the twentieth century seems increasingly complex. Experts, each with his own special canons of selection and judgment, dominate their fields. There is so much to be known. And even if we knew it, who would really dare to judge and, more, to propose alternatives? Our real problem is not so much that we lack requisite knowledge, but that the values from which we might build have ceased to exist in the public mind. The advocate, reformer, or myth maker faces an almost superhuman task: he must first of all unearth the very values that he will then attempt to develop, illustrate, enhance, and implement. Faced with this task, humility is the only possible response; and the most probable—although by no means the only possible—behavior is withdrawal into some private domain where the job to be done has more defined and attainable ends.

Finally, a somewhat different type of obstacle to positive myth exists: the relative *absence of concepts* appropriate to, adequate for, or expressive of either the felt evils of the contemporary world or the vague aspirations for a better world. If it is true, as I have argued, that the imminence of an age of affluence means a complete reappraisal of what is wrong and what should be right in the world, this revaluation has yet to be made.

Preoccupied by their specialist endeavors, immersed in the improvement of the techniques for this and that, or, at best, nostalgically reliving the wisdom of a happier past, men have yet to give adequate diagnoses of our present situation. The concepts by which we interpret our contemporary world are by and large those of the past century—a century not only more confident but also considerably more impoverished than our own.

The changes that have taken place are not merely changes in quantity or degree, a little more here and a little less there. They amount to *absolute* alterations of our social, cultural, and, in many ways, our human condition. We do not only have more of the goods of life; for the first time many of us *have enough,* and barring world disaster, we can be relatively confident that we will continue not to want. We not only have less confidence in our powers to evaluate and change society; many of us have *none* and see little possibility of regaining our hope. We not only face the possibility of a somewhat more destructive war than the last, but the real chance that another war would mean *total* annihilation of life on our earth. These transformations are absolute; their understanding requires new concepts, new ways of thinking; their judgment requires new values, new positive myths; and the solution of the problems they bring requires new utopias, defined this time with a surer understanding of the means by which they may be at least partially attained.

Language is a prerequisite of cure. One way of looking at individual psychotherapy is to view it as a means of acquiring an adequate language (in the broadest sense of the word) for hitherto unexpressed feelings and impulses. If this is inadequate as a total explanation of the process of cure, the development of a language partially adequate to symbolize the roots of illness and the stages and goals of cure is at least a prerequisite to any successful therapy. Regardless of whether such a language really exists for the cure of the individual,* we clearly lack concepts adequate to the diagnosis of a world in which poverty is for many an ancestral recollection and in which limited war is merely a statement of hope. To our older vocabulary we owe a paradoxical debt: it enabled us to approach the solution of our former problems and thus led to our present condition. But in our present condition, this vocabulary merely blinds us to our realities.

Doubtless many other factors help produce our current repression of any positive myth, utopia, morality, or value. But the fears and humilities and inadequacies of intelligence mentioned may partly explain why we

---

* Even here I doubt that most of our current definitions of "adjustment," "mental health" or even "maturity" are fully adequate. The search for universal standards in this area has led to definitions of health as the absence of psychic or social tension or conflict—to many an unappetizing and dull prospect. That each individual might have his own unique form of the fullness of life, and that for many the continual overcoming of tensions and conflicts might be the key to zest and vigor—these thoughts have received too little attention.

now find it so difficult to give adequate articulation to the foundations of
our dissatisfactions. Lacking such expressions of what we aspire to, our
discontents can only be alienations, seldom even protests. For those whose
creativity will not be stifled, private concerns remain. There is a direct
relation between the decline of political ardor and the rise of the arts. The
ratio of paeans on the private poetic act to praise of the future estates of
mankind approaches infinity. Without an affirmative vision of what is actively desired as an alternative to alienation, creative change is difficult for
the individual and impossible for the society.

The reconstruction of commitment.   If these reflections on the roots of
alienation in our society are valid, any comments on how alienation might
be translated into reform or apathy into commitment are bound to be
inadequate. They would be inadequate not only because in this day any
attempt to express affirmation is bound to seem inadequate, but because
the problem of alienation is coextensive with the martial and moral crisis
of our civilization and as such can be resolved only by generations of men
dedicated to the reconstruction of commitment. Therefore my comments
will of necessity be directed toward what might be done to create circumstances more favorable to the alleviation of alienation, and not to the un-
formulated myths that could provide new objects of individual and social
commitment.

In considering the factors conducive to alienation and its most characteristic American form, youth culture, I contrasted views of childhood and
adulthood. To change the facts that underlie these felt and resented discontinuities and our ensuing unwillingness to accept the disadvantages of
maturity," far-reaching modifications of our present conceptions of work,
human relations, and leisure will be needed. As production per se ceases to
be a valid social goal, we can now afford to recall the original aims of
production, and to ask whether these humanitarian goals, if still viable,
are being served by a system in which sheer "output" has become an end
in itself. It is not enough to provide in leisure a dissociated escape from
the monotony, abstraction, and specialization required of work—especially if the use of leisure time, in the absence of any other criterion, is
subject to rigid canons of conformity.

Given the increasing ingenuity, appeal to vanity, avarice, lust, and
even patriotism required to cajole, entice, browbeat, or seduce consumers
into accepting products they do not want, we must ask whether our natural and psychological resources might not be better spent in altering work
itself, so as to make it more inherently rewarding to the worker, in addition to (or, if necessary, rather than) making it more efficient. It might
even be, for example, that men could perform more than one specialized
operation in their jobs, that they might be given work that taxes imagina-

tion instead of patience, that they might reacquire some understanding of and contact with the final use of their work and some pride in the quality of what they do. Then perhaps some men might even rejoice that they had work they could "take home with them" instead of plunging directly into the oblivion of the television set, recreation room, or home workshop. And perhaps our proverbial American ingenuity could devise ways of accomplishing these humane aims, utopian as they may seem, without totally wrecking our sometimes overproductive industrial productivity.

In other areas, too, we have only begun to conceive of alternatives to our present definitions of the lives men and women must lead. The tremendous ambitions and talents of our vast entertainment industry have never been known to study the aesthetic, psychological, or moral effects of their output with the same eagerness as they now scan indices of the number of listeners, readers, or viewers per product. But they might; and if they did, a revolution in the use and effects of leisure would ensue. Or again, we have never been able to, or not really wanted to, teach our children that knowledge, learning, and wisdom were rewarding, demanding, and inherently valuable pursuits. Were we interested in allocating a greater portion of our wealth toward creating different conditions for learning, our children might be better prepared to understand and live amidst the necessary ambiguities of adulthood, and to choose with less anxiety from among the variety of careers, spouses, convictions, and styles of life that compete for their enthusiasm. Or to take a final example, we now have too much time and too little idea of how to play in a way that invigorates and refreshes. We have hardly begun to imagine the possibilities that may exist for a more enhancing interaction between our love, our work, and our play.

If all of these questions could be answered by proposals deemed desirable and feasible, and if the proposals were successfully implemented, commitment to our society might be more enticing. To be sure, the chances are small that even such general suggestions as these could result in either completely desirable or completely feasible reforms. Indeed, this is not the point—it is that we think too seldom of how we might change ourselves and our society, and we reflect too attentively on the minor interstices of existing fabrics. Our slowly increasing understanding of man and society, inadequate though it remains, is seldom applied to problems such as these: we experiment with what we know or are indifferent to, and not with what might concern us more centrally as human beings.

Yet specific proposals such as these merely touch the surface of the problem and are therefore bound to be inadequate. Concrete reforms, however desirable, will remain extemporizations in the absence of an explicit positive myth, ideology, faith, or utopia. Indeed, no lasting or potent reform is ever possible except as men can be roused from their disaffection and indifference by the prospect of a world more inviting than that in which they now apathetically reside. Our deepest need is not to propose specific reforms, but rather to create an intellectual and cultural atmosphere in which it is possible for men to attempt affirmation without undue fear that valid constructions will collapse through neglect, ridicule, or their own inherent errors. Such an ethos can only be built slowly and piecemeal, yet it is already clear what some of its preconditions must be.

For one, we need a more generous tolerance for synthetic and constructive formulations. Instead of concentrating on the possible bad motives from which they arise (the genetic fallacy) or on the possible bad consequences that might ensue from their misinterpretation (the progenitive fallacy), we must learn to assess them in terms of their present relevance, depth, and appropriateness. To accomplish this is a double work. Destructively, we must subvert the methodologies of reduction that now dominate intellectual life. Constructively, we must replace these with more just measures of relevance, subtlety, and wisdom, learning to cherish the enriching complexity of motives and interests that will necessarily underlie and support any future myths.

Second, we must reappraise our current concepts and interpretations of man and society. It is characteristic of the intellectual placidity of this period, obviously different in so many ways from former times, that we continue to operate with language more apposite to past generations than to our own. We require a radical reanalysis of the present, one which, starting from uncritical openness to the experience, dissatisfactions, and joys of men today, can gradually develop frames of reference that can more totally comprehend us. The sharp analysis, fine discrimination, and imaginative interpretation needed are available; but we have yet to focus them on the problem.

But above and beyond a generous atmosphere and an adequate comprehension of our time, ordinary human courage is needed. To criticize negativism openly requires a strong heart when negativism is ubiquitous; only a man of mettle will propose a novel interpretation of facts now arranged in entrenched categories. And no matter how eagerly the audience awaits or how well-prepared the set, only courage can take the performer to the stage. There are many kinds of courage; needed here is the courage to risk being wrong, to risk doing unintentional harm and, above all, the courage to overcome one's own humility and sense of finite inadequacy. This is not merely diffuse "courage to be" without protest in a world of inherent uncertainty and anxiety, but the resolve to be *for* something despite the perishability and transience of all human endeavors.

Despite the difficulties that stand before even partial realization of these preliminary goals, there is reason not to despair. Here is a purpose worthy of the highest talent, a dedication for those who claim such causes no longer exist. And if this reasoning is correct, such dedication, if it bears fruit, will not be without its appreciators—those who now sense their lack of aim or aspiration. Nor need we begin from an utter void to create a universe *ex nihilo*. Instead we need the human wisdom to shape new understandings of who and what we are, and the courage and foresight to voice our own and our fellows' dimly sensed aspirations. Ironically, we can hope for such new commitments in the future only if men now resolve their alienations by committing themselves—through the analysis, synthesis, and reform of their own lives and worlds—to the preparation for new utopias. Perhaps then we will move nearer that world of creative individual fulfillment within self-renewing cultural vitality for which men have always longed.

The Speed-up of Change

This essay, written in 1962, is the first of several in which I point to the profound psychological effects of the accelerating rate of social change. I returned to this theme in The Uncommitted *(1965) and then again in "Youth, Change and Violence" (1968), reprinted here. In recent years others have explored the topic: Margaret Mead's* Culture and Commitment *and Alvin Toffler's* Future Shock *have helped expand and popularize the concept of an unprecedented speed-up of history in the twentieth century.*

Despite these works, however, I think it remains true that we too seldom realize how profoundly the acceleration of change affects us. Although in this essay I comment largely on the outlooks of the educated young, the impact of historical acceleration is much more devastating on those who are less resilient and adaptable. Those many "middle Americans" who today are frightened, angry, and confused are reacting in good part, I think, to the feeling of living in a world they never made, and for which they are quite unprepared. Thus the common complaint that youths or blacks or experts are no longer obeying "the [old] rules of the game" reflects the speed-up of history no less than does the present orientation of dissenting youth.

In retrospect, then, this essay seems fragmentary and incomplete. But it points to what I consider one of the most important and psychologically disruptive characteristics of the modern world, and to a topic that I think still deserves much further discussion.

EVERY society tends to ignore its most troublesome characteristics. Usually these remain unfathomed precisely because they are taken for granted, because life would be inconceivable without these traits. And most often they are taken for granted because their recognition would be painful to those concerned or disruptive to the society. Active awareness would at times involve confronting an embarrassing gap between social creed and social fact; at other times, the society chooses to ignore those of its qualities that subject its citizens to the greatest psychological strain. Such pluralistic ignorance is usually guaranteed and disguised by a kind of rhetoric of pseudo awareness, which, by appearing to talk about the characteristic and even to praise it, prevents real understanding far more effectively than could an easily broken conspiracy of silence.

Such is often the case with discussions of social change in America. From hundreds of platforms on Commencement Day, young men and women are told that they go out into a rapidly changing world, that they live amidst unprecedented new opportunities, that they must continue the innovations that have made and will continue to produce an ever-improving society in an ever-improving world. Not only is social change here portrayed as inevitable and good, but, the acoustics of the audience being what they are, no one really hears, and all leave with the illusory conviction that they have understood something about their society. But it occurs to none of the graduating class that their deepest anxieties and most confused moments might be a consequence of this "rapidly changing world."

More academic discussions of social change often fail similarly to clarify its meaning in our society. Most scholarly discussions of innovation concentrate either on the primitive world or on some relatively small segment of modern society. No conference is complete without panels and papers on "New Trends in X," "Recent Developments in Y," and "The New American Z." But commentators on American society are usually so preoccupied with specific changes—in markets, population patterns, styles of life—that they rarely if ever consider the over-all impact of the very fact that our entire society is in flux. And however important it may be to understand these specific changes in society, their chief importance for the individual is in that they are merely part of the broader picture of social change in all areas.

Even when we do reflect on the meaning of change in our own society, we are usually led to minimize its effects by the myth that familiarity breeds disappearance—that is, by the belief that because as individuals and as a society we have made an accommodation to social change, its effects have therefore vanished. It is of course true that the vast majority of Americans have made a kind of adaptation to social change. Most would feel lost without the technological innovations with which industrial managers and advertising men annually supply us: late-model cars, TV sets, refrigerators, women's fashions, and home furnishings. And, more important, we have made a kind of peace with far more profound non-technological changes; new conceptions of the family, of sex roles, of work and play cease to shock or even to surprise us. But such an adaptation, even when it involves the expectation of and the need for continuing innovation, does not mean that change has ceased to affect us. It would be as true to say that because the American Indian has found in defeat, resentment, and apathy an adaptation to the social changes which destroyed his tribal life, he has ceased to be affected by these changes. Indeed, the acceptance and anticipation of social change by most Americans is itself one of the best indications of how profoundly it has altered our outlooks.

Thus, though barraged with discussions of "our rapidly changing world" and "recent developments," we too easily can remain incognizant of the enormous significance, and in many ways the historical uniqueness, of social change in our society. Rapid changes in all aspects of life mean that little can be counted on to endure from generation to generation, that all technologies, all institutions, and all values are open to revision and obsolescence. Continual innovation as we experience it in this country profoundly affects our conceptions of ourselves, our visions of the future, the quality of our attachment to the present, and the myths we construct of the past. It constitutes one of the deepest sources of strain in American life, and many characteristically "American" outlooks, values, and institutions can be interpreted as attempts to adapt to the stress of continual change.

Social Change in America

Many of the outlooks and values of American youth can be seen as responses to the social changes that confront this generation. But merely to point out that society is changing and that youth must cope with the strains thus created is to state a truth so universal as to be almost tautological. Social change is the rule in history: past ages which at first glance appear to have been static usually turn out on closer study to have been merely those in which conflicting pressures for change were temporarily canceled out. Indeed, the very concept of a static society is usually a mistake of the shortsighted, a hypothetical construct which facilitates the analysis of change, or a myth created by those who dislike innovation. All new generations must accommodate themselves to social change; indeed, one of youth's historic roles has been to provide the enthusiasm—if not the leadership—for still further changes.

And even if we add the qualifier "rapid" to "social change," there is still little distinctive about the problems of American youth. For though most historical changes have been slow and have involved little marked generational discontinuity, in our own century at least most of the world is in the midst of rapid, massive, and often disruptive changes, and these may create even greater problems for the youth of underdeveloped countries than they do for Americans. Thus, to understand the responses of American youth to the problems of social change, we must first characterize, however tentatively and impressionistically, the most striking features of social change in this country.

Social change in America is by no means *sui generis;* in particular, it has much in common with the process of innovation in other industrialized countries. In all industrially advanced nations the primary motor of social change is technological innovation: changes in nontechnological areas of society usually follow the needs and effects of technological and scientific advances. But though our own country is not unique in the role technology plays, it is distinguished by the intensity of and the relative absence of restraint on technological change. Probably more than any other society, we revere technological innovation, we seldom seek to limit its effects on other areas of society, and we have developed complex institutions to assure its persistence and acceleration. And, most important, because of the almost unchallenged role of technology in our society, our attitudes toward it spread into other areas of life, coloring our views on change in whatever area it occurs. This country closely approximates the ideal type of unrestrained and undirected technological change which pervades all areas of life; and in so far as other nations wish to or are in fact becoming more like us, the adaptations of American youth may augur similar trends elsewhere.

Our almost unqualified acceptance of technological innovation is historically unusual. To be sure, given a broad definition of technology, most major social and cultural changes have been accompanied, if not produced, by technological advances. The control of fire, the domestication of animals, the development of irrigation, the discovery of the compass—each innovation has been followed by profound changes in the constitution of society. But until recently technological innovation has been largely accidental and usually bitterly resisted by the order it threatened to supplant. Indeed, if there has been any one historical attitude toward change, it has been to deplore it. Most cultures have assumed that change was for the worse; most individuals have felt that the old ways were the best ways. There is a certain wisdom behind this assumption, for it is indeed true that technological change and its inevitable social and psychological accompaniments produce strains, conflicts, and imbalances among societies as among individuals. Were it not for our own and other modern societies, we might ascribe to human nature and social organization a deep conservatism which dictates that changes shall be made only when absolutely necessary and after a last-ditch stand by what is being replaced.

But in our own society in particular, this attitude no longer holds. We value scientific innovation and technological change almost without conscious reservation. Even when scientific discoveries make possible the total destruction of the world, we do not seriously question the value of such discoveries. Those rare voices who may ask whether a new bomb, a new tail fin, a new shampoo, or a new superhighway might not be better left unproduced are almost invariably suppressed before the overwhelming conviction that "you can't stop the clock." And these attitudes extend beyond science and technology, affecting our opinions of every kind of change—as indeed they must if unwillingness to bear the nontechnological side effects of technological innovation is not to impede the latter. Whether in social institutions, in ideology, or even in individual character, change is more often than not considered self-justifying. Our words of highest praise stress transformation—dynamic, expanding, new, modern, recent, growing, current, youthful, and so on. And our words of condemnation equally deplore the static and unchanging—old-fashioned, outmoded, antiquated, obsolete, stagnating, stand-still. We desire change not only when we have clear evidence that the *status quo* is inadequate, but often regardless of whether what we have from the past still serves us. The assumption that the new will be better than the old goes very deep in our culture; and even when we explicitly reject such notions as that of progress, we often retain the implicit assumption that change per se is desirable.

Given this assumption that change is good, it is inevitable that institutions should have developed which would guarantee change and seek to accelerate it. Here, as in other areas, technology leads the way. Probably the most potent innovating institution in our society is pure science, which provides an ever-increasing repertoire of techniques for altering the environment. An even greater investment of time and money goes into applied science and technology, into converting abstract scientific principles into concrete innovations relevant to our industrialized society. The elevation of technological innovation into a profession, research, and development is the high point of institutionalized technological change in this country and probably in the world. And along with the institutionalized change increasingly goes planned obsolescence, to assure that even if the motivation to discard the outmoded should flag, the consumer will have no choice but to buy the newest and latest, since the old will have ceased to function.

But the most drastic strains occur only at the peripheries of purely technological innovation, because of changes in other social institutions which follow in the wake of new commodities and technologies. Consider the effects of the automobile, which has changed patterns of work and residence, transformed countryside with turnpikes and freeways, all but destroyed public transportation, been instrumental in producing urban blight and the flight to the suburbs, and even changed techniques of courtship in America. Further examples could be adduced, but the point is clear: unrestrained technological change guarantees the continual transformation of other sectors of society to accommodate the effects and requirements of technology. And here, too, our society abounds with planning groups, special legislative committees, citizens' movements, research organizations, and community workers and consultants of every variety whose chief task is, as it were, to clean up after technologically induced

changes, though rarely if ever to plan or co-ordinate major social innovations in the first place. Thus, citizens' committees usually worry more
about how to relocate the families dispossessed by new roadways than
about whether new roads are a definite social asset. But by mitigating
some of the more acute stresses indirectly created by technological
change, such organizations add to the stability of the society.

One of the principle consequences of our high regard for change and
of the institutionalization of innovation is that we have virtually assured
not only that change will continue, but that its pace will accelerate. Since
scientific knowledge is growing at a logarithmic rate, each decade sees still
more and more revolutionary, scientific discoveries made available to industry for translation into new commodities and techniques of production.
And while social change undoubtedly lags behind technological change,
the pace of social innovation has also increased. An American born at the
turn of the century has witnessed in his lifetime social transformations
unequaled in any other comparable period in history: the introduction of
electricity, radio, television, the automobile, the airplane, atomic bombs
and power, rocketry, the automation of industry in the technological area,
and equally unprecedented changes in society and ideology: new conceptions of the family, of the relations between the sexes, of work, residence,
leisure, of the role of government, of the place of America in world affairs.
We correctly characterize the rate of change in terms of self-stimulating
chain reactions—the "exploding" metropolis, the "upward spiral" of living
standards, the "rocketing" demands for goods and services. And unlike
drastic social changes in the past (which have usually resulted from pesti-
lence, war, military conquest, or contact with a superior culture), these
have taken place "in the natural course of events." In our society at
present, "the natural course of events" is precisely that the rate of change
should continue to accelerate up to the as-yet-unreached limits of human
and institutional adaptability.

The effects of this kind of valued, institutionalized, and accelerating
social change are augmented in American society by two factors. The first
is the relative absence of traditional institutions or values opposed to
change. In most other industrialized nations, the impact of technology on
the society at large has been limited by pre-existing social forces—aristocratic interests, class cleavages, or religious values—opposed to unrestrained technological change. Or, as in the case of Japan, technological
changes were introduced by semifeudal groups determined to preserve
their hegemony in the new power structure. Technologically induced
changes have thus often been curbed or stopped when they conflicted
with older institutions and values, or these pretechnological forces have
continued to exist side by side with technological changes. The result has
been some mitigation of the effects of technological innovation, a greater

channeling of these changes into pre-existing institutions, and the persistence within the society of enclaves relatively unaffected by the values of a
technological era. But America has few such antitechnological forces.
Lacking a feudal past, our values were from the first those most congenial
to technology—a strong emphasis on getting things done, on practicality,
on efficiency, on hard work, on rewards for achievement not birth, on
treatment of all men according to the same universal rules.

A second factor that increases the effect of technological change is our
unusual unwillingness to control, limit, or guide the directions of industrial
and social change—an unwillingness related to the absence of institutions
opposing innovation. Most rapid changes in the world today involve far
more central planning or foreknowledge of goal than we are willing to
allow in America. At one extreme are countries like China and Russia,
which attempt the total planning of all technological, industrial, and social
change. While unplanned changes inevitably occur, central planning
means that the major directions of change are outlined in advance and
that unplanned changes can frequently be redirected according to central
objectives. Furthermore, most underdeveloped nations are aiming at developing a highly technological society; in so far as they succeed, the direction of their changes is given by the model they seek to emulate. Given
three abstract types of change—planned, imitative, and unguided—our
own society most closely approximates the unguided type. We do little to
limit the effects of change in one area of life on other aspects of society,
and prefer to let social transformations occur in what we consider a "free"
or "natural" way, that is, to be determined by technological innovations.
As a result, we virtually guarantee our inability to anticipate or predict the
future directions of social change. The Russian knows at least that his
society is committed to increasing production and expansion; the Nigerian
knows that his nation aims at increasing Westernization; but partly by our
refusal to guide the course of our society, we have no way of knowing
where we are headed.

The Phenomenology of Unrestrained
Technological Change

Man's individual life has always been uncertain: no man could ever
predict the precise events which would befall him and his children. In
many ways we have decreased existential uncertainty in our society by
reducing the possibilities of premature death and diminishing the hazards
of natural disaster. But at the same time, a society changing in the way
ours is greatly increases the unpredictability and uncertainty of the life
situation shared by all the members of any generation. In almost every
other time and place, a man could be reasonably certain that essentially

the same technologies, social institutions, outlooks on life, and types of people would surround his children in their maturity as surrounded him in his. Today we can no longer expect this. Instead, our chief certainty about the life situation of our descendants is that it will be drastically and unpredictably different from our own.

Few Americans consciously reflect on the significance of social change; as I have argued earlier, the rhetoric with which we conventionally discuss our changing society usually conceals a recognition of how deeply the pace, the pervasiveness, and the lack of over-all direction of change in our society affect our outlooks. But nonetheless, the very fact of living amidst this kind of social transformation produces a characteristic point of view about the past and future, a new emphasis on the present, and above all an altered relationship between the generations which we can call the phenomenology of unrestrained technological change.

The major components of this world view follow from the characteristics of change in this country. First, the past grows increasingly distant from the present. The differences between the America of 1950 and that of 1960 are greater than those between 1900 and 1910; because of the accelerating rate of innovation, more things change, and more rapidly, in each successive decade. Social changes that once would have taken a century now occur in less than a generation. As a result, the past grows progressively more different from the present in fact, and seems more remote and irrelevant psychologically. Second, the future, too, grows more remote and uncertain. Because the future directions of social change are virtually unpredictable, today's young men and women are growing into a world that is more unknowable than that confronted by any previous generation. The kind of society today's students will confront as mature adults is almost impossible for them or anyone else to anticipate. Third, the present assumes a new significance as the one time in which the environment is relevant, immediate, and knowable. The past's solution to life's problems are not necessarily relevant to the here-and-now, and no one can know whether what is decided today will remain valid in tomorrow's world; hence, the present assumes an autonomy unknown in more static societies. Finally, and perhaps of greatest psychological importance, the relations between the generations are weakened as the rate of social innovation increases. The wisdom and skills of fathers can no longer be transmitted to sons with any assurance that they will be appropriate for them; truth must as often be created by children as learned from parents.

This mentality by no means characterizes all Americans to the same degree. The impact of social change is always very uneven, affecting some social strata more than others, and influencing some age groups more than others. The groups most affected are usually in elite or vanguard positions: those in roles of intellectual leadership usually initiate innovations and make the first psychological adaptations to them, integrating novelty with older values and institutions and providing in their persons models which exemplify techniques of adaptation to the new social order. Similarly, social change subjects different age groups to differing amounts of stress. Those least affected are those most outside the society, the very young and the very old; most affected are youths in the process of making a lifelong commitment to the future. The young, who have outlived the social definitions of childhood and are not yet fully located in the world of adult commitments and roles, are most immediately torn between the pulls of the past and the future. Reared by elders who were formed in a previous version of the society, and anticipating a life in a still different society, they must somehow choose between competing versions of past and future. Thus, it is youth that must chiefly cope with the strains of social change, and among youth it is "elite" youth who feel these most acutely.

Accordingly, in the following comments on the outlooks of American youth, I will emphasize those views which seem most directly related to the world view created by unrestrained change and will base my observations primarily on my observations over the past decade of a number of able students in an "elite" college. While these young men are undoubtedly more articulate and reflective than most of their contemporaries, I suspect they voice attitudes common to many of their age mates.

Outlooks of Elite Youth

One of the most outstanding (and to many members of the older generation, most puzzling) characteristics of young people today is their apparent *lack of deep commitments to adult values and roles.* An increasing number of young people—students, teenagers, juvenile delinquents, and beats—are alienated from their parents' conceptions of adulthood, disaffected from the main streams of traditional public life, and disaffiliated from many of the historical institutions of our society. This alienation is of course one of the cardinal tenets of the beat generation; but it more subtly characterizes a great many other young people, even those who appear at first glance to be chiefly concerned with getting ahead and making a place for themselves. A surprising number of these young men and women, despite their efforts to get good scholarships and good grades so that they can get into a good medical school and have a good practice, nonetheless view the world they are entering with a deep mistrust. Paul Goodman aptly describes their view of society as "an apparently closed room with a rat race going on in the middle." Whether they call it a rat race or not is immaterial (though many do); a surprising number of apparently ambitious young people see it as that. The adult world into which they are headed is seen as a cold, mechanical, abstract, specialized, and emotionally meaningless place in which one simply goes through the motions, but without conviction that the motions are worthy, humane, dignified, relevant, or exciting. Thus, for many young people, it is essential to stay "cool"; and "coolness" involves detachment, lack of commitment, never being enthusiastic or going overboard about anything.

This is a bleak picture, and it must be partially qualified. For few young people are deliberately cynical or calculating; rather, many feel forced into detachment and premature cynicism because society seems to offer them so little that is relevant, stable, and meaningful. They wish there were values, goals, or institutions to which they could be genuinely committed; they continue to search for them; and, given something like the Peace Corps, which promises challenge and a genuine expression of idealism, an extraordinary number of young people are prepared to drop everything to join. But when society as a whole appears to offer them few challenging or exciting opportunities—few of what Erikson would call objects of "fidelity"—"playing it cool" seems to many the only way to avoid damaging commitment to false life styles or goals.

To many older people, this attitude seems to smack of ingratitude and irresponsibility. In an earlier age, most men would have been grateful for the opportunities offered these contemporary young. Enormous possibilities are open to students with a college education, and yet many have little enthusiasm for these opportunities. If they are enthusiastic at all, it is about their steady girl friend, about their role in the college drama society, about writing poetry, or about a weekend with their buddies. Yet, at the same time, this apparently irresponsible generation is surprisingly sane, realistic, and levelheaded. They may not be given to vast enthusiasms, but neither are they given to fanaticism. They have a great, even an excessive, awareness of the complexities of the world around them; they are well read and well informed; they are kind and decent and moderate in their personal relations.

Part of the contrast between the apparent maturity and the alienation of the young is understandable in terms of the phenomenology of unrestrained change. For the sanity of young people today is partly manifest in their awareness that their world is very different from that of their parents. They know that rash commitments may prove outmoded tomorrow; they know that most viewpoints are rapidly shifting; they therefore find it difficult to locate a fixed position on which to stand. Furthermore, many young men and women sense that their parents are poor models for the kinds of lives they themselves will lead in their mature years, that is, poor exemplars for what they should and should not *be*. Or perhaps it would be more accurate to say, not that their parents are poor models (for a poor model is still a model of what not to be), but that parents are increasingly irrelevant as models to their children. Many young people are at a real loss as to what they should seek to become: no valid models exist for the as-yet-to-be-imagined world in which they will live. Not surprisingly, their very sanity and realism sometimes lead them to be disaffected from the values of their elders.

Another salient fact about young people today is their relative *lack of rebelliousness* against their parents or their parents' generation. Given their unwillingness to make commitments to the "adult world" in general, their lack of rebellion seems surprising, for we are accustomed to think that if a young man does not accept his parents' values, he must be actively rejecting them. And when the generations face similar life situations, emulation and rejection are indeed the two main possibilities. But rebellion, after all, presupposes that the target of one's hostility is an active threat: in classical stories of filial rebellion, the son is in real danger of being forced to become like his father, and he rebels rather than accept this definition of himself. But when a young man simply sees no possibility of becoming like his parents, then their world is so remote that it neither tempts nor threatens him. Indeed, many a youth is so distant from his parents, in generational terms if not in affection, that he can afford to "understand" them, and often to show a touching sympathy for their hesitant efforts to guide and advise him. Parents, too, often sense that they appear dated or "square" to their children; and this knowledge makes them the more unwilling to try to impose their own values or preferences. The result is frequently an unstated "gentleman's agreement" between the generations that neither will interfere with the other. This understanding acknowledges a real fact of existence today; but just as often it creates new problems.

One of these problems appears very vividly in the *absence of paternal exemplars* in many contemporary plays, novels, and films. One of the characteristic facts about most of our modern heroes is that they have no fathers—or, when they do have fathers, these are portrayed as inadequate or in some other way as psychologically absent. Take Augie March or Holden Caulfield, take the heroes of Arthur Miller's and Tennessee Williams' plays, or consider the leading character in a film like *Rebel without a Cause*. None of them has a father who can act as a model or for that matter as a target of overt rebellion. The same is true, though less dramatically, for a great many young people today. One sometimes even hears students in private conversations deplore the tolerance and permissiveness of their exemplary parents: "If only, just once, they would tell me what *they* think I should do." Young people want and need models and guardians of their development; and they usually feel cheated if they are not available. The gentleman's agreement seldom works.

It would be wrong, however, to infer that parents have suddenly become incompetent. On the contrary, most American parents are genuinely interested in their children, they try hard to understand and sympathize with them, they continually think and worry about how to guide their development. In other, more stable times, these same parents would have been excellent models for their children, nourishing their growth while recognizing their individuality. But today they often leave their children with a feeling of never really having had parents, of being somehow cheated of their birthright. The explanation is not hard to find. Even the most well-intentioned parent cannot now hope to be a complete exemplar for his children's future. A man born in the 1910's or 1920's and formed during the Depression already finds himself in a world that was inconceivable then; his children will live in a world still more inconceivable. It would be unrealistic to hope that they would model their lives on his.

Another aspect of the psychology of rapid change is the *widespread feeling of powerlessness*—social, political, and personal—of many young people today. In the 1930's, there was a vocal minority who believed that society should and, most important, *could* be radically transformed; and there were more who were at least convinced that their efforts mattered and might make a difference in politics and the organization of society. Today the feeling of powerlessness extends even beyond matters of political and social interest; many young people see themselves as unable to influence any but the most personal spheres of their lives. The world is seen as fluid and chaotic, individuals as victims of impersonal forces which they can seldom understand and never control. Students, for example, tend not only to have a highly negative view of the work of the average American adult, seeing it as sterile, empty, and unrewarding, but to feel themselves caught up in a system which they can neither change nor escape. They are pessimistic about their own chances of affecting or altering the great corporations, bureaucracies, and academies for which most of them will work, and equally pessimistic about the possibility of finding work outside the system that might be more meaningful.

Such feelings of powerlessness of course tend to be self-fulfilling. The young man who believes himself incapable of finding a job outside the bureaucratic system and, once in a job, unable to shape it so that it becomes more meaningful will usually end up exactly where he fears to be—in a meaningless job. Or, a generation who believes that it cannot influence social development will, by its consequent lack of involvement with social issues, in fact end up powerless before other forces, personal or impersonal, which *can* affect social change. In a generation, as in individuals, the conviction of powerlessness begets the fact of powerlessness. But, however incorrect, this conviction is easy to comprehend. The world has always been amazingly complex, and with our widening understanding comes a sometimes paralyzing awareness of its complexity. Furthermore, when one's vantage point is continually shifting, when the future is in fact more changeable than ever before, when the past can provide all too few hints as to how to lead a meaningful life in a shifting society—then it is very difficult to sustain a conviction that one can master the environment.

The most common response to this feeling of helplessness is what David Riesman has called "privatism." Younger people increasingly emphasize and value precisely those areas of their lives which are least involved in the wider society, and which therefore seem most manageable and controllable. Young men and women today want large families, they are prepared to work hard to make them good families, they often value family closeness above meaningful work, many expect that family life will be the most important aspect of their lives. Within one's own family one seems able to control the present and, within limits, to shape the future. Leisure, too, is far more under the individual's personal control than his public life is; a man may feel obliged to do empty work to earn a living, but he can spend his leisure as he likes. Many young people expect to find in leisure a measure of stability, enjoyment, and control which they would otherwise lack. Hence their emphasis on assuring leisure time, on spending their leisure to good advantage, on getting jobs with long vacations, and on living in areas where leisure can be well enjoyed. Indeed, some anticipate working at their leisure with a dedication that will be totally lacking in their work itself. In leisure, as in the family, young people hope to find some of the predictability and control that seem to them so absent in the wider society.

Closely related to the emphasis on the private spheres of life is the *foreshortening of time span.* Long-range endeavors and commitments seem increasingly problematical, for even if one could be sure there will be no world holocaust, the future direction of society seems almost equally uncertain. Similarly, as the past becomes more remote, in psychological terms if not in actual chronology, there is a greater tendency to disregard it altogether. The extreme form of this trend is found in the "beat" emphasis on present satisfactions, with an almost total refusal to consider future consequences or past commitments. Here the future and the past disappear completely, and the greatest possible intensification of the present is sought. In less psychopathic form, the same emphasis on pursuits which can be realized in the present for their own sake and not for some future reward is found in many young people. The promise of continuing inflation makes the concept of a nest egg obsolete, the guarantee of changing job markets makes commitment to a specialized skill problematical, the possibility of a war, if seriously entertained, makes all future planning ridiculous. The consequence is that only the rare young man has life goals that extend more than five or ten years ahead; most can see only as far as graduate school, and many simply drift into, rather than choose, their future careers. The long-range goals, postponed satisfactions, and indefinitely deferred rewards of the Protestant ethic are being replaced by an often reluctant hedonism of the moment.

A corollary of the emphasis on the private and the present is the *decline in political involvement* among college youth. To be sure, American students have never evinced the intense political concerns of their Continental contemporaries, and admittedly, there are exceptions, especially in the "direct-action" movements centered around desegregation. But the general pattern of political disengagement remains relatively unchanged or, if anything, has become more marked. Those familiar with elite college students in the 1930's and in the late 1950's contrast the political activity of a noisy minority then with the general apathy now before world problems of greater magnitude. Instead of political action, we have a burgeoning of the arts on many campuses, with hundreds of plays, operas, poems, and short stories produced annually by college students. Underlying this preference of aesthetic to political commitment are many of the outlooks I have mentioned: the feeling of public powerlessness, the emphasis on the private and immediate aspects of life, the feeling of disengagement from the values of the parental generation. But most important is the real anxiety that overtakes many thoughtful young people when they contemplate their own helplessness in the face of social and historical forces which may be taking the world to destruction. It is perhaps significant that Harvard students began rioting about Latin diplomas the evening of a relatively underattended rally to protest American intervention in Cuba, a protest to which most students would have subscribed. So high a level of anxiety is generated by any discussion of complex international relations, the possibilities of nuclear war, or even the complicated issues of American domestic policies that all but the extraordinarily honest or the extraordinarily masochistic prefer to release their tensions in other ways than in political activity. And in this disinvolvement they are of course supported by the traditional American myth of youth, which makes it a time for panty raids but not for politics.

In general, then, many college students have a kind of *cult of experience*, which stresses, in the words of one student, "the maximum possible number of sense experiences." Part of the fascination which the beat generation holds for college students lies in its quest for "kicks," for an intensification of present, private experiences without reference to other people, to social norms, to the past or the future. Few college students go this far, even in the small group that dresses "beat," rides motorcycles, and supports the espresso bars; for most, experience is sought in ways less asocial than sex, speed, and stimulants. But travel, artistic and expressive experience, the enjoyment of nature, the privacy of erotic love, or the company of friends occupy a similar place in the hierarchy of values. Parallel with this goes the search for self within the self rather than in society, activity, or commitment, and a belief that truth can be uncovered by burrowing within the psyche. The experience sought is private, even solipsistic; it involves an indifference to the beckonings of the wider society. To be sure, Teddy Roosevelt, too, was in his way a seeker after experience; but unlike most contemporary American youths, he sought it in frantic extroversion, in bravado, and in heroic action; and its rewards were eventual public acclaim. But for most college students today, T.R. and the values of his era have become merely comic.

Youth Culture and Identity

Many of these outlooks of youth can be summed up as a sophisticated version of the almost unique American phenomenon of the "youth culture," that is, the special culture of those who are between childhood and adulthood, a culture which differs from both that of the child and that of the adult. To understand the youth culture, we must consider not only the increasing gap between the generations but the discontinuity between childhood and adulthood. Generational discontinuities are gaps in time, between one *mature* generation and the next; but age-group discontinuities are gaps between different age groups at the *same* time. The transition from childhood to adulthood is never, in any society, completely continuous; but in some societies like our own there are radical discontinuities between the culturally given definitions of the child and of the adult. The child is seen as irresponsible, the adult responsible; the child is dependent, the adult is independent; the child is supposedly unsexual, the adult is interested in sex; the child plays, the adult works, etc. In societies where these age-group discontinuities are sharpest, there is usually some form of initiation rite to guarantee that everyone grows up, that the transition be clearly marked, and that there be no backsliding to childish ways.

But in our society we lack formalized rites of initiation into adulthood; the wan vestiges of such rites, like bar mitzvah, confirmation, or graduation-day exercises, have lost most of their former significance. Instead, we have a youth culture, not so obviously transitional, but more like a waiting period, in which the youth is ostensibly preparing himself for adult responsibilities, but in which to adults he often seems to be armoring himself against them. The essence of the youth culture is that it is not a rational transitional period—were it one, it would simply combine the values of both childhood and adulthood. The youth culture is not always or explicitly antiadult, but it is belligerently *non*adult.

To understand this subculture we must consider its relation to both the discontinuities between age groups and the discontinuities between generations. Childhood is seen as (and often really is) a time for the full employment of one's talents and interests, a time when work, love, and play are integrally related, when imagination is given free play, and life has spontaneity, freedom, and warmth. Adulthood obviously suffers by comparison, and it is understandable that those who are being rushed to maturity should drag their feet if this is what they foresee. The youth culture provides a kind of way station, a temporary stopover in which one can muster strength for the next harrowing stage of the trip. And for many the youth culture is not merely one of the stops, but the last stop they will really enjoy or feel commitment to. Thus, the youth culture is partially a consequence of the discontinuity of age groups, an expression of the reluctance of many young men and women to face the unknown perils of adulthood.

But the gap between childhood and adulthood will not explain why in our society at present the youth culture is becoming more and more important, why it involves a greater and greater part of young men's and women's lives, or why it seems so tempting, compared with adulthood, that some young people increasingly refuse to make the transition at all. Rock 'n' roll, for example, is probably the first music that has appealed almost exclusively to the youth culture; catering to the teenage market has become one of the nation's major industries. And, as Riesman has noted, the very word "teenager" has few of the connotations of transition and growing up of words like "youth" and "adolescent," which "teenager" is gradually replacing.

The youth culture not only expresses youth's unwillingness to grow up but serves a more positive function in resolving generational discontinuities. Erik H. Erikson would characterize our youth culture as a psychosocial moratorium on adulthood, which provides young people with an opportunity to develop their identity as adults. One of the main psychological functions of a sense of identity is to provide a sense of inner selfsameness and continuity, to bind together the past, the present, and the future into a coherent whole; and the first task of adolescence and early adulthood is the achievement of identity. The word "achieve" is crucial here, for identity is not simply given by the society in which the adolescent lives; in many cases, and in varying degree, he must make his own unique synthesis of the often incompatible models, identifications, and ideals offered by society. The more incompatible the components from which the sense of identity must be built and the more uncertain the future for which one attempts to achieve identity, the more difficult the task becomes. If growing up were merely a matter of becoming "socialized," that is, of learning how to "fit into" society, it is hard to see how anyone could grow up at all in modern America, for the society into which young people will some day "fit" remains to be developed or even imagined. Oversimplifying, we might say that socialization is the main problem in a society where there are known and stable roles for children to fit into; but in a rapidly changing society like ours, identity formation increasingly replaces socialization in importance.

Even the achievement of identity, however, becomes more difficult in a time of rapid change. For, recall that one of the chief tasks of identity formation is the creation of a sense of self that will link the past, the present, and the future. When the generational past becomes ever more distant, and when the future is more and more unpredictable, such continuity requires more work, more creative effort. Furthermore, as Erikson emphasizes, another of the chief tasks of identity formation is the development of an "ideology," that is, of a philosophy of life, a basic outlook on the world which can orient one's actions in adult life. In a time of rapid ideological change, it seldom suffices for a young man or woman simply to accept some ideology from the past. The task is more difficult; it involves selecting from many ideologies those essential elements which are most relevant and most enduring. Such an achievement takes time, and sometimes the longest time for the most talented, who usually take the job most seriously.

The youth culture, then, provides not only an opportunity to postpone adulthood, but also a more positive chance to develop a sense of identity which will resolve the discontinuity between childhood and adulthood on the one hand, and bridge the gap between the generations on the other. Of course, a few young men and women attempt to find an alternative to identity in other-direction. Unable to discover or create any solid internal basis for their lives, they become hyperadaptable; they develop extraordinary sensitivity to the wishes and expectations of others; in a real sense they let themselves be defined by the demands of their environment. Thus, they are safe from disappointment, for, having made no bets on the future at all, they never have put their money on the wrong horse. But this alternative is an evasion, not a solution, of the problem of identity. The other-directed man is left internally empty; he has settled for playing the roles that others demand of him. And role-playing does not satisfy or fulfill; letting the environment call the shots means having nothing of one's own. Most young people see this very clearly, and only a few are tempted to give up the struggle.

There is another small group, the so-called beats and their close fellow travelers, who choose the other alternative, to opt out of the system altogether and to try to remain permanently within the youth culture. In so doing, some young people are able to create for themselves a world of immediate, private, and simple enjoyment. But leaving the system also has its problems. The search for self which runs through the youth culture and the beat world is not the whole of life, and to continue it indefinitely means usually renouncing attainments which have been traditionally part of the definition of a man or a woman: intimacy and love for others; personal creativity in work, ideas, and children; and that fullness and roundedness of life which is ideally the reward of old age. So, though many young people are tempted and fascinated by the beat alternative, few actually choose it.

The vast majority of young people today accept neither the other-directed nor the beat evasion of the problem of identity. In many ways uncommitted to the public aspects of adult life, they are willing nonetheless to go through the motions without complete commitment. They have a kind of "double consciousness," one part oriented to the adult world which they will soon enter, the other part geared to their version of the youth culture. They are not rebellious (in fact they like their parents), but they feel estranged and distant from what their elders represent. They often wish they could model themselves after (or against) what their parents stand for, but they are sensible enough to see that older people are often genuinely confused themselves. They feel relatively powerless to control or to influence the personal world around them, but they try to make up for this feeling by emphasizing those private aspects of life in which some measure of predictability and warmth can be made to obtain. They often take enthusiastic part in the youth culture, but most of them are nonetheless attempting to "graduate" into adulthood. And though many hesitate on the threshold of adulthood, they do so not simply from antagonism or fear, but often from awareness that they have yet to develop a viable identity which will provide continuity both within their lives and between their own, their parents', and their future children's generations. And in each of these complex and ambivalent reactions young people are in part responding to the very process of unrestrained change in which they, like all of us, are involved.

Evaluations and Prospects

In these comments so far I have emphasized those attitudes that seem most directly related to the stresses of unrestrained change, neglecting other causal factors and painting a somewhat dark picture. I have done this partly because the more sanguine view of youth—which stresses the emancipations, the sociological understandability of youth's behavior, the stability of our society despite unprecedented changes, and the "adaptive" nature of youth's behavior—this more encouraging view has already been well presented elsewhere. But furthermore, if we shift from a sociological to a psychological perspective and ask how young people themselves experience growing up in this changing society, a less hopeful picture emerges. Rightly or wrongly, many young people experience emancipations as alienations; they find their many freedoms burdensome without

criteria by which to choose among equally attractive alternatives; they
resent being "understood" either sociologically or psychologically; and
they often find the impressive stability of our society either oppressive or
uninteresting. Furthermore, what may constitute an "adaptation" from
one sociological point of view (e.g., the American Indian's regression in
the face of American core culture) may be not only painful to the individual but disastrous to the society in the long run. A sociological and a
psychological account of youth thus give different though perhaps complementary pictures and lead to different evaluations of the outlook of
American youth. Despite the stability of American society and the undeniable surfeit of opportunities and freedoms available to young people
today, many of youth's attitudes seem to me to offer little ground for
optimism.

The drift of American youth, I have argued, is away from public in-
volvements and social responsibilities and toward a world of private and
personal satisfactions. Almost all young people will eventually be *in* the
system—that is, they will occupy occupational and other roles within the
social structure—but a relatively large number of them will never be *for*
the system. Their vision and their consciousness will be split, with one eye
on the main chance and the other eye (the better one) on some private
utopia. This will make them good organizational workers, who labor with
detachment and correctness but without the intensity or involvement
which might upset bureaucratic applecarts. And they will assure a highly
stable political and social order, for few of them will be enough committed to politics to consider revolution, subversion, or even radical
change. This orientation also has much to commend it to the individual:
the private and immediate is indeed that sphere subject to the greatest
personal control, and great satisfaction can be found in it. The "rich full
life" has many virtues, especially when contrasted with the puritanical and
future-oriented acquisitiveness of earlier American generations. And I
doubt if commitment and "fidelity" will disappear; rather, they will simply
be transferred to the aesthetic, the sensual, and the experiential, a transfer
which would bode well for the future of the arts.

Yet the difficulties in this split consciousness seem to me overwhelming, both for the individual and for the society. For one, few individuals
can successfully maintain such an outlook. The man who spends his working day at a job whose primary meaning is merely to earn enough money
to enable him to enjoy the rest of his time can seldom really enjoy his
leisure, his family, or his avocations. Life is of a piece, and if work is
empty or routine, the rest will inevitably become contaminated as well,
becoming a compulsive escape or a driven effort to compensate for the
absent satisfactions that should inhere in work. Similarly, to try to avoid
social and political problems by cultivating one's garden can at best be

only partly successful. When the effects of government and society are so ubiquitous, one can escape them only in the backwaters, and then only for a short while. Putting work, society, and politics into one pigeonhole, and family, leisure, and enjoyment into another creates a compartmentalization which is in continual danger of collapsing. Or, put more precisely, such a division of life into nonoverlapping spheres merely creates a new psychological strain, the almost impossible strain of artificially maintaining a continually split outlook.

Also on the demerit side, psychologically, is the willful limitation of vision which privatism involves, the motivated denial of the reality or importance of the nonprivate world. Given the unabating impact of social forces on every individual, to pretend that these do not exist (or if they do exist, have no effect on one) qualifies as a gross distortion of reality. Such blindness is of course understandable: given the anxiety one must inevitably feel before a volatile world situation, coupled with the felt inability to affect world events, blinders seem in the short run the best way to avoid constant uneasiness. Or similarly, given the widespread belief that work is simply a way of earning a living, refusal to admit the real importance to one's psychic life of the way one spends one's working days may be a kind of pseudo solution. But a pseudo solution it is, for the ability to acknowledge unpleasant reality and live with the attendant anxiety is one of the criteria of psychological health. From a psychological point of view, alienation and privatism can hardly be considered ideal responses to social change.

From a social point of view, the long-range limitations of these "adaptations" seem equally great. Indeed, it may be that, through withdrawal from concern with the general shape of society, we obtain short-run social stability at the price of long-run stagnation and inability to adapt. Young people, by exaggerating their own powerlessness, see the system, whether at work, in politics, or in international affairs, as far more inexorable and unmalleable than it really is. Consider, for example, the attitude of most American youth (and most older people as well) toward efforts to direct or restrain the effects of social change. Partly by a false equation of Stalinism with social planning, partly on the assumption that unrestrained social change is "natural," and partly from a conviction that social planning is in any case impossible, young people usually declare their lack of interest. Apart from the incorrectness of such beliefs, their difficulty is that they tend to be self-confirming in practice. Given a generation with such assumptions, social changes will inevitably continue to occur in their present haphazard and unguided way, often regardless of the needs of the public. Or again, it seems likely that if any considerable proportion of American students were to demand that their future work be personally challenging and socially useful, they would be able to create or find such work and would revolutionize the quality of work for their fellows in the process. But few make such demands. Or, most ominous of all, if the future leaders of public opinion decide that they can leave the planning of foreign policy to weapons experts and military specialists, there is an all too great chance that the tough-minded "realism" of the experts will remain unmitigated by the public's wish to survive.

In short, an alienated generation seems too great a luxury for us. To cultivate one's garden is a stance most appropriate to times of peace and calm, and least apposite to an era of desperate international crisis. It would be a happier world than this in which men could devote themselves to personal allegiances and private utopias. But it is not this world. International problems alone are so pressing that for any proportion of the ablest college students to take an apolitical stance seems almost suicidal. And even if world problems were less horrendous, there is a great deal to be done in our own society, which to many, young and old, still seems corrupt, unjust, ugly, and inhuman. But to the extent that the younger generation loses interest in these public tasks, remaining content with private virtue, the public tasks will remain undone. Only a utopia can afford alienation.

In so far as alienation and privatism are dominant responses of the current college generation to the stresses of unrestrained change, the prospects are not bright. But for several reasons I think this prognosis needs qualification. For one, I have obviously omitted the many exceptions to the picture I have sketched—the young men and women who have the courage to confront the problems of their society and the world, who have achieved a sense of identity which enables them to remain involved in and committed to the solution of these problems. Furthermore, for most students alienation is a kind of *faute de mieux* response, which they would readily abandon could they find styles of life more deserving of allegiance. Indeed, I think most thoughtful students agree with my strictures against privatism and accept withdrawal only as a last resort when other options have failed. But, most important, I have omitted from my account so far any discussion of those forces which do or might provide a greater sense of continuity, despite rapid change. Discussion of these forces may correct this perhaps unnecessarily discouraged picture.

Throughout this account, I have suggested that Americans are unwilling to plan, guide, restrain, or coordinate social change for the public good. While this is true when America is compared with other industrialized nations, it is less true than in the past, and there are signs that many Americans are increasingly skeptical of the notion that unrestrained change is somehow more "free" or more "natural" than social planning. We may be beginning to realize that the decision not to plan social changes is really a decision to allow forces and pressures other than the public interest to plot the course of change. For example, it is surely not more natural to allow our cities to be overrun and destroyed by the technological requirements of automobiles than to ask whether humane and social considerations might not require the banning or limiting of cars in major cities. Or to allow television and radio programming to be controlled by the decisions of sponsors and networks seems to many less "free" than to control them by public agencies. If we are prepared to guide and limit the course of social change, giving a push here and a pull there when the "natural" changes in our society conflict with the needs of the public, then the future may be a less uncertain prospect for our children. Indeed, if but a small proportion of the energy we now spend in trying to second-guess the future were channeled into efforts to shape it, we and our children might have an easier task in discovering how to make sense in, and of, our changing society.

I have also neglected the role that an understanding of their situation might play for the younger generation. Here I obviously do not mean that students should be moralistically lectured about the need for social responsibility and the perversity of withdrawal into private life. Such sermonizing would clearly have the opposite effect, if only because most young people are already perfectly willing to abandon privatism if they can find something better. But I do mean that thoughtful students should be encouraged to understand the meaning and importance of their own stage in life and of the problems which affect them as a generation. The emphasis on individual psychological understanding, which characterizes many "progressive" colleges, can provide only a part of the needed insight. The rest must come from an effort to end the pluralistic ignorance of the stresses confronting all members of the current younger generation. Here colleges do far too little, for courses dealing with the broad social pressures that impinge on the individual often deliberately attempt to prevent that personal involvement which alone gives insight. But one can imagine that a concrete understanding of the psychosocial forces that affect a generation might have some of the same therapeutic effects on the more reflective members of the generation that insight into psychodynamic forces can give the thoughtful individual.

And finally, I have underplayed the importance that values and principles can and do play in providing continuity amid rapid change. If one is convinced that there are guiding principles which will remain constant—and if one can find these enduring values—life can be meaningful and livable despite rapid change. But here we need to proceed cautiously. Technologies, institutions, ideologies, and people—all react by extremes when faced with the fear of obsolescence. Either they firmly insist that *nothing* has changed and that they are as integrally valid as ever before or—and this is equally disastrous—they become so eager to abandon the

outmoded that they abandon essential principles along with the irrelevant. Thus, parents who dimly fear that they may appear "square" to their
children can react either by a complete refusal to admit that anything has
changed since their early days or (more often) by suppressing any expression of moral concern. The second alternative seems to me the more prevalent and dangerous. An antiquated outlook is usually simply ignored by
the young. But person or institution that abandons its essential principles
indirectly communicates that there are no principles which can withstand
the test of time and thus makes the task of the young more difficult.

Yet the bases for the continuity of the generations must of necessity
shift. Parents can no longer hope to be literal models for their children;
institutions cannot hope to persist without change in rite, practice, and
custom. And although many of the essential principles of parents, elders,
and traditional institutions can persist, even those who seek to maintain
the continuity of a tradition must, paradoxically, assume a creative and
innovating role. We need not only a rediscovery of the vital ideals of the
past, but a willingness to create new ideals—new values, new myths, and
new utopias—which will help us to adapt creatively to a world undergoing continual and sweeping transformations. It is for such ideals that
young people are searching: they need foundations for their lives which
will link them to their personal and communal pasts and to their present
society but which at the same time will provide a trustworthy basis for
their futures. The total emulation or total rejection of the older generation
by the young must be replaced by a re-creation in each generation of the
living and relevant aspects of the past, and by the creation of new images
of life which will provide points of constancy in a time of rapid change.

The Political Revival

Even before Berkeley it was clear that a new political mood was growing among American students. By 1963, when this essay was written, the Civil Rights Movement had become nationally visible, and a small but vocal antiwar movement was also emerging. But at the same time, the overwhelming majority of American students remained apathetic, silent, or acquiescent vis-à-vis the surrounding society.

In discussing this "political revival," I attempted to place the unexpected (and to me welcome) appearance of a small but vocal group of activists in the context of a long tradition of student acceptance of American society. One reason for the absence of a vivid tradition of student activism in America is the traditional image of the student as apprentice, the apolitical self-definition of American youth culture, and the American myth that ours is a society in which anyone with drive, ambition, and a modicum of intelligence can quickly work his way to the Top. These images, definitions, and myths effectively depoliticized discontent and helped prevent the emergence in America of the radical student movements that had, in other nations, accompanied industrialization.

The "political revival," then, was correlated with the rejection by growing numbers of students of the older definition of studenthood as apprenticeship, and the emergence of a less vocational, more "academic," or intellectual, conception of the personal meaning of higher education. Although the style of the youthful opposition has changed greatly since 1963, I think it is still difficult to understand the rhetoric of the oppositional young without appreciating their rejection of vocationalism and their basic acceptance of a broadly academic, intellectual, identity-seeking definition of the meaning of their education. Paradoxically, even the "anti-intellectualism" some observers find rampant among the young is the kind of objection to the misuse of the intellect that only disillusioned intellectuals can formulate.

THE apolitical stance of American youth is something of a puzzle. Our liberal political tradition once led us to believe that intelligent political concern went hand in hand with public well-being and education; and yet despite prosperity and the highest level of education in the world, our young men and women remain overwhelmingly uninterested in the state of the nation and the world. Even in a time of "political revival" and "revolt on the campus," the highest estimates of politically active students range around 10 per cent; while at most colleges, 90, or 95, or 99 per cent of the student body take no active part in any cause or organization that could truly be called political. In other nations—both the highly industrialized and the rapidly developing—a much larger proportion of educated young men and women are involved in political life, actively debate the issues of the day, and demonstrate their vigorous approval or disapproval of the trends of the times. In Korea and Turkey successful revolutions have recently been led by students; in Japan, as in Latin America and Africa, student demonstrations can affect national policy; and even in industrialized Europe educated youth is more politically conscious and active than in America. It almost appears that affluence and education have a negative effect on political involvement, at least in America.

The puzzle is deepened when we recall the close historical association between rapid social change and a politically active youth. It is an axiom of historical observation that drastic social change puts enormous stresses on the individual, that the aspirations of young people often—indeed usually—outrun the facts of society during such periods, and that a radically altered social scene makes impossible any easy continuity between the generations. All of these factors increase the likelihood that young men and women will attempt to change the society to conform with their own democratic and often radical aspirations. And in this country during the past hundred years we have witnessed precisely the kind of social transformations that elsewhere led to a politically active youth. Beginning with the spurt of industrialization after the Civil War, American society has undergone and continues to undergo deep transformations, no less drastic because they are no longer reflected in the indices of economic output, and no less affecting because we have grown used to them. Yet despite this American youth is predominantly apolitical, and has been so almost without interruption since the foundation of this nation.

A full explanation of the predominantly apolitical outlook of American youth—as of the active participation in politics of an increasing few—would involve nothing less than a social and psychological history of this nation. Here I can only suggest one or two factors that have played a role in the development of this outlook and then, in the light of these factors, try to assess the meaning and prospects of the recent "revival" of political interest among students.

Traditional Images of Youth

To understand so current a topic as the campus "political revival" and the inert student masses against which this "revival" takes place, we must take a long step backward to consider some of the factors that distinguish American social development from that of most other nations; for in them, I think, lies the key to understanding the apolitical outlook of today's young. For one, as many commentators on American life have noted, America never had a feudal past to overcome. If we define "feudal" broadly, so that it includes not only established aristocracies but land- and mine-owning oligarchies and colonial rulers, then there are only a handful of former British colonies that had the same fresh start that we did. Concretely, this has meant that Americans, from the beginning, have lacked clear and obvious targets for rebellion. Young people growing up in this country have, for 150 years, found themselves *already* living in a nation whose major public values are still the mottoes of revolution elsewhere— equal rights, equal opportunities, justice under law, and so on. Not that these values are always practiced—but at least they are subscribed to almost universally and probably practiced to a greater extent than in many countries. Thus, generations of young Americans awakened to consciousness to find themselves already living in a "postrevolutionary" world. If they remained dissatisfied, impoverished, or underprivileged, there were no aristocrats, landowners, or colonial rulers to rebel against. Instead, Americans have always perceived their chief obstacle as some quality of their own like ignorance, laziness, bad luck, or inexperience, chains that could be cast off by effort, by education, or, in our own time, by psychotherapy.

A second relevant constant in American life is the anti-ideological bias of American life. Even Tocqueville commented in the 1830's that Americans' passion for grand ideas was not matched by any parallel passion for translating these ideas into practice. And it has remained true, in general, that ideological speculations in this country have been a kind of game played by intellectuals who themselves often doubted their practicality on a large scale. For example, even though the founders of the utopian communities that dotted the countryside in the 1800's were discontented with the *status quo,* they did not attempt to change the whole society through revolution or political action as they might have done in an ideological nation like France or Germany. Rather, they withdrew from the wider society to set up their own private utopias. Americans who were explicitly disaffected have rarely attempted political action on a grand scale but have chosen instead for withdrawal, emigration, or exemplary self-reform. As a nation we are not only hostile to the translation of grand schemes into political reality, but, more important, it seldom even occurs to most of us that ideological (or even intellectual) considerations have much to do with the workings of political life.

This characteristic American distrust of grand political schemes, coupled with our fresh start as a nation, has given a peculiar and perhaps unique coloring to Americans' attitudes toward social change. It has meant that the burden of proof has always been on those who opposed or sought to direct the economic and social transformations of the nation. In countries with Establishments, whether of title, education, race, or conquest, it has seemed quite natural that the original Establishment or its latter-day successor should seek to direct the changes of the nation's social face. And in such countries the vestiges of the older "feudal" orders have often served as foci of opposition to the new, the modern, and the untried. But in America, lacking such foci and mistrusting social planning, we have consistently preferred to let society run its "natural course," which has in practice meant that the needs of a burgeoning industry have usually been most heeded. To this fact we owe part of our industrial accomplishments and our high standard of living, which could not have been achieved without a people who were convinced that the new, the modern, the "latest" were good, and that what was old and established was "old-fashioned," "obsolete," and "outmoded." Concretely, this has meant that each new product, institution, custom, or even value has been eagerly seized by a nation rushing to outgrow its yesterdays and hurrying to enter a future ever brighter than the present. In a word, Americans have been and continue to be on the side of change, and have considered it their obligation to make whatever accommodations were necessary to Progress.

In this continuing context of unopposed, undirected, and highly valued social change, the last four generations of Americans have been formed. And, more important, their conceptions of themselves and their tasks as youths have been shaped by social definitions of youth that have been broadly consonant with this context of social change. Such social definitions exist unnoticed in every society, dictating what kinds of behavior are legitimate for youth—and when not legitimate, then expected, and when not expected, then at least comprehended by other members of society as signs of protest, illness, or divine favor. A young man or woman who lives within the confines of these definitions is understandable and predictable to his fellows and (even more important to an adolescent) understandable and "normal" to himself; whereas one who deviates from the sheltering confines of such images is considered strange, erratic, weird (in our society, "un-American"), and eventually begins to wonder about his own normality. To "work" in the broader context of society, an image of youth must be broadly consonant with the basic values of the society, and, furthermore, it must help the young to grow into adulthood, resolving the peculiar stresses of adolescence in that society and strengthening in each youth an attachment to the tasks that maturity will require.

In a complex and changing society like ours, two basic definitions of youth exist, each with many subvariants. These two images, which I will call youth as *apprenticeship for social mobility* and youth as *youth culture,* are very different in most ways. But both are consistent with American values about social change; both permit the resolution of some of the major problems created by rapid change, and—most relevant to this context—both discourage political activity among the young.

To understand the role played by these definitions of youth, we must consider in more detail the specific directions of social change in this country over the past hundred years or so. And on this point there is a good deal of consensus among historians and sociologists. Put very generally, we are moving from an economy of scarcity to one of relative affluence, from the takeoff point of rapid industrialization to an era of mass consumption, from basic production to service industries. Sociologically, this has meant a relative shift from individual entrepreneurship to bureaucratic corporations limited by government regulation, from the rugged competitiveness of the Protestant ethic in the last century to the smoother group orientation of the social ethic in this century, and, on the family front, from the more authoritarian entrepreneurial family to the newer, more team-minded bureaucratic family. And most important for the understanding of youth has been the shift in social character first discussed by Riesman—a shift from an organization of character based on internal standards of personal worth that lead to competitive achievement, from this inner-direction to the newer, other-directed character based on sensitivity to the feelings of others and on interpersonal standards of worth.

The heyday of the older entrepreneurial society seems to have occurred in the northern United States during the decades of rapid industrialization following the Civil War; these years saw the transformation of this country from an agrarian into an industrial society. These were decades of very rapid social mobility, of fortunes quickly made and quickly lost in the next panic—a time much like our own when adults found themselves living in a kind of society their own parents had never dreamed of, and hence had not been able to prepare their children for. Comparable periods in Germany and Japan saw the rise of militant youth groups aiming at radical changes in the social organization of the nation; but of course in America there has never been any such movement.

Part of the explanation for the quiescence of American youth undoubtedly lies in the facts I have already mentioned: in America there was no feudal, preindustrial order to block the advancement or frustrate the democratic aspirations of the young; but in Japan and Germany such an order did exist and did frustrate the dreams of radical youth. But even more important, I think, was the existence in this country of another mythical and to some extent real alternative to politics for youth—rapid social mobility. Horatio Alger is probably the best-known spokesman for this view. Recall the basic plot of his stories: his heroes were poor but honest lads who were befriended by a wealthy older man, a man successful and prosperous *within* the existing social order. The lads, partly by dint of their own drive and energy, but also with large amounts of assistance from the obliging older man, eventually take over the bank or company, marry the older man's lovely, rich daughter, and become roaring successes. The presence of the helping older man is crucial here. Horatio Alger implies that if one's parents are inadequate models, others will act in their stead. Indeed Horatio Alger, like the motto "From rags to riches," positively *urges* the young to abandon their rag-ridden parents and follow other, more modern and successful elders into the new world of riches. Generational discontinuity is of course one of the chief problems of rapid social change, in that parents can seldom serve as exemplars to their children; but here it is made a virtue. The young are told that the remedy for discontent is hard work *within* the existing system, which will reward the deserving according to their industry, ambition, and honesty.

Although probably only a few young men took Horatio Alger literally, the general moral of his stories was widely accepted. Youth was defined as an apprenticeship for adulthood; the specific task of youth was to cultivate the many virtues and acquire the few skills needed for success in the upward road ahead. And so long as it remained credible, this definition of youth worked fairly well. It enjoined the young to answer discontent with hard work, to abandon the past willingly for greater goods ahead, and to view college as if it were the Pennsylvania Railroad Station, in Edgar Z. Friedenberg's phrase: its function was to teach the route and timetable for the journey ahead. The only problem for a young man (although it was not always a small problem) was to locate the right track and stay on it to his destination. Education was above all a matter of memorizing the map and timetable, and getting out as quickly as possible for the main journey ahead. Furthermore, as long as many young men believed in the possibility and desirability of upward mobility and success, this definition of youth assured the society a goodly reserve of eager young men who were determined to abandon the past, quick to learn the techniques of the new society, convinced that it was to their own benefit to work hard, and sustained even in poverty by fantasies of success, luck, and a helping hand ahead. And, finally, by transforming potential discontent and unrest into the struggle to get ahead *within* the system, this image of youth effectively prevented political involvement among the young.

But as we all now know, there were not enough kindly and helping bankers to go around, or enough thriving businesses to take over, or enough lovely bosses' daughters to marry. And, more important, American society has changed since Horatio Alger's day, so that its most visible, prestigious positions are no longer the conspicuous castles of bank presidents and robber barons, but rather the discreetly restrained steel-and-glass offices of executive vice presidents, technical advisers, scientists in business, and even, occasionally, a college professor with a government grant. Increasingly in our present society the older "entrepreneurial" virtues of thrift and determination, grit and gumption, are no longer enough; the newer requirements for prestige are at least a B.A., a certain personal sophistication, specialized technical competence, an acceptable wife, and at least a good imitation of a "genuine interest in people." Then, too, the intensity of the drive to success and prestige has itself lessened. In a day of middle-class affluence the push to escape the poverty and restriction of slum, farm, or immigrant background has lessened, and people worry more, and longer, about *how* to live the rich full life with the goods they *already* possess—and even sometimes question whether it is all worth the effort to begin with. Horatio Alger and "from rags to riches" are tokens of a fast-disappearing day; and with them, the image of youth as an apprenticeship for upward mobility is waning too.

Youth Culture

The definition of youth that in many places has replaced this older image is harder to pin down, harder even to find an adequate name for. I can only call it, in a cumbersome way, the image of youth as youth culture, and then try to make clear what I mean. The youth culture is the special set of mores, customs, roles, and values of youth considered as a distinctive, separate age group. In many primitive societies youth is not so considered; on the contrary, youths are seen either as old children or as young adults, not as members of an age group who—simply because they are adolescents—are expected to behave in a way distinct from both children and adults. But in other societies, especially those like our own where the transition from childhood to adulthood is difficult, late adolescents and early adults are expected to behave in special, idiosyncratic ways that are symptomatic of their age.

In America it is probably best to speak of many youth cultures, rather than one, for under this rubric we must subsume a great many different phenomena: teen-agers, "Joe College" students, youthful beatniks, rock'n'-rollers, juvenile delinquents. But, at the same time, all of these distinct cultures have certain common features. Talcott Parsons lists emphasis on physical attractiveness, irresponsibility, interest in athletics, repudiation of adult things—and to this list I would add other common characteristics, for example, a kind of hedonism of the moment, a reluctance to undertake long-range commitments, a high value placed on sensation, experience, and excitement. F. Scott Fitzgerald's picture of Princeton before and after the First War came to epitomize an earlier, "flaming youth" version of youth culture. In our own day, we have more various and contrasting versions, ranging from the black-jacketed delinquent to the oversensitive Catcher in the Rye, from the misunderstood James Dean to the fun-and-football fraternity man. The particular group most relevant to a discussion of student politics is what could be called "elite youth"—that is, those educationally privileged young men and women who correspond in talent and intelligence to the most politically active students in other nations. It is from this group that tomorrow's leaders will most likely be drawn; and these young men and women usually act as pace-setting models to other students. Although such "elite" students are more articulate than most of their contemporaries, they often voice aspirations and ideas implicit in other versions of the youth culture.

I have earlier discussed some of the characteristics of today's able young people: lack of deep commitment to adult values, absence of overt rebelliousness, lack of admired paternal figures, a sense of social power-lessness, privatism, foreshortening of time span, the cult of experience. (See "The Speed-up of Change," pp. 66–72.) At best, their youth culture has important virtues for the individual as for the society, providing what Erik Erikson calls a "psycho-social moratorium," that is, a sanctioned time and place when the young can decide how, where—and even whether—they will fit into society. And, above all, it provides a breathing spell between childhood and adulthood, time to develop a sense of personal identity that will link the problematical individual social and national past with the uncertain future, and, hopefully, will enable the young to develop their own guidelines for commitment and action. Thus, the definition of youth as youth culture helps the young to cope with the stresses and strains created by rapid social change and, at the same time, to do so in a thoroughly apolitical way that will not rock the social or political boat.

The transition from apprenticeship to youth culture is, of course, far from a completed fact. At many colleges, especially those that recruit primarily working-class and lower-middle-class students, the apprentices still dominate the scene. And even in so-called elite colleges, some students still view their education as an occupational passport and resist involvement with both the youth culture and the academic enterprise. Furthermore, as I will suggest below, I think we are witnessing the emergence of yet a third conception of youth, which differs from both apprenticeship and youth culture. So the shift in images of youth is complex and far from complete.

Nor do I want to imply that young men and women are either *simply* apprentices or *simply* youth culturists. To do so would be to leave out what is probably the central fact about most college students—namely, their *ambivalence toward their own youth*. A great deal has been said and written about the ambivalence of older people toward adolescents—the mixture of envy, respect, fear, titillation, exaggeration, and hope with which nonyouths perennially eye the younger generation. But much less has been said about the ambivalence of the young toward themselves, their fluctuation between a view of themselves as free and reckless participants in the most irresponsible of youth cultures, and the alternate image of themselves as sober and dedicated apprentice citizens. Indeed, a controversy rages between those observers who see American youth as wild and irresponsible, and those who see only the deferential and conformist side of youth.

The point is, I think, that these observers are usually looking at two sides of the very same people, mistaking the part for the whole. Such oversimplification is especially hard to avoid because young people themselves present now one and now another face, all the while maintaining that there is no more than meets the eye. Not that they deliberately deceive older people as to what they are like—on the contrary, when a young man or woman is with representatives of the adult world (teachers, ministers, admissions officers, polltakers) he not only acts like a future citizen of America, he really *feels* that way. And the same youths under other circumstances—when with friends, at Fort Lauderdale or Newport, in campus coffee houses, fraternities and sororities or dormitories—really *feel* like hoods, beatniks, College Joes or Dekes. But in each of these stances some of the same ambivalence exists, despite the frequent insistence of the young (with a characteristic adolescent combination of ambivalence and intolerance for ambivalence) that there is only one side to the coin.

However complex, shifting, and ambivalent these definitions of youth, they have in common a fundamental indifference to politics. Indeed, they do more than suggest indifference to politics; they make it virtually abnormal for a young man of standard middle-class background to become passionately involved with national or international issues. Not surprisingly, those few who have violated the implicit prohibition on politics in these images have often come from atypical milieus—usually either from recent European immigrant stock or from upper-class backgrounds capable of resisting the dominant American mores. And also not surprising is the array of reinforcing and supporting customs that have buttressed the apolitical outlook of American students. Among these buttressing customs two seem to me especially important today: what is usually referred to as campus politics, and what is often called the legacy of McCarthyism. Both of these are commonly misunderstood.

"Campus politics," as most Americans use the term, refers primarily to the intramural politics of American undergraduate life—the quarrels over elections to student legislatures and student judiciary councils, over the role of the dean of women and over that traditionally most vexing of college problems, the hours at women's dormitories. Thus, "campus politician" is a slightly pejorative term for a would-be manipulator of campus factions—and it seldom refers to a young person interested in broader political issues. Indeed, the substantive issues of campus politics seldom resemble the topics of what I will henceforth call "true politics"—that is, active concern with state, national, and international issues. But because of similarities in outward form (both have elections, issues, parties, candidates, campaigns, and parliaments), campus politics is usually seen as a "training for democracy," as a preparation for political responsibility in later life. In fact, however, I think that campus politics acts as a subtle deterrent to true political activity.

Campus politics usually short-circuits energy from political activity on the broader scene—much as, among adults, passionate arguments about new roads, school-bond issues, and fluoridation distract attention from more pressing and affecting national and international affairs. Once the energies of young men and women are channeled into such matters as the relationship between fraternity members and nonmembers, or 2 A.M. signouts from women's dormitories, they are seldom likely to be rechanneled into broader matters. The topics about which students are concerned are often quite important, but the point is that such intramural politics are often a substitute for, rather than a complement to, truly political interests. This short-circuiting is often abetted by frightened college administrators who distinguish between "on-campus" issues which are deemed within the competence of the young, and "off-campus" issues about which they cannot express themselves publicly. Such a distinction of course merely reinforces the definitions of youth that make it a time for preparation or panty raids, but not for real political interests.

But so-called student politics is a deterrent to true politics for another, more important reason: it implicitly suggests that individuals are not capable of making important decisions about the general welfare. To make this point clearer, assume that under the guise of "training for democracy" we were seeking to convince a generation of young Americans that they lacked the wisdom to make policy decisions, and that omnicompetent officials alone possessed this wisdom. It would be hard to find a better system than student politics. We would begin in grade school by gradually giving to students all the minor decisions with which the grownups did not want to be bothered—dances, class elections, crossing streets, bond drives, and so on. At the same time, however, we would reserve all of the major decisions for the grownups, met in secret council of the Tuesday Teachers' Meeting or in private session of the Board of Regents. To make sure that a complete feeling of incompetence ensued, we would make all student decisions, no matter how trivial, subject to review by some higher adult body. By these techniques, I think we could create in all but the most independent and strong-willed a subtle feeling—perhaps the more effective because never openly stated—that they were incapable of making any but the most trivial decisions, and even these, only if subject to review by higher authority. A generation so trained would feel powerless and helpless with major issues and would be inclined to leave truly political matters—things that really mattered—in the hands of higher-ups, whether they be principals, deans, Pentagons, or National Security Councils. In short, campus politics is too often instead of, rather than in addition to, true politics: it subtly convinces students that they are incapable of dealing with the major issues of national welfare and survival that ultimately affect them far more deeply than most campus issues.

Another factor that conspires with our apolitical images of youth—indeed is reinforced by them—is the fear remaining from the McCarthy period. When such fear is mentioned, we usually think of a youth who refuses to take part in some political activity in which he believes lest it "go on his record" and subsequently be "used against him." In fact, however, I think that the fear of later reprisal is small compared to that special American fear of one's own idealism and innocence, against which the "disclosures" of the McCarthy period reverberated. Americans, and especially American men, have always been afraid of being a "sucker," of being "taken in," of being "had," or of being "duped"—of becoming the unwilling and unknowing instrument of another's will. One of the revealing peculiarities of American speech illustrates this fear in a more general context—it is good for a man to make something, but never to be made— whether it be to be made *to do* something, to be made *into* something, or, worst of all, simply to *be made*.

Thus, the "disclosures" of the Red baiters, and their world of "unwitting dupes," "front organizations," "inconscient tools," "pseudo Reds," "hapless victims," etc., activated a not-too-latent fear in many young Americans that their idealism, tender-mindedness, sensitivity, or innocence might mislead them into the position of the "sucker." When students give reasons for refusing to sign political petitions with which they fully agree, they usually cite their doubts as to the backers and sponsors of the petition, worrying about the uses to which their names might be put. It is a mistake to assume that these students are really considering future security clearance; rather, in an age of conspiratorial interpretations of history, all but the most resolute or insensitive tremble lest they too become the pawns of conspiracy. Given such nagging doubts, and the impossibility of ever being *sure* about the credentials of any petition, individual, or group, inaction is often the safest and easiest course. But by taking this course, young men and women merely confirm that image of youth that deems youthful political activity somehow "un-American."

Given these apolitical images of youth, and the distractions and fears that have supported them, it is not surprising that until recently few lights have broken the political darkness on most American campuses. To be sure, in the thirties there were flickers of left-wing political groups in metropolitan and "elite" colleges, but their total membership was small; and although the students involved were talented and vocal far beyond their numbers, they found few answering voices among the majority of their fellow students. Further, the ardor of even these students was first channeled into the war and then cooled by the Cold War, so that by 1950 left-wing groups had disappeared from most American campuses. The Mc-Carthy period brought no student political protest, although students as a group were far more opposed to indiscriminate Red-hunting than the general population. Nor did student organizations like the Young Republicans and Young Democrats constitute real exceptions. Small as these groups were, their claimed membership was swollen by inactive members who joined in search of an extracurricular activity for the nonathletic; and their active membership included a disproportionate number of ex-debaters and future lawyers, including not a few seeking prepolitical apprenticeships and free visitors' passes to the next National Convention.

The New Political Minority

In the past two years, however, there have been signs of increasing political activity on a number of campuses. And although I should re-emphasize that by foreign standards the students involved are very few in number, they are of interest both for the unprecedented attention they receive and for their possible role as forecasts of things to come. The two most visible new groups are the right-wing organizations usually associated with Young Americans for Freedom (Y.A.F.) and the single-issue groups, usually left wing, organized around such issues as desegregation, disarmament and loyalty oaths. It is generally agreed that right-wing groups elicit less support from most student bodies than the single-issue groups, and that they are not always spontaneous student creations. But on the basis of very unsystematic acquaintance with such right-wing groups and their literature and with one or two current studies of their membership, I think that they are bringing into political activity a kind of youth who has previously been politically inactive—a type we can call the displaced apprentice.

Such students continue to view college, and youth, in terms of an older apprentice image. At liberal arts colleges, however, they increasingly find no timetable to memorize, no maps of the terrain ahead, but instead a heavy pressure to make a commitment to the youth culture or even the academic enterprise itself. They frequently come from small conservative towns; and their parents' teachings and sacrifices have given them an outlook and a character that would have fit them well for upward mobility in the older, more entrepreneurial society. These students at many liberal arts colleges now find themselves in a minority, viewed with puzzlement by their contemporaries and teachers; furthermore, they usually see that academic rewards and prestige go to the more sensitive, searching, and interpersonally minded. The broader political scene also affects them: during the Eisenhower Administration, there still seemed a place for the inner-directed in the counsels of state and power; but the Kennedy Administration, with its surrounding phalanxes of college professors, suggests that the days of the old-fashioned entrepreneur are numbered. From several points of view, the displaced apprentice faces the unpleasant alternative of accepting his college's and by extension his society's judgment of him as out-of-date—or else of finding a way to repudiate the values and the people that deem him outmoded.

A group like Y.A.F. seems to provide an answer to some such students. For one, it offers a meeting place with other like-minded young men and women, and a sense of belonging to a group with powerful backers and a conspiratorial air. But more important, the ideology of a group like Y.A.F., which ascetically calls for a return to a purer, harder, and tougher America, gives the displaced apprentice a voice for repudiating the soft-minded liberals, college professors, bureaucrats, and others who epitomize the newer America in which he is characterologically obsolescent. And, not least of all, belonging to such a group permits a student of conservative background to retain and reinforce his loyalty to his parents and home town, and perhaps even to contemplate going home again to run for office on a conservative ticket.

But if the so-called resurgent right can be partly understood in terms of traditional American definitions of youth, the single-issue groups that are more prominent on most college campuses do not fit these definitions. To understand these groups we must posit the emergence of a third American definition of youth, one that is only now beginning to take shape, and one whose future remains uncertain. This new conception of youth, which I will call "academic," has as its distinctive feature a commitment to intellect, to knowledge, to scholarship and the academic enterprise, relatively unheard-of in earlier American college generations. At the same time, it involves considerable generational self-consciousness—awareness of oneself as a member of a distinctive age group rather like the youth culture—and also a basic acceptance of the traditional values of our society: those values that, although not always practiced by parents and elders, are at least preached.

The emergence of the academic image of youth is in part a conse-

quence of the changing complexion of student bodies. As admission standards rise, the caliber of college applicants rises with them, so that more
and more students arrive at college well prepared, already committed to
the values and vices of the academic community, more genuinely interested in getting an education (if necessary for its own sake), less patient
with both vocationalism and fraternities. Most teachers will testify that
these students are still in a minority; but they are a growing minority that
at some colleges will soon become the majority. Their level of sophistication and awareness is extremely high, probably higher than that of any
previous college group; and while they are not immune to the pressures
against political commitment in this country, they are at the same time
more realistically aware of the importance of national and international
issues for their own and their generation's future.

To be sure, the outlooks of such students are not necessarily political.
Often their interests are rather narrowly academic; and for some, ascent of
the ladders of academic specialization and promotion will merely replace
older forms of status-seeking, leaving little time for politics. And when
they are politically committed, such academic students are seldom radical
or revolutionary; rather, they are interested in basic and unexceptionable
American values like peace, equality, and freedom. Their differences with
their parents are seldom over matters of basic value, but rather over the
implementation of these values, as with the Negro students active in the
sit-in movement who have shocked older Negro leaders—including their
own parents—by trying to achieve in practice the rights that their elders
had always affirmed but never dared to demand. And, finally, the distinctive political style of such students is restrained, reflective, cautious, intellectual, and even pedantic.

Only some, and perhaps only a few, of the students active in the single-
issue groups fit this picture; but there are enough, I think, to color the style
of these groups. One sees the restraint of these students in their picketing
and petitions rather than protests and parades, in their carefully planned
study-and-discussion groups, in their debates at which they give their opponents the platform, and above all in the nonviolence and self-control of
the Negro sit-in movement. Such students resist efforts to organize them in
the service of some general ideological program, so that attempts of radical
groups to capture the student peace movement or the Negro sit-in movement have been remarkably unsuccessful. And the academic style of such
students was manifest during the recent peace march on Washington in
their original (if not invariably successful) effort to present carefully
studied and reasoned arguments to Congressmen and government officials.

The recent political activity of "academic" students is due to a variety
of factors. For one, the number of such students is increasing, so that the

reservoir of students intelligently aware of "true politics" has increased. And, for another, the relative success and restraint of the Negro sit-in movement has inspired white students in the North to supporting action which, once begun, was easily redirected into other activities like disarmament and anti-House Un-American Activities Committee groups. But most important has been the change of administration in Washington. Unlike its predecessor, the Kennedy Administration has been solicitous of the good opinion of future voters and responsive to student demonstrations— at least to the extent of "symbolic" pots of coffee, if not to changes in policy. And most crucial to students of academic outlook has been the presence of a number of academic, academically respected men on the President's staff. If the entrepreneurial apprentice found justification for inactivity in the golf-links-and-shooting-brake ethos of the Eisenhower regime, the academic student finds a spur to activity in the Harvard-Senior-Common-Room mentality of Kennedy's immediate entourage. Not even the touch football of the Kennedy clan, which reminds him uncomfortably of his own lack of athletic prowess, subdues his hopes that his kind may yet have a say in Washington.

But for all of the interest and publicity aroused (and sought) by the new political activists on American campuses, the fact remains that few students are involved, and that most of them are concentrated at a few of the most selective institutions like California, Harvard, Michigan, Antioch, etc. The vast majority—at "elite" colleges more than 90 per cent and at most colleges probably more than 99 per cent—remain uninvolved with true politics beyond perhaps a perfunctory membership in the local branch of the Young Republicans. So in considering the future of student politics, the critical question is whether these "inert masses" are destined to become more active than they have been traditionally.

The Future of Students in Politics

The future is, of course, something that is determined by men and groups of men. And it follows that the shape of the future is not merely something to be guessed at, but, if we have hopes, something to be molded in accordance with these hopes. There are many, of course, who hope that American youth will remain unconcerned with politics. Political apathy, it is said, prevents the radical youth movements that plague other governments; and in more sophisticated sociological terms, essentially the same argument is phrased in terms of social stability and social solidarity. It is probably apparent by now that my own hopes differ. For one, I see little likelihood of American students ever playing a radical role, much less a revolutionary one, in our society. And, even if they did, it would be far from a calamity, given the almost total absence of radical or fundamental criticism of American society at present. On the contrary, I am more impressed with the dangers of political inactivity, ignorance, and helplessness, especially in an era when the future of civilization or of life itself depends on a few words spoken into a red telephone in the Rockies or the Urals. In such a time, the greatest danger is not student ferment but resignation from concern with the shape of the wider world—the delegation of responsibility for survival to experts, weapons specialists, generals, and even to Presidents and their academic advisers.

More important, then, than guessing at the future of student politics is the effort to suggest ways of increasing political involvement and activity on college campuses. And here the academic community seems to be bound to play a major role. I noted earlier that the form and style of the "academic" definition of youth was still indeterminate. Just as the real-life counterparts of Horatio Alger's bankers helped form the concept of apprenticeship, and just as the peer group and mass media helped define the youth culture, so the members of the academic community will have an especially large part in forming the outlooks of the emerging "academic" student, determining among other things the extent to which these students consider political concern and activity appropriate and necessary to their lives.

Here teachers can do a number of things. For one, I think we must increasingly question our traditional American opposition to ideology. To be sure, everyone is against narrow and blind dogmatism; but if by ideology we merely mean a coherent political program that embraces many sectors of society, then common sense dictates an ideological approach to politics. All of the recent evidence from the social sciences suggests how difficult it is to deal with single issues in isolation. To deal with only one issue at a time is rather as if the physician agreed to treat only the external symptoms of a disease, or the psychiatrist pledged himself to discuss only the current manifestations of a neurosis. Social and political issues are complex, complexly interrelated; and sometimes the best way to alleviate one problem is to ignore it and start with another. A commitment to a single-issue approach or inflexible opposition to ideology is too often a commitment to ineffectuality or opposition to fundamental cure.

Secondly, and at a very different level, far more can be done to encourage students to understand their own position in the world and their role in society. Here I obviously do not mean that students should be lectured about social responsibility and the perversity of privatism. Such preaching would have the opposite effect, if only because privatism is already a kind of *faute de mieux* response, a compensation on the part of young men and women who would quickly seize a beautiful or noble or challenging purpose if they could but find one. Nor do I mean that students should be required to take more courses in political science and international relations. Instead, or in addition, I think that intelligent young people should be encouraged and helped to explore their own positions and places in society, to understand better the conflicts and stresses that beset them, not only as individuals, but as members of a generation, a nation, and the twentieth century. Here most colleges do far too little, for those courses that deal with our society and our motivations often deliberately seek to prevent personal involvement, soul-searching, and application of knowledge to one's own life—in short, they seek to prevent that participation that alone can give insight. But one can imagine—in fact many of us have seen it happen—that a real awareness of the psychosocial forces that confront their generation can give students a vastly heightened sense of their political responsibilities and powers.

And, finally, teachers must be aware of their growing role not only as imparters of information and techniques to their students, but as personal exemplars. This is a role that most teachers consciously dislike, but students cast their teachers as heroes or villains in the best of times. Even the most anti-intellectual undergraduate finds among his instructors models of ivory-tower withdrawal and narrow pedantry that he determines *not* to emulate. But when society by and large lacks adequate paternal exemplars, students become more inclined to seek them among their teachers. And in the coming years as more and more students arrive in college already committed to academic interests and values, they will be even more likely to search for epitomes of the good (academic) life among their instructors. Less insulated against emulation by a contempt for the "merely academic" and by a loyalty to the youth culture, they will be more inclined to find their teachers worthy unless proved otherwise, and probably more likely to emulate them even when they are not worthy.

All of this means that an increased responsibility (and to most teachers an unwanted one) falls on the academic community in shaping the self-definitions and ideals of youth. The academic community has two mutually exclusive possibilities, which lead to very different outcomes in terms of student politics. One is pedantry—a narrow concentration on subspecialties within fenced-off fields, hostility to general interests, to speculation, and to broad commitments. The other I would call intelligence at its best, and it is marked by social and political concern and by openness to the nonacademic world, which is after all the ultimate *raison d'être* of the college and university. Which possibility prevails seems to me very important; for what is ultimately at issue is our own personal survival and the survival of civilization in the world. Not that these issues will be decided by or at American colleges—far from it; but if we are granted so much time, they will be decided in part by young men and women who have attended these colleges. And just as past generations of Americans have patterned themselves on earlier images of youth, so the coming generation will be formed by the conceptions of youth, and life, available to them.

At worst, a narrow academicism of the young could result, made more intolerant and vicious by the fusion of personal ambition and a pseudopatriotism that thinks we can "harness brainpower" to beat the Russians. At best, an academic generation might become a truly intelligent generation, animated by public concern and guided by political understanding. In helping to shape such a concept, the most that teachers can do (and it is a great deal) is to suggest possibilities, to hold open doors, to criticize the false and spurious, and to support the true—and above all to try to embody in their own lives that humane political concern and openness of social vision that is the mark of true intelligence.

Faces in the Lecture Room

*In an issue on "The Contemporary University," the Journal of the American
Academy of Arts and Sciences,* Daedalus, *included articles about virtually
every aspect of modern higher education—except students. When the
time came to transform the* Daedalus *issue into a book, the absence of any
discussion of students was noted, and several articles on the topic were
commissioned.*

*My essay, "Faces in the Lecture Room" (1966), starts by asking how
it could be that students, presumably one important reason for higher
education, could be neglected in most discussions of the university. But
my chief purpose here is to present a typology of American students based
upon an historical analysis of the changing concept of the student.
Expanding the discussion in "The Political Revival," I argued that each of
the major student types visible on American campuses has its origins in a
distinct historical period, and that only as we near the present, with the
appearance on a mass scale of an academic-intellectual definition of
higher education, do we begin to find any significant number of students
prepared to take a critical stance toward the society in which they live.*

*Typologies of students come and go: in later writings (see "What's
Bugging the Students?") I abandoned this particular one, which reflected
a moment in the 1960's. But the general principle on which this typology
is based seems to me valid and important. For it continues to be true that
the human types found in any complex and changing society are a kind of
psychological sedimentation of historical conditions. Most of the conflicts
between groups with different orientations and values in modern American
society seem to me conflicts between groups attached to a different
historical definition of society, and psychologically adapted to that society.
The problem is that men, at least today, are rarely able to change as fast
as technologies, international conditions, values, or even institutions, with
the result that millions of us are psychologically "adapted" to historical
societies that disappeared long ago. When this happens, our adaptations
become maladaptations, and what were once vital life styles and
personality organizations are apt to become mean, frightened, intolerant,
and defensive.*

IT is easier to describe an institution than an individual or a generation. For institutions, like universities, at least have formal organizational
charts, constant aims, established traditions, continuing programs, and
chronically troubled relations with state and national governments. But
individuals like students are by virtue of their stage in life changeable and
changing, malleable yet often intransigent. Thus, for every statement we
make about "the contemporary student," there is a readily available coun-
terstatement, often backed by imposing evidence. To emphasize the activism of some highly vocal students seems to neglect the lack of commitment of the quieter majority. And to speak of the "seriousness" of many
students is to ignore the frivolity evidenced by many others.

Furthermore, characterizations of students have a special way of being
self-fulfilling or self-defeating, but rarely simply apt. To write about
students today is also to write *for* students; no audience of adults awaits so
eagerly the latest poll, the latest analysis, or the latest description of
"students today." And to write for students is to write for a group who,
rather than be nothing, may all too readily accept the latest label—silent,
beat, activist, rebellious, cool, explosive, committed. But, at other times,
students may unpredictably react *against* a label—resisting characterization, defying pigeonholing, refusing to be what they are told they are.
Indeed, one factor behind the increasingly vocal activism of some students
today may be their desire to reject the epithet of "silent" bequeathed them
by students in the late 1950's. The process of characterization affects the
characterized; an incorrect label may be accepted slavishly; a correct description may inspire a reaction that soon invalidates it.

In a society changing at a dizzying pace, we no sooner arrive at a
tentative characterization of a generation of students than we become
aware that our generalization is no longer valid. Since the end of World
War II, at least a half-dozen "generations" have been labeled and described, only to disappear before a new and different "generation." This
points to one of the crucial facts about students today: their characteristics
change extremely rapidly; they are extraordinarily responsive to the fluc-
tuating pressures of American society. To the universal fact that young
adults are always capable of rapid change simply by virtue of their stage
in life is added the historical fact that American students are also responding to a rapidly changing society. All of this gives today's students an
unusually mercurial and protean quality.

Areas of Ignorance

Anyone who tries to discuss American students is confronted with immense areas of ignorance. For, despite years of systematic research using

students as subjects, there is astonishingly little knowledge of students as people. On the whole, American psychology and sociology have been more interested in "universal" relationships between operationally defined variables than in human lives—or even in asking whether relationships discovered among college sophomores who happen to be taking Psychology 1a are necessarily true for all mankind. Students are *used* in psychological research but rarely studied qua students. Only in the past decade have longitudinal studies of students' development in relation to their educational institutions begun in earnest, and most of the results are not yet in.

The state of current knowledge about students is ably summarized in Nevitt Sanford's massive compendium *The American College*. But we may well leave this opus more confused than we began it: virtually every article tells the same story of positive findings matched by negative findings and concludes by calling for further, more sophisticated, research. Most important, there have still been very few studies of student development and student characteristics as they relate to the university. And the few important exceptions to this generalization suffer because the colleges studied were usually small, private, and intensely academic liberal-arts colleges. Just as the first sociologists to investigate social class in America studied towns where class lines were extremely rigid, so those who have studied student development have selected small liberal arts colleges where students *do* develop. But one review of research on changing values in college suggests that such colleges may be the *exception* to the general rule that most American students are manifestly unaffected by their education.

Even in the private, academic, liberal arts college it is not clear whether the college produces change or merely happens to be the setting where it occurs, for such colleges characteristically recruit the most able freshmen, who arrive already eager to discard outworn outlooks and acquire new values. Perhaps these students are already so firmly launched on a trajectory of self-transformation that even in a nonacademic college they would have insisted upon changing. Doubtless both factors—the motivations and talents of entering freshmen *and* the characteristics of the college—co-operate to produce the senior and the adult. But of how these factors interact, and of how they should be weighed, we know very little.

One fact about American students today is of course clear: there are more of them than there have ever been before in any nation of the world. Not only is the college age group larger, but every year a greater proportion of this age group attends college. Already more than 50 per cent of high school graduates go on for higher education; and in some states this figure approaches 75 per cent. Yet the vast hordes of students attending colleges and graduate schools merely add to the difficulties in characterizing "the student." American college youth is becoming more and more synonymous with American youth in general, and the study of students as a group assumes all of the complexity of the study of national character.

Furthermore, the enormous increase in the numbers of students in college and graduate school has led to a greater variety both in the types of students attending college and in the types of colleges they attend. The influx of students also permits a kind of specialization not only among academic programs but among student bodies. At the same time that the diversity of American universities has increased, the homogeneity of students within each university has probably increased as well.

This specialization most obviously affects the "elite" colleges. One consequence of the flood of students has been an increase in the intellectual caliber of those who attend the most selective colleges. Such institutions have been unable or unwilling to expand their facilities to match the growing pressure on their admissions offices. Admissions standards have therefore become increasingly selective: each new freshman class is routinely "the best in history." And more stringent entrance requirements have widened the intellectual gap between the student bodies of selective colleges and those at the bottom of the intellectual scale. Some American colleges now recruit their entire student bodies from among the most talented 5 per cent, 3 per cent, or even 1 per cent of the college age group: they are able as never before to specialize in educating only the very intelligent and well prepared. But other, less selective colleges bear the main burden of educating that growing proportion of young Americans of average and less-than-average intellectual ability who at least begin college.

What is true of talent that can be measured by IQ tests is equally true of other talents, aptitudes, and outlooks that are harder to quantify. Students of similar personality type clearly tend to be concentrated in colleges that "specialize" in educating (or failing to educate) just that type. But we know very little about how to define these types precisely— of the characteristics of those who attend the new municipal and junior colleges, or of what distinguishes students at private Protestant denominational colleges, urban Catholic universities, or major and minor technological institutes. Moreover, not all colleges and universities of the same apparent category draw the same type of student. Within a broad category like city colleges or denominational colleges, student bodies range from intense academic commitment to complete vocationalism or narrow fundamentalism. Useful ways of describing and contrasting colleges and their student bodies are only beginning to be found.

Furthermore, colleges and student bodies are continually changing. The growing admissions pressure on selective colleges has generated a kind of academic fallout on secondary schools and less selective colleges.

Parents who live in suburban middle-class areas are notoriously eager to have their children admitted to "good" colleges: they exert pressure on local school boards to create more advanced programs in secondary schools. The result is paradoxical, for since more students arrive each year at college gates with advanced standing, high achievement scores, and rigorous academic training, academic gate-keepers must raise their entrance hurdles still higher, generating new pressures on secondary schools to upgrade still further, and so on.

The result—more and more students with superior secondary-school training—indirectly changes less selective and less academic colleges. Since only a few of these well-qualified students can be admitted to "elite" colleges, the rest must go to institutions of second and third choice. Many a college which one generation ago had no admissions standards whatsoever now finds itself able to pick and choose among its applicants. Without any expenditure, effort, or improvement of program or faculty, thousands of highly motivated students appear on campus, well trained and chafing at the academic bit. These students can sometimes effect a real improvement in the quality of the colleges they attend, but they have also created an unprecedented phenomenon on some American campuses—a tension between a second-rate faculty and an academically committed student body.

In general, there is a considerable "match" between the characteristics of a university or college and the characteristics of its students. The "better" colleges obviously get the high-IQ, high-performance students: admissions tests alone can guarantee this. Similarly, the most academically motivated students tend to find their way to liberal arts colleges that provide a maximum of intellectual stimulation. And high school graduates who still view college as "learning to get along with other people" usually enter institutions where fun, social life, fraternities, and sororities still dominate the campus. But precisely how and why this matching of student to college takes place remains unclear. Certainly the "image" of a college has a great deal to do with the selective application of the "right" type of student. But in no college is the match between student needs and capacities and the institution's provisions and demands perfect.

Nor should a perfect match be viewed as the ideal. Education, after all, aims at inducing change in students; and some disparity between what the entering freshman is and what the college thinks he should become by graduation is necessary if college is to be more than stagnation or play. But no one really knows how to define the optimal disparity. If the gap between what the student wants and expects and what the college provides and asks is too great, then frustration, a sense of failure, or discontent is likely to result. But if what the student brings with him to college and what the college expects from him are too perfectly matched, the

result is likely to be that stagnation which some observers think characteristic of student development at many major American colleges.

Furthermore, an ideal match for men students may not be at all ideal
for women; yet little is known about the educational differences between
the sexes. Most studies concentrate on one or the other sex, yet generalize
to both. But anyone who has taught both sexes can personally document
the enormous difference between their educational outlooks, concerns,
and motivations. It is not yet clear, for example, to what extent student
development as described in two classic studies of Bennington and Vassar
should be generalized to most students, most liberal arts students, most
female students, or most female liberal arts students. Other accounts of
contemporary students seem relevant primarily to me; thus, for example,
very few of the "activists" in the present generation are drawn from
among coeds. Whether we consider it a result of anatomy or social condi-
tioning, women view their educations and their lives very differently than
do men.

Many discussions of contemporary students have an implicitly historical or cross-cultural perspective, comparing students today and yesterday,
here and abroad. Yet our historical and cultural ignorance about students
is once again more impressive than our knowledge. Today, at least, we
have public-opinion polls and a number of on-going studies of student
development. About the past, however, we have only impressionistic and
journalistic accounts. When researchers attempt to compare today's
students with their forebears, they are inevitably forced to rely on studies
of alumni, where the effects of aging are almost impossible to distinguish
from real generational differences. Cross-cultural studies, too, are in their
infancy. Everyone knows that American students are different even from
students in Western Europe, to say nothing of the developing nations.
Americans are less politicized, less ideological, and more concerned with
the practical and private aspects of life. But how much of this difference is
due to the different selectivity of universities abroad, how much to differences in national style and character, how much to different stages of national economic and political development, how much to specifically educational influences—all these questions remain unanswered.

Still another unanswered question concerns the role of masses and
elites in the contemporary American university. Whatever the modal characteristics of any given student body as reflected in a public-opinion poll,
every campus has its deviants, its leaders, and its subcultures. In some
cases, these may be of greatest interest to the college psychiatrist. But in
other cases, markedly atypical students may be the leaders of their generation. In retrospect, for example, extreme left-wing students in the 1930's
were clearly in a minority. But their articulateness, visibility, and energy
have left their mark on the entire generation. Similarly, student activists,

beatniks, and voluntary dropouts constitute a minority of the more than 5 million students attending college today. Yet these students have a disproportionate influence, not only on the public image of students as transmitted through the mass media, but also on students' images of themselves. Even more than other age groups, students are prone to vicarious identification with others; and many an apathetic student on a vast campus where only a few dozen classmates are active in civil rights work considers himself a member of an "activist" generation.

Nor should this judgment be considered automatically invalid when it is not substantiated by a public-opinion poll. Most revolutions are made by small elites that are ahead of the masses; yet revolutions do occur. The Bolsheviks were but a fringe of a faction in Russian radical thought, but they eventually dominated the Russian Revolution. In this respect, public-opinion surveys can be misleading, for, in characterizing students, we need to know not only what is typical, but what is salient, visible, and prominent in students' judgments of themselves.

The next decade is likely to bring some light into these areas of ignorance. At a number of American colleges and universities, research now underway will help characterize more exactly the variety of American colleges and student bodies, helping distinguish between men and women, the past and the present, here and abroad, the typical and the salient. But as of today one group of American students seems likely to remain almost completely unstudied. Most commentators on the contemporary university at least recognize that undergraduates and undergraduate education remain an "unsolved problem." But graduate students are discussed, if at all, as if theirs was but the idyllic reward for superior college performance. In fact, however, the plight of graduate students is probably more dire than that of any other student group. Undergraduates may be ignored and neglected, but neglect at least gives those who desire it a certain freedom. The graduate student, in contrast, is often pressured, judged, graded, indentured, and exploited in a way that has few parallels in the annals of civilized oppression. He is, at present, the forgotten man in American education: no one is even studying him.

However we may explain it, this considerable body of ignorance about the contemporary student is symbolic of, if not a reflection of, one of the crucial facts about students today. In discussions of the university, the education of students is too often relegated to the end of the list of unsolved problems. And most American universities devote vastly more attention to every conceivable research question than they do to trying to understand their own students. To be sure, everyone acknowledges that without students there can be no university; and so, too, "education" is widely admitted to be one of the functions of a university. Yet the characteristics of students—the fact that they have commitments, aspirations, values, dreams, needs, psyches, and perhaps souls even *before* being admitted to college—are largely ignored in the concentration on more easily describable features of the university. To many administrators and to some faculty members, students remain a kind of unleavened lump to be molded by the university, blank cards on which education will punch imperishable information, shapeless ingots to be pressed into useful forms by "the college experience." All too often students must bring their real existence forcibly to the attention of college administrators through demonstrations, misbehavior, or vocal misery. The university remains, while student bodies change; the lecture room endures, only slowly eroded by time, whereas the faces in the lecture room change year by year and hour by hour.

Just as our attention is more readily caught by the institutions that students attend than by the students who attend them, so students themselves often feel lost in the contemporary university and in contemporary society. This fact, and all it portends about both university and society, is probably the central fact about American students today. They are embedded from kindergarten to the grave in the complex, organized, specialized, professional, bureaucratized, and impersonal institutions of American life. Whether we like it or not, we all—student and teachers alike—live in the most advanced technological nation of the world; and in such a society, as in its educational institutions, individuals tend to feel lost and to have to devise new ways to assert their individuality and justify their lives.

Even in the absence of solid information which would make a definitive portrait of American students possible, we must attempt to understand the contemporary student. For much of what goes on in a university goes on among students; and education is not merely the molding of an inert lump, but a transaction between an institution on the one hand and students on the other. In this transaction, the characteristics of students are as crucial as those of the university; only in so far as the university understands the potentials, commitments, and needs of those it teaches can it really educate them well.

In the remarks to follow, I will attempt to characterize, however impressionistically, one segment of American students—those who attend the more selective and traditionally more pace-setting colleges and universities. I will be talking largely of students at the great state universities like California and Michigan, the great private universities and university colleges on the East and West coasts, and the small private liberal arts colleges across the nation. I will be dealing largely with the problems and outlooks of men students and will stress what seems to me characteristically different about today's student. Thus, I will be comparing the contemporary student with the student of previous generations, and not with students abroad. And I will draw not only on the research and impressions of others, but also upon my own subjective impressions.

From Gentleman to Professionalist

Even within a relatively homogeneous liberal arts college, it is impossible to speak of *the* student: we meet instead a variety of clearly distinguishable *types* of students. These can be classified in various ways, according to intelligence, field of concentration, social background, future profession, and the like. But the most useful classification, if we are interested in what is new about students today, will be historical. Any American university contains student types whose origins lie at different points in American history: there is a kind of historical stratification within American student bodies, each layer originating in a distinct historical era, having outlooks dating from that era, partaking of a different historical style of life. The past never disappears or fades away: it is merely submerged under the present. And the representatives of past ways of life continue to live in today's society, only gradually being buried under more contemporary types. Thus, a historical typology of students can serve as an introduction to the distinctly contemporary student.

Two centuries ago advanced education was largely the prerogative of the most privileged groups in American society. Colleges like Harvard, Yale, or William and Mary existed primarily to educate the religious leaders, future merchants, and "gentlemen" of society. Education was intimately involved with the way of life embodied in the established Protestant churches, the descendants of Anglo-Saxon settlers, and the Federalist establishment. Often aping the manners of European aristocrats, this group emphasized Christianity in religion, prosperity in commerce, and aristocratic disdain for the masses, tempered by commitment to social service.

Students of this era were thus largely *gentlemen-in-waiting*. Some later became parsons, others merchants, and still others scholars and teachers; but, for all, education was not so much a preparation for a specific vocation as a refinement of the gentlemanly qualities. Nor did education "make" a gentleman: to be educated at all, one had first to possess gentlemanly antecedents. But education was a finishing school, a way of acquiring polish, knowledge of the world, familiarity with the classics—all topped off with a Grand Tour. In this sense, education was dispensable: since gentlemen are born, not made, advanced schooling has never been a necessity for upper-class Americans. Striving and "achievement" motivation were largely irrelevant; going to college could not make a student into something he was not. Nor did it really provide useful vocational training for anyone but the parson-to-be. Rather, education merely confirmed a gentleman in what he already was, perhaps teaching him how to express it better.

With the extension of democratic rights in the first half of the nineteenth century and the ensuing decline of the Federalist establishment, a new conception of education began to emerge. Education was no longer a confirmation of a pre-existing status, but an instrument in the acquisition of higher status. For a new generation of upwardly mobile students, the goal of education was not to prepare them to live comfortably in the world into which they had been born, but to teach them new virtues and skills that would propel them into a different and better world. Education became training; and the student was no longer the gentleman-in-waiting, but the journeyman *apprentice* for upward mobility.

In the nineteenth century a college education began to be seen as a way to get ahead in the world. The founding of the land-grant colleges opened the doors of higher education to poor but aspiring boys from non-Anglo-Saxon, working-class, and lower-middle-class backgrounds. The myth of the poor boy who worked his way through college to success drew millions of poor boys to the new campuses. And with this shift, education became more vocational: its object was the acquisition of practical skills and useful information.

For the gentleman-in-waiting, virtue consisted above all in grace and style, in doing well what was appropriate to his position; education was merely a way of acquiring polish. And vice was manifested in gracelessness, awkwardness, in behaving inappropriately, discourteously, or ostentatiously. For the apprentice, however, virtue was evidenced in success through hard work. The requisite qualities of character were not grace or style, but drive, determination, and a sharp eye for opportunity. While casual liberality and even prodigality characterized the gentleman, frugality, thrift, and self-control came to distinguish the new apprentice. And while the gentleman did not aspire to a higher station because his station was already high, the apprentice was continually becoming, striving, struggling upward. Failure for the apprentice meant standing still, not rising.

In the early twentieth century still another type of student began to appear. As American society became more developed economically and more bureaucratized, upward mobility was no longer guaranteed by ambition, drive, and practical knowledge. In addition, those who aspired to success had to possess the ability to make friends and influence people. Mastering the human environment became more important than mastering the physical and economic environment. The function of education thus became not vocational training, but teaching the ability to be likable and persuasive and to get along with all kinds of people. College life was increasingly seen as an informal training ground for social skills; virtue was defined as popularity; and a new type, exemplified by the *Big Men on Campus,* began to emerge.

Students who sought popularity and skill in dealing with people were naturally likely to emphasize the social rather than the academic or vocational aspects of higher education. Fraternities, student governments, even casual walks across the college campus, calling friends by name and saying "Hi" to strangers, were the new classrooms. Vocational skills became secondary—or, more precisely, the most important skills in *any* vocation were the capacity to make oneself respected, well liked, and a leader. The new sin was not gaucheness or standing still, but unpopularity. To the Big Man on Campus, academic and intellectual interests were irrelevant: whatever intelligence he possessed went into a rather calculated effort to please and impress others, win their respect, and dominate them without their knowing they were being dominated.

The emergence of the Big Man on Campus as an ideal type among American students coincided with the appearance of a distinctively non-academic youth culture. The gentleman and the apprentice were both oriented primarily to the adult world: their most relevant models were adults —either the parental generation of gentlemen or the older generation of upwardly mobile and successful entrepreneurs. For the Big Man on Campus, however, the adult world was less immediately important. He looked mainly to his peers, for only by establishing his popularity in their eyes could he demonstrate his merit. Thus student cultures became more and more insulated both from academic culture and from adult society, developing their own rites, rituals, and traditions. The world of students became a separate world, not merely a reflection of or a preparation for adulthood. And as many observers have noted, the outlooks of this world were clearly distinguishable from the outlooks of adulthood—the student youth culture emphasized immediacy, enjoyment of the moment, popularity, attractiveness, sports, daring, and intellectual indifference. Walls, barricades, and fences of apathy, deafness, and blindness were built between students and the more academic, intellectual values of their teachers. The power of these fortifications is suggested by the monotonous finding of research done before World War II that so many students were so little affected by the values their colleges sought to promote.

Since that time, yet another type of student has begun to emerge. Today "superior academic performance" is a prerequisite for admission to any desirable college, let alone graduate school. Grace, ambition, and popularity have fallen into secondary position, for, without good grades and the ability to do well on IQ tests, the gentlemanly, ambitious, or popular student is not even considered by the admissions office. From an early age students are therefore exposed and overexposed to academic demands: they are taught from kindergarten onward that prestige and rewards are impossible without intellectual competence, cognitive efficiency, intellectual skill, and a high degree of specialization.

But these pressures within American education themselves reflect and are made weightier by comparable pressures in American society at large. The growth of the pressure for academic performance coincides with the full development of a technological society, with a new set of technological virtues. Even our new technological heroes, the astronauts, are a carefully selected and screened group of experienced professional pilots, all of whom have IQ's of 130 and over and a B.S. in engineering. And though they may be heroes in the eyes of the nation, heroism plays little part among their own motives. One study finds that "they are less concerned with abstractions and ideas as such than with the application of thought to problems solvable in terms of technical knowledge and professional experience." Even their trust in their fellow men "seems to depend largely on their sharing common standards of professional and technical competence with co-workers. It is faith in the *expertness* of the man, rather than dependence on the *man* himself, that allows them to accept interdependence without suspicion."

The virtues of the astronauts are the ascendant virtues of the technological age. Our contemporary heroes are not men of mere aristocratic lineage, driving ambition, or social skill, but men of intense technical competence, high professional expertise, and careful specialization. These qualities are the prerequisites for a responsible position in adult society; and, without them, aristocrats, robber barons, or grown-up Big Men on Campus get nowhere. Although aristocratic grace, drive, and popularity naturally remain helpful, their relative importance has waned before the need for highly developed intelligence, competence, and expertise—the capacity to be "really good" in a professional field.

In our bureaucratized and organized society it is the professional who counts. And the jobs that students at selective colleges will eventually take are almost without exception professional jobs. They will become research scientists, government administrators, accounts managers, research and development experts. They will be tomorrow's corporation lawyers, aeronautical engineers, medical specialists, and the up-and-coming professors of the "knowledge industry." For these students "success" in the old sense is no longer an issue at all: fewer and fewer students strive to get ahead in the world, but more and more labor to become experts. And failure for today's students is not awkwardness, lack of ambition, or unpopularity; rather, the new sin is underachievement. The burden of institutional sanctions falls most heavily not upon the rebellious, the mischievous, or the selfish, but upon those who "fail to live up to their potential."

The last two decades have seen a slow shift from a predominantly social view of education to an increasingly academic and preprofessional view. The major trend on most American campuses is away from the old pattern of a fun, football, and fraternity student culture that subverted the intellectual efforts of the faculty, and toward student bodies that sometimes demand more intellectual challenge and individual instruction than faculties are willing or able to provide. Both students and colleges have changed in the past decades: increasingly, the new campus hero is becoming the committed *professionalist* who is "really good in his field."

Although each of these four student types originates in a different historical period, all four continue to coexist on most American campuses. Furthermore, these types are differently distributed among institutions. Today's jaded gentlemen are to be found largely in a few Ivy League colleges, often prepared at those few Eastern boarding schools that still consider it their primary function to instill Christian values and concepts of *noblesse oblige* into the children of the upper class. The Big Man on Campus today finds his most natural home in the state universities of the South and in some fraternity subcultures of large public universities in the North. The apprentice also can be found in the large public universities and, increasingly, in municipal and technical colleges. And the new academic and professionalist student is most visible at the more selective private universities and liberal arts colleges.

Moreover, modern society has required changes in each of these earlier types. The gentleman-in-waiting, deprived of an aristocratic society which respects his status, has increasingly been forced to emphasize the outward tokens of upper-class position: membership in the Social Register, debutante parties, belonging to exclusive clubs. At best, such students possess a lack of status anxiety that gives them great personal openness and helps them excel in the more reflective, artistic, and humanistic fields; at worst, they seem merely pretentious to their more academic contemporaries. Similarly, the apprentice who today gains admission to a selective college must inevitably display the cognitive skills and technical competence of the professionalist. But he continues to be distinguished by his drive to succeed and move up in the world, and by his view of education as a passport to social mobility. The Big Man on Campus, if he attends an academic college, increasingly construes popularity itself as the acquisition of specialized competence in interpersonal manipulation, gained through a study of the behavioral sciences, industrial administration, or "human relations." And, though he may succeed in his scientific quest for campus popularity, he often secretly fears that his less popular and more academic classmates (who refuse fraternity and football for library and laboratory) will end up better equipped for life in a technological age.

What is new about American students today, then, is the growing number of academically committed young men and women who value technical, intellectual, and professional competence above popularity, ambition, or grace. And while the transition from older student types is far from complete, it is the professionalist whom we must examine if we are to understand what is distinctive about American students today.

Profile of the Professionalist

The academically committed preprofessional student is a product of postwar American affluence. Born during or after World War II, he moves easily and familiarly in a world of communications revolutions, population explosions, thermonuclear bombs, brush-fire wars, interstate highways, and emerging nations. The era of the 1920's and 1930's—when his own parents were formed, educated, married, and launched on careers—seems as remote as the medieval past. He is a distinctive creature of the longest period of uninterrupted peace and prosperity in American history.

His parents are usually professional people themselves—teachers, doctors, lawyers, administrators, officials, advertising men, or businessmen who have learned the hard way that a glad hand and a burning desire to succeed are no substitute for really knowing your business. Whether the business is teaching college or selling Buicks, what counts is skill, competence, and professionalization. Indeed, the fathers of today's students have sometimes found that lack of specialization, inability to keep up with "new developments," has meant frustration or inadequacy in their work. Thus, although they themselves may have neglected school work for social life or the football field, they are determined that their children will not make this mistake. While sometimes frustrated by their lack of training, these fathers are usually quite successful in their professions, earning between $10,000 and $20,000 per year, living in a pleasant suburban area, commuting every day to the office—and consistently urging their children to do well in school.

The contemporary student who is headed for a professional career is therefore inevitably faced with repeating the outward life-pattern of his parents. Unlike the apprentice or the Big Man on Campus, he is not attempting to change his station in life, but merely to upgrade his skills. The past provides today's students with little poverty to escape from, little anxiety about income, little fear of not getting a job, and little need for social mobility. In one way, the professionalist is like the gentleman-in-waiting, for he too was born into the status to which he aspires, and his public goals are only to do better the same kind of thing that his father did. To be sure, in an era of rapid technological change, no young man can hope simply to repeat the life pattern of his father: even to keep up, skills, intellectual ability, and cognitive talent must be continually improved. But, on the whole, today's students are not characterized by a burning ambition to "succeed"; their financial and vocational goals are relatively modest; and they anticipate living the same professional, suburban lives now lived by their parents.

To achieve even this modest goal today requires continual diligence and performance in school. College therefore becomes less and less a "moratorium" on adulthood, and more and more a training ground for it. There is less energy or interest left for fraternities, hazing, and the tribal rites of the student culture; there is less room for experimentation, risk-taking, making mistakes, and taking false tacks. Only the exceptionally talented young man can excel academically without effort and be left free to use his energies as he chooses. For most students, the academic competition is too stiff; and they must work far harder in college than their parents ever thought of working.

Partly for this reason, the professionalist must devote himself with great seriousness to intellectual and academic matters. College grading is an important business; and a failed course or a bad year may mean an inferior graduate school or none at all. This academic seriousness is not the self-justifying eagerness of the "grade hound," for good grades are but an instrumental rung on the academic ladder to graduate school, a postdoctoral fellowship, and a specialized job after graduation. Nor is it typically the seriousness of the committed intellectual, for whom the pursuit of knowledge and understanding is a goal in its own right. Indeed, students often unhappily admit to a fear of "getting too interested" in their work, because it might jeopardize the detachment they could otherwise bring to getting good grades. To their teachers today's students appear unprecedentedly dedicated, well trained, intelligent, and devoted; they study hard and do well; they "perform." But they are often disappointingly unwilling to become excited about ideas and, if pressed, will often admit they cannot afford the luxury of enthusiasm when the next admissions office lies only around the corner.

In all men there is a distinction between public and private life; but for today's young professionalist, the gap between public persona and private self is very great. Publicly, his goals are intellectual performance, the acquisition of expertise, making the academic grade. Thus he is a serious, unfrivolous, and often quite humorless student. But privately, he is often very different. One of the peculiar characteristics of the quest for intellectual competence and professional expertise is that attaining these goals helps so little in defining the ultimate aims of existence. Being a gentleman was a way of life with a world view attached; struggling to be successful could occupy a man's entire existence; and even the search for popularity could be integrated into an ideology of interpersonal relations. But expertise, skill, and professional competence are difficult to ideologize: they are clearly instrumental goals, useful only in the service of something else, and they were never intended to answer ultimate questions about life's meaning. The student whose daily life is almost inevitably spent in the pursuit of intellectual competence must therefore elaborate a private life to justify his existence. The demanding and often tedious round of courses, examinations, and admissions committees requires compensation and a rationale.

The result is that peculiar confusion often noted among able American students and variously termed a "search for meaning," a "quest for identity," a "pursuit of significance." In only a few students does this take the form of an implicit quest for a "philosophy of life." Although most students believe at least nominally in God, and some attend church, religion plays no important role in the professionalist's attempt to "find out what really matters." Exposed from early childhood by schools and mass media to the vast variety of human conviction, such students are likely to be ethical relativists. If they think philosophically, they think in terms of "existential leaps" rather than "absolute values," prefer Tillich to St. Thomas, and read Camus for inspiration but not Marx. Unable to rationalize their convictions in ultimate metaphysical terms, they speak often of "personal commitment" and "authentic acts." And, in the end, those who arrive at an articulate philosophy of life are relatively few in number. The rest *wish* they could find some principled purpose but accept the fact that in modern American society such purposes are hard to come by.

Most students therefore turn to private life as both compensation and justification for their public activities. In the here-and-now, some respite from the demanding round of academic work can be found through friendship, love, artistic experience, and self-expression. And, as a future goal, "the rich full life"—defined as private life—promises to provide justification for the often demanding round of professional activities. To be sure, there are many students who expect to enjoy their future careers and pursue their educations precisely because they lead to these careers. But, even among future physicians, public servants, and teachers, relatively few students bring high idealism or an expectation of deep personal fulfillment to their future professions. And those few who do are usually taught during graduate and professional school that love of suffering mankind does not make a doctor, nor zeal for the commonweal a government official, nor love of teaching a professor.

The resulting privatism is therefore evident both in college life and in students' visions of their futures. In college, noncurricular activities assume a new meaning as part of a search for self-definition and self-fulfillment. Most of the students' waking hours during the week must necessarily be spent in academic work. But in the hours that remain, on weekends and holidays, students can really be themselves—or, more precisely, search to find themselves. The vehicle for this search is inevitably personal and expressive: friendship, music, art, sports, dramatics, or even poetry.

Nor are these activities enjoyed in a frivolous and lighthearted way: the most casual friendship may involve a painful search for self-definition; and reading, walking in the country, or listening to music can become part of the "quest for identity." Extracurricular activities are thus losing their traditional meaning as safety valves and outlets for the exuberance of youth: they too become more serious, more intense, more involved in the search for significance.

This same seriousness also pervades the relations between the sexes: the new professionalist takes these relations earnestly, even morally. Bravado is still sometimes apparent in his accounts of his own adventures to his cronies and competitors. But scratch the surface, and the same student usually turns out to be sincerely concerned with defining an ethic of interpersonal and sexual relations. The old question of "Whether to or not" is rapidly succumbing to a new effort to define the precise circumstances under which sexual relations are meaningful and honorable. Sex itself is rarely the main issue; instead, sex is increasingly ancillary to intimacy, understanding, communication, and mutual self-definition.

The academically committed student is therefore not a gay, frivolous, or abandoned person. His public life is regulated by the need to maintain his academic rank; his private life is an effort to discover or create some rationale for his public life; and his inner life is dominated by his attempt to create some synthesis of public and private selves. American students generally lack the levity, gaiety, wit, and whimsey that characterize their counterparts of equal academic attainment in universities abroad. Simply to acquire the necessary expertise requires great effort from all but the most brilliant; and to figure out why one is making this effort—to justify the struggle, to find something worth living for—takes the rest of the effort. There is less and less time just to have fun.

Part of the apparent desperation in this search for significance comes from ambivalence about parents and their lives. Despite their conviction that their future lives will resemble those of their parents (indeed, perhaps because of this conviction), preprofessional students are often filled with subtle unease about the world they grew up in. One reason for this is that rapid social change has widened the gap between the generations, making it more and more difficult for parents and children to understand each other. But, more important, parents often appear to their sons and daughters as frustrated and unfulfilled men and women. When students speak candidly about their mothers and fathers, they often show a surprising compassion and even pity. Despite the suburban split-level, two cars in the garage, and a respected position in the community, there is often something bleak, flat, empty, and barren about parents' lives as portrayed by their children. Some of this may be merely the perennial intolerance of youth for the staidness of middle age; and some often has to do with the idiosyncratic unhappinesses of individual parents. But much is related to the vast sameness of the American social landscape—the lack of excitement, beauty, intense feeling, high indignation, passion, or idealism in the lives of affluent American parents.

Furthermore, many American parents convey a subtly negative image of adult life and adult work to their offspring. A "dad" whose happiest moments are those he shares with his wife and children, who frequently comments that he "feels really human" only on vacation, and who "lives for the weekend" is unwittingly engaging in social criticism, suggesting that work is something to be escaped from whenever possible. He indirectly tells his son that the work which will occupy most of his waking hours as an adult is merely a price he must pay for "really living" on weekends. Since many students already feel this about much of their academic work, it is understandable that progress to the final commencement inspires uneasy jokes about the "rat race" beyond.

But this uneasiness does not lead most students to an overt rejection of their parents or to an attack on middle-class professional values and outlooks. Despite their sense of distance from their parents, most students feel too much genuine sympathy for their plight to repudiate them or their world. Parents are seen as victims, not villains; and when students dread long vacations at home, it is more often because they feel sorry for their parents than because they despise them. Furthermore, to repudiate what parents stand for would involve an ideological commitment of a sort students generically distrust. In any case, many students are not quite sure what their parents *do* stand for, such is the tentativeness and diffidence of American parents toward their children. Perhaps because the explicit values of parents have so often had to be compromised by the facts of American life, and certainly because of the fashionable distrust of ideology in modern America, most students are disinclined to grand ideas, global commitments, global repudiations, or blanket rejections of anything.

Yet the subtle disquiet is there, and it expresses itself in countless ways —in an often frantic search for meaning within the psyche, in fantasies that family, friendship, and leisure will provide all of life's meaning, in jokes about the "death" that lies beyond the last professional degree, and on the occasional winter morning when the student awakes to wonder what he is doing here but forgets the question unanswered. A vague, inarticulate, formless discontent with the pattern of present and future life is common. But none of this means that the professionalist is in any general way opposed to American society. Indeed, his focus on *private* experience and *personal* commitment acts to divert discontent from the broader social scene. Even if the meaning of his studies and his ultimate profession is not clear, meaning can be sought in personal life. And the student who fails to find this meaning usually ends by blaming himself.

But the gap between public and private life is rarely completely closed. For the meaning found in privatism often fails to justify the public activities and plans of the student. The widespread use of the term "performance" reflects this dilemma, for a "performance" is enacted on a stage for the benefit of others, and it suggests playing an alien role that is detached from the real self. This same detachment between activity and self is suggested by many of the favorite expressions of college students— "come on like," "make like," "turn on," all of which suggest a tenuous connection between deed and inclination. And the laudatory epithet "cool" indicates the same lack of emotional involvement in external surroundings and deeds. The problem is that the logical corollary of privatism is retirement from public life at the age of twenty, not continuing academic and professional exertion.

The student I have called the professionalist reflects many of the dilemmas of life in modern American society. Hard-working, earnest, diligent in his academic work, he is publicly committed to the acquisition of expertise in a university. But in his private search for meaning, he mirrors the problem of a society where expertise counts more than individuality, and where even the most talented may feel they are but replaceable cogs in a bureaucratic, academic, or industrial machine. Similarly, the solution of such students is the solution of most Americans: they turn their best energies away from the public world onto the private, manageable, controllable world of personal experience and individual expression. The intellectual style of such students—anti-ideological, pragmatic, empirical, and distrustful of doctrine—is, of course, the traditional style of America. And the inner tension of such students is the tension of American society itself, the problem of reconciling technological development with human fulfillment, the problem of individuality and meaning in an impersonal society.

Three Minority Views

Every generation has its innovators, its deviants, and its self-defined failures. The emergence of the professionalist has brought with it new types of student dissent, marginality, and misery. These students are not main-line professionalists, but neither are they the deviants and dissenters of earlier generations. Instead, they are those who have not been able to resolve so happily the fundamental tension of the professionalist, the schism between public performance and private meaning. All of them are in a sense professionalists *manqués,* and, although they constitute but a statistical minority of American students, it is these students who today make the headlines, dominate the popular image of the college generation, and help define students to themselves.

There are at least three new types of "deviant" students, who have appeared as recognizable groups only in the past decade or so. I shall call them the activist, the disaffiliate, and the underachiever. The *activist* is the much-discussed student demonstrator, who protests against some segment of the university or society which seems in urgent need of reform. The *disaffiliate* is the nonpolitical but culturally alienated student who rejects totally the offerings and values of his society. The *underachiever* is the student who accepts the values of the university and the society but, with them, his own inadequacy. Despite their important differences from the professionalist, each of these types shares the same dilemmas and many of the same characteristics.

Today's student activist is primarily concerned with some specific issue. He is emphatically not an ideologue; and herein lies the enormous difference between activism now and activism in the thirties. His commitment is not a commitment to a way of life or to a coherent set of political beliefs; rather it is "existential" in its emphasis on simple personal expressions of moral indignation. Camus and William Golding, rather than Marx or the novelist of social protest, are the spokesmen for such students. The particular issue in question is always one of apparent moral simplicity: civil rights, "free speech" on campus, the abolition of college paternalism, peace, the promotion of a devoted teacher. Moreover, the activist's initial commitment normally extends no further than a single cause. The student Civil Rights Movement has, on the whole, steadfastly refused to take positions on other issues. The Free Speech Movement in Berkeley disbanded when the university grudgingly granted the legitimacy of its demands.

To student activists, demonstrations are usually precisely that—acts whose primary motive is to demonstrate and express where the student stands. The original impulse is to make a statement about one's convictions and one's indignation; instrumental activity follows primarily from this expression of indignation and is almost always limited to the achievement of relatively short-range objectives. To be sure, when "demonstrating" students meet strong opposition from a university administration or the "power structure," they are often forced to evolve organized plans for action. But these programs are usually *ad hoc,* short-range, pragmatic, and empirical. Once the technique of demonstration has been learned, of course, it can be used in other areas. Even more important, once the student begins to demonstrate his indignation over one issue, he may feel morally compelled to express his stand on other matters as well. Thus, students who protest campus policies or foreign policies are likely to have been "trained" in the Civil Rights Movement. But what unites these demonstrations is not a coherent ideology of protest or reform, much less an organized political group, but a personal sense of ethical obligation to take a visible stand against injustice or oppression.

Compared to his classmates, the typical activist tends to be a better-than-average student, a committed and dedicated "intellectual," ethically or even religiously oriented, and a relatively well-balanced and well-liked person. He is rarely a "failure" in his own eyes or in the eyes of the college community. The better his grade average, the more likely that he will be involved in and/or support student activism; the less vocational his personal values, the greater his propensity for activism. Indifference and opposition to activism come primarily from students and colleges where the older success and popularity outlooks prevail. In contrast, humanists and social scientists at highly academic liberal arts colleges and universities are those most disposed toward active expressions of dissent.

Despite much that has been written about the motivating role of student dissatisfaction with the impersonal "multiversity," few participants in campus demonstrations seem outstandingly dissatisfied with their academic experience. On the contrary, most of these better-than-average students probably find more stimulation in their academic work and closer relations with the faculty than do their nonactivist classmates. Nor is it really necessary to search for hidden motives and discontents to explain their activism: the goals of most campus demonstrations are understandable, specific, and often legitimate. Admittedly, some of the leaders of the Free Speech Movement, the Student Non-violent Coordinating Committee, or Students for a Democratic Society occasionally issue indictments of the entire multiversity, the "power structure," or the "military-industrial complex." This handful of students of the New Left does have a vague ideology of dissent, based on writers like C. Wright Mills, Paul Goodman, and Michael Harrington. What Goodman calls the "Organized System" is clearly bad. But what is good, how to reform the multiversity, precisely what "far-reaching changes in the power structure" are needed—these are never made quite clear. In practice, even this small dissenting group usually spends more time and energy trying to build community organizations among Mississippi Negroes or tutoring slum children in Northern ghettos than in ideological debates.

The personal background of the rank-and-file activist is usually an ordinary, middle-class background. His activism is more often *premised* upon the liberal values of his parents and the creedal values of American society than *opposed* to them. Indeed, if there is any single psychological thread that runs through student activism today, it is this "identification with parental values." When parents and their activist offspring disagree, it is usually not over principle but over practice; and when these students criticize their parents, it is not for what their parents believe, but for their failure to practice the beliefs they drummed into their children's ears from an early age. Thus, "generational conflict" and "rebellion against parents" are gross oversimplifications as applied to these students: most of them get along moderately well with their parents, and most of their parents feel compelled—at least in principle—to support their children's activism. Overt conflict enters only because parents commonly feel that "discretion" might dictate a less active pursuit of the values they themselves taught their children.

There has been much misunderstanding of student activism, some of it originating with Mississippi sheriffs and Alabama mayors, some coming (less forgivably) from frightened college administrators. These students are not, with rare exceptions, Maoists or Castroites, professional rebels, beatniks, or hooligans. Nor do the self-disciplined nonviolent students in the Civil Rights Movement in any way resemble the undisciplined student rowdies who periodically riot on resort beaches during spring vacation. Furthermore, student activists generally *are* students: the much-touted "nonstudents" involved usually turn out to be graduate students, plus a few students on leave of absence, ex-students, and students' wives. Whatever evidence is available—and increasing amounts are—consistently suggests that student activists are selectively drawn from among the most talented and committed students in the humanities and social sciences, that they are largely concentrated at the most academic colleges and universities, and that in most cases their professed public motives are quite adequate to explain their behavior. Perhaps the basic motive of such activists is their desire to make public their private convictions, indignations, and sense of moral outrage—and to change specific sectors of society so that they will no longer be so outrageous.

A second deviant response to the new academic climate is disaffiliation, resentful withdrawal from American society, repudiation of conventional adulthood. Like activists, disaffiliates are often inconscient existentialists; but their existentialism is that of Heidegger, not Camus. Such students are too pessimistic and too firmly against the system to demonstrate their disaffiliation in any organized public way. Their demonstrations are private: these are the residual beatniks, the Bohemians, and the "LSD crowd" that exist on many American campuses. Often capable and imaginative, sensitive and hyperaware, they usually manage to do passable academic work, though their hearts are in their alienation.

As people, disaffiliates tend to be disorganized. They generally lead unconventional lives and are unwilling or unable to conform to conventional social expectations. In their personal lives, one sometimes finds considerable psychological disturbance; and they are vehemently at odds with the values of their parents, which are the values of conventional middleclass life. Their rejection of American society is based less upon personal idealism and outraged indignation than upon temperamental disaffinity for the requirements and rewards of American society—and for their fathers who epitomize this society to them.

Now that the bright lights of the beat generation have been dimmed by publicity and advancing age, disaffiliates increasingly turn to the psychedelic drugs—such as LSD, psilocybin, mescaline, and marijuana—in their search for intensification of experience. The promise of free passage through the doors of perception and the intense interpersonal cultism that surrounds the use of these drugs provide a provisional identity for many who cannot achieve one on the surface of campus life. The most striking feature of these cults is the virtually complete withdrawal of significance from public life—only intense, drug-assisted subjectivity is real; the rest is but role-playing. In this group the schism between public and private is resolved by denying the reality of the public.

The third deviant type, the underachiever, differs from the activist and disaffiliate in that he rejects himself rather than part or all of society. Such students often do poorly, drop out of college, or see to it that they are thrown out by failing academically; but simple lack of intellectual ability will rarely suffice to explain their "failure." Indeed, excessive seriousness and desperate academic effort often block their academic success more than lack of intelligence does. They characteristically take the requirements of the academic system very earnestly; and, as a result, they find it impossible to take shortcuts, to manipulate and calculate for good grades, and to "work the system."

Of all American students underachievers find it most difficult to weld the connection between their own personal search for meaning and the continual academic pressures they face in their college lives. Often ambitious and intellectually mobile, they may be overwhelmed upon entering a college where most of their freshman class is culled, as they are, from the top 1 per cent of high school graduates. If they do less than outstanding academic work, they begin to feel that they are failing—failing their parents, failing to live up to their potential, failing themselves. Once this feeling develops, its common consequences are depression, confusion, increasing but futile efforts to study harder, and a mounting sense of disaster which may eventually reach panic proportions. Many students who fit this type do not actually drop out of college; but, if they remain, they do so with a self-conforming suspicion that they are not so good as they had hoped, that they are not "really first-rate." They almost always blame themselves, not college or society; indeed, they generally lack enough critical detachment from the colleges they attend to be able to criticize them at all.

The background of the underachiever, like that of the activist and the disaffiliate, tends to be staunchly middle-class. But in the underachiever's personal history there is often especially great familial pressure to achieve, and strong parental emphasis on academic performance as an indicator not merely of intellectual competence but of moral and human worth. Far from rejecting these values, the underachiever overaccepts them, using them as weapons against himself when his performance flags. He comes to feel that he is inadequate and intellectually incompetent, and that low grades are a sign of moral failure. Society merely confirms his self-deprecation by deeming underachievement mistaken, cowardly, short-sighted, lazy, weak, and an insult to the national economy.

But underachievement is often a motivated act, and, although self-deprecation and a sense of personal inadequacy predominate in conscious-ness, the same student is often engaged in a desperate unconscious man-euver to slough off standards of performance that remain unconnected with his private purposes. The underachiever is thus often involved in an unconscious (and usually self-defeating) protest against parental, aca-demic, and social pressures. When this is true, dropping out of college may be a useful act of self-assertion that allows a student to return (or not to return) on his own terms and for his own reasons. The unhappy under-achiever is, paradoxically, the student who most exaggerates the signifi-cance of the public values of intellectual achievement and is therefore unable to elaborate a valued autonomous private self. In this respect, he is the polar opposite of the disaffiliate.

In practice, of course, no individual student ever fits any type per-fectly; nor are these types always clearly distinguishable from the main-line professionalist. Most professionalists, for example, at least *consider* dropping out of college; many identify with and occasionally join activists; and some are secretly fascinated by the cult of disaffiliation, perhaps to the extent of a puff of marijuana. Nor are these dissenting types always clearly distinguishable one from the other: the activist may harbor doubts about his own adequacy, and the disaffiliate is increasingly likely to become a fringe member of a protest group. Only as an oversimplification, perhaps justified as an effort to underline recurring themes and dilemmas among American students, can we speak of ideal types at all.

Students and the University

If these interpretations are correct, they suggest that the faces in the lecture room are the faces of a new generation, in many respects qualita-tively different from previous student generations in America. The old faces are of course still there, scattered across the room: the gentlemen devoted to being gentlemen, the apprentices committed to making good, the Big Men on Campus who want to be popular. But increasingly they are outnumbered by serious, academically committed students who are headed for a career in the professions, and by their first cousins, the dem-onstrating activists, the withdrawn disaffiliates, and the self-deprecating underachievers.

All of these new types have a great deal in common. All are nonideo-logical or anti-ideological; all oppose or despair about large-scale political and social planning; all distrust "politicians" and dogmatists in societal matters. Furthermore, all are essentially privatistic: they start not from a desire to reform society nor from a blueprint for the future, but from a personal or existential statement; the activist emphasizes personal demonstration, the disaffiliate emphasizes personal withdrawal, and the underachiever emphasizes personal blame. Paradoxically, for a generation whose most publicized members are often termed "social activists," the broader social scene rarely exists as a clearly defined or sharply articulated entity. Instead, its significant existence is denied altogether by the disaffiliate, globally and unselectively overaccepted by the underachiever, forgotten by the typical activist's emphasis on a "single issue," or blurred by a few activist leaders in vague indictments of the "Organized System."

The absence of a differentiated picture of American society, coupled with a lack of overriding ideology, is important in appraising the future of American students. For without a clear specification of what is good and what is bad about American society, coupled with a coherent ideology of social reform, few individuals can sustain for long the mishaps and disappointments that inevitably plague anyone who seeks to improve society. The motive of "personal demonstration" by itself is not likely to endure: two hours a week in a slum area, two months in Mississippi during the summer, or two years in Afghanistan with the Peace Corps may serve to dissipate rather than confirm the student's "activism." Once he has demonstrated where he stands, there is little need for further involvement: the demonstration has been made, idealistic impulses have been exhausted, and he can resume his course up the academic stepladder, putting aside all thoughts of social reform in the interests of a Ph.D., a professional job, and a rich full life.

The "expressive" and anti-ideological outlook of students today suggests that those who anticipate a coming generation of adults committed to social reform are mistaken. Peace Corps graduates generally return from two years of working with deprived nations to enter graduate and professional schools, where they give little thought to their own deprived status as graduate students, much less to the greater deprivations of other Americans. To be sure, a few dedicated workers in the Civil Rights Movement, largely Negro students, have made a commitment to reform that extends far beyond a few months' work in the field. But, in general, there seems little need to worry (or rejoice) that students are becoming so involved in "causes" that they will neglect their studies or turn against their society. One socialist onlooker at the Berkeley demonstrations put it this way: "Ten years from now most of them will be rising in the world and in income, living in the suburbs from Terra Linda to Atherton, raising two or three babies, voting Democratic, and wondering what on earth they were doing in Sproul Hall—trying to remember, and failing."

In the end the vast majority of American students remains privatistic.

Even for the student activist, the main tension is not the effort to realize a vision of social reform, but the tension between his private search for meaning and his public activities. To attribute this tension solely to the bureaucratization, impersonality, and bigness of the university is an over-simplification and an evasion, for the university only reflects the character-istics of American society. The divorce of public from private reflects all too faithfully the demands of a society that expects of its responsible citi-zens extraordinary objectivity, impersonality, competence, control, and cognitive efficiency and leaves little room in public life for private com-mitment, idealism, passion, zeal, indignation, and feeling. What matters to most students is not that they do not know their professors, but that they find it hard to integrate their private search for meaning with their public quest for professional competence. Even the activist, who temporarily links the two spheres of life, usually lapses back to privatism once his final examinations near—few student demonstrations take place at the end of the semester.

Yet it would seem that one of the functions of the liberal arts college and of the university might be to help mend this schism by providing an education and an environment that encourage students to gather intellect, ethical sense, and action into one related whole. And it would also seem that graduate and professional education might assist the preprofessional to weld close connections between his inner self and the vocation that will occupy his life for the next fifty years. But this too rarely happens. Each university is a part of the educational system, and the most determined effort of any one university cannot cancel the fact that another admissions committee usually lies around the corner. Grades or no grades, tutorial or teaching by television, the student knows what graduate schools expect, and he may feel driven anyway. It takes extraordinary efforts to reduce the pressure to perform.

One reason so few universities even try, I think, is a too narrow inter-pretation of the functions of American universities. Everyone grants that education should ultimately serve the community, but it is widely thought that this obligation is fully discharged by producing millions of well-trained, technically competent, and professionally skilled young men and women to man the American economy. But another even more important need of American society is for men and women with a capacity for criti-cal detachment from their communities, a sense of ethics above traditional piety, a capacity to articulate new goals, and a sustained determination to work toward the realization of these goals. These qualities differ from pro-fessional skills in that a university cannot guarantee them, but can only provide a setting where they may flourish. Moreover, their development requires time, freedom from external pressure, the chance to make mis-takes, and the opportunity to experiment—none of which is readily available on most American campuses. And, perhaps crucial, these qualities are controversial, impolitic, and unpopular with many state legislators and boards of trustees.

Yet there are hopeful signs. This student generation probably has a greater potential for informed detachment, a high sense of ethics, articulateness, and determination than any before it. Today's students have been exposed to ideas from kindergarten onward with an intensity that has no American precursor. Their minds are well trained; they are well informed; they deal easily with both the abstract and the concrete. They are less plagued than any previous generation by status anxiety and the dread of poverty. Most important, they are eager to find some way of reconciling their private lives with their academic activities. And some few succeed. A few activists find in social service and action an enduring and informed commitment that will not easily be dissipated. Even the voluntary dropout may be creating a new way to escape the pressures of academic routine for long enough to connect education to his life. And there are, I think, increasing numbers of students who are led so often to the trough of knowledge that they finally stay to drink—not merely for the sake of an admissions committee, but because of the heady taste of enlightenment. Once real connections between disciplined intellect, inner self, and outer activity are made, the result will likely be a determination to retain these connections throughout the rest of life. Despite the pressures of American higher education, individual students are often able to marry the parts of their lives into a lasting union.

Nor is the institutional picture completely bleak. For any system that can expose so many students so intensively to so many ideas has great potential—even though it may be dismayed when students want their universities and their society to practice ideas they teach. Furthermore, there are dozens of colleges across America that push their students not merely to perform well on examinations, but to think independently, to connect intellect with the rest of life. Such colleges—some ancient and famous, others recent and unknown—can help provide students with a respite from pressure, a chance to experiment, grow, and connect what they learn with their future lives. Some few professional schools, too, contribute to real enlightenment even while they teach professional skills. By admitting the genuinely inquiring, by encouraging intellectual curiosity, diversity, innovation, and speculation, they create an atmosphere in which their students can link their personal goals to their professional careers. To be sure, all of this runs against the main academic tide, and it still happens rarely. But it suggests that American universities could easily do more than provide professional man power for the economy.

In essence, I am arguing that American colleges too often simply mirror the pressures and human schisms of American society. We need to ask whether a major goal of a great university should not be to provide a countervailing center to the immediate trends of society. We need to recognize that all human development is discontinuous and that one prime function of the university is to provide for its students a moratorium from adult pressures, rather than a caricature of them. Perhaps our society's greatest long-range need is not for more skilled engineers, lawyers, scientists, and physicians, but for more whole and integrated men and women who can bring educated minds to both personal and public life. Perhaps the university serves both society and its students best when it serves neither directly but attempts to create a friendly culture for the growth of critical intelligence, the joining of reason and action, and that detachment from the daily pressures of society which has always characterized educated men. If so, and if American universities can move toward these goals, they will find today's students more ready and able to follow them than any previous generation.

The University as Critic

In 1967, the American Council on Education chose "Whose Goals for American Higher Education?" as the theme of its annual conference. The choice of this topic reflected, I think, a growing fear that American higher education, by trying to be all things to all men, had seriously jeopardized its integrity, its credibility, and its effectiveness—to say nothing of its sources of income. Several writers were asked to discuss the traditional triumvirate of university functions—teaching, research, and public service. My commission was to consider a possible "new function" of the university —the critical function.

This request gave me a chance to develop some of the ideas about higher education as a countervailing center to the dominant pressures of society that I had introduced in the previous essay. In essence, I argue that "socialization" can no longer adequately describe the functions of the university in a rapidly changing society whose fundamental values and purposes are constantly in question. As a result, the American university has already become a major and probably the major critic of American society. And I maintain that this change is for the good, in the long run, for both students and society.

In the few years since this essay was written the role of higher education and of its products as critics of modern society has become even more clear, as has the public revulsion against the exercise of this role. Nevertheless, on rereading this essay, I think I did not distinguish sharply enough between the university as I think it should be (and as it comes close to being at a few of the more privileged institutions) and American higher education as it actually is. While I disagree with the charge of some radicals that universities are nothing but "service stations" for the status quo, neither do I believe that it is accurate to describe the "critical university" as the real university in America. In fact, American higher education is partly service station and partly critical university. The implication of my argument here is that it should become less of the former and more of the latter.

A comprehensive account of the achievements and failures of American higher education in the exercise and defense of its role as critic could

well be the topic of a lengthy volume. But I do not think that we can
understand the emergence of a new youthful opposition—above all from
the universities of the industrialized nations—unless we appreciate the
extent to which higher education has in fact become the center for
criticism of existing societies. Nor will the vitality of these societies long
endure unless we are prepared to justify and protect that critical function
to a public that too often sees criticism as subversion and dissent as treason.

AMONG the major functions of the modern university, criticism is surely the most neglected. In the spate of recent treatises on the goals of higher education, much has been said about the transmission, extension, and application of knowledge, about teaching, research, and public service, and occasionally even about "innovation." But the critical function of the university is mentioned, if at all, in an apologetic aside, rather as if the critical comments of students and faculty members were merely the price the public must pay ("academic freedom") for the *other* valuable services performed by the university.

Were we to rely solely on these prevalent theories of higher education, we would find it impossible to understand most popular accounts of the American university. For in newspapers, weeklies, and monthlies, on radio and television, the critical voices that emanate from our universities receive by far the greatest amount of attention. Student rebellion and protest are breakfast-table topics; faculty teach-ins and petitions are headline news; the critical stance of "university intellectuals" toward government policies is constantly discussed; and the definition of the rights of university members to criticize our society preoccupies the public. Nor could we infer from most recent discussions of our universities that in the past fifty years American higher education has become the prime source for critical analyses of our society. When criticism is discussed by the theorists of higher education, it is largely in an aside—to minimize its importance and prevalence ("Most students are basically apathetic; most of our faculty are Republicans"), to explain it as a result of remediable defects within the university ("We must learn to pay more attention to our students as individuals"), or to defend it lamely and apologetically ("Academic freedom includes the right to be wrong").

Criticism, then, is the cuckoo's egg in the otherwise harmonious nest of traditional university functions. There can be no doubt that criticism is an actual function of the American university; indeed, our society has come to rely upon and to need higher education to exercise this role. How much we take the critical role of the university for granted can be seen by attempting to imagine our society if all students and faculty members were to be transformed overnight into uncritical apologists for the *status quo*. America would not only be quieter and less interesting, but unimaginably less vital and less promising. To the traditional triumvirate of teaching, research, and public service, a fourth function has been added: that of criticism—a function that is much discussed and maligned by the general public but passed over in embarrassed silence by most articulate spokesmen for higher education.

In the remarks to follow, I will consider some of the reasons for the emergence of criticism as a major function of American higher education, some of the qualifications of the university for the exercise of this function, and some of the limitations upon its exercise. But before turning to these topics, I should underline that in speaking of the critical function I am not discussing what is ordinarily referred to as "public service" or "innovation." By criticism I mean above all the analysis, examination, study, and evaluation of our society at large; of its directions, practices, institutions, strengths, weaknesses, ideals, values, and character; of its consistencies and contradictions; of what it has been, of what it is becoming, of what is becoming of it, and of what it might at best become. The critical function involves the examination of the purposes, practices, meanings, and goals of our society. It entails not merely the description of the past, the characterization of the present, and the attempt to predict the future, but the evaluation of the past, present, and probable future, and the right to prescribe solutions, alternatives, and new directions, and to act in support of them.

Criticism, then, is distinguished from simple analysis and description by the presence of judgment. A critic not only characterizes but condemns and praises according to his values. In this measure he commits himself to a position vis-à-vis the object of criticism and to the values from which his position springs. Moreover, the responsible critic will usually do more than analyze and evaluate; he will propose, recommend, and advocate action that accords with his judgments and promotes his ideals, and he will condemn, oppose, and reject what he judges worthless or evil. Criticism implies commitment to a position, and its natural consequence is action. To separate critical thought from action is therefore to be blind to the fact that ideas have behavioral implications; to seek to promote the first but suppress the second is to try to unman the critical intelligence. Similarly, to attempt to distinguish between "objective" and "partisan" criticism is to ignore the role of judgment and values in the critical process, for all judgments and values can be deemed "partisan" by those who reject them. What can be asked of criticism is not that it be objective, but that it be informed, regardful of facts, profound, generous, and intelligent. But to expect that it can be objective, confined to thought, or uncontroversial is to ask that it cease to be criticism.

One reason for the theoretical neglect of the critical function by spokesmen for American higher education is relatively obvious. The most articulate interpreters of the American university have been university administrators, who are responsible to multiple constituencies—among others, to their fellow college administrators, to their faculties and students, and, most relevant to this topic, to boards of trustees, alumni, state legislators, and citizens with an interest in supporting education. To this constituency the traditional university functions are readily understood: they deserve support and grateful remuneration. But in his search for the support upon which his university depends, the administrator is embarrassed by dissenting students and protesting faculty members. He is therefore likely to excuse rather than to justify their existence. Students are said to be young, searching, and uninformed; they will settle down; and, in any case, dissenters are few in number. Faculty members are notably cantankerous and eccentric; but they contribute to the public good in *other* ways. The public must learn to accept a few weeds of criticism in the rich harvest of American higher education.

This neglect or dismissal of the critical function of the university, however, not only fails to describe accurately the present role of higher education but defensively slights what should be viewed as one of the most valuable functions of universities in our rapidly changing and complex society. Indeed, the emergence of criticism as a major function of the university is intimately related to the changing nature and needs of American life. In modern society the simple "transmission" of knowledge must increasingly give way to a critical re-examination of that knowledge; the extension of knowledge presupposes a critical analysis of what is worth extending; and the application of knowledge requires a critical study of which knowledge can be applied to what.

Social Change, Diversity, and Socialization

The traditional model of higher education is essentially a model of socialization. The task of education is commonly said to be the "transmission" or "communication" to the next generation of the skills, techniques, knowledge, and wisdom of the past. In libraries, archives, and the minds of faculty members, universities have accumulated profound knowledge and insight about the past and present; teaching involves "passing on" this knowledge and insight to the next generation. Similarly, the traditional model of research involves either the study of the past in order to disinter its enduring wisdom or the study of nature in order to uncover its eternal laws. And the traditional image of public service presupposes an established body of knowledge, facts, and techniques that can be applied to the solution of social problems—in short, a kind of technical assistance to the community. In all of these views the older generation is seen as possessing knowledge, skills, and insights which can be transmitted in an uncomplicated way to the receptive young.

There are, to be sure, many variations on this traditional model. Some view the functions of higher education narrowly as training, as the simple transmission of skills to those who will eventually use them. We hear much today, for example, about the services of higher education in providing a reservoir of "skilled man power" for the national economy. By others, proponents of the liberal arts, education is viewed less as the transmission of skills and more as a way of teaching students how to ask questions, how to analyze problems, and how to look at the world. Similarly, within the model of socialization, there is much disagreement as to the amount of "adjustment" to the existing society that should be encouraged. Some few would argue that universities should teach their students to "work within" the existing society; others would define the goals of higher education as having to do with "the good life," a life that may not involve immediate acceptance of community standards. But in each of these views, higher education is said to serve its students and society best when it transmits to them skills, facts, competences, techniques of analysis, or values that originate in the past and are assumed to be important and relevant for the present and future.

The durability of the model of socialization is easy to understand, for the assumptions upon which it rests have until recently been valid. For many centuries the university was the prime repository of the learning and wisdom of the past; and scholars have traditionally been those who examined this past with an eye to distilling its implications for the present. As a description of the medieval university, the Renaissance university, or even the religiously oriented British university of the eighteenth and nineteenth centuries, the traditional model is largely accurate. Yet increasingly, "socialization" no longer describes what happens or what should happen in higher education. For to assume that higher education can simply socialize youth presupposes social conditions that are fast disappearing from American society. For one, the increasing pace of social change invalidates the assumption that the skills, wisdom, and knowledge of one generation can be uncritically "transmitted" to the next; in addition, the growing complexity of our society raises with urgency the question "Which society should the young be socialized to?" Increasingly, higher education, if it is to serve either its students or society, must assist the former in a critical examination of what they inherit.

The model of socialization remains relevant to the education of youth in static and simple societies. In most primitive societies, for example, social change occurs slowly and almost imperceptibly, when it occurs at all. In such societies the wisdom of the past is clearly relevant to the present and future; the skills, life styles, and values that were good enough for a man's father are good enough for him and will continue to be relevant to his offspring. Such traditional societies are highly resistant to change, and "higher education" (initiations, age-graded learning, apprenticeships,

etc.) can appropriately consist in teaching youth the traditional, prescribed, and socially established ways. Indeed, in most traditional societies
any form of education that leads youth to challenge the established ways
only produces misfits.

Other characteristics of most traditional societies are homogeneity,
uniformity, and the absence of individual choice. In many primitive societies, for example, there are only a very few adult roles available to each
sex—for a man, to be a hunter, a fisherman, or a tiller of the land; for a
woman, to be a wife and mother, with prescribed economic duties.
Equally important, traditional societies tend to be monolithic in religion,
ideology, and life style. The questions "What shall I do with my life?" and
"What shall I believe?" are answered before they arise by the wider society, not left up to the choices of the individual. And even in those traditional societies where a variety of adult roles exists, entry into these positions is rarely influenced by the desires of the individual but is instead
dictated by the accidents of birth to clan, caste, and guild. In any society
where the "options" are few or nonexistent, educative agencies can appropriately limit themselves to "training" youth for the clearly defined slots
they will fill as adults. There is no need to assist the young in choosing
wisely in societies where they have no choices to make.

Increasingly, however, in modern American society, as in other advanced nations, the preconditions for the validity of socialization no
longer obtain. In our society, change is the rule rather than the exception.
We have learned to welcome the revolutionary transformations that have
repeatedly altered our physical, technological, social, and moral orders.
Far from being able to predict that the wisdom and skills of the past will
continue to be relevant into the future, our best prediction today is that
the future will be different from both present and past. Who, a generation
ago, could have anticipated the material conditions of life, the social problems, the moral revolutions, the changing values and standards, or the
international dilemmas of today? And who can predict the technologies of
tomorrow? Which skills, values, outlooks, and information taught to college students today will be useful and relevant to them in thirty years?
Which job skills dare we uncritically "transmit" to youth? Which perspectives and values can we merely "communicate" in full confidence of their
enduring validity?

Nor does modern American society meet the requirement of homogeneity. Indeed, the very term "society"—with its connotations of consistency and coherence—requires major redefinition as we move from the
primitive to the modern world. Our social order is stratified, organized,
differentiated, and compartmentalized in a hundred ways. Instead of one
homogeneous society, we confront highly articulated sets, groupings,
classes, regions, enclaves, and clusters of people who happen to live within

the same national boundaries, but who may otherwise possess few common values, patterns of life, and norms of behavior. Even those values once firmly associated with the "American way of life" have been vigorously challenged from within our own society. Indeed, virtually every generalization about America now requires qualification; every rule has its important exception; and every value ardently held by one group is as ardently rejected by another.

Thus, even if our society were unchanging, it would not be clear which part, portion, or subculture higher education is supposed to "socialize" students to. In *which* world will tomorrow's students live? The white upper class of the Eastern seaboard? The Bohemian subcultures of New York or San Francisco? The academic environment of the small liberal arts college? The urban Negro ghetto? The world of the Wall Street lawyer? Clearly the answer will vary from student to student. Or, if we consider the traditional functions of transmitting values from the past, *which* values do we mean? Those of scientific optimism and progress? The romantic rejection of industrial-technological society? The values of free enterprise? The tradition of protest against social injustice? In our incredibly heterogeneous society it becomes virtually impossible to define precisely the institutions and values to which youth are to be socialized.

Few would deny that the content of higher education must change in a changing and heterogeneous society. But my argument here implies that in modern technological societies the functions of education must change as well. In so far as higher education today means merely the uncritical "transmission" of knowledge to students who are taught passively to "assimilate" this knowledge, it will prepare a new generation that has absorbed indiscriminately the obsolete along with the enduring. In so far as research today consists merely of an uncritical digging in the past for principles that will be extended automatically into the future, research will often be irrelevant to that future. And in so far as public service is defined only to mean the uncritical application of existing techniques to uncritically accepted community goals, the university will fail to serve the community well in the long run. Most important, in so far as higher education encourages in today's students an outlook of acquiescent assimilation, it will fail to prepare them for a modern world in which the ability to select, evaluate, examine, and criticize is a vital necessity.

I am arguing, then, that to the traditional triumvirate of teaching, research, and public service a fourth function, that of criticism, must be added. To assist the next generation in the development of viable life plans, choices, commitments, and values, it is not enough to present the past on a silver platter. By example and by direct precept the university must teach its students to become informed, wise, sensitive, and humane critics of their legacy. Learning the facts must be but the preface to examining them critically; assimilating the past, if that past is to be useful, must be followed by analyzing, judging, and selecting the best from it. Indeed, recent years have suggested that many able American students are far ahead of our theories of higher education: they demand the right to judge, to criticize, to select, and to act in accordance with the results of their critical judgment. They insist, with increasing firmness, that their educations be relevant to them and to the last third of the twentieth century. A vocal and able minority has begun to point out with increasing indignation the gaps between what our society and our universities practice and what we preach. Although we may at times be distressed by the occasional shallowness of student criticism or embarrassed by its stridency, we cannot hope to silence the critical spirit of the younger generation. Nor should we try: our task as teachers and administrators should be to ally ourselves with the critical intelligence of our students, demonstrating and teaching that criticism can be informed, wise, and deeply responsible.

Indeed, if there is any danger that faces the next generation, it is not that today's students will become the irresponsible revolutionaries of the next decades, but that through our failure to educate our students in the proper and responsible uses of criticism, we will deprive the next generation of a critical intelligence that they will desperately need. For the modern world brings with it not only enormous opportunities but aggravated problems and terrifying risks. What should concern us most is that we, as educators, may not sufficiently justify and strengthen the critical function of the university and the critical spirit of the young, training a generation that is blind to the problems and risks of the twentieth century. If we not only allow but encourage and teach them to be intelligent, informed, and selective critics of the modern world and the legacies of the past, if we accept this as a proper and legitimate function of the modern university, we will serve them and the future of our society well.

Time Span and the Wider Society

The critical function of higher education is by no means exhausted with a consideration of teaching students. On the contrary, over the last decades American universities have also come to exercise this function in a far more direct way—by collectively acting as the watchdogs, gadflies, defenders, Jeremiahs, and at times Cassandras of our society. Increasingly, the university has become the prime institutional source of ideas about the nature, strengths, weaknesses, and future of our society as a whole.

Among the distinctive problems of modern American society are those of appraising, assessing, understanding, evaluating, controlling, and guiding the directions of social change. These problems can scarcely arise in a static society where, since change rarely occurs, there is little need to reflect upon their meaning. Nor does the question of who "controls" social change arise in the same form in planned and totalitarian states, whose political regimes are not subject to the changing moods of the electorate, and where state planning boards are responsible for the shape of change. Our own society, in contrast, has resisted efforts to plan and co-ordinate social change on a governmental level. As a result, the question of who is to evaluate, assess, predict, and attempt to direct the long-range directions of our society has become more urgent. And increasingly, the university has stepped in to provide a critical commentary on the transformations of our social order.

In the past decades it has become apparent that unplanned social revolutions have sometimes been destructive in a way that human intelligence might have prevented or corrected. We have become increasingly aware that the chronic transformations of our society have left a wake of avoidable or remediable social wreckage: the structural exclusion from our affluent society of a significant portion of the poor, the destruction of the core of our major cities, the defacement of the beauty of our countryside, and our frequent support of political regimes abroad whose values are antithetical to our own.

In this critical examination of modern society American universities have quietly but nonetheless decisively assumed the leading role. Higher education has become the chief source of analyses, evaluations, and judgments of our society: our proposals for reform, our critiques and defenses of the *status quo*, our prophecies of doom, and our utopias almost invariably originate from the Academy. With but few exceptions our modern vocabulary of social analysis, our rhetoric of social criticism and reform are the products of higher education. The university has given us our most powerful understandings of American social character, of the economy, of our psychology as a nation. Academics have analyzed our emergent patterns of consumption and leisure, the human implications of the technological revolutions of the past decades, and the meaning and portent of our new role in the world. The most cogent voices of criticism, rejection, and protest have emanated from the universities. So, too, the most powerful defenses of American life, of our ideals as a society, and of the viability of our traditions have come from centers of higher education. And university students and teachers have intensified our reluctant awareness of the many gaps between the ideals we profess and the way we live.

The reasons for the pre-eminence of higher education as the "critical center" of American society are not difficult to understand. The modern university at its best encourages a lengthier time span and a more inclusive scope of concern than does any other major American institution; and the experience and temperament of the academic community at its best encourages a concern with the next generation and a critical view of the existing society that permits the academic to stand back from immediate pieties and verities to search for more enduring principles and ideals.

Like individuals, social institutions may be thought of as possessing time spans of greater or lesser length, and scopes of concern that are more or less inclusive. In our society most institutions apart from the university are ill-equipped to exercise the critical function with regard to the long-range directions of society as a whole, because they are bound by their objectives and internal arrangements to a short time span and a scope of concern that is limited to one defined sector of society. Industry and technology, perhaps the prime motors of social change in America, tend to plan no more than five or ten years ahead. Similarly, political parties, despite their rhetoric of concern for the long-range welfare of our society, tend in practice to emphasize short-range electoral planning (four years and less), and therefore to be minimally competent in exerting long-range strategic influences over society as a whole. Even governmental planning agencies and regulatory bodies are incapacitated as social critics or planners because of their fiscal dependence upon legislative moods and the replacement of their top leaders with every change in political administration.

Compared to most other institutions in American society, then, universities more often permit at least some of their members to reflect in a relatively unpressured way upon the long-range meaning and implications of society as a whole. To be sure, universities have short-range and restricted objectives as well: grading students, publishing or perishing, convincing the state legislature of the need for an increase in the budget. And the academic may, of course, define his concerns in a narrow and departmentally limited way; most academics do. But it is also possible for the university professor to take a broad view, to study the implications of one topic for another, to reflect, analyze, and evaluate in a leisurely and unpressured manner. The academic is probably better placed and more strongly motivated than other comparable professionals in our society to take a long-range view of things, and to attempt to understand not only the intricacies of some small microcosm, but the macrocosm of our society and the modern world as a whole.

Apart from its relatively long time span and inclusive scope of concern, the modern American university possesses other characteristics that have led it to come to be the chief center of criticism of our society. The motivations and role of the academic profession allow it, when it desires, a more intimate involvement with the next generation than that afforded any other professional group. And to this encounter with youth the academic brings a critical mind inclined to stand aside from the traditional pieties of any particular embodiment of the community. To be sure, these same qualities often make the academic community appear seditious, disloyal, and dangerous to those who identify themselves with the *status quo*. But these qualities also enable at least some academics, at some times, to stand back from the immediate interests of their own position and time to consider the welfare of the next generation.

Most adults are, of course, in one way or another preoccupied with the next generation. As parents, we are concerned with our children; and in most vocations at least some adults undertake to pass on to their juniors the values and standards of their vocation. Yet in most situations the concern of the older generation for the young is attenuated. Parents are linked to their children not only by concern and identification but by ambivalence, frustration, disappointment, and hurt, which may impede understanding and sympathy. Similarly, in most American occupations a sense of responsibility to the next generation is often balanced or outweighed by an even greater sense of obligations to the previous generation, as embodied by the boss, the board of directors, or the traditions of the occupation. Indeed, in much of American society the young and the old meet largely on the latter's terms: the new generation must accommodate itself to that which preceded it.

It sometimes happens in universities, however, that the relative weight of the younger generation is increased. At least some academics have chosen their vocation because of their special concern with youth, and this concern sensitizes them to those they teach. It is not always mere lip service when academics comment on how much they learn from their students; nor is it an accident that the most accurate characterizations of today's youth often come from their teachers. Between teachers and their students there can exist deep but generally unstated ties of understanding, sympathy, and identification. In recent years these ties have been reflected in the frequency with which faculty members have allied themselves with dissenting students, as in the reluctance of students to attack openly their teachers. Whatever the actual merits of the case, it is the administration, not the faculty, that must generally bear the brunt of student dissatisfaction.

The academic vocation also allows—indeed demands—of the teacher an intensive exposure to those whom he seeks to educate. And it requires considerable imperviousness to remain unaware of the very real differences between this student generation and those which preceded it. Many faculty members *are* just that impervious; but others are able to perceive the changing outlooks and needs of college students. Some of what the academic sees in his students is, of course, all too familiar from the years of his own late adolescence and early adulthood. But today, much of what he sees is also unfamiliar; and his vicarious participation in the outlooks of his students permits him to see the modern world not only through his own eyes, but through the eyes of his students as well. This "double vision" in turn disposes at least some members of the academic community to a special preoccupation with the world in which their students will live, to heightened sensitivity to the factors that will help determine the options, resources, and dilemmas that will confront their students as adults, and to a strengthened investment in guaranteeing that the society they will live in is adequate to their needs and potentialities. This intensified concern with the adequacy of tomorrow's society to the next generation contributes to the willingness of the American university to examine critically the future shape and direction of our society.

Finally, the university's assumption of a critical role vis-à-vis American society is related to the intellectual style and outlook of those who choose an academic vocation. A generation of research has shown a distinctive correlation between "anti-authoritarianism," the possession of a critical mind, and the choice of an academic career. The extent of this correlation is daily witnessed in the skeptical, iconoclastic, and questioning outlook of many of the teachers and scholars who inhabit the major university centers of this country. More than other professionals, such men and women are disposed to challenge authoritative views, to trust the power of human reason in ameliorating human difficulties, to identify with the underdog rather than with the powerful, to hold a complex view of the world, and to question any solution that presents itself as final or beyond question.

In underlining the critical temperament of academics, I do not mean to suggest that all faculty members are equally endowed with "critical minds," much less that the academic is characterized by a sweet reasonableness. Nor do I mean to dismiss the valid criticisms frequently made of "the academic mind" and the "academic liberal." To those of us who pride ourselves on being members of the academic community, it is chastening to recall that the term "academic" is usually preceded by the word "merely": all too often, our views are in fact trivial, irrelevant, superficial, or uninformed. And surely only a minority of academics are as sensitive to the moods and outlooks of their students as those I have here described. But I do mean to suggest that during the past decades American universities have gathered within their protective boundaries an unusual number of men and women whose temperaments and outlooks incline them to view the contemporary community and the modern world in a critical rather than an acquiescent spirit, and that this concentration of critical minds in the modern university helps explain its pre-eminent role as critic of our society.

In brief, then, the institution of higher education in America has become the major source of analysis, commentary, critique, defense, and reform in our society. It has come to occupy this position partly in response to our growing awareness that the unexamined and unguided logic of technological change has not automatically produced a humane, decent, beautiful, and just society or world. Compared to other institutions in America, higher education allows its members an unusual freedom to consider the long-range trends of society in a broad and inclusive perspective. Compared to other professionals, academics are likely to be particularly sensitive to and concerned with the next generation, and with the social and human preconditions for their welfare. By temperament, the members of the academic community are inclined toward skepticism, toward questioning, toward the examination of what has been given, and toward faith in the power of human intelligence to resolve human problems. For all these reasons, then, the modern American university has become the prime critic of our society.

Who Is to Criticize What?

Even if we grant that the exercise of the critical function by American universities is valid and essential both with regard to students and with regard to the wider society, the important practical questions still remain. Who is to criticize what? Should individual universities align themselves with particular criticisms of the wider society or become lobbyists for social reform? Under what circumstances is criticism legitimate and by whom? Are there no limits on the exercise of the critical function? Should not the university be objective rather than partisan?

To clarify these questions, we must distinguish between three meanings of the term "the university"; for according to our definitions our answers will differ. First, we may think of the university as equivalent to "higher education," that is, as a social institution on a par with other major social institutions like the family, the law, and industry. In my comments so far I have largely been referring to the university in this broad sense. But second, we may think of the university as a particular organization— as Eastern Michigan University, the University of Mississippi, Johns Hopkins University. In this second sense, a university contains an administrative structure, carries on relations with other organizations, has financial needs, sets admission standards, hires faculty members, etc. And finally, we may think of the university as the university community, the set of students, faculty members, administrators, and others who are associated with particular universities. In this sense, the university consists of a group of individuals who are united by the fact that they hold roles in a special kind of organization.

I trust I have made abundantly clear my reasons for arguing that the university as a social institution—higher education in America—not only does but must continue to exercise a critical function in educating students and in commenting on the wider society. And in defining the critical function, I have noted that the exercise of this function entails not only "objec-

tive" analyses of existing institutions, values, and practices, but the evaluation, judgment, rejection, and acceptance of what exists, coupled frequently
with a commitment to alternatives to the *status quo*. In this sense,
then, if the critical function is to be exercised by higher education, it entails the possibility of commitments, judgments, and activities by students
and faculty members that will be taken as partisan. Thus, to justify the
critical function, we must be prepared to justify its inevitable corollaries—
evaluation, judgment, and commitment to action; to do otherwise would
be to make criticism merely "academic" in the worst sense of the term. As
one of the major social institutions in modern American society, then, the
university must be critical, which includes the right to be partisan.

I have also indicated my conviction that the members of the university
community not only have made but must continue to make critical contributions to our society. To be sure, the right to analyze critically, to evaluate, to defend and oppose, to propose and reject, to campaign for and
against is not limited to members of the academic community; it is a right
that we possess simply by virtue of our citizenship in a democracy. But for
reasons I have attempted to explain, members of the university community are disposed to exercise this right with special vehemence and vigor,
and with results that are very much to the long-range advantage of our
society.

The university as an organization, however, is in a very different position. As organizations, universities should act primarily to protect and promote the major functions of the institution of higher education—teaching,
research, public service, and criticism. Thus, the tasks of the individual
university must be distinguished sharply from the functions of higher education in general: the tasks of the former are to maintain a climate in
which, among other things, the critical spirit can flourish. For individual
universities as organizations officially to align themselves with specific critical analyses, views, judgments, or reforms would undermine their ability
to defend the critical function itself. Acting as a lobby or pressure group
for some particular judgment or proposal, a university effectively closes its
doors to those whose critical sense leads them to disagree and thus destroys itself as an environment in which the critical spirit can truly flourish.
The task of the university as an organization, then, is to be neutral, objective, and dispassionate in order to preserve an atmosphere in which students and faculty members can discuss, evaluate, criticize, judge, commit
themselves, and, when they choose, decide to act.

This view implies that the university as an organization should not take
upon itself the burden of enforcing community laws and standards. To be
sure, members of the university are members of the wider community and
are subject to its laws, just as they are free to strive to change these laws.
But for the university as an organization to implement or enforce commu-

nity codes and regulations, acting as a substitute for law-enforcement agencies, is to assume functions that are not properly those of higher education. One of the many disadvantages of the *in loco parentis* doctrine is that, under the guise of protecting students, it identifies the university as an organization with a particular set of community values and thus, once again, closes its doors to those who would question or reject these values. Similarly, for the university as an organization to align itself with the deprecation or rejection of community values would undermine the free expression of those whose critical judgment leads them to stand staunchly behind these values.

In one respect, however, the university as an organization must be vigorously partisan and committed—to the defense of its right to exercise its own proper functions. A university must insist vigorously on its freedom to teach students what is known, to confront them with multiple viewpoints (with a variety of distinct partisanships), to encourage them to reflect upon, analyze, and criticize what they learn. It must forthrightly justify the freedom of its faculty members to pursue their researches without community harassment, and regardless of where these researches may lead. It must insist upon its own authority to decide when service to the community is consistent with its other goals. And, perhaps most important today, it must adamantly resist all efforts to limit the freedom of students and faculty members as individuals to comment upon, evaluate, criticize, and attempt to change the surrounding world. Specifically, this entails defense of the rights of faculty members to hold deviant views and propose unpopular actions, of students to comment on off-campus issues and take part in off-campus causes, and of both students and faculty to "mount action" that overflows the ivied walls of the Academy. In all of these respects the university qua organization should be a partisan proponent of the unencumbered exercise of its own functions and of the rights of its members.

Furthermore, each university has the obvious right to regulate its own internal affairs. Like any organization, a university must have standards regarding the quality of its efforts: of teaching, research, public service, and criticism. It has the right to demand honesty and decency from its members. It has the obligation to insist upon high standards of attainment and integrity from students and faculty members. It must attempt to develop patterns of self-government that embody within the university the ideals of free inquiry, discussion, and criticism. And inevitably, universities will differ, depending upon their traditions and circumstances, in their definitions of decency, in their standards of attainment, and in the ways they choose to govern themselves. But in this regard, it is easiest to err in the direction of excessive limitation, to be unduly fearful of the consequences of freedom. The steady movement toward allowing students more meaningful self-regulation and more consequential self-government, for example, has not brought with it chaos or license but, rather, growing opportunities for responsible self-control.

Increasingly, then, the critical function must be added to the traditional triumvirate of teaching, research, and public service. Criticism must be seen not as the price to be paid for the services of higher education, but as one of the most crucial of these services. As our century progresses, as our society and the world become more complex, as the pace of social change accelerates, higher education that is not eminently critical will be increasingly useless. More and more, our society and the world will need young men and women who have not only assimilated the past and made themselves familiar with the present, but who have become articulate, informed, and thoughtful critics of both.

The Sources of Student Dissent

By 1967, there had been enough "trouble" on American campuses to interest the editors of The Journal of Social Issues *in an issue on student activism. Writing for that issue gave me a chance to review the then-meager literature on student radicals, on institutions where protests occurred, and on the conditions under which protests were most likely. The ideas put forward here were essentially those I tested, and sometimes found wanting, in a later study of antiwar radicals (see "Radicals: Renewal of the Tradition").*

In this essay I again argue that no single factor suffices to explain the unexpected emergence of a youthful opposition in the 1960's. For example, simply to point to the changes in personalities and individual values is not enough, for it neglects the importance of the issues. Yet equally, simply to note the validity of the issues neglects the fact that only some students respond to these issues, while most ignore them. In brief, only an analysis that deals simultaneously with psychological, institutional, cultural, historical, and political trends, and examines their interaction, can adequately explain the phenomenon of student dissent.

I also emphasize here the lack of monolithic unity within what was then called "the Movement." Dissenting students are often seen as "all of a kind"; but, in fact, there are many kinds of dissenters. Specifically, I point to the tension between two poles of dissent—political radicalism and cultural alienation. Those at the extremes of radicalism and alienation have distinct personal styles, different values, and contrasting backgrounds. The internal dynamic and the evolution of the oppositional youth culture, I believe, can be understood only in terms of the constant tension between these two poles—Woodstock vs. Weatherman, drugs vs. demonstrations, new consciousness vs. new politics.

Here as elsewhere (see "Vulnerabilities of the Counterculture") I tend to be critical of the "cultural" revolt, partly because it too often simply caricatures the privatism of American life, but also because it turns its back on social, economic, international, and political problems that desperately need solution. The strength of the new oppositional culture, I think, lies in its ability to tolerate the tension between cultural

*and political revolution. When a purely "political" position is chosen, we
have the pop Marxism of the Progressive Labor faction of SDS or the
romance with violence of the Weathermen; when the purely "cultural"
stance is taken, we end with speed freaks, teenyboppers or the Rolling
Stones at Altamonte—where murder was virtually staged for the
forthcoming Hollywood film. The power of the new youth culture comes
from the effort to make a "revolution" that is both cultural and political,
that combines new ways of living with fundamental social and political
change. No one can say whether that effort will succeed. But it is clearly
a noble and important effort.*

THE apparent upsurge of dissent among American college students is
one of the more puzzling phenomena in recent American history. Less
than a decade ago, commencement orators were decrying the "silence" of
college students in the face of urgent national and international issues; but
in the past two or three years the same speakers have warned graduating
classes across the country against the dangers of unreflective protest, irresponsible action, and unselective dissent. Rarely in history has apparent
apathy been replaced so rapidly by publicized activism, silence by strident dissent.

This "wave" of dissent among American college students has been
much discussed. Especially in the mass media—popular magazines, newspapers and television—articles of interpretation, explanation, deprecation,
and occasionally applause have appeared in enormous numbers. More important, from the first beginnings of the student Civil Rights Movement,
social scientists have been regular participant-observers and investigators
of student dissent. There now exists a considerable body of research that
deals with the characteristics and settings of student dissent. To be sure,
most of these studies are topical (centered around a particular protest or
demonstration), and some of the more extensive studies are still in varying
stages of incompletion. Yet enough evidence has already been gathered to
permit tentative generalizations about the varieties, origins, and future of
student dissent.

In the remarks to follow, I will attempt to gather together this evidence (along with my own research and informal observations) to provide tentative answers to three questions about student dissent today.
First, what is the nature of student dissent in American colleges? Second,
what are the sources of the recent "wave of protest" by college students?
And third, what can we predict about the future of student dissent?

Two Varieties of Dissent

Dissent is by no means the dominant mood of American college
students. Every responsible study or survey shows apathy and privatism

far more dominant than dissent. On most of our 2,500 campuses, student protest, student alienation, and student unrest are something that happens elsewhere or that characterizes a mere handful of "kooks" on the local campus. However we define "dissent," overt dissent is relatively infrequent and tends to be concentrated largely at the more selective, "progressive," and "academic" colleges and universities in America. Thus, Peterson's study of student protests finds political demonstrations concentrated in the larger universities and institutions of high academic caliber, and almost totally absent at teachers colleges, technical institutes, and nonacademic denominational colleges. And even at the colleges that gather together the greatest number of dissenters the vast majority of students—generally well over 95 per cent—remain interested onlookers or opponents rather than active dissenters. Thus, whatever we say about student dissenters is said about a very small minority of America's 7 million college students. At most colleges dissent is not visible at all.

Partly because the vast majority of American students remain largely uncritical of the wider society, fundamentally conformist in behavior and outlook, and basically "adjusted" to the prevailing collegiate, national, and international order, the small minority of dissenting students is highly visible to the mass media. As I will argue later, such students are often distinctively talented; they "use" the mass media effectively; and they generally succeed in their goal of making themselves and their causes highly visible. Equally important, student dissenters of all types arouse deep and ambivalent feelings in nondissenting students and adults—envy, resentment, admiration, repulsion, nostalgia, and guilt. Such feelings contribute both to the selective overattention dissenters receive and to the often distorted perceptions and interpretations of them and their activities. Thus, there has developed through the mass media and the imaginings of adults a more or less stereotyped—and generally incorrect—image of the student dissenter.

The "stereotypical" dissenter as popularly portrayed is both a Bohemian and political activist. Bearded, be-Levi-ed, long-haired, dirty, and unkempt, he is seen as profoundly disaffected from his society, often influenced by "radical" (Marxist, Communist, Maoist, or Castroite) ideas, an experimenter in sex and drugs, unconventional in his daily behavior. Frustrated and unhappy, often deeply maladjusted as a person, he is a "failure" (or as one U. S. Senator put it, a "reject"). Certain academic communities like Berkeley are said to act as "magnets" for dissenters, who selectively attend colleges with a reputation as protest centers. Furthermore, dropouts or "nonstudents" who have failed in college cluster in large numbers around the fringes of such colleges, actively seeking pretexts for protest, refusing all compromise and impatient with ordinary democratic processes.

According to such popular analyses, the sources of dissent are to be found in the loss of certain traditional American virtues. The "breakdown" of American family life, high rates of divorce, the "softness" of American living, inadequate parents, and, above all, overindulgence and "spoiling" contribute to the prevalence of dissent. Brought up in undisciplined homes by parents unsure of their own values and standards, dissenters channel their frustration and anger against the older generation, against all authority, and against established institutions.

Similar themes are sometimes found in the interpretations of more scholarly commentators. "Generational conflict" is said to underly the motivation to dissent, and a profound "alienation" from American society is seen as a factor of major importance in producing protests. Then, too, such factors as the poor quality and impersonality of American college education, and the large size and lack of close student-faculty contact in the "multiversity" are sometimes seen as the latent or precipitating factors in student protests, regardless of the manifest issues around which students are organized. And still other scholarly analysts, usually men now disillusioned by the radicalism of the 1930's, have expressed fear of the dogmatism, rigidity, and "authoritarianism of the Left" of today's student activists.

These stereotyped views are, I believe, incorrect in a variety of ways. They confuse two distinct varieties of student dissent; equally important, they fuse dissent with maladjustment. There are, of course, as many forms of dissent as there are individual dissenters; and any effort to counter the popular stereotype of the dissenter by pointing to the existence of distinct "types" of dissenters runs the risk of oversimplifying at a lower level of abstraction. Nonetheless, it seems to me useful to suggest that student dissenters generally fall somewhere along a continuum that runs between two ideal types—first, the political activist or protester, and second, the withdrawn, culturally alienated student.*

The activist. The defining characteristic of the "new" activist is his participation in a student demonstration or group activity that concerns itself with some matter of general political, social, or ethical principle. Characteristically, the activist feels that some injustice has been done and attempts to "take a stand," "demonstrate," or in some fashion express his convictions. The specific issues in question range from protest against a paternalistic college administration's actions to disagreement with American Vietnam policies, from indignation at the exploitation of the poor to anger at the firing of a devoted teacher, from opposition to the Selective Service laws, which exempt him but not the poor, to—most important— outrage at the deprivation of the civil rights of other Americans.

---

* In an earlier account (see "Faces in the Lecture Room," pp. 121–22), I discussed a third deviant type: the "underachiever." But since he rejects himself rather than society, he does not belong in a discussion of dissenters.

The initial concern of the protester is almost always immediate, *ad hoc,* and local. To be sure, the student who protests about one issue is likely to feel inclined or obliged to demonstrate his convictions on other issues as well. But whatever the issue, the protester rarely demonstrates because his *own* interests are jeopardized, but rather because he perceives injustices being done to *others* less fortunate than himself. For example, one of the apparent paradoxes about protests against current draft policies is that the protesting students are selectively drawn from that subgroup *most* likely to receive student deferments for graduate work. The basis of protest is a general sense that the Selective Service rules and the war in Vietnam are unjust to others with whom the student is identified, but whose fate he does not share. If one runs down the list of "causes" taken up by student activists, in rare cases are demonstrations directed at improving the lot of the protesters themselves; identification with the oppressed is a more important motivating factor than an actual sense of immediate personal oppression.

The anti-ideological stance of today's activists has been noted by many commentators. This distrust of formal ideologies (and at times of articulate thought) makes it difficult to pinpoint the positive social and political values of student protesters. Clearly, many current American political institutions, like *de facto* segregation, are opposed; clearly, too, most students of the New Left reject careerism and familism as personal values. In this sense, we might think of the activist as (politically) "alienated." But this label seems to me more misleading than illuminating, for it overlooks the more basic *commitment* of most student activists to other ancient, traditional, and creedal American values like free speech, citizens' participation in decision-making, equal opportunity, and justice. In so far as the activist rejects all or part of "the power structure," it is because current political realities fall so far short of the ideals he sees as central to the American creed. And in so far as he repudiates careerism and familism, it is because of his implicit allegiance to other human goals he sees, once again, as more crucial to American life. Thus, to emphasize the "alienation" of activists is to neglect their more basic allegiance to creedal American ideals.

One of these ideals is, of course, a belief in the desirability of political and social action. Sustained in good measure by the successes of the student Civil Rights Movement, the protester is usually convinced that demonstrations are effective in mobilizing public opinion, bringing moral or political pressure to bear, demonstrating the existence of his opinions, or, at times, in "bringing the machine to a halt." In this sense, then, despite his criticisms of existing political practices and social institutions, he is a political optimist. Moreover, the protester must believe in at least minimal organization and group activity; otherwise, he would find it impossible to take part, as he does, in any organized demonstrations or activities. De-

spite their search for more truly "democratic" forms of organization and
action (e.g., participatory democracy), activists agree that group action is
more effective than purely individual acts. To be sure, a belief in the value
and efficacy of political action is not equivalent to endorsement of prevalent political institutions or forms of action. Thus, one characteristic of
activists is their search for new forms of social action, protest, and political
organization (community organization, sit-ins, participatory democracy)
that will be more effective and less oppressive than traditional political
institutions.

The alienated. In contrast to the politically optimistic, active, and socially concerned protester, the alienated student is far too pessimistic and
too firmly opposed to the system to wish to demonstrate his disapproval in
any organized public way. His demonstrations of dissent are private:
through nonconformity of behavior, ideology, and dress, through personal
experimentation, and above all through efforts to intensify his own subjective experience, he shows his distaste and disinterest in politics and society. The activist attempts to change the world around him, but the
alienated student is convinced that meaningful change of the social and
political world is impossible; instead, he considers "dropping out" the
only real option.

Alienated students tend to be drawn from the same general social
strata and colleges as protesters. But psychologically and ideologically,
their backgrounds are often very different. Alienated students are more
likely to be disturbed psychologically; and although they are often highly
talented and artistically gifted, they are less committed to academic values
and intellectual achievement than are protesters. The alienated student's
real campus is the school of the absurd, and he has more affinity for pessimistic existentialist ontology than for traditional American activism. Furthermore, such students usually find it psychologically and ideologically
impossible to take part in organized group activities for any length of
time, particularly when they are expected to assume responsibilities for
leadership. Thus, on the rare occasions when they become involved in
demonstrations, they usually prefer peripheral roles, avoid responsibilities,
and are considered a nuisance by serious activists.

Whereas the protesting student is likely to accept the basic political
and social values of his parents, the alienated student almost always rejects his parents' values. In particular, he is likely to see his father as a man
who has "sold out" to the pressures for success and status in American
society: he is determined to avoid the fate that overtook his father. Toward their mothers, however, alienated students usually express a very
special sympathy and identification. These mothers, far from encouraging
their sons toward independence and achievement, generally seem to have

been oversolicitous and limiting. The most common family environment of
the alienated-student-to-be consists of a parental schism supplemented by
a special mother-son alliance of mutual understanding and maternal control and deprecation of the father.

In many colleges alienated students often constitute a kind of hidden
underground, disorganized and shifting in membership, in which students
can temporarily or permanently withdraw from the ordinary pressures of
college life. The alienated are especially attracted to the hallucinogenic
drugs like marijuana, mescaline, and LSD, precisely because these agents
combine withdrawal from ordinary social life with the promise of greatly
intensified subjectivity and perception. To the confirmed "acid head,"
what matters is intense, drug-assisted perception; the rest—including politics, social action, and student demonstrations—is usually seen as "role-
playing." *

The recent and much-publicized emergence of "hippie" subcultures in
several major cities and increasingly on the campuses of many selective
and progressive colleges illustrates the overwhelmingly apolitical stance of
alienated youth. For although hippies oppose war and believe in interra-
cial living, few have been willing or able to engage in anything beyond
occasional peace marches or apolitical "human be-ins." Indeed, the hippie's emphasis on immediacy, "love," and "turning-on," together with his
basic rejection of the traditional values of American life, innoculates him
against involvement in long-range activist endeavors, like education or
community organization, and even against the sustained effort needed to
plan and execute demonstrations or marches. For the alienated hippie,
American society is beyond redemption (or not worth trying to redeem);
but the activist, no matter how intense his rejection of specific American
policies and practices, retains a conviction that his society can and should
be changed. Thus, despite occasional agreement in principle between the
alienated and the activists, cooperation in practice has been rare and

---

* The presence among student dissenters of a group of "nonstudents"—that is,
dropouts from college or graduate school who congregate or remain near some academic center—has been much noted. In fact, however, student protesters seem somewhat *less* likely to drop out of college than do nonparticipants in demonstrations, and
there is no evidence that dropping out of college is in any way related to dissent from
American society. On the contrary, several studies suggest that the academically gifted
and psychologically intact student who drops out of college voluntarily has few distinctive discontents about his college or about American society. If he is dissatisfied at
all, it is with himself, usually for failing to take advantage of the "rich educational
opportunities" he sees in his college. The motivations of students dropping out of
college are complex and varied, but such motivations more often seem related to personal questions of self-definition and parental identification or to a desire to escape
relentless academic pressures than to any explicit dissent from the Great Society. Thus,
although a handful of students have chosen to drop out of college for a period in order
to devote themselves to political and societal protest activities, there seems little reason
in general to associate the dropout with the dissenter, whether he be a protester or
an alienated student. The opposite is nearer the truth.

usually ends with activists accusing the alienated of "irresponsibility," while the alienated are confirmed in their view of activists as moralistic, "up-tight," and "uncool."

Obviously, no description of a type ever fits an individual perfectly. But by this rough typology I mean to suggest that popular stereotypes which present a unified portrait of student dissent are gravely oversimplified. More specifically, they confuse the politically pessimistic and socially uncommitted alienated student with the politically hopeful and socially committed activist. To be sure, there are many students who fall between these two extremes, and some of them alternate between passionate search for intensified subjectivity and equally passionate efforts to remedy social and political injustices. And as I will later suggest, even within the student movement one of the central tensions is between political activism and cultural alienation. Nonetheless, even to understand this tension we must first distinguish between the varieties of dissent apparent on American campuses.

Furthermore, the distinction between activist and alienated students as psychological types suggests the incompleteness of scholarly analyses that see social and historical factors as the only forces that "push" a student toward one or the other of these forms of dissent. To be sure, social and cultural factors are of immense importance in providing channels for the expression (or suppression) of dissent, and in determining *which* kinds of dissenters receive publicity, censure, support, or ostracism in any historical period. But these factors cannot, in general, change a hippie into a committed activist, or a SNCC field worker into a full-time "acid head." Thus, the prototypical activist of 1966 is not the "same" student as the prototypical student Bohemian of 1956 but is rather the politically aware but frustrated, academically oriented "privatist" of that era. Similarly, as I will argue below, the most compelling alternative to most activists is not the search for kicks or sentience but the quest for scholarly competence. And if culturally sanctioned opportunities for the expression of alienation were to disappear, most alienated students would turn to private psychopathology rather than to public activism.

Stated more generally, historical forces do not ordinarily transform radically the character, values, and inclinations of an adult in later life. Rather, they thrust certain groups forward in some eras and discourage or suppress other groups. The recent alternation in styles of student dissent in America is therefore not to be explained so much by the malleability of individual character as by the power of society to bring activists into the limelight, providing them with the intellectual and moral instruments for action. Only a minority of potential dissenters fall close enough to the midpoint between alienation and activism so that they can constitute a "swing vote" acutely responsive to social and cultural pressures and styles.

The rest, the majority, are characterologically committed to one or another style of dissent.

What I have termed "alienated" students are by no means a new phenomenon in American life, or for that matter in industrialized societies. Bohemians, "beatniks," and artistically inclined undergraduates who rejected middle-class values have long been a part of the American student scene, especially at more selective colleges; they constituted the most visible form of dissent during the relative political "silence" of American students in the 1950's. What is distinctive about student dissent in recent years is the unexpected emergence of a vocal minority of politically and socially active students. Much is now known about the characteristics of such students, and the circumstances under which protests are likely to be mounted. At the same time, many areas of ignorance remain. In the account to follow, I will attempt to formulate a series of general hypotheses concerning the sources of student activism.*

It is abundantly clear that no single factor will suffice to explain the increase of politically motivated activities and protests on American campuses. Even if we define an activist narrowly, as a student who (a) acts together with others in a group, (b) is concerned with some ethical, social, ideological, or political issue, and (c) holds liberal or "radical" views, the sources of student activism and protest are complex and interrelated. At least four kinds of factors seem involved in any given protest. First, the individuals involved must be suitably predisposed by their personal backgrounds, values, and motivations. Second, the likelihood of protest is far greater in certain kinds of educational and social settings. Third, socially directed protests require a special cultural climate, that is, certain distinctive values and views about the effectiveness and meaning of demonstrations, and about the wider society. And finally, some historical situations are especially conducive to protests.

* Throughout the following, I still use the terms "protester" and "activist" interchangeably, although I am aware that some activists are not involved in protests. Furthermore, the category of "activist" is an embracing one, comprising at least three subclasses. First, those who might be termed *reformers,* that is, students involved in community organization work, the Peace Corps, tutoring programs, Vista, etc., but not generally affiliated with any of the New Left organizations. Second, the group of *activists proper,* most of whom are or have been affiliated with organizations like the Free Speech Movement at Berkeley, Students for a Democratic Society, the Student Non-violent Coordinating Committee, or the Congress of Racial Equality. Finally, there is a much publicized handful of students who might be considered *extremists,* who belong to doctrinaire Marxist and Trotskyite organizations, like the now-defunct May Second Movement. No empirical study with which I am acquainted has investigated the differences between students in these three subgroups. Most studies have concentrated on the "activist proper" and my remarks will be based on a reading of their data.

The Protest-Prone Personality

A large and still-growing number of studies, conducted under different auspices, at different times, and about different students, presents a remarkably consistent picture of the protest-prone individual. For one, student protesters are generally outstanding students; the higher the student's grade average, the more outstanding his academic achievements, the more likely it is that he will become involved in any given political demonstration. Similarly, student activists come from families with liberal political values; a disproportionate number report that their parents hold views essentially similar to their own, and accept or support their activities. Thus, among the parents of protesters we find large numbers of liberal Democrats, plus an unusually large scattering of pacifists, socialists, etc. A disproportionate number of protesters come from Jewish families; and if the parents of activists are religious, they tend to be concentrated in the more liberal denominations—Reform Judaism, Unitarianism, the Society of Friends, etc. Such parents are reported to have high ethical and political standards, regardless of their actual religious convictions.

As might be expected of a group of politically liberal and academically talented students, a disproportionate number are drawn from professional and intellectual families of upper-middle-class status. For example, compared with active student conservatives, members of protest groups tend to have higher parental incomes, more parental education, and less anxiety about social status. Another study finds that high levels of education distinguish the activist's family even in the grandparental generation. In brief, activists are not drawn from disadvantaged, status-anxious, underprivileged, or uneducated groups; on the contrary, they are selectively recruited from among those young Americans who have had the most socially fortunate upbringings.

The basic value commitments of the activist tend to be academic and nonvocational. Such students are rarely found among engineers, future teachers at teachers colleges, or students of business administration. Their over-all educational goals are those of a liberal education for its own sake, rather than specifically technical, vocational, or professional preparation. Rejecting careerist and familist goals, activists espouse humanitarian, expressive, and self-actualizing values. Perhaps because of these values, they delay career choice longer than their classmates. Nor are such students distinctively dogmatic, rigid, or authoritarian. Quite the contrary, the substance and style of their beliefs and activities tends to be open, flexible, and highly liberal. Their fields of academic specialization are nonvocational—the social sciences and the humanities. Once in college, they not only do well academically but tend to persist in their academic commitments, dropping out *less* frequently than most of their classmates. As might be expected, a disproportionate number receive a B.A. within four years and continue on to graduate school, preparing themselves for academic careers.

Survey data also suggest that the activist is not distinctively dissatisfied with his college education. As will be noted below, activists generally attend colleges which provide the best, rather than the worst, undergraduate education available today. Objectively then, activists probably have less to complain about in their undergraduate educations than most other students. And subjectively as well, surveys show most activists, like most other American undergraduates, to be relatively well satisfied with their undergraduate educations. Thus, dissatisfaction with educational failings of the "impersonal multiversity," however important as a rallying cry, does not appear to be a distinctive cause of activism.

In contrast to their relative satisfaction with the quality of their educations, however, activists *are* distinctively dissatisfied with what might be termed the "civil-libertarian" defects of their college administrations. While no doubt a great many American undergraduates distrust "University Hall," this distrust is especially pronounced amongst student protesters. Furthermore, activists tend to be more responsive than other students to deprivations of civil rights on campus as well as off campus, particularly when political pressures seem to motivate on campus policies they consider unjust. The same responsiveness increasingly extends to issues of "student power": i.e., student participation and decisions affecting campus life. Thus, bans on controversial speakers, censorship of student publications, and limitations on off-campus political or social action are likely to incense the activist, as is arbitrary "administration without the consent of the administered." But it is primarily perceived injustice or the denial of student rights by the administration—rather than poor educational quality, neglect by the faculty, or the impersonality of the multiversity—that agitates the activist.

Most studies of activists have concentrated on variables that are relatively easy to measure: social class, academic achievements, explicit values, and satisfaction with college. But these factors alone will not explain activism: more students possess the demographic and attitudinal characteristics of the protest-prone personality than are actually involved in protests and social-action programs. Situational, institutional, cultural, and historical factors (discussed below) obviously contribute to "catalyzing" a protest-prone personality into an actual activist. But it also seems that, within the broad demographic group so far defined, more specific psychodynamic factors contribute to activism.

In speculating about such factors, we leave the ground of established fact and enter the terrain of speculation, for only a few studies have explored the personality dynamics and family constellation of the activist, and most of these studies are impressionistic and clinical. But certain facts are clear. As noted, activists are *not*, on the whole, repudiating or rebelling against explicit parental values and ideologies. On the contrary, there is some evidence that such students are living out their parents' values in practice; and one study even suggests that activists may be somewhat *closer* to their parents' values than nonactivists. Thus, any simple concept of "generational conflict" or "rebellion against parental authority" is clearly oversimplified as applied to the motivations of most protesters.

It does seem probable, however, that many activists are concerned with *living out expressed but unimplemented parental values.* Solomon and Fishman, studying civil rights activists and peace marchers, argue that many demonstrators are "acting out" in their demonstrations the values which their parents explicitly believed, but did not have the courage or opportunity to practice or fight for. Similarly, when protesters criticize their fathers, it is usually over their fathers' failure to practice what they have preached to their children throughout their lives. Thus, in the personal background of the protester there is occasionally a suggestion that his father is less than "sincere" (and even at times "hypocritical") in his professions of political liberalism. In particular, both careerism and familism in parents are the objects of activist criticisms, the more so because these implicit goals often conflict with explicit parental values. And it may be that protesters receive both covert and overt support from their parents because the latter are secretly proud of their children's eagerness to implement the ideals they as parents have only given lip service to. But whatever the ambivalences that bind parents with their activist children, it would be wrong to overemphasize them: what is most impressive is the solidarity of older and younger generations.

While no empirical study has tested this hypothesis, it seems probable that in many activist-producing families, the mother will have a dominant psychological influence on her son's development. I have already noted that the protester's cause is rarely himself, but rather alleviating the oppression of others. As a group, activists seem to possess an unusual *capacity for nurturant identification*—that is, for empathy and sympathy with the underdog, the oppressed, and the needy. Such a capacity can have many origins, but its most likely source in upper-middle-class professional families is identification with an active mother whose own work embodies nurturant concern for others. Flacks' finding that the mothers of activists are likely to be employed, often in professional or service roles like teaching and social work, is consistent with this hypothesis. In general in American society, middle-class women have greater social and financial freedom to work in jobs that are idealistically "fulfilling" as opposed to merely lucrative or prestigious. As a rule, then, in middle-class families, it is the mother who actively embodies in her life and work the humanitarian, social, and political ideals that the father may share in principle but does not or cannot implement in his career.

Given what we know about the general characteristics of the families of protest-prone students, it also seems probable that the dominant ethos of their families is unusually equalitarian, permissive, "democratic," and highly individuating. More specifically, we might expect that these will be families where children talk back to their parents at the dinner table, where free dialogue and discussion of feelings is encouraged, and where "rational" solutions are sought to everyday family problems and conflicts. We would also expect that such families would place a high premium on self-expression and intellectual independence, encouraging their children to make up their own minds and to stand firm against group pressures. Once again, the mother seems the most likely carrier and epitome of these values, given her relative freedom from professional and financial pressures.

The contrast between such protest-prompting families and alienating families should be underlined. In both, the son's deepest emotional ties are often to his mother. But in the alienating family the mother-son relationship is characterized by maternal control and intrusiveness, whereas in the protest-prompting family, the mother is a highly individuating force in her son's life, pushing him to independence and autonomy. Furthermore, the alienated student is determined to avoid the fate that befell his father, whereas the protesting student wants merely to live out the values that his father has not always worked hard enough to practice. Finally, the equalitarian, permissive, democratic, and individuating environment of the entire family of the protester contrasts with the overcontrolling, oversolicitous attitude of the mother in the alienating family, where the father is usually excluded from major emotional life within the family.

These hypotheses about the family background and psychodynamics of the protester are speculative, and future research may prove their invalidity. But regardless of whether *these* particular speculations are correct, it seems clear that in addition to the general social, demographic, and attitudinal factors mentioned in most research, more specific familial and psychodynamic influences contribute to protest-proneness.

The Protest-Promoting Institution

However we define his characteristics, one activist alone cannot make a protest: the characteristics of the college or university he attends have much to do with whether his protest-proneness will ever be mobilized into actual activism. Politically, socially, and ideologically motivated demonstrations and activities are most likely to occur at certain types of colleges; they are almost unknown at a majority of campuses.

In order for an organized protest or related activities to occur, there must obviously be sufficient *numbers* of protest-prone students to form a group, these students must have an opportunity for *interaction* with each other, and there must be *leaders* to initiate and mount the protest. Thus, we might expect—and we indeed find—that protest is associated with institutional size, and particularly with the congregation of large numbers of protest-prone students in close proximity to each other. More important than sheer size alone, however, is the "image" of the institution: certain institutions selectively recruit students with protest-prone characteristics. Specifically, a reputation for academic excellence and freedom, coupled with highly selective admissions policies, will tend to congregate large numbers of potentially protesting students on one campus. Thus, certain institutions do act as "magnets" for potential activists, but not so much because of their reputations for political radicalism as because they are noted for their academic excellence. Among such institutions are some of the most selective and "progressive" private liberal arts colleges, major state universities (like Michigan, California at Berkeley, and Wisconsin), which have long traditions of vivid undergraduate teaching and high admissions standards, and many of the more prestigious private universities.

Once protest-prone students are on campus, they must have an opportunity to interact, to support one another, to develop common outlooks and shared policies—in short, to form an *activist subculture* with sufficient mass and potency to generate a demonstration or action program. Establishing "honors colleges" for talented and academically motivated students is one particularly effective way of creating a "critical mass" of protest-prone students. Similarly, inadequate on-campus housing indirectly results in the development of off-campus protest-prone subcultures (e.g., co-op houses) in residences where student activists can develop a high degree of ideological solidarity and organizational cohesion.

But even the presence of a critical mass of protest-prone undergraduates in an activist subculture is not enough to make a protest without leaders and issues. And in general, the most effective protest leaders have not been undergraduates, but teaching assistants. The presence of large numbers of exploited, underpaid, disgruntled and frustrated teacher assistants (or other equivalent graduate students and younger faculty members) is almost essential for organized and persistent protest. For one, advanced students tend to be more liberal politically and more sensitive to political issues than are most undergraduates—partly because education seems to have a liberalizing effect, and partly because students who persist into graduate school tend to be more liberal to start than those who drop out or go elsewhere. Furthermore, the frustrations of graduate students, especially at very large public universities, make them particularly sensitive to general problems of injustice, exploitation, and oppression. Teaching assistants, graduate students, and young faculty members also tend to be in daily and prolonged contact with students, are close enough to them in age to sense their mood, and are therefore in an excellent position to lead and organize student protests. Particularly at institutions which command little institutional allegiance from large numbers of highly capable graduate students will such students be found among the leaders of the protest movement.

Finally, issues are a necessity. In many cases these issues are provided by historical developments on the national or international scene, a point to which I will return. But in some instances, as at Berkeley, "on-campus" issues are the focus of protest. And in other cases off-campus and on-campus issues are fused, as in the recent protests at institutional cooperation with draft-board policies considered unjust by demonstrating students. In providing such on-campus issues, the attitude of the university administration is central. Skillful handling of student complaints, the maintenance of open channels of communication between student leaders and faculty members, and administrative willingness to resist public and political pressures in order to protect the rights of students—all minimize the likelihood of organized protest. Conversely, a university administration that shows itself unduly sensitive to political, legislative, or public pressures, that treats students arrogantly, ineptly, condescendingly, hypocritically, or above all dishonestly, is asking for a demonstration.

Thus one reason for the relative absence of on-campus student protests and demonstrations on the campuses of private, nondenominational "academic" colleges and universities (which recruit many protest-prone students) probably lies in the liberal policies of the administrations. Liberal students generally attend nonrestrictive and "libertarian" colleges. Given an administration and faculty that supports or tolerates activism and student rights, student activists must generally find their issues off-campus. The same students, confronting an administration unduly sensitive to political pressures from a conservative board of regents or state legislature, might engage in active on-campus protests. There is also some evidence that clever administrative manipulation of student complaints, even in the absence of genuine concern with student rights, can serve to dissipate the potentialities of protest.

Among the institutional factors often cited as motivating student protest is the largeness, impersonality, atomization, "multiversitification," etc., of the university. I have already noted that student protesters do not seem distinctively dissatisfied with their educations. Furthermore, the outstanding academic achievements and intellectual motivations of activists concentrate them, within any college, in the courses and programs that provide the most "personal" attention: honors programs, individual instruction, advanced seminars, and so on. Thus, they probably receive relatively *more* individual attention and a *higher* caliber of instruction than do nonprotesters. Furthermore, protests generally tend to occur at the best, rather than the worst colleges, judged from the point of view of the quality of undergraduate instruction. Thus, despite the popularity of student slogans dealing with the impersonality and irrelevance of the multiversity, the absolute level of educational opportunities seems, if anything, positively related to the occurrence of protest: the better the institution, the more likely demonstrations are.

Nor can today's student activism be attributed in any direct way to mounting academic pressures. To be sure, activism is most manifest at those selective colleges where the "pressure to perform" is greatest, where standards are highest, and where anxieties about being admitted to a "good" graduate or professional school are most pronounced. But the impact of academic pressure on activism seems negative rather than positive. Protest-prone students, with their superior academic attainments and strong intellectual commitments, seem especially vulnerable to a kind of academic professionalism that, because of the enormous demands it makes upon the student's energies, serves to cancel or preclude activism. Student demonstrations rarely take place during exam periods, and protests concerned with educational quality almost invariably seek an improvement of quality, rather than a lessening of pressure. Thus, though the pressure to perform doubtless affects *all* American students, it probably acts as a deterrent rather than a stimulus to student activism.

What probably does matter, however, is the *relative* deprivation of student expectations. A college that recruits large numbers of academically motivated and capable students into a less-than-first-rate education program, one that oversells entering freshmen on the virtues of the college, or one that reneges on implicit or explicit promises about the quality and freedom of education may well produce an "academic backlash" that will take the form of student protests over the quality of education. Even more important is the gap between expectations and actualities regarding freedom of student expression. Most entering freshmen have extremely high hopes regarding the freedom of speech and action they will be able to exercise during college: most learn the real facts quickly and graduate thoroughly disabused of their illusions. But since activists, as I have argued above, are particularly responsive to these issues, they are apt to tolerate disillusion less lightly, and to take up arms to concretize their dashed hopes. Compared to the frustration engendered by disillusionment regarding educational quality, the relative deprivation of civil libertarian hopes seems a more potent source of protests. And with regard to both issues, it must be recalled that protests have been *fewest* at institutions of low educational quality and little freedom for student expression. Thus, it is not the absolute level either of educational quality or of student freedom that matters, but the gap between student hopes and institutional facts.

The Protest-Prompting Cultural Climate

Even if a critical mass of interacting protest-prone students forms in an institution that provides leadership and issues, student protests are by no means inevitable, as the quiescence of American students during the nineteen fifties suggests. For protests to occur, other, more broadly cultural, factors, attitudes, and values must be present. Protest activities must be seen as meaningful acts, either in an instrumental or an expressive sense; and activists must be convinced that the consequences of activism and protest will not be overwhelmingly damaging to them. During the 1950's, one much-discussed factor that may have militated against student activism was the conviction that the consequences of protest (blacklisting, F.B.I. investigations, problems in obtaining security clearance, difficulties in getting jobs) were both harmful to the individual and yet extremely likely. Even more important was the sense on the part of many politically conscious students that participation in left-wing causes would merely show their naïveté, gullibility, and political innocence without furthering any worthy cause. The prevailing climate was such that protest was rarely seen as an act of any meaning or usefulness.

Today, in contrast, student protesters are not only criticized and excoriated by a large segment of the general public, but—more crucial—actively defended, encouraged, lionized, praised, publicized, photographed, interviewed, and studied by a portion of the academic community. Since the primary reference group of most activists is not the general public, but rather that liberal segment of the academic world most sympathetic to protest, academic support has a disproportionate impact on protest-prone students' perception of their own activities. In addition, the active participation of admired faculty members in protests, teach-ins, and peace marches acts as a further incentive to students. Thus, in a minority of American colleges, subcultures have arisen where protest is felt to be both an important existential act—a dignified way of "standing up to be counted"—and an effective way of "bringing the machine to a halt," sometimes by disruptive acts (sit-ins, strikes, etc.), more often by calling public attention to injustice.

An equally important, if less tangible, "cultural" factor is the broad climate of social criticism in American society. One of the enduring themes of American society is the pressure toward "universalism," that is, an increasing extension of principles like equality, equal opportunity, and fair protection of the law to all groups within the society (and in recent years, to all groups in the world). As affluence has increased in American society, impatience at the slow "progress" of nonaffluent minority groups has also increased, not only among students, but among other segments of the population. Even before the advent of the student Civil Rights Movement, support for racial segregation was diminishing. Similarly, the current student concern for the "forgotten fifth" was not so much initiated by student activists as it was taken up by them. In this regard, student activists are both caught up in and in the vanguard of a new wave of extension of universalism in American society. Although the demands of student activists usually go far beyond the national consensus, they nonetheless reflect (at the same time that they have helped advance) one of the continuing trends in American social change.

A contrasting but equally enduring theme in American social criticism is a more fundamental revulsion against the premises of industrial—and now technological—society. Universalistic-liberal criticism blames our society because it has not yet extended its principles, privileges, and benefits to all: the complaint is injustice, and the goal is to complete our unfinished business. But alienated-romantic criticism questions the validity and importance of these same principles, privileges, and benefits—the complaint is materialism, and the goal is spiritual, aesthetic, or expressive fulfillment. The tradition of revulsion against conformist, antiaesthetic, materialistic, ugly, middle-class America runs through American writing from Melville through the "lost generation" to the "beat generation" and has been expressed concretely in the Bohemian subcultures that have flourished in a few large American cities since the turn of the century. But today the power of the romantic-alienated position has increased: one response to prosperity has been a more searching examination of the technological assumptions upon which prosperity has been based. Especially for the children of the upper middle class, affluence is simply taken for granted, and the drive "to get ahead in the world" no longer makes sense for students who start out ahead. The meanings of life must be sought elsewhere, in art, sentience, philosophy, love, service to others, intensified experience, adventure—in short, in the broad aesthetic or expressive realm.

Since neither the universalistic nor the romantic critique of modern society is new, these critiques affect the current student generation not only directly but indirectly, in that they have influenced the way many of today's college students were raised. Thus, a few of today's activists are children of the "radicals of the 1930's," and Flacks comments on the growing number of intellectual, professional upper-middle-class families who have adopted "deviant" views of traditional American life and embodied these views in the practices by which they brought up their children. Thus, some of today's activists are the children of Bohemians, college professors, etc. But in general, the explanation from parental "deviance" does not seem fully convincing. To be sure, the backgrounds of activists are "atypical" in the statistical sense, and thus might be termed empirically "deviant." It may indeed turn out that the parents of activists are distinguished by their emphasis on humanitarianism, intellectualism, and romanticism, and by their lack of stress on moralism. But it is not obvious that such parental values can be termed "deviant" in any but a statistical sense. "Concern with the plight of others," "desire to realize intellectual capacities," and "lack of concern about the importance of strictly controlling personal impulses"—all these values might be thought of as more normative than deviant in upper-middle-class suburban American society in 1967. Even "sensitivity to beauty and art" is becoming increasingly acceptable. Nor can the socioeconomic facts of affluence, freedom from status anxiety, high educational levels, permissiveness with children, training for independence, etc., be considered normatively deviant in middle-class America. Thus, the sense in which activists are the deviant offspring of subculturally deviant parents remains to be clarified.

Another explanation seems equally plausible, at least as applied to some student activists—namely that their activism is closely related to the social and cultural conditions that promote high levels of psychological flexibility, complexity, and integration. Social scientists may be too reluctant to entertain the possibility that some political and social outlooks or activities are symptomatic of psychological "health," while others indicate "disturbance." In fact, many of the personal characteristics of activists—empathy, superior intellectual attainments, capacity for group involvement, strong humanitarian values, emphasis on self-realization, etc.—are consistent with the hypothesis that, as a group, they are unusually "healthy" psychologically. Similarly, the personal antecedents of activists —economic security, committed parents, humanitarian, liberal, and permissive home environments, good education, etc.—are those that would seem to promote unusually high levels of psychological functioning. If this is correct, then former SDS president Tom Hayden's words may be a valid commentary on the cultural setting of activism:

Most of the active student radicals today come from middle- to upper-middle-class professional homes. They were born with status and affluence as facts of life, not goals to be striven for. In their upbringing, their parents stressed the right of children to question and make judgments, producing perhaps the first generation of young people both affluent and independent of mind.

In arguing that activists may be more psychologically "healthy" as a group than nonactivists, I am aware of the many difficulties entailed by this hypothesis. First, complexity, flexibility, integration, high levels of functioning, etc., are by no means easy to define, and the criteria for "positive mental health" remain vague and elusive. Second, there are obviously many individuals with these same "healthy" characteristics who are not activists; and within the group of activists there are many individuals with definite psychopathologies. In any social movement a variety of individuals of highly diverse talents and motivations are bound to be involved, and global descriptions are certain to be oversimplified. Third, the explanation from "psychological health" and the explanation from "parental deviance" are not necessarily opposed. On the contrary, these two arguments become identical if we assume that the preconditions for high levels of psychological functioning are both statistically and normatively deviant in modern American society. This assumption seems quite plausible.

Whatever the most plausible explanation of the sociocultural sources of activism, the importance of prevailing attitudes toward student protest and of the climate of social criticism in America seems clear. In the past five years a conviction has arisen, at least among a minority of American college students, that protest and social action are effective and honorable. Furthermore, changes in American society, especially in middle-class child-rearing practices, mean that American students are increasingly responsive to both the universalistic and romantic critique of our society. Both strands of social criticism have been picked up by student activists in a rhetoric of protest that combines a major theme of impatience at the slow fulfillment of the creedal ideals of American society with a more muted minor theme of aesthetic revulsion at technological society itself. By and large, activists respond most affirmatively to the first theme and alienated students to the second; but even within the student protest movement, these two themes coexist in uneasy tension.

The Protest-Producing Historical Situation

To separate what I have called the "cultural climate" from the "historical situation" is largely arbitrary. But by this latter term I hope to point to the special sensitivity of today's student activists to historical events and trends that do not immediately impinge upon their own lives. In other nations and in the past student protest movements seem to have been more closely related to immediate student frustrations than they are in America today. The "transformationist" (utopian, Marxist, universalistic, or democratic) aspirations of activist youth in rapidly developing nations often seem closely related to their personal frustrations under oppressive regimes or at "feudal" practices in their societies; the "restorationist" (romantic, alienated) youth movements that have appeared in later stages of industrialization seem closely connected to a personal sense of the loss of a feudal, maternal, and "organic" past. Furthermore, both universalistic and romantic youth movements in other nations have traditionally been highly ideological, committed either to concepts of universal democracy and economic justice or to particularistic values of brotherhood, loyalty, feeling, and nation.

Today's activists, in contrast, are rarely concerned with improving their own conditions and are highly motivated by identification with the oppressions of others. The anti-ideological bias of today's student activists has been underlined by virtually every commentator. Furthermore, the historical conditions that have produced protest elsewhere are largely absent in modern America; and the student "movement" in this country differs in important ways from student movements elsewhere. In many respects, then, today's American activists have no historical precedent, and only time will tell to what extent the appearance of organized student dissent in the 1960's is a product of locally American conditions, of the psychosocial effects of a technological affluence that will soon characterize other advanced nations, or of widespread changes in identity and style produced by psychohistorical factors that affect youth of all nations (thermonuclear warfare, increased culture contact, rapid communications, etc.).

But whatever the historical roots of protest, today's student protester seems uniquely sensitive to historical trends and events. In interviewing student activists I have been impressed with how often they mention some world-historical event as the catalyst for their activism—in some cases, witnessing via television of the Little Rock demonstrations over school integration, in another case, watching rioting Zengakuren students in Japan protesting the arrival of President Eisenhower, in other cases, particularly among Negro students, a strong identification with the rising black nationalism of recently independent African nations.

Several factors help explain this sensitivity to world events. For one, modern means of communication make the historical world more psychologically "available" to youth. Students today are exposed to world events and world trends with a speed and intensity that has no historical precedent. Revolutions, trends, fashions, and fads are now world-wide; it takes but two or three years for fashions to spread from Carnaby Street to New York, New Delhi, Tokyo, Warsaw, Lagos, and Lima. In particular, students who have been brought up in a tradition that makes them unusually emphatic, humanitarian, and universalistic in values may react more intensely to exposure via television to student demonstrations in Japan than to social pressures from their fellow seniors in Centerville High. Finally, this broadening of empathy is, I believe, part of a general modern trend toward the *internationalization of identity*. Hastened by modern communications and consolidated by the world-wide threat of nuclear warfare, this trend involves, in vanguard groups in many nations, a loosening of parochial and national allegiances in favor of a more inclusive sense of affinity with one's peers (and non peers) from all nations. In this respect, American student activists are both participants and leaders in the reorganization of psychosocial identity and ideology that is gradually emerging from the unique historical conditions of the twentieth century.

A small but growing number of American students, then, exhibit a peculiar responsiveness to world-historical events—a responsiveness based
partly on their own broad identification with others like them throughout
the world, and partly on the availability of information about world
events via the mass media. The impact of historical events, be they the
world-wide revolution for human dignity and esteem, the rising aspirations of the developing nations, or the war in Vietnam, is greatly magnified upon such students; their primary identification is not their unreflective national identity, but their sense of affinity for Vietnamese peasants,
Negro sharecroppers, demonstrating Zengakuren activists, exploited migrant workers, and the oppressed everywhere. One of the consequences
of security, affluence, and education is a growing sense of personal involvement with those who are insecure, nonaffluent, and uneducated.

The Future of Student Activism

I have argued that no single factor can explain or help us predict the
future of the student protest movement in America: active expressions of
dissent have become more prevalent because of an *interaction* of individual, institutional, cultural, and historical factors. Affluence and education
have changed the environment within which middle-class children are
raised, in turn producing a minority of students with special sensitivity to
the oppressed and the dissenting everywhere. At the same time technological innovations like television have made available to these students
abundant imagery of oppression and dissent in America and in other nations. And each of these factors exerts a potentiating influence on the
others.

Given some understanding of the interaction of these factors, general
questions about the probable future of student activism in America can
now be broken down into four more specific questions: Are we likely to
produce (a) more protest-prone personalities? (b) more institutional settings in which protests are likely? (c) a cultural climate that sanctions and
encourages activism? and (d) a historical situation that facilitates activism? To three of the questions (a, b, and d), I think the answer is a
qualified yes; I would therefore expect that in the future, if the cultural
climate remains the same, student activism and protest would continue to
be visible features on the American social landscape.

Consider first the factors that promote protest-prone personalities. In
the coming generation there will be more and more students who come
from the upper-middle-class, highly educated, politically liberal professional backgrounds from which protesters are selectively recruited. Furthermore, we can expect that a significant and perhaps growing proportion
of these families will have the universalistic, humanitarian, equalitarian,
and individualistic values found in the families of protesters. Finally, the

expressive, permissive, democratic, and autonomy-promoting atmosphere of these families seems to be the emerging trend of middle-class America: older patterns of "entrepreneurial-authoritarian" control are slowly giving way to more "bureaucratic-democratic" techniques of socialization. Such secular changes in the American family would produce a growing proportion of students with protest-prone personalities.

Institutional factors, I have argued, are of primary importance in so far as they bring together a critical mass of suitably protest-predisposed students in an atmosphere where they can interact, create their own subculture, develop leadership, and find issues. The growing size of major American universities, their increasing academic and intellectual selectivity, and the emphasis on "quality" education (honors programs, individual instruction, greater student freedom)—all seem to promote the continuing development of activist subcultures in a minority of American institutions. The increasing use of graduate-student teaching assistants in major universities points to the growing availability of large numbers of potential "leaders" for student protests. Admittedly, a sudden increase in the administrative wisdom in college deans and presidents could reduce the number of available "on-campus" issues; but such a growth in wisdom does not seem imminent.

In sharp contrast a maintenance of the cultural climate required for continuation of activism during the coming years seems far more problematical. Much depends on the future course of the war in Vietnam. Continuing escalation of the war in Southeast Asia will convince many student activists that their efforts are doomed to ineffectuality. For as of mid-1967, antiwar activism has become the primary common cause of student protesters. The increasing militancy and exclusivity of the Negro student Civil Rights Movement, its emphasis on Black Power and on grass-roots community organization work (to be done by Negroes) is rapidly pushing white activists out of civil rights work, thus depriving them of the issue upon which the current mood of student activism was built. This fact, coupled with the downgrading of the war on poverty, the decline of public enthusiasm for civil rights, and the increasing scarcity of public and private financing for work with the underprivileged sectors of American society, has already begun to turn activists away from domestic issues toward an increasingly singleminded focus on the war in Vietnam. Yet at the same time, increasing numbers of activists overtly or covertly despair of the efficacy of student attempts to mobilize public opinion against the war, much less to influence directly American foreign policies. Continuing escalation in Southeast Asia has also begun to create a more repressive atmosphere toward student (and other) protesters of the war, exemplified by the question "Dissent or treason?" Already the movement of activists back to full-time academic work is apparent.

Thus, the war in Vietnam, coupled with the "rejection" of white middle-class students by the vestigial black Civil Rights Movement, is producing a crisis among activists, manifest by a "search for issues" and intense disagreement over strategy and tactics. At the same time the diminution of support for student activism tends to exert a "radicalizing" effect upon those who remain committed activists—partly because frustration itself tends to radicalize the frustrated, and partly because many of the less dedicated and committed activists have dropped away from the movement. At the same time most activists find it difficult to turn from civil rights or peace work toward "organizing the middle class" along lines suggested by alienated-romantic criticisms of technological society. On the whole, activists remain more responsive to universalistic issues like peace and civil rights than to primarily expressive or aesthetic criticisms of American society. Furthermore, the practical and organizational problems of "organizing the middle class" are overwhelming. Were the student movement to be forced to turn away from universalistic issues like civil rights and peace to a romantic critique of the "quality of middle-class life," my argument here implies that its following and efficacy would diminish considerably. Were this to happen, observations based on student activism of a more "universalistic" variety would have to be modified to take account of a more radical and yet more alienated membership. Thus, escalation or even continuation of the war in Vietnam, particularly over a long period, will reduce the likelihood of student activism.

Yet there are other, hopefully more permanent, trends in American culture that argue for a continuation of protests. The further extension of affluence in America will probably mean growing impatience over our society's failure to include the "forgotten fifth" in its prosperity: as the excluded and underprivileged become fewer in number, pressures to include them in American society will grow. Similarly, as more young Americans are brought up in affluent homes and subcultures, many will undoubtedly turn to question the value of monetary, familistic, and careerist goals, looking instead toward expressive, romantic, experiential, humanitarian, and self-actualizing pursuits to give their lives meaning. Thus, in the next decades, barring a major world conflagration, criticisms of American society will probably continue and intensify on two grounds: first, that it has excluded a significant minority from its prosperity, and second, that affluence alone is empty without humanitarian, aesthetic, or expressive fulfillment. Both of these trends would strengthen the climate conducive to continuing activism.

Finally, protest-promoting pressures from the rest of the world will doubtless increase in the coming years. The esteem revolution in developing nations, the rise of aspirations in the impoverished two-thirds of the world, and the spread of universalistic principles to other nations—all of these trends portend a growing international unrest, especially in the developing nations. If young Americans continue to be unusually responsive to the unfulfilled aspirations of those abroad, international trends will touch a minority of them deeply, inspiring them to overseas activities like the Peace Corps, to efforts to "internationalize" American foreign policies, and to an acute sensitivity to the frustrated aspirations of other Americans. Similarly, continuation of current American policies of supporting anti-Communist but often repressive regimes in developing nations (particularly regimes anathema to student activists abroad) will tend to agitate American students as well. Thus, pressures from the probable world situation will support the continuance of student protests in American society.

In the next decades, then, I believe we can foresee the continuation, with short-range ebbs and falls, of activism in American society. Only if activists were to become convinced that protests were ineffectual or social action impossible is this trend likely to be fundamentally reversed. None of this will mean that protesters will become a majority among American students; but we can anticipate a slowly growing minority of the most talented, empathic, and intellectually independent of our students who will take up arms against injustice both here and abroad.

Throughout this discussion I have emphasized the contrast between two types of students, two types of family backgrounds, and two sets of values that inspire dissent from the Great Society. On the one hand, I have discussed students I have termed alienated, whose values are apolitical, romantic, and aesthetic. These students are most responsive to "romantic" themes of social criticism; that is, they reject our society because of its dehumanizing effects, its lack of aesthetic quality, and its failure to provide "spiritual" fulfillment to its members. And they are relatively impervious to appeals to social, economic, or political justice. On the other hand, I have discussed activists who are politically involved, humanitarian, and universalistic in values. These students object to our society not because they oppose its basic principles, but because it fails to implement these principles fully at home and abroad.

In the future the tension between the romantic-alienated and the universalistic-activist styles of dissent will probably increase. I would anticipate a growing polarization between those students and student groups who turn to highly personal and experiential pursuits like drugs, sex, art, and intimacy, and those students who redouble their efforts to change American society. In the past five years activists have been in the ascendant, and the alienated have been little involved in organized political protests. But a variety of possible events could reverse this ascendency. A sense of ineffectuality, especially if coupled with repression of organized dissent, would obviously dishearten many activists. More important, the inability of the student protest movement to define its own long-range objectives, coupled with its intransigent hostility to ideology and efficient organization, means that *ad hoc* protests are too rarely linked to the explicit intellectual, political, and social goals that alone can sustain prolonged efforts to change society. Without some shared sustaining vision of the society and world they are working to promote, and frustrated by the enormous obstacles that beset any social reformer, student activists would be likely to return to the library.

How and whether this tension between alienation and activism is resolved seems to me of the greatest importance. If a growing number of activists, frustrated by political ineffectuality or a mounting war in Southeast Asia, withdraw from active social concern into a narrowly academic quest for professional competence, then a considerable reservoir of the most talented young Americans will have been lost to our society and the world. The field of dissent would be left to the alienated, whose intense quest for *personal* salvation, meaning, creativity, and revelation dulls their perception of the public world and inhibits attempts to better the lot of others. If, in contrast, tomorrow's potential activists can feel that their demonstrations and actions are effective in molding public opinion and, more important, in effecting needed social change, then the possibilities for constructive change in postindustrial American society are virtually without limit.

II. Faces of Dissent

IF the oppositional youth culture is a heterogeneous group—diverse in values, backgrounds, and personality types—then any effort to define a unitary "counterculture," to pinpoint the defining characteristics of all young dissenters, or to identify the new "consciousness" that unifies the youthful opposition is inevitably bound to be an oversimplification. To be sure, we often need such oversimplifications; and works that try to define the central core of the new youth culture often deserve their popularity, for they help us recognize aspirations and values that are indeed shared by many of the dissenting young. Yet the fact that such definitions, whether approving or disapproving, are invariably oversimplifications must never be forgotten.

One good way to counteract the tendency to oversimplify about "the young" is by staying in close contact with them. Over the past fifteen years my primary research has involved intensive work with students of a variety of backgrounds, outlooks, and political persuasions. This research is the ground to which I refer in thinking more generally about the youth culture; it is a useful though not always adequate corrective to my own tendency to oversimplify by treating "the students" as a homogeneous mass.

The essays that follow are the product of a series of intensive studies of small groups of young men and women, most of them students. They are collective biographies of young people who share some common characteristic: one group who was heavily involved in the use of drugs; another group who chose to drop out of an Ivy League college for no obvious financial, psychiatric, or academic reason; another group of deeply committed political radicals, and so on. In each instance the research data comes from prolonged, unstructured, exploratory interviews. This method of doing research is of course open to much criticism, including that of subjective bias, sampling error, lack of "controls," and so on. But in my experience no other method so readily enables me to understand a particular person, since no other method so directly allows that person to tell his own story, to emphasize what is important, to take issue with me, and to explain his own experience. Thus, I find no method (including the allegedly "harder" methods of experimental manipulation or quantitative design) quite so appropriate for understanding in depth the real experience of other people. And finally, no method I know of has been as helpful in disabusing me of so many of my own misconceptions about people.

The portraits that follow are largely portraits of the faces of dissent, of students who, if not unhappy with themselves, are critical of the surrounding society, find the colleges they attend inadequate to their needs, consider the traditional avenues toward experience and self-understanding unrewarding, or have an agonized awareness of the disparity between their personal values and the public practices of the world. Since the need for confidentiality and anonymity prevents the detailed discussion of any one person, most of these essays involve collective biographies, efforts to define the shared psychological and historical themes in the group studied.

Working with students constantly impresses me with the fact that individuals always live and develop in a social, cultural, and historical setting, and cannot be understood apart from that setting. The radicals I studied in the summer of 1967 were what they were not only because of their familial past and their private fantasies, but because of the current status of the movement of which they formed an important part. Drug-using students are in some sense reacting not only to their personal needs, but to the whole social and political history of their generation. Students who drop out of college are making a statement not only about their present discontents, but about their college and its inadequacy to meet their needs. In each case, then, in studying individuals I have tried to understand them in a matrix that includes their social, cultural, and historical world, but that also acknowledges their unique and unrepeatable individuality. All of this is a way of saying that my daily research convinces me of the psychohistorical nature of human experience and encourages me to try to understand people in a context that is at once individual and historical.

The Alienated: Rejection of Conventional Adulthood

This essay, written in 1964, grew out of the study of the psychological origins of alienation I conducted at Harvard in the late 1950's and early 1960's. As that study progressed I began to realize that whatever the psychological similarities between alienated students, their alienation was a reaction not only to their personal pasts but to the society around them. Psychological alienation resulted from an interaction between a complex, sometimes troubled childhood, and an equally complex, even more troubled society. The essay that follows is a summary of the first part of that equation.

Were I writing about these "alienated" students today, I would emphasize two issues that I did not sufficiently appreciate at the time. First, I would stress more than I did the developmental function of alienation, and I would view the permanent choice of an alienated position as an example of development gone awry—as the response of a growing individual to the experienced failure of his search for people, ideals, groups, and institutions that genuinely merit his commitment. Second, I would emphasize more than I did the historical context in which alienation unfolds and expresses itself. For in the years since this research was completed, I have worked with many other students of comparable background and psychological makeup whose behavior and professed ideology differed, for cultural and historical reasons, from those of these students. For example, had psychedelic drugs been widely available during the years this study was conducted, I think these alienated students would have been strongly drawn to them. And, in the late 1960's, students of comparable psychological outlook were often immersed in a "hippie" subculture that adopted, at least on the surface, an ideology of love, openness, and genuine relatedness, instead of an ideology of distrust and cynicism. Indeed, one can view the hippie movement in part as a kind of informal (and often effective) therapy for alienated people, a subculture that expresses the discontents of the alienated while trying to provide new, communal, and loving ways of resolving their deep mistrust and frustration.

Whatever the limitations of this account, I think that the psychological type I defined here is an enduring type, and that its occurrence in highly industrialized societies underlies many social movements now and in the future. The particular manifestations of this kind of psychological alienation will doubtless change in the years ahead. But its underlying roots lie deep in the structure of industrialized society, and until or unless that structure is changed, we will continue to have alienated youth.

THE term "alienation" has become a fashionable catchword for the varied problems and malaises of our age. The term's meanings are extremely diverse: "alienation" has been used to describe such diverse conditions as the separation of spirit from nature, man's loss of relationship to his work, the individual's estrangement from some deep and productive part of himself, his loss of his own sanity, disillusionment with politics and politicians, the violational behavioral norms, and a variety of other conditions. Many writers have attempted to disentangle the meanings of "alienation"; this will not be my topic here. My point is rather that the term "alienation" is today so ill-defined that anyone who sets out to study the psychology of "alienated" individuals must begin by defining carefully what it is he is studying.

Especially since the beginning of the Industrial Revolution, historians and social commentators have noted that intellectuals, artists, writers, and students have often rejected the major value assumptions of bourgeois, industrial, capitalist, or technological society. Indeed, one of the most salient characteristics of "the intellectual" in modern society is his skeptical, critical, or repudiative attitude toward much of his culture. Such men and women are often said to be "alienated"; and it is in this sense of the term that I will use the word in this report. Alienation will mean "an explicit rejection of what are seen as the dominant values of the surrounding society."

Given this definition of alienation, it becomes possible to develop empirical measures (questionnaires, ratings, tests) that will give us some rough index of the degree to which any individual is alienated. And once such measures have been developed, it is then possible to study the distinctive characteristics of those who are highly alienated, contrasting them with those who are less alienated or extremely *non*alienated. For it follows from this definition of alienation that not all men and women are equally alienated from their society; on the contrary, in modern American society explicit and vehement rejection of the surrounding culture is the exception rather than the rule. Thus, we can reasonably ask why some individuals are alienated from their society while others are not. The study to be summarized here is an effort to answer that question for a group of highly talented male American college students.

In essence, the study consisted of three parts. First, empirical measures of alienation were developed and the correlates of alienation were studied systematically in personality tests, in background factors, in fantasy, and in interpersonal behavior. Second, a group of extremely alienated students was identified and chosen for intensive psychological study. And finally, the understanding of individual alienation required a more speculative inquiry into the social and historical factors which cooperate with psychological factors to produce alienation in some, but not all, young Americans. In this essay I will be primarily concerned with the second part of the research, that is, with the psychology of a small group of intensively studied and extremely alienated students.

The Alienation Syndrome

In order to study alienated individuals, we must first have some reliable way of identifying them. Over a period of several years my colleagues and I developed a series of highly intercorrelated questionnaire scales that enabled us to identify extremely alienated students. In the course of this study, we were able to define thirteen related alienated outlooks. If a student held one of these outlooks, he was extremely likely to hold the rest as well; if he disagreed with one, he was likely to disagree with the rest. These attitudes constitute a kind of empirical cluster or "alienation syndrome."

Amplifying the earlier work of Henry Murray and Anthony Davids, we eventually ended with the following thirteen alienation scales: (1) distrust ("Expect the worst of others and you will avoid disappointment"); (2) pessimism ("There is little chance of ever finding real happiness"); (3) resentment ("At times, some people make you feel like killing them"); (4) egocentricity ("You will certainly be left behind if you stop too often or too long to give a helping hand to other people"); (5) anxiety ("Whether he admits it ar not, every modern man is a helpless victim of one of the worst ailments of our time—neurotic anxiety"); (6) interpersonal alienation ("Emotional commitments to others are usually the prelude to disillusion and disappointment"); (7) social alienation ("Trying to cooperate with other people brings mainly strains, rivalry, and inefficiency; consequently I much prefer to work by myself"); (8) cultural alienation ("The idea of trying to adjust to society as it is now constituted fills me with horror"); (9) self-contempt ("Any man who has really known himself has had good cause to be horrified"); (10) vacillation ("I make few commitments without some inner reservation or doubt about the wisdom of undertaking the responsibility or task"); (11) subspection ("First impressions cannot be relied upon; what lies beneath the surface is often utterly different"); (12) outsider ("I feel strongly how different I am from most people, even my close friends"); (13) unstructured universe ("The notion that man and nature are governed by regular laws is an illusion based on our insatiable desire for certainty"). Together these scales constitute the empirical definition of the "alienation syndrome."

These scales enabled us to select a small group of subjects for intensive clinical study. From a large group of volunteers, eighty-three male Harvard College sophomores with satisfactory academic standing were chosen for testing and were given these alienation scales and other questionnaires. On the basis of their scores three groups were selected for intensive clinical study: (1) a highly alienated group; (2) a highly nonalienated group; and (3) a third "comparison" group of students with medium scores on alienation. Including students drawn from this group and earlier groups, eleven alienated undergraduates, ten nonalienated undergraduates, and a comparison group of a dozen students were studied. The modal alienated student was in the most alienated 8 per cent of the college population; the typical nonalienated student was in the least alienated 8 per cent; and the members of the comparison group stood very near the middle.

All of these undergraduates took part in at least one year of the research study, and most of them were studied throughout the last three years of their college careers. During this time they gave approximately two hours a week to the research, for which they were paid. The research ranged over a wide variety of topics. All students wrote a lengthy autobiography and a detailed statement of their basic values and beliefs. All were repeatedly interviewed about matters autobiographical, ideological, vocational, ethical, and experimental. All took the Thematic Apperception Test (T.A.T.), a test of fantasy in which students make up imaginative stories to twenty ambiguous pictures. In addition, all of the research subjects took part in a great variety of other specific psychological experiments. By the end of the three-year period, large amounts of information had been collected about almost every aspect of the individual's life.

The clinical study of alienation focused on the following questions:

1. What is the ideology of alienation as seen in these students? Written statements of basic values, interview material, and added questionnaire material helped answer this question.

2. What common characteristics of behavior and life style do these alienated students possess? Systematic studies of behavior in experimental groups, interview materials, and informal observations of the students in college helped answer this question.

3. What features of past life (infancy, family characteristics, childhood, adolescence) do these alienated students share? Written autobiographies and interviews provided most of the data here.

4. What are the central features of the fantasy life of alienated students? The T.A.T., reports of fantasies and dreams, and imaginative pro-

ductions like poems, short stories, plays, and drawings were the basis for efforts to answer this question.

5. What hypotheses can be advanced that might explain the psychological basis of alienation? Here I sought for interpretations and hypotheses that might enable me to construct a coherent explanation of how alienation develops within the individual.

In an attempt to answer these questions the case records of each student were first studied independently. Then alienated students were systematically contrasted with the nonalienated and with the comparison group. In certain respects, of course, all three groups were similar: for example, all students in all three groups were intelligent and academically oriented, and most were from relatively privileged social backgrounds. But in the account to follow I will emphasize only those characteristics of the alienated students which were not found to the same degree among the nonalienated or the comparison group.

The Ideology of Alienation

Statistical studies had suggested that distrust was a primary variable in the alienation syndrome. Clinical investigations confirmed this finding. For alienated students distrust extends far beyond a low view of human nature; they also believe that intimacy ends in disillusion, that attachment to a group entails the loss of individuality, and that all appearances are untrustworthy. Nor can American culture be trusted: it is mechanical, boring, trashy, cheap, conformist, and dull. Any kind of positive commitment is viewed negatively: life is such that the alienated can never be sure of anything; every choice precludes equally desirable alternatives.

In addition, most alienated students are native existentialists. Few of them, when they began the research study, had read existentialist philosophers; yet they had often spontaneously arrived at a view of the world close to that of the most pessimistic existentialists like Sartre. And when later in their college careers they read such writers, it was usually with a sense of *déjà vu*. From middle adolescence on, alienated students had become increasingly aware of the darkness, isolation, and meaninglessness of life. The human condition as they had come to see it provides the basis for universal anxiety. The universe itself is dead, lacking in structure, inherently unpredictable and random. Individual life, too, is devoid of purpose and preordained form. Consequently, any meaning or truth that an individual finds is inevitably subjective and solipsistic. The "truth" that one man creates is not necessarily that of his fellows; and in writing about their "philosophies of life," the alienated stress that these are merely expressions of subjective and arbitrary belief. Morality, too, is seen as inevitably egocentric, arbitrary, and individualistic. Given the unpredictability of the future, long-range ethical idealism is impossible; the present becomes overwhelmingly important. Alienated students are usually moral "realists," who see immediate feeling, mood, and pleasure as the only possible guidelines for action.

Alienated undergraduates do not react stoically to this view of the world. On the contrary, their response is scorn, bitterness, and anger. Love and hate, they insist, are inseparable. Their own hostilities and resentments are close to awareness, and their scorn is especially intense when they confront those who are not alienated. They do not suffer fools gladly, and they consider most of their fellows fools. Indeed, their anger is so corrosive that it extends even to themselves. True to the logic of their position, they maintain that the consequences of self-knowledge are self-contempt and are quick to admit their own self-revulsion. Similarly, their resentment is expressed in their conviction that all men inevitably use each other for their own purposes, whatever their altruistic rationalizations.

Much of the explicit philosophy of these students is negative. They are, like Nietzsche (one of their favorite writers), philosophers with hammers, whose favorite intellectual sport is exposing the hypocrisy of others. They distrust all positive thinking and therefore find it almost impossible to agree with any questionnaire statement that clearly expresses an affirmative view. But despite the negative cast of their explicit views, the alienated share an implicit positive search in a common direction. Their philosophies emphasize the value of passion and feeling, the search for awareness, the cultivation of responsiveness, the importance of solitude, and the need somehow to express their experience of life. Their main values are therefore "expressive" or aesthetic, in that their main focus is the present, their main source is the self, and their main aim is the development of awareness, responsiveness, expressiveness, and sentience. Rejecting the traditional American values of success, self-control, and achievement, they maintain that passion, feeling, and awareness are the truest forces at man's disposal. For most of them the primary objective in life is to attain and maintain openness to experience, contact with the world, and spontaneity of feeling. Anything that might fetter or restrain their responsiveness and openness is opposed: the goal, as one student puts it, is "circumscribing my life as little as possible." And the same student goes on to say that he will some day be able to "express all or part of what I feel about life."

These alienated outlooks contrast sharply with "traditional" American views about the self, life, others, society, and the universe. Indeed, each alienated view is a rejection of the conventional wisdom of our society. Thus, the unifying theme of the ideology of alienation is the rejection of what are seen as dominant American values, an unwillingness to accept the trusting, optimistic, sociocentric, affiliative, interpersonally oriented, and culturally accepting values which were, in less troubled times, the foundations of the American world view.

Alienation as a Style of Life

When we turn from alienated views of the world to the everyday life of alienated students, we find much less surface distinctiveness. Formal socioeconomic and demographic variables do not distinguish these students from their classmates, nor does a casual search through college records, high school records, or even police records. The alienated do not look different from their classmates, and the overt pattern of their daily activities shows relatively little that is distinctive. But if we examine not what they do but *how* they do it, we soon discover that the alienated have a characteristic life style that reflects and complements their alienation.

One crucial feature of this style of life is intellectual passion. In their approach to intellectual matters, these students are distinguished by their passionate concentration on a few topics of intense personal concern. They pursue their intellectual interests with such singleminded dedication that they almost completely disregard the conventional distinction between "work" and "goofing off" made by most of their classmates. Their capacity for intense intellectual concentration stands them in good stead during the last days before examinations, when they are capable of accomplishing extraordinary amounts of work. Moreover, when they are challenged in their work, and above all when their assignments strike some deep personal chord, they can become totally absorbed in intellectual work. Thus, despite erratic performances before examinations, the over-all averages of these students are about what was predicted for them on arrival in college.

Alienated students, when they become involved in extracurricular activities, are specifically drawn to those that allow them to express their artistic and "aesthetic" interests. But in whatever they do the style of their participation is alienated: it characteristically involves a preference for the role of the observer. Thus, as a group, they avoid positions of responsibility or, when accorded them, repudiate them immediately. One student, elected to an important national position, confounded everyone from his parents to his classmates by dropping out of college on the eve of assuming his new office. Since the alienated see all groups as destructive of individuality, they distrusted even the beatnik group which, during the years they were studied, flourished around the college: they found beatniks conformists and "not serious."

Their favored stance as detached observers led these students into semisystematic wanderings. Whenever they were confronted with a problem or conflict, they were likely to "take off," sometimes for a long walk at night, sometimes for a few years out of college. In all of these wanderings they seem to have been searching not so much for escape, as to immerse themselves in intense experience. Sometimes they found such experience. In their interviews and autobiographies there are occasional mentions of epiphanies, mystical experiences, and revelations of Everything in the garish pennants of a filling station, in the way the light of the setting sun falls through an archway, or in the smell of burning leaves.

Only on rare occasions did the alienated become active participants. In intellectual discussions in small groups, however, they are active, dominant, negative, and hostile, interrupting and correcting their fellows, impressing others with their scorn and contempt. But in stressful two-person situations, when confronted with an experienced and skilled antagonist, they find it difficult to express their anger at the time but later lapse into enduring resentment. Thus, direct expression of hostility to another person is not easy for these students; they find it most comfortable to channel their annoyance into intellectual discussions.

But despite their outward appearance of detachment from others, alienated undergraduates are highly though ambivalently involved with them. They are often simultaneously attracted to and somewhat fearful of an admired person—tempted to emulate him, but afraid that emulation might mean the sacrifice of their inner integrity. Given this ambivalence, it is understandable that these students tend to ruminate, often obsessively, about all close personal relationships. No friendship escapes detailed analysis from every point of view; every relationship becomes a matter of the preservation of identity. This ambivalent examination of relationships is especially pronounced with girls. Almost invariably, alienated students choose girls who are either profoundly dissatisfying to them or else strongly rejected by some crucial portion of their background. Thus, when they do become close to a girl, it is either to one who is described as passive, dependent, and subservient, or to one who is so totally unacceptable to their parents as to precipitate a complete break between the student and his family. In these relationships with girls, as in most of their relationships with other people, they combine an agonizing desire for closeness with a great fear of it.

In interviews as in questionnaires, alienated students are quick to admit their confusions, angers, anxieties, and problems. Given a list of neurotic symptoms, they check them all, describing themselves as confused, depressed, angry, neurotic, hostile, and impulsive. Yet the inference that these students are grossly disturbed can only be made with reservations. For one, they reject the value assumptions upon which most questionnaire measures of "maturity," "ego strength," and "good mental health" are based. Furthermore, they make a great effort to undermine any "defenses" that might protect them from unpleasant feelings. For most of these students, openness to their own problems and failings is a cardinal virtue;

and they make a further point of loudly proclaiming their own inadequacies. Their drive to be totally honest with themselves and others makes them consistently put their worst foot forward.

But even when we make due allowance for the tendency of alienated students to exaggerate their own failings, many of these students are in fact confused, disoriented, and depressed. In interviews, their public face of contempt often gives way to private admissions of unhappiness and apprehension. Secretly, some harbor doubts that this unhappiness may be of their own making, rather than merely a consequence of the human condition. Thus, many alienated students can be aptly described in Erikson's terms as in a state of more or less intense identity diffusion. Their sense of themselves seems precarious and disunified; they often doubt their own continuing capacity to cope; they have little positive sense of relatedness to other people; the boundaries of their own egos are diffuse and porous. Strong in opposition, these students are weak in affirmation; unable to articulate what they stand for, they have little sense of self to stand on. As a group, then, alienated students are not characterized by happiness, optimism, tranquillity, or calm; they are more notable for the intensity of their convictions, the vehemence of their scorn, the passion behind their search for meaning.

Alienation and the Personal Past

A careful examination of what alienated students tell us about their families and their earlier lives shows a remarkable consistency in their views. When discussing their mothers, for example, they frequently emphasize the renunciations and sacrifices their mothers have made. To their sons, these women appear to have been talented, artistic, intense, and intelligent girls who gave up promise and fulfillment for marriage. They also seem to their sons vivid, sensuous, and magnetic; and alienated students often wonder aloud "whether marriage was worth it" to their mothers. Throughout, these students express their special sympathy for and identification with their mothers and their sadness at their mothers' lack of fulfillment.

But the mothers of alienated sons have another set of common characteristics—dominance, possessiveness, excessive involvement with their sons, oversolicitude. The typical alienated student tells of his mother's intrusiveness, of her attempts to limit, supervise, and restrict his independence and initiative. And although few of the alienated admit that their mothers have been successful in controlling *them,* they do on the whole believe that their mothers have succeeded in controlling their fathers. Thus, it was Mother who paid Dad's way through college, it was Mother who made Dad's mind up to marry her, it is Mother who somehow decides how things are done in the family. Seen through her son's eyes, she emerges as a woman who has turned her considerable energies to the domination of her family.

About their fathers, alienated students volunteer less information than do most undergraduates. We already know that fathers are usually seen as dominated by mothers. Fathers are also described as men who, despite public success, are "failures in their own eyes," "apostates," disappointed, frustrated, and disillusioned men. But often, in addition, their college-age sons portray them as having once had youthful dreams which they were unable to fulfill, as idealists whose idealism has been destroyed by life. The precise agent of this destruction varies: sometimes it was Mother; sometimes it was the father's own weakness, particularly his inability to stand up against social pressures. So, despite their frequent scorn for their dominated fathers, alienated students retain much sympathy for the same fathers as they might have been—a covert identification with the fantasy of a youthful idealistic father.

In characterizing their fathers at present, however, the alienated again and again emphasize qualities like detachment, reserve, inability to express affection, loneliness, and withdrawal from the center of the family. Contrasted with the expressive, emotional, controlling, and dynamic mother, the father appears weak, inactive, detached, and uninterested. The greater portion of these students' current sympathies goes to their mothers, whose frustrations are seen as imposed from without, while their fathers are more often directly blamed for their failure to live up to their youthful dreams.

In their earliest memories alienated students make unusually frequent references to "oral" themes, that is, to issues of consuming, being nurtured and cared for, to food aversions, feeding problems, and in one student, to the assumption that his voracious nursing produced breast cancer in his mother. In these memories women are always present; men are striking by their absence. Although these subjects' fathers were usually present during their early childhood, it was the mother or other women who appeared to have mattered. Especially striking are idyllic recollections of happy times alone with Mother on vacations or family expeditions when Father was away from home. All of these memories suggest an unusually intense attachment between mother and son in early life.

In primary and secondary school alienated students, like most undergraduates at Harvard College, were capable intellectually and interested in their schoolwork. But they differ from many of their classmates in that they seem consistently to have preferred imagination, thought, and staying at home to outgoing activities with others; they speak less than most students of group activities and "running with the gang"; they usually describe themselves as quiet, homebound, unrebellious, and obedient children.

But during adolescence alienated students seem to have undergone even greater turmoil than most of their classmates. The symptoms of their turmoil are extremely varied: intense asceticism, tentative delinquency, vociferous rebellion, speeding, drinking, and, in one case, a halfhearted suicide attempt. From other evidence it seems that the arrival of adult sexuality was unusually disturbing to these young men. In discussing their sexual fantasies as college students, they emphasize to an unusual degree their desire for passivity, oblivion, and tranquillity, and often mention difficulties about being initiating and "aggressive" with women. Only a few alienated students have found sexual relationships fully satisfying, and many mention enduring feelings of anxiety, discomfort, or apprehension connected with sex. All of this suggests that one of the major problems in adolescence was especially great anxiety about assuming the traditional male sex role.

There is no mention of overt alienation in the life histories of these students until midadolescence—about the age of sixteen. At this age we hear accounts of growing feelings of cynicism, distance, estrangement, and scorn—initially for school classmates, later for parents and teachers, finally for all of society. In most cases these feelings appeared spontaneously, though sometimes they were precipitated by the views of a friend, a trip abroad, or some other specific event. This growing sense of alienation usually contrasted sharply with continuing academic and social success; and the contrast between inner alienation and outer success led to increasing feelings of estrangement from all those who accepted them merely at face value. Their alienation developed more or less in isolation and more or less spontaneously; it was usually only after they became alienated that these students sought out books and people who would confirm and support them in their alienation. Among the students studied, alienation could not be explained as the result of identification with an alienated parent; on the contrary, it always seemed to involve a sharp repudiation of perceived parental values.

Alienation in Fantasy

The fantasies of alienated students, as seen on the T.A.T., are different from the fantasies of other students both in style and in content. Stylistically, alienated fantasies are rich, vivid, imaginative, antisocial, unconventional, and sometimes bizarre. The typical alienated fantasy involves an inferior or unusually sensitive hero who becomes involved in a difficult relationship with another person. The relationship goes from bad to worse, leading to great resentment and hurt, especially on the hero's side. Efforts to repair the relationship invariably fail, and the hero is profoundly and adversely affected. This plot format contrasts sharply with the typical stories of nonalienated students, whose competent and superior heroes enter into positive and enduring relationships from which all concerned profit and grow.

Within this general plot format the alienated characteristically tells stories reflecting one or both of two major themes. The first of these is the loss of Eden. Alienated fantasies are distinctively concerned with the loss of supplies, with starvation, with forcible estrangement, and with a yearning to return to bliss. Sometimes these fantasies involve isolated heroes who die of starvation; more often they entail a hero who seeks to regain his union with a lost loved one, usually a woman. Alienated fantasies are a catalogue of yearnings for the past: undertakers enamored of their female subjects, ghoulish grave robbers, heroes obsessed with the recovery of the lost gods, grief-stricken husbands who crawl into their wives' graves, detectives searching for missing persons, lovers mourning the dead, husbands who kill themselves on their wives' coffins.

The same theme of reunion with a lost love is reflected in other stories where the hero loses himself in some warm, fluid, or embracing maternal medium. Some heroes are lured to their deaths by warm and friendly voices speaking from the sea or calling from the air. Other fantasies involve heroes who dive to the bottom of the ocean, never to return. Developmentally, these often archaic and weird stories seem to refer to an unconscious obsession with the lost early relationship with the mother. The fantasy of fusion with the lost maternal presence—a fantasy which exists somewhere in the hearts of all men—constitutes an obsessional theme for these college students.

A second important motif in alienated fantasy is the theme of a Pyrrhic Oedipal victory. Most college students, when given the Thematic Apperception Test, are at some pains to avoid stories which involve competitive rivalrous triangles: rivalry between men is usually minimized, and struggles between two men for the love of a woman are especially rare. The alienated, in contrast, take rivalrous triangles for granted, often importing them into stories where the picture in no way suggests this theme. Even more striking is the peculiar form and outcome of such fantasies. Again and again, it is the younger man who defeats the older man, but only to be overcome himself by some extraneous force. Attacks on fathers and father figures are almost inevitably successful: the father dies, the Minister of Interior Affairs is assassinated, the boss who has propositioned the hero's wife is killed. Or, in the many stories of political revolution told by these apolitical students, the established regime is seen as weak, corrupt, and easily overthrown. Traditional male authority topples at the first push.

Yet these stories of rebellion, rivalry, and revolution are, paradoxically, cautionary tales. The revolution succeeds, but it is followed by a disaster: the revolutionary murderer is assassinated by his own men; the revolutionary regime turns into a despotism worse than that which it overthrew; the avenged cuckold is killed in an automobile accident. These fantasies suggest that although traditional male authority is weak, its destruction leads to a new and worse tyranny.

These fantasies are consistent with the hypotheses that the rebellious son believes that he indeed succeeded in deposing his father, but that this deposition was followed by a new maternal tyranny. The victor was neither father nor son, but mother, who now dominates them both. Supporting this hypothesis is the fact that most alienated fantasies portray adult women as active, controlling, and possessive. In particular they restrain men's sexuality, aggressiveness, and nonconformity: they try to keep their sons from going out with girls; they keep men from fighting; they try to make their husbands settle down and conform—and almost invariably they succeed.

The dominant theme of relations between the sexes, then, is not love and intimacy but the control of men by women. When intimacy begins to seem possible, the story usually ends disastrously. Furthermore, women are not only seen as controlling and possessive but, on occasion, as murderous and destructive: as lizard goddesses who eat their victims, apparently lovable ladies who murder their husbands, as emasculating and destructive figures. Fathers and older men, in contrast, are almost always portrayed as weak, corruptible, absent, or damaged. Men are controlled by women, and even men who initially appear strong eventually turn out to be fraudulent and weak.

Hypotheses about the Psychological Sources of Alienation

The themes of ideology, life style, past history, and fantasy summarized here are of course open to many different interpretations. In some respects the psychological origins of alienation are different for each alienated individual, and no composite account can hope to do justice to the uniqueness of each person. Nonetheless, the existence of many shared strands of belief, present feeling, past experience, and imagination suggests that in so far as we can take these students' accounts as an adequate basis for an explanation, general hypotheses about the psychological origins of alienation are possible.

One of the most striking findings of this study is the great similarity in the families of alienated students. Both parents seem to have been frustrated and dissatisfied. The mother's talents and emotionality found little expression within her marriage; the father's idealism and youthful dreams were crushed by the realities of his adult life. The mothers of alienated students seem to have turned their drive and perhaps their own frustrated needs for love onto their sons. Often, these mothers explicitly deprecated or disparaged their husbands. And confronted with this deprecation, the fathers of alienated students seem to have withdrawn from the family, becoming detached, embittered, and distant. Forced to choose between their families and their work, they almost to a man turned their energies outside of the family, leaving mother and son locked in a special alliance of mutual understanding and maternal control.

This basic family constellation is reflected and elaborated in fantasy. Unconsciously, alienated students seem to believe that they defeated their fathers, who are therefore seen as weak and inadequate models of male adulthood. Probably like most small boys, they attempted a "revolution" within the family in order to overthrow the tyrannical father and gain the exclusive love of the mother. But unlike most, these boys believe that their revolution succeeded in destroying male authority. Yet paradoxically, their apparent victory did not win them maternal love but maternal control, possessiveness, and oversolicitude. Furthermore, by displacing their fathers, they lost the right of every boy to a father he can admire. The son thus gained something very different from what he had wanted. At least in fantasy he found himself saddled with the possessive and intrusive mother, and he lost the youthful, idealistic father he could respect.

If these hypotheses are correct, they may help us explain some of the other characteristics of these alienated students. For such a childhood experience would clearly leave a boy or even a college student with the unconscious assumption that apparently admirable men were really weak and impotent; and that apparently nurturing and loving women were really controlling, possessive, and even emasculating. Conventional adulthood as epitomized by the father—that is, the dominant value assumptions about adulthood in American society—would also seem unattractive and have to be rejected. Adult closeness with women would be frightening, as it would evoke fears of being dominated, controlled, and emasculated. Similarly, competition and rivalry would be avoided in everyday behavior, not out of the fear of failure, but from a fear of another Phyrric victory. Furthermore, the inability of our subjects' mothers to love them as sons, coupled with the apparently sudden change in the sons' image of the mother from that of a nurturer to an emasculator might help explain the persistence into early adulthood of recurrent fantasies about fusion with the maternal presence, the dominance of the theme of loss of Eden.

The pyschological factors that predisposed these students toward alienation are thus complex and interrelated. The sense and the stance of alienation are partially reflections of the unconscious conviction of these subjects that they are outcasts from a lost Eden, alienated forever from their mothers' early love. Then, too, the repudiation of conventional adulthood, of the dominant values of American society, is closely related to their unconscious determination not to let what happened to their fathers happen to them, and to covert identification with the fantasy of a youthful, idealistic father before he was "broken" by life. Similarly, the centrality of distrust in the emotional lives and ideologies of alienated students is probably in part a reflection of an early family situation in which neither parent turned out to be what he or she had seemed to be. In a variety of ways, then, these students were prepared by their past experience and by the fantasies through which they interpreted this experience to be alienated from American culture.

Nonpsychological Factors in Alienation

An account of the psychological factors that predispose certain individuals to be alienated is by no means a complete or adequate account. For one, such an account will have, to many readers, an implicitly "reductive" quality: it may seem to suggest that alienation is "nothing but" a reflection of a particular kind of family constellation and childhood experience. It is far from my intention to "reduce" alienation to childhood history here; on the contrary, while the links between early experience and later alienation are clear, these links in no way entail that alienation is "nothing but" a reflection of unfortunate childhood. On the contrary, the childhood events and fantasies I have discussed here could be viewed as the fortunate and enabling factors that permitted these students to be aware of the very real deficiencies in their society to which their less alienated fellows remain obdurately blind.

Furthermore, this psychological account is, even in its own terms, far from complete. It is probable that the family factors I have outlined will dispose a young man to *some* kind of hesitancy about or repudiation of conventional adulthood. But these family factors alone do not suffice to explain why this hesitancy took the particular form of cultural alienation. For further explanations we would need to consider the early propensity of these students to solve problems with their imaginations rather than with their fists, their generally privileged social backgrounds, their very high talent, intelligence, and imaginativeness, and their very great sensitivity to the evils in themselves and in the world around them. We would have to consider the impact of talented and often artistic mothers on their eldest or only sons, and we would have to prepare a more adequate catalogue not only of the major psychological themes of alienation, but of the specific strengths and weaknesses of alienated students.

Another dimension omitted from this psychological account of alienation is even more important—it is the social and historical context and traditions within which these students live. Alienation of the sort here described is by no means an exclusively contemporary phenomenon; especially during the past two centuries in the Western world, many of the most creative men and women have been highly alienated from their own cultures. Furthermore, the precise forms, manifestations, and content of alienation are always given by the surrounding society; for example, during the years these students were studied, the late 1950's and early 1960's, there were few available student movements of social change and reform into which alienation might have been channeled. At least a few of these alienated students, had they been in college six years later, might have found a channel for the constructive expression of their alienation in the Civil Rights Movement or the peace movement.

Finally, this account of alienation is incomplete in the most fundamental way of all. Although alienated students are especially sensitized and predisposed toward alienation by their pasts, their alienation itself is a reaction *to* and *against* the society in which they live. In other words, alienation is a transaction between an individual and his society, and we can understand it adequately by examining not only the individual and his psychology, but the characteristics of the wider society as they impinge upon students like him. To attempt to characterize the major trends and pressures of American society is far beyond my topic here. But it should be said that the pressures and demands of modern American society seem to me profoundly alienating in many respects. Thus, we could with full justice ask of the *non*alienated why their individual psychology so blinds them to these "alienating" aspects of our society which the alienated perceive so sharply.

Alienation, then, as studied in this small group of talented college students, is the product of a complex interaction of psychological, sociological, cultural, and historical factors within the experience of each individual. It is not enough to attribute alienation solely to the characteristics of modern technological society—such an explanation makes it impossible for us to account for the majority of Americans who are not alienated. But it would be equally misleading to see alienation purely as an expression of individual psychology. Like most outlooks, alienation is the product of the inner world and the outer world as they come together in the developing individual's experience.

Dropouts: Development
through Discontinuity

*This study of a group of college dropouts was the direct outgrowth of the
previous study of alienated students. For among the alienated, I had noted
that a disproportionate number dropped out of college before graduating.
And dropping out seemed, almost by definition, a form of alienation.*

*Partly for this reason, I joined in a study of dropouts with two
psychiatric colleagues at Yale: Drs. Stephen J. Hirsch and Robert A.
Nemiroff. Virtually all of my initial hypotheses about college dropouts
turned out to be wrong. For example, I expected to find among dropouts
a high degree of rejection of American society, along with a pattern of
maternal overinvolvement and paternal absence similar to that observed
in alienated students. As this clinical study shows, actual work with
dropouts demonstrated the inaccuracy of these hypotheses. We found no
general pattern of psychological alienation, but rather a developmental
search for self-definition, which the student felt he could not achieve
within a college setting. And dropouts, unlike alienated students, usually
began and ended their research interviews with us by talking about their
fathers and about what we came to see as their "spoiled identification"
with them. One danger of clinical research is that the researcher will
simply confirm, through selective perception, what he expects to find. My
experience in this study suggests that the opposite may also happen: if one
remains open to the people one studies, they may profoundly disconfirm
the expectations with which one approaches them.*

*In this study, written with Dr. Hirsch in 1966, the focus is once again
not only upon the individual, but upon his relationship to social institutions
—in this case, to the liberal arts college he attended. The article was
written for a psychiatric journal and uses the language of psychodynamics
and at times, of psychopathology. But we argue that it is a serious mistake
to view dropping out simply as a neurotic form of conflict resolution. For
many of the students we studied, dropping out was an exercise in personal
courage and a major step toward accepting, often for the first time,
responsibility for the conduct of their own lives. Finally, dropping out*

*seemed to us to have as much to do with the college as with the student—
it reflected not only the student's inability to find what he wanted in
college, but the college's inability to respond to the students'
developmental needs.*

OF all freshmen who enter four-year colleges in America, considerably
less than half graduate from the same colleges four years later. If the
term "dropout" is defined as any student who interrupts or discontinues his
education, there are far more dropouts than nondropouts, although the
reverse is usually cited as the "typical" condition. Even at colleges with
highly selective admissions policies, approximately 20 per cent of all entering freshmen do not graduate with their class. The issue of educational
discontinuity has obvious importance for understanding American students and American higher education. The present study is an effort to
develop hypotheses about psychosocial issues involved in the decision to
withdraw from college.

An extensive but unfocused literature has attempted to define factors
associated with withdrawal from college. But most studies are limited by
focusing on a small number of easily defined demographic variables, by
failing to distinguish between different kinds of dropouts, by calling dropouts "academic casualties" or "mortalities," by neglecting the role of institutional factors in dropping out, or by failing to consider dropping out in
the light of the student's over-all development.

Recently, a number of studies have begun to ask more sophisticated
questions about dropouts. Trent and Medsker, in a four-year study of
more than 10,000 high school graduates, showed that persistence in college is related to a variety of factors, including intellectual ability, personal motivation, family background, and academic (nonvocational) orientation. They conclude that "the indications are strong that the academic
orientation necessary for successful completion of college is extensively
derived from very early family environment and beginning school experiences." Pervin, Reik, and Dalrymple provide an overview on the issue of
withdrawal from college and also point to the role of psychological factors
in withdrawal from college. Suczek and Alfert differentiated between
students who dropped out of two California colleges for academic and nonacademic reasons and found that students who left college in good academic standing were more intellectual, innovative, autonomous, and tolerant of ambiguity than those who persisted for four years in college. In
general, then, there is some consensus that "psychological" factors play an
important role, along with social and demographic factors, in leading
some students to withdraw from college.

There is less consensus, however, on precisely what these factors are.
Studies of psychological factors in withdrawal from college have concen-

trated on single institutions and are therefore difficult to generalize to other colleges. Most thoroughly studied have been dropouts from "elite" (highly selective and academically challenging) institutions. Nicholi, in a study of Harvard College dropouts, emphasizes that dropouts have consulted the university psychiatric service more often than have nondropouts. Wertenbaker, in an anecdotal account, stresses issues of identity diffusion in Harvard dropouts. Pervin, in a recent clinical paper, has emphasized problems of "counteridentification" in dropouts seen in psychotherapy at Princeton. Levenson and his associates, in a series of papers, have emphasized among other things the "unauthenticity" of the parents of dropouts seen in individual and group therapy. Many dropouts, they find, appear to be re-enacting a parental pattern of dropping out, in response to covert parental instigation. Wright, in two comprehensive studies of Harvard College dropouts, finds that a major determinant of withdrawal from Harvard is lack of integration with the college community coupled with high subjective stress.

Still another approach to the study of college dropouts is the "transactional" orientation advocated by Pervin. This approach sees the probability of dropping out as a function of the lack of congruence or "fit" between the student and his college. Stern, for example, found that authoritarian students tended to withdraw from the University of Chicago, a nonauthoritarian institution. And Pervin and Rubin report that the discrepancy between self-image and image of the college predicts intention to drop out. This approach to the study of dropouts focuses not on the personality characteristics of the students *in vacuo*, but on these characteristics as related to the characteristics of the college environment. It thus helps explain why findings on the psychological characteristics of students who withdraw from college have differed so much from one college to another.

In seeking to develop further hypotheses in this area of investigation, we used a study sample consisting of a group of academically talented, psychologically intact, male college undergraduates who withdrew from college for "personal" reasons. Taking the point of view of the clinician rather than the demographer, we will emphasize: first, the characteristic feelings, attitudes, and fantasies of students in our study sample considering withdrawal from college; second, the most salient psychosocial issues observed in dropouts; and finally, our general hypotheses concerning the "transaction" between the timing of individual psychological development and the timetable of college life.

Subjects and Methods

Forty Yale College undergraduates were studied as they decided whether or not to withdraw from college. Of these, 31 actually did drop out, almost all for "personal" reasons. We interviewed 25 of the 40 students personally. Of these, approximately 15 were seen for from three to twenty interviews, while 10 were interviewed only once or twice. Case reports and records of the remaining students in the sample were made available by colleagues in the university health service.

Subjects were recruited by asking all residential college deans to refer to us students who consulted them about withdrawal from college for nonacademic reasons. Since our study was conducted during 1965–1966, when growing Selective Service pressures led to an unusually low voluntary dropout rate, only 11 students were directly referred to us.* The remaining 29 students in our sample were self-referred. Of these, two-thirds came to the university psychiatric service for consultation about their decision to withdraw from college, while the remainder was seeking psychotherapy, in the course of which dropping out of college became the central issue.

We also interviewed a small number of students with acute psychiatric disturbances who were given medical leaves of absence because of incapacitating symptoms. Since dropping out was not "voluntary" for these students, we have not included them in this discussion.

Within the study sample, then, students came to us for three reasons: (1) one group of students agreed to be interviewed primarily to assist our research study; (2) another group of students sought to clarify their own decision whether to withdraw from college; (3) another group of students sought psychotherapy for personal problems focused on dropping out. The lines between these groups were shifting and blurred, and since we noted no important differences in other areas among these three groups, they are treated as one group in the following discussion.

None of the students in our sample who withdrew from college was required to do so for academic, disciplinary, or medical reasons. Administratively, their withdrawals were classified as "withdrew for personal reasons." All left college in good academic standing, and none had compelling financial reasons for dropping out. Almost all of these students viewed dropping out as a *temporary* interruption of their college careers. Furthermore, these students, like their classmates at Yale as a group, had the social, attitudinal, and demographic characteristics that have been shown in other studies to be associated with persistence in college—for example,

* During the four years preceding 1965–1966, an average of between 200 and 250 students withdrew from Yale College each year, while approximately 150 returned. Thus, the cumulative dropout rate (which does not consider the returnees) over a four-year period was approximately 20–25 per cent of each class of 1,000 men. Of those who leave college, a majority do so during the summer, not during the college term itself. And approximately 65 per cent of those dropping out do so for nonmedical, nonacademic reasons. During the year of our study the proportions of students returning and leaving were reversed, with 150 leaving and 250 returning, as a result of Selective Service pressures.

extremely high aptitudes, parental support for continuing higher education, high socioeconomic status, a nonvocational orientation to college,
early decision to attend college. We did not find in the group studied an
unusual incidence of drug use, sociopolitical activism, or disturbances in
sexual functioning or orientation, or any specific character structure. The
study sample, then, is an elite male group whose withdrawal from college
cannot readily be explained on social, economic, financial, or medical
grounds.

Several informal comparison groups were also available to us. One of
the authors (KK) had previously interviewed ten returnees (voluntary
nonacademic dropouts) about their reasons for leaving college and their
experiences while away; twelve students in an experimental program involving a year of work in a developing nation between sophomore and
junior years were being studied concurrently; and the regular nondropout
patient load of one of the authors (SH) made possible comparisons between dropouts and psychiatric patients who were continuing as undergraduates.

Our interviews were unstructured and nondirective, aimed primarily at
assisting each student to explore and clarify the factors that had made him
question continuation at college. In addition, we sought to explore the
individual's perception of the college environment, and his fantasies and
plans about dropping out and the years to come. We did not attempt to
influence the individual's decision but tried to help him understand better
the factors that lay behind it.

The Dropout Crisis

The decision to leave college was in none of our subjects conflict-free,
lighthearted, or hedonistic. On the contrary, deciding whether to leave
college was, for all of the students we interviewed, a *crisis* in every sense
of the word—a moment of intensified anxiety and stress, a turning point,
and the culmination of a long process of reflection and growing dissatisfaction. Although our subjects reported a great variety of conscious reasons for leaving college, we came to recognize a characteristic set of feelings in the students we interviewed.

Withdrawal from academic work—work paralysis.   For most of our
subjects, dropping out was the culmination of a longer, more gradual
process of withdrawal from academic work. Some students reported growing problems of concentration, while others, who had kept abreast of their
assignments, reported little interest, enthusiasm, or zest in their work. Still
others found it increasingly difficult to attend classes, do assigned reading,
or complete required papers. Pre-dropouts commonly reported feeling

that they were "just going through the motions" or "wasting my own time and my parents' money." Renewed efforts to apply themselves academically by the use of "will power" generally proved futile and led instead to growing feelings of despair. Although none of the students we interviewed failed out, confronting the decision of whether to withdraw from college was usually the cognitive reflection of a *prior* loss of interest in academic work.

Collapse of time perspective. Concern over time, particularly a marked collapse of future orientation, was prominent among all our subjects. On the one hand, they reported not having enough time to study, enjoy themselves, or read, but on the other hand, they often felt that they were wasting time. To some, it seemed as if they were living in a gray and featureless present, and that their college lives lacked connection both to their future goals and to their past endeavors. For many, previously cherished plans had now lost much of their relevance—in particular, our subjects reported having abandoned earlier vocational commitments.

Sense of urgency. The feeling of stagnating in an empty present often led to a great sense of urgency, occasionally bordering on panic, about leaving college. For a few students, to remain in college one day longer or to reflect upon their motives for leaving or their plans on withdrawal seemed extremely difficult. Many potential dropouts felt that they had "no time" to reflect, but must act immediately and even impulsively in order to break out of an increasingly impossible situation.

Feelings of meaninglessness. Some of the urgency felt by dropouts was related to feelings of hollowness, emptiness, and meaninglessness of the present. In a few instances these feelings involved mild states of depersonalization and estrangement from others. More often, students reported a loss of interest in their immediate surroundings and an incapacity to relate themselves to their activities, both academic and nonacademic. Relationships with friends and roommates, girl friends, and extracurricular activities had also lost their savor; life seemed profitless, stale, and tasteless. For most, the entire college environment became tainted with "nonreality": our subjects habitually contrasted their current lives with "really" living in the "real" world. "Really living" usually involved the fantasy of some manual, practical, nonintellectual activity requiring simple motor skills and leading to a useful and visible finished product, often in a faraway place.

Self-reproach—altered self-conception. Feelings of inadequacy and changed self-conception were frequent among potential dropouts. In only a few students did these feelings reach severe despondency and depression; but in almost all others we observed milder feelings of self-blame and worthlessness and a heightened sense of inadequacy. Although some students were critical of the college, in none did criticism of the college outweigh self-criticism. In particular, growing loss of interest in academic work, frequently accompanied by inability to concentrate, had led many potential dropouts to question their academic and intellectual competence and, in some cases, their basic worth as human beings. Thus, the students often thought that their consideration of the possibility of dropping out of college was a symptom of intellectual and/or psychological inadequacy, and a few students wondered aloud whether dropping out was a sign of clinical mental illness. Although many articulate critics of Yale College exist among Yale undergraduates, they were not overrepresented in our dropout sample.

Evocation of earlier problems. Students considering dropping out discussed their pasts, and particularly their relationships with their parents, with an immediacy, a concreteness, and an abundance of feeling that are uncommon even among students consulting a college psychiatric service. Partly, no doubt, this can be explained by the intense contact with parents (telephone calls, consultations, parental visits) that often ensued when the student announced that he was considering leaving college. But in addition, the reactivation of the past seemed part of a more general intensification of conscious concern about ambivalent and in some cases mutually incompatible feelings about others, and especially parents. Problems, conflicts, and troubled relationships which had been covered over and "forgotten" before the dropout crisis were reactivated during this period and brought into consciousness. Our subjects experienced former crises and present conflicts with an intensity that surprised and sometimes frightened them.

Eagerness to talk—need for contact. Regardless of their reasons for seeing us and despite their urgent need to act, potential dropouts were as a group very willing to explore their motives and eager to maintain contact with us as researcher-therapists. Part of this eagerness for contact reflects the fact that dropping out was experienced by all students as a major conscious crisis in their lives, which evoked painful personal feelings regarding unresolved conflicts. Thus, many students sought support, clarification, and reassurance in their interviews—support for a prior decision to drop out, clarification of the motives that had brought them to this decision, reassurance about their own psychological intactness. But, in addition, the eagerness with which students who had "definitely" decided to drop out sought appointments with us, like the faithfulness with which they kept these appointments, seemed to express one side of their ambivalence about dropping out. Not only did we offer an opportunity for students to clarify their feelings, motivations, and plans, but our interviews also allowed many students to express indirectly their desire for continuing contact with the institution they were planning to leave. It was not unusual for students who had their suitcases packed to delay their departure for days and even weeks in order to participate in our study.

Search for a new self. We have so far emphasized our subjects' desire to withdraw from a situation that was becoming increasingly meaningless or unpleasant to them. For most potential dropouts, however, leaving college was not merely an "escape" but an attempt at solution. To be sure, the sense of urgency felt by many dropouts often prevented their formulating coherent and specific plans for their extra-academic experience. But in the course of our interviews, it became clear that many students who are anticipating leaving college have similar fantasies about their goals. The prototypical fantasy involved the hope that after a period of rest and recoupment of strength, the dropout would obtain a job, would travel and so forth, and eventually would return to college to complete his formal education.

Some students emphasized a wish to regain lost self-confidence and to try to understand what had "gone wrong"—in short, a desire to reconstitute a self that had become undermined during the dropout crisis. Others spoke of more affirmative developmental goals—becoming more independent, learning to live on their own, becoming less affected by public opinion and social pressures, articulating more positive commitments, and gaining self-understanding, perspective, and maturity. The precise goals of the student naturally varied with his formulation of his major difficulties; but to a greater or lesser extent for all our subjects, dropping out was viewed not only as an escape, but as a step *toward* the formulation of a more competent, integrated, directed, and adequate self. As one student put it, dropping out for him represented the possible fulfillment of a desire for a more "vibrant, exciting, and alive experience" than he had found in college.

In so far as our sample was representative, then, we concluded that the undergraduate myth of the carefree, happy, hedonistic, and unconcerned dropout is largely fictitious. For our subjects, at least, conscious thoughts of dropping out came at the end of a painful period of growing aimlessness, sense of disconnection, and intensification of personal conflicts. To most students dropping out seemed a possible way to resolve this personal crisis, rather than its prima facie cause.

In general, the feelings we observed in dropouts have much in common with Erikson's descriptions of the phenomenology of intense identity diffusion. Thus, work paralysis, diffusion of time perspective, a search for a "rock bottom," and role diffusion are characteristic of both syndromes. We do not believe that "identity diffusion" alone is specific enough to explain college dropouts, but it is noteworthy that these students manifest many of the characteristics of this condition.

In more conventional psychiatric diagnostic terms, the feelings of potential dropouts are similar to the symptoms of an agitated depression. Feelings of meaninglessness, hollowness, unconnectedness to previously enjoyed activities and relationships, barrenness of the present, and loss of future goals and values were frequent. Sleep, appetite, and concentration problems were also common. The response to these feelings was agitation, a sense of urgency, a need to act, a feeling that the present situation was completely unendurable, and the search for an alternative. The depression found in our subjects may be partly explained by the impending loss of their relationship with the college. But in most students depression had preceded and to a certain extent determined the decision to withdraw from college, so that the impending loss of a connection with the college does not adequately explain their depression.

The feelings of dropouts are of course not specific to students who withdraw from college: similar feelings can be observed in many undergraduates who do not drop out. To begin to understand why some students withdraw from college while others with similar feelings remain, it is necessary to examine some of the more specific themes of family relationship, adaptive style, and perception of the college found in our subjects.

Psychosocial Issues among Dropouts

Before undertaking our study, we had hoped that it would prove possible to define a single set of psychological and sociological factors that would sharply distinguish dropouts from nondropouts. We were encouraged in this hope by the work of other researchers who have related dropping out to such factors as parental inauthenticity, identity crises, problems of identification and counteridentification, and reenactment of parental "dropouts."

Our interviews, however, soon led us to conclude that no single factor or set of factors could enable us to "explain" dropping out in all of our subjects. The students in our sample were extremely diverse, and we were unable to define clean psychological or sociological "types." Issues that appeared central in understanding one student's decision were peripheral in other students. Thus, while we found other studies helpful in explaining the motives of *some* of our subjects, none of these studies provided a framework adequate for explaining *all* of our sample. As our study progressed, we came to doubt that it is possible to provide a single explanation for dropping out.

We were, however, impressed by the frequency and urgency with which three issues were discussed in our interviews. A preliminary formulation of these issues midway through our study found confirmation from subjects interviewed subsequently. The importance and salience of each issue varied from student to student; furthermore, each of these issues is often raised by students who are *not* considering dropping out. But the themes we describe below were raised with particular insistence by dropouts, and after comparing our research group to "normal" and patient populations, we have hypothesized that the three issues below are more salient in the dropout group than in otherwise similar college populations.

Family relationships: problems of identifying with the father. The issue most frequently discussed by potential dropouts was their ambivalent relationship with their fathers.* Our subjects characteristically made conflicting and contradictory statements about their fathers, damning with faint praise, alternating between praise and criticism, or recounting a history of growing disillusionment, disenchantment, and disappointment with a father toward whom they had once felt very close. Most commonly, dropouts were struggling to come to terms with a father whom they had recently learned to view as inadequate, weak, or for some other reason impossible to accept as a model.

For some potential dropouts problems of relationship with the father had been intensified by some recent specific event. Several students, for example, reported that their fathers had contracted incurable or terminal illnesses within the past year. Other students had become conscious, during the preceding months, of a crisis in their father's life, often involving depression and dissatisfaction with his life work. In such cases the son's previous image of his father as adequate, healthy, and competent and as an exemplar for the son had been challenged and perhaps undermined by critical events in the father's own life. These students, further, acted as if they had lost not only their unqualifiedly positive conscious image of their fathers, but an important part of themselves as well.

In another group of subjects illustrating this same theme, we found no specific event in the father's life that had precipitated the son's crisis.

---

* Our emphasis on problems of identification with the father is a reflection of the material as it was presented to us in relatively unstructured interviewing. The relative absence of discussion of the mother in these interviews obviously does not indicate that she played an unimportant role in the son's development or in his decision to drop out. It does, however, point to the prominence in the conscious and preconscious thinking of future dropouts of their relationships with their fathers. More intensive interviewing would have undoubtedly revealed a more complex picture of family dynamics.

Rather, the son had gradually become aware of inadequacies or deficiencies in his father to which he had previously been blind. This revised perception of the father was often precipitated by new developmental demands upon the son and seemed to involve increased awareness of previously repressed, disassociated, or denied feelings that had existed long before the son's disillusionment became conscious. The need to choose a field of college concentration or a career, for example, sometimes served to make the son realize that he did not wish to emulate his father's life. In other cases the father's insistence that the son prepare himself to enter the father's profession had forced the son to confront his ambivalent image of his father.

In some of our subjects the father-son relationship seemed characterized by a particular "stickiness." A number of these fathers had shown for years a special intrusiveness into their sons' lives—for example, by seeking confidences or sharing intimate feelings in a way that is generally considered inappropriate for parents of college-age sons. Other fathers in this group seemed unusually oversolicitous and apprehensive about their sons' welfare, sometimes to a degree that suggested anxious or hostile dependency on the son rather than genuine paternal concern. Several of these fathers had direct contact with us in the course of our study. They sometimes wrote us long, introspective letters about themselves, their sons, and the father-son relationship; they requested interviews with members of our research group; they voiced the fear that their sons were becoming all too like themselves. In such fathers it was clear that the father's own ambivalence about himself extended to his image of the son and had affected the son's image both of his father and of himself. The following example illustrates some of these elements.

One freshman, whose father is a college history teacher, began to question his own choice of history as a field of early concentration. This field was not as attractive to him as he had thought it would be: "I feel that my interest in history was inspired by my father, not me." He added that before coming to college, he had been dealing with "big ideas," and that having to get down to the actual business of "routine scholarly research" had made him fear he was not really motivated for history. He considered dropping out "to see whether I can reorient myself better by getting out of the educational world and focusing on day-to-day life, and trying to fill in some of the void in my own life."

Further consultation revealed that this student's repudiation of history represented not a simple rebellion against his father, but rather a preconscious awareness of his father's inadequacy as a model. The father himself requested an interview with us, in which he discussed his disappointment and disillusionment after having assumed what had promised to be a challenging new position in the past year. This disillusionment had represented a massive blow to the father's self-esteem, and he expressed a desire to enter psychotherapy. Although the father had never discussed his unhappiness or his need for therapy with his son, we inferred that the son's unexpressed awareness of his father's growing dissatisfaction with his life work had helped to undermine the son's perception of the father as an adequate, competent model, and to create the "void in my own life."

In the course of his interviews with us, the son began to become more conscious of his previously unexpressed reservations about his father's life. As he expressed these reservations, he seemed to be mourning the loss of an important component of his own developing identity, namely, those commitments which had been based upon identification with a strong and admirable father. As he put it, "I guess, before I can distinguish myself *at* Yale, I'll have to try to distinguish myself *from* Yale, and from those things at Yale that are allied with my father and his interests. I've got to find my *own* real interests." He dropped out.

In still another group of our subjects the problem of relationship with the father was primarily complicated by parental strife, discord, divorce, or separation. These parents had told their sons of their discontent with their marriage, and implicitly (or sometimes explicitly) each parent had warned the potential dropout not to emulate the spouse, threatening rejection and withdrawal of love should the son "take after" him or her. Often, too, each parent had used the son as the primary means of communicating with the other, and the parental struggle had been translated into an indirect attempt to gain the son's exclusive affection and loyalty.

Students with such backgrounds had understandable difficulties in making life commitments and vocational choices. To emulate the father by choice of vocation, graduate school, field of concentration, or even the topic of a term paper reactivated the student's conflictual relationships with his parents. To choose any option that might be approved of by the father inevitably meant running the risk of displeasing the mother, and vice versa. Conscious (and unconscious) efforts at synthesis of conflicting parental pressures were made difficult by the adamant hostility of each parent to the other, which was translated into internal conflict in our subjects. It was as if, for these students, any choice, commitment, or decision was sure to displease one of the internalized parents; no major decision could be made without intense conflict and ambivalence. For example: Such a student was a twenty-one-year-old senior who had recently learned of a serious rift between his parents. At the time he was seen by us he was in the throes of trying to choose between what he perceived to be two conflicting directions for his future life. He expressed a feeling of "being torn apart" and "less than whole"—very probably a reflection of his internalization of the interpersonal struggle between his parents. For this student the family disruption was effectively blocking identity synthesis.

In attempting to understand the subjects' characteristic problems in relationship with the father (and sometimes with the mother as well), we were impressed with the students' unsuccessful struggle to reconcile sharply contrasting identifications derived from a split in the conscious and unconscious image of the father. On the one hand, the father (especially in the past) appeared strong, competent, capable, caring, and emulable; on the other hand, the father appeared weak, impotent, ineffectual, dependent, and bad. The resolution of this conflictual identification was usually impeded by the fact that the students' ambivalence was not fully conscious and sometimes emerged only indirectly in the brief course of our interviews. And in some instances, the son clearly felt guilty over abandoning his identification with his father, partly because of his genuine affection for him and partly because of his awareness of his father's dependency.

Furthermore, for many subjects, to become fully conscious either of the father's own defects or of the extent of filial ambivalence entailed a major sense of loss, sometimes intensified during our brief contact with these subjects. The comfort and direction that had been given by an unambivalently positive view of the father was now lost, and this loss was often accompanied by a devaluation of an important part of the student's own personality.

Our clinical observation agrees in substance with Pervin's discussion of identification and "counteridentification" (i.e., the effort to resist identification with the father) among dropouts. It is also consistent with many of the issues of family dynamics discussed by Levenson and his colleagues. Our students had reached, we believe, a developmental impasse, such that further growth was temporarily blocked by an inability to resolve or synthesize an ambivalent identification with the parents, particularly the father. Their depression seems related to the "spoiling" of their positive identification with their fathers, and to their preconscious sense of having lost an important and valued component of themselves. And their sense of stagnation and emptiness may reflect in part a preconscious recognition of the blocking of development. The feeling that continuing attendance at college was undesirable or impossible reflected a covert acknowledgment of submerged difficulties, of vague dissatisfactions and yearnings, and of unresolved problems of identification that impeded the individual's further psychological growth within the college environment. One major issue in the dropouts we studied was thus an inability to accomplish one of the major developmental tasks of adolescence—the need to free one's self from childhood identifications and the fantasies connected with them in order to make room for new objects, relationships, and commitments. As far as their strongest feelings were concerned, the students we interviewed seemed bound to their parents.

As we noted earlier, we do not believe that the concept of "identity crisis" is sufficiently specific to account for the particular psychodynamic issues we encountered in our subjects. Rather, for the potential dropout, identity formation itself had been truncated. Our students seemed to be grappling with earlier issues of identification—to be unable thus far to move beyond identifying. Having been unable to achieve differentiation from their parents, they had not yet been able to gain that critical distance which makes possible the selection, rejection, and modification of earlier identifications, and their subsequent synthesis into a unique identity. Bound by their earlier identifications, our students were not yet able to become what Erik Erikson calls "circumscribed individual[s] in relation to a predictable universe which transcends the circumstances of childhood." For students for whom role experimentation has been seriously inhibited from within and without, the decision to leave college may represent, for virtually the first time, an exercise of individual choice and the first step toward the development of an autonomous selfhood.

While the problem of reconciling conflicting and ambivalent identifications to the parent of the same sex is a normative problem during adolescence, and adult identity normally develops from the resolution of this problem, we would speculate that most college students confront and begin to resolve this problem before they arrive at college. The discovery that one's parents have "feet of clay" commonly occurs among talented middle-class American adolescents during the high-school years. Thus, we might think of potential dropouts as lagging behind their classmates in terms of their psychosocial development. At the same time, there are many college students who manifest a similar "developmental lag," but do *not* seriously consider dropping out of college. Thus, we must examine other issues in our subjects in order to attempt to explain why they decided to leave college.

Adaptation: disengagement in response to conflict.   Given our finding that the active confrontation of the possibility of dropping out was almost always preceded by a prolonged period of intensifying crisis, it is tautological to describe dropping out as a manifestation of leaving the field in response to conflict. But several observations led us to conclude that many or most dropouts, long before ever considering dropping out, exhibited a pattern of disengagement, active withdrawal, avoidance, and "leaving the field" as a characteristic response to stress, crisis, and conflict. We have already noted that the voluntary decision to drop out was almost always preceded by a longer period during which the student *involuntarily* lost interest and connection with his academic work, his extracurricular activities, his college friends, his teachers and advisors, and his previous commitments to the future. Upon inquiry, it further emerged that many of our subjects had also exhibited a similar pattern of disengagement when confronted with earlier conflicts. In some instances this pattern was apparent in relationships with girls; in a few other cases the student had previously dropped out of secondary school or even college. In still other instances the student had avoided difficult confrontations with parents and others by "taking off," going away, seeking a new environment, and so on. Thus, on a variety of levels, we observed a tendency to turn away from difficult or conflict-arousing situations.

In some students the origins of this pattern of avoidance could be discerned. In a few cases we encountered the syndrome described by Levenson wherein the son vengefully identifies with and re-enacts a pattern of parental dropping out. Specifically, some of our subjects had fathers (or, more rarely, mothers) who had themselves dropped out of college. This "acting out" of parental history often had an ambivalent and even hostile quality: the parents of such students seemed exceptionally distressed by their son's decision to drop out, perhaps because his decision repeated a pattern the parents deplored in themselves. Since, however, college dropouts have for many decades been more numerous than students who completed their B.A.'s without interruption, by chance alone we would expect over 75 per cent of all students whose parents both began college to have a dropout father, mother, or both.

In other cases avoidance seemed to have been learned in childhood as a means of coping with conflicting demands within the student's family. For example: One student, after attempting to act as a mediator and go-between for his warring parents, finally informed both parents that he no longer wished to discuss their relationship with them and insisted on avoiding their quarrels, often by leaving home during parental fights. Now, confronted with a college that, in his view, was full of internal contradictions, he again contemplated absenting himself from the scene of perceived conflict.

Other students seemed to have been confronted by family situations best described as "double binds." For example, a number of fathers had pushed their sons to enter their own fields, but at the same time indicated their profound dissatisfaction with their own lives. Repeatedly confronted with such conflicting messages from the father, some students had long ago concluded that their best hope was to "leave the field" altogether. When these students were faced, during college, with a reintensification of earlier problems in a new setting, they seem to have fallen back on an adaptation that had served them well in the past.

Theoretically, adaptations to stress and conflict can be classified into three types: *autoplastic* adaptations, which involve transforming the self so as to cope with conflict; *alloplastic* adaptations, which involve efforts to transform the environment so as to make it less stressful; and *avoidant* adaptations, which seek to increase the distance between the individual and the source of stress. At Yale, most students confronted with acute developmental crises choose either autoplastic or alloplastic adaptations, rather than avoidance. For example, one response to stress around academic work is alloplastic: a determined effort to modify academic programs, change courses, or even join one of several student groups concerned with promoting educational reform in the college. Another common reaction to stress is to seek to change one's self: by seeking psychotherapy in order to overcome "study problems"; by programs of self-reform, hard work, or "self-analysis"; or by the use of drugs that alter consciousness. Our dropout sample chose neither of these two general options. Their disengagement from academic life seemed far too profound to be remedied by changes of courses or even of majors. Nor were these students especially vociferous critics of the college, much less educational reformers. Similarly, most of those in our sample who sought therapy did so not in order to overcome the difficulties that led them to consider dropping out, but to understand better why they were dropping out.

By emphasizing the importance to these students of disengagement as a response to conflict, we do not mean to suggest that dropping out is necessarily an "escape" or a maladaptive choice. For many of the students we interviewed, the decision to resign from college was part of a preconscious effort to master, actively and effectively, the conflicts which led up to the crisis. The decision to leave college transformed a prior involuntary and conflict-laden work paralysis into an act for which the student accepted full personal responsibility. In principle, many dropouts might have been capable of a solution chosen by some of their classmates as a reaction to personal crisis during college—namely, to continue "going through the motions" of academic work in order to secure passing grades, while turning their major energies toward some noncurricular activity such as dating, bridge playing, or immersion in sociopolitical activism. As compared with the latter solutions, leaving college seemed an equally "active" and direct confrontation of the students' difficulties. Nor was it self-evident to us that students' problems were such that psychotherapy, with the student remaining in college, clearly constituted the best way of resolving them.

Thus, although our observations led us to hypothesize that disengagement is a preferred adaptation to stress among college dropouts, we would not conclude that dropping out is for that reason always a maladaptive decision. On the contrary, our impression is that for many or most of our subjects the decision was probably justified, although rarely fully thought through. It would be a mistake to lionize the college dropout, seeing him as a creative dissenter against an oppressive educational machine. But for at least some of the students we studied, dropping out clearly did represent an exercise in courage. For them the road to graduation might have been smoother had they been content to slide by with passing grades, seeking a psychosocial moratorium within the college rather than outside its walls. But remaining in an unrewarding academic environment is not necessarily the road to intellectual and emotional maturity, much less to the development of creative potential. In more clinical terms there may be value to allowing the student who is struggling with the idea of dropping out to use this tentative mode of conflict resolution, recognizing that its neurotic aspects may perhaps best be seen as developmental steps toward healthier patterns of adaptation.

Institutional: transference to the college. Dropping out of college is obviously a transaction between an individual and an institution, and to consider only the familial and adaptive factors of this act is to study but part of the picture. It is beyond the scope of our study to try to characterize the curriculum and climate of Yale College; in any case, an earlier study suggested that Yale students actively considering dropping out of college were not characterized by any distinctive view of or complaint about the college. Our interviews in general confirmed this finding.

We were, however, impressed with the way in which our subjects' idiosyncratic images of the college paralleled their equally idiosyncratic descriptions of their parents and family life. More than most students, they seemed to have a family transference to the institution, involving a selective and even projective perception of those aspects of the college environment that corresponded to characteristics of their early family situation. Although such institutional transferences were rarely evident to our subjects themselves, the parallels between their descriptions of their families and of the college were impressive to us. For example: One sophomore's idiosyncratic view of the college as being harsh and repressive, yet devoid of real strength and moral purpose, found a striking parallel in his description of his own family. His father's surface violence and brutality served to veil an underlying passivity and dependency that was betrayed by chronic alcoholism. This student's reasons for dropping out were complex, but his dissatisfaction with the college's lack of underlying purpose and strength was important among them.

In promoting such transferences, the attitude of the student's family toward the college is important. For example, among our subjects there were some whose fathers (and sometimes grandfathers and great-grandfathers) had attended Yale College. A family tradition that is a source of ambivalent pride and respect to the son can foster a strong positive transference to the institution, which may in turn motivate him to stay in college regardless of his discontents. Such positive transferences were evident even in our dropout sample among those whose initial decision to attend Yale College had been premised on the assumption that it was in some sense a reflection of a valued part of their family tradition. But when these students began to question their families' values and heritage or to feel oppressed by their families' traditions, they also began to see dropping out as a means of repudiating the families' values. Once again, we are dealing with genuine ambivalence rather than simple hostility: attending Yale in the first place was an expression of the student's positive feelings about his father and his family tradition; withdrawing from Yale was an expression of the negative side of his ambivalence.

Similar family pressures affected students whose fathers were not graduates of Yale College. Some parents had strongly urged their sons to apply to Yale because of its academic and social prestige. For these parents, having a son admitted to Yale was the fulfillment of a long-standing dream in which they vicariously expressed their own strivings for intellectual and social status. And in other cases, attending Yale was an expression by the son of parental and suburban ideals that value (and overvalue) an Ivy League education. For such students dropping out of Yale was, among other things, a way of repudiating not only parental identifications and values but a suburban, middle-class way of life.

In marked contrast to these students are other undergraduates, not in our dropout sample, whose view of the college is more unambivalently positive. They, too, relate to the institution as if it were a family. And for them, as well as for dropouts, the internalized representation of the college is complex, overdetermined, and an important determinant of their behavior vis-à-vis the institution. But for many students the college is like a *new* family that provides a chance to learn, explore, and develop in a way that was not possible within the confines of their original families. And for still others the college is valued because it is *like* certain positive aspects of the family: for example, it encourages independence, learning, curiosity, and autonomy.

Our interviews with dropouts have impressed us with the importance of the intrapsychic meaning of institutions to individuals. In some of our subjects we would have found it almost impossible to understand the students' motives for leaving college without considering this factor. In many cases the college stood psychologically *in loco parentis*—despite its determined institutional effort to avoid a parental role. To be sure, positive transferences to the institution undoubtedly make dropping out less likely. Furthermore, there are students who do *not* appear to identify the college with their families. But for those who do, and who perceive their families as constricting, destructive, or subversive of further personal development, the probability that they will drop out is increased. It may be that in colleges that deliberately assume a parental role, institutional transferences are even more frequent.

Toward a Developmental Transactionalism

All our observations focus on one overriding theme: the way in which differential rates of psychological development mesh with or fail to mesh with the changing opportunities and pressures that impinge upon the student within the college context. To put this another way, the act of dropping out seems basically related to the incongruence between the student's own developmental timetable and the normative timetable of demands and opportunities of the college setting at each point in the student's college career.

Many investigators of student development have insisted that institutional characteristics must be considered along with psychological variables in understanding student phenomena. Dropping out is, as we have noted, a "transaction" between the individual and his college: in principle, an ideal institution for one student may be abhorrent to another, who may be impelled to leave college partly because of his distaste for that particular college. Despite the obviousness of these propositions, studies that relate dropping out to explicit discontent with the college experience or to a characteristic perception of the college (e.g., as impersonal, authoritarian, excessively demanding, or too frivolous) have been relatively few. Only Pervin and Rubin, using a variation of the semantic differential test, have reported significant relationships between perceived discrepancy between self and college and stated willingness to drop out. Our own research suggests the fruitfulness of this approach, which focuses on the lack of congruence of college and student rather than upon independent characteristics of either. Dropouts, as we have studied them, appear to have few shared personal characteristics or complaints about the college; what they do share is a sense that whatever their own developmental needs and goals, these cannot be fulfilled within the college context.

But in interpreting our findings, it is crucial to recall that students are not homogeneous and static bundles of traits who interact with a simple and unchanging environment. Any approach that merely "matches" self-characterizations with college characteristics at one point in time is at best a first approximation to the extremely complex and changing transactions between student and college. With regard to the student, naïve transactionalism overlooks two crucial student characteristics: first, students change in the course of their college careers; second, students have inner tensions, ambivalences, alternations in behavior and mood, and unconscious mental processes that cannot be adequately summarized in their conscious self-conceptions. The psychological assets and qualities of students change in complex ways at many levels as students pass through a "typical" college education. These changes, for example, are reflected in the problems students present to their counselors. In a university psychiatric service freshmen present a disproportionate number of problems concerning separation from parents and first adaptations to the college environment. Once an initial adaptation to college has been more or less achieved, a new set of problems assumes prominence. These "crises" of the middle college years, often summarized as "sophomore slump," characteristically revolve around problems of commitment and choice of a philosophy of life; of a field of concentration; of friends, roommates, and girls; of a congenial subculture and life style. Finally, during the last years in college the focus of student concern is on the "unfinished business" of a college career that has not always yielded what the student had hoped for, and on "the next phase"—hopes, expectations, and plans for the future. And in all of these problems the student brings to his development not only the pressures and psychological tasks of the college years themselves, but the conscious and unconscious legacy of his past.

On the other side of the equation the college is also a dynamic and often contradictory culture, not easily summarized in a brief set of questionnaire responses. Educational institutions are no less complex and changing than individuals: furthermore, they invariably have their own timetables of demands, challenges, and opportunities they place before the student as he passes through college. For example, freshmen are not thought ready to make a choice of majors, but sophomores are. Sophomores are not usually expected to do independent work, but seniors sometimes are. Colleges, then, make implicit assumptions about the timing of the intellectual and psychological development of their students, and these assumptions are embodied in the class-graded demands of the curriculum and the college's informal culture. "The college" that confronts a senior is often extremely different in its psychological meanings and demands from "the college" that confronts a freshman in the same institution at the same time. And students who respond successfully to one set of class-graded college demands may not be as successful with later college pressures.

Finally, not only is the college a dynamic culture which the student encounters variously in the course of his career, but at each stage of his college life the student may experience a "college" very different from that experienced by his classmates. Academic demands on the student in history may differ vastly from those in physics or sociology. Even more important, the freshman whose assigned roommate is a dedicated football aspirant has a different experience than his classmate with a hippie, bridge player, socialite, radical, or intellectual for a roommate.

The basic hypothesis we derive from our study, then, is that dropping out of college is indeed a transaction between the student and his institution, but it is a transaction that cannot be adequately understood without considering the constantly changing relationship between the developmental schedule of the student and the college's timetable of demands on him as he passes through it. Our observations are confined to one highly selective liberal arts college. At other colleges the nature and phasing of institutional demands and opportunities at each stage of a college career will often be different. But all institutions of higher education presuppose the attainment of a certain level of psychological development if the student is to thrive at any given point in college. For example, to enter a residential college a freshman must have sufficiently separated himself from his parents so as to be able to live without their physical presence. Survival of the first year at many competitive colleges presupposes a capacity to endure the almost universal blows to self-esteem that accompany freshman grades. At academically demanding colleges, the relatively conflict-free use of highly developed ego functions is clearly a prerequisite for continuing successful academic performance. In some colleges the steady increase in freedom of choice given students as they progress through the four years of college requires, at the psychological level, an increase in the capacity to make vital choices and commitments without undue ambivalence and internal conflict. Finally, the ability to "allow" one's self to graduate may presuppose that the individual feels ready to make further commitments after graduation. In each case the changing demands of the college environment must be matched by new developmental accomplishments in the student. For example: One student whose own unfinished developmental business interfered with his readiness to "commence" on his own was a twenty-one-year-old senior for whom the idea of becoming a Yale graduate was terrifying: graduating represented the expectation that he would "go on to bigger and better things," a commitment to himself and to the world which he did not yet feel ready to make. This student's relationship with his family had always been a tenuous one, marked by lengthy physical as well as psychological separations because of his father's missionary profession. These separations and discontinuities had interfered with the student's achievement of differentiation from his parents and had prevented the consolidation of identity fragments into a new organization. It was his preconscious awareness of this unfinished developmental business which he seemed to be attempting to convey by his felt need "to go back before I can move forward," to "try to find my real self, my capacities, and goals," before once and for all committing himself to the status of graduate.

We would hypothesize that other students who are equally "behind schedule" as compared to the timetable of college life are also subjected to great psychological stress. Similarly, students who are developmentally "ahead of schedule" may be subjected to equal stress in colleges that do not permit them to "accelerate" or that persist in treating them as psychologically less adult than they are.* According to this hypothesis, given a psychologically heterogeneous student body whose members are developing at different rates, the best way to produce dropouts is to create a curriculum and an informal culture that make inflexible demands upon the student. Indeed, the concept of a regular and uninterrupted four-year progression from freshman year to the B.A. bears little relationship to what we know about the extreme variability in the rates of individual psychological development during late adolescence and early adulthood.

While our study strongly supports an emphasis upon the interaction between the student and the college as an important determinant of persistence or withdrawal from college, we have concluded that, to be useful, a transactional approach must be both *developmental* and *dynamic*. Changes in the student's psychological assets, accomplishments, vulnerabilities, and conflicts as he progresses through college must be taken into account, along with the role in current behavior of often unconscious themes and conflicts whose origins lie in earlier life. Similarly, educational institutions invariably make class-graded demands on students and provide changing opportunities as they progress through college. Our study confirms that students drop out of college for many different conscious reasons, but in our sample, the outcome of the dropout crisis depended not only on the student's psychosocial capacities but on the ability of the college environment to provide him with the resources and support he needed to continue his personal growth.

Conclusions

There are many kinds of "dropouts," and this study is focused on only one kind: the talented male undergraduate who withdraws in good academic standing and without incapacitating psychiatric symptoms from a residential liberal arts college. Even within this narrowly defined sample we found great diversity. So it is only by way of oversimplified hypotheses that we can discuss the "typical" student we interviewed. It was nonetheless impressive to us that the talented college dropouts we studied tended to have intense conflicts centering around ambivalent or spoiled identifications with their fathers, and that many had had a longstanding pattern of disengagement as a response to conflict. Our students generally had a "negative transference" to the college, which they saw as possessing many of the bad features of their families and therefore as a place where their own further development was impossible. Finally, the issues around which

* We have observed this phenomenon in some students who have returned to college after a prolonged leave of absence during which they have more than "caught up" with their classmates. To such students, accustomed to and ready for a high degree of self-determination, freedom, and responsibility, the regulations, constraints, and life style of a residential liberal arts college may seem "childish" and restrictive.

students tended to drop out seemed closely related to the implicit developmental timetable of the college itself—dropping out was most likely at times when the college demanded of the student a level of psychological development he had not attained.

Many of the problems we observed in college dropouts seemed to us more characteristic of early and middle adolescence than of late adolescence. Thus, the intensified problems of identification we found in dropouts are probably very common in students in high school, but less common in college students. Similarly, the students' inability to differentiate the psychosocial aura of the college from that of their families also might be interpreted as a sign of developmental lag. Because dropouts seemed developmentally out of phase with the demands of the college, the actual decision to drop out often seemed, from our perspective, a sound one.

Our study convinces us that most views of college dropouts advanced in the literature err on the side of excessive simplification. Although we interviewed very few parents, it does not seem sufficient to say that dropouts are uniformly "acting out" a covert parental wish or re-enacting some characteristic of the father's life. Nor do those formulations that link dropping out with "identity diffusion" seem adequately explanatory to us. We found problems of identification more central than issues of identity in our subjects: indeed, autonomous identity development often seemed blocked in most students by their inability to synthesize ambivalent identifications.

Despite our emphasis on the problems of dropouts, we do not believe that dropping out is always most usefully viewed in the context of psychiatric disorder. Whatever the personal discomfort and sense of crisis experienced by our students, we came to believe that most of them, with minimal help and average good luck, would eventually be able to resolve their psychological conflicts, thus "catching up" with those of their classmates whose progression through college was continuous. Although our interviews with returnees were few in number, they supported this impression. Returnees, although seldom able to explain fully what had happened psychologically during their time away from college, generally believed that their dropout experience had been personally useful. The sense of urgency and depression with which they had left college had abated; their "hang-ups" either had been satisfactorily resolved or seemed not to matter so much. For many of these students the mere act of withdrawing from college has been itself an important accomplishment. At the time they left, their expressed desire for a sense of autonomy and control, coupled with an inner need to see their behavior as defiant and rebellious, had made it difficult for them to perceive even supportive authorities as potentially helpful. Upon their return, they were much more able to view their college experience as an instrument in their *own* personal and intellectual growth. The returnees we interviewed were not, in general, eager to "rake up the past"; they preferred to discuss their present activities and future goals rather than their past difficulties and conflicts, many of which they had now "forgotten." This attitude, coupled with greater tranquillity and with generally improved academic performance, suggests that for these students dropping out of college had been an adaptive step, allowing them to escape the pressures of an academic routine long enough to connect their education to their lives.

Finally, given the increase in the diversity of social and cultural backgrounds from which college students are drawn, we believe that the relationship of the changing demands and rewards of college curricula and college life with the student's developmental needs, schedules, and accomplishments must be examined more closely. Colleges that systematically seek heterogeneous student bodies must increasingly plan systematically for students who arrive at college with a wide variety of developmental timetables. Dropping out of college may be, in part, one way in which students with "atypical" developmental schedules and problems can cope with the pressures of a college geared to the "typical" student. The high proportion of college students who discontinue or interrupt their education may in part reflect the fact that most college students are, in terms of their colleges, "atypical."

Radicals: Renewal of
the Tradition

*This essay summarizes a study of a small group of young radicals who led
Vietnam Summer 1967, a national antiwar organizing project. Some of
what I found was approximately what I had been led to expect by the
research of others (see "The Sources of Student Dissent"). But in many
other respects, I learned much from this study. For example, I had
expected far more suspicion than I actually encountered; in 1967, the
mistrust of the student Left toward social scientific research had not
developed to its present extent. More important, I had expected to find
among radicals a very deep identification with a nuturant, humanitarian
mother. But as this report chronicles, what was impressive in these radicals
was instead their deep and ambivalent ties to their fathers, and in
particular their identification with their fathers' and their families' ideals.*

This study, published at greater length as Young Radicals, *has been
criticized by both radicals and conservatives. To some radicals it seemed
a typically "liberal" (or even "counterrevolutionary") effort to explain
away radicalism by examining its psychological roots. Some conservatives
have considered the study little more than an apology for the people I
studied. This charge is correct if it means that I liked and respected the
people I studied, and that I did not attempt to hide these feelings in
reporting the study. These radicals were markedly different from the
popular stereotype of the wild-haired drug fiend or the nihilistic anarchist
that was current even in 1967 and that has become even more current
since. The portrait I drew of these students was as accurate as I could
make it in 1967, and my later contact with these men and women has not
led me to want to revise that portrait.*

*What has most annoyed some critics is that I not only rejected the view
that these radicals were unusually neurotic, paranoid, filled with Oedipal
hatred, or involved in adolescent rebellion, but I went on to suggest that by
many criteria of "mental health," these young men and women did not
lack it. By and large, other scholars, using more "objective" research
methods than my own, have come to the same conclusion. None*

of this was meant to deny that young radicals had "hang-ups"—which they discussed with great openness with me. Nor do I believe that the psychological health or lack thereof of an individual enables one to judge the merits of his views. It is as incorrect to adopt a point of view because those who hold it are "psychologically healthy" as it is to reject a view because those who put it forward have psychological problems. But to understand a social movement it is important to understand something about those who are among its leaders; and whether they are severely disturbed human beings is, at least in this century, one question we inevitably ask.

With these particular young men and women, studied in 1967, what was most impressive was not their rebellion against their parents or American society, but their ultimate fidelity to both—their principled acceptance of the core values of their families, which in almost every case were humanitarian, intellectual, liberal, democratic, and very American. Compared to these traditional values, our actual society seemed to these young radicals (as it does to me) grossly wanting. My experience with these young men and women has thus shaped and informed my own understanding of the new youthful opposition: I see it not simply as a wholesale rejection of the creedal values of American society but also as a selective effort to implement and renew these values.

ONE afternoon in May, 1967, I received a long-distance telephone call asking me if I wanted to take part in a study called Vietnam Summer. The caller explained that this summer project would attempt to organize new groups to oppose the war in Southeast Asia. Several social scientists and journalists were being urged to study the development and effectiveness of the summer project.

After some hesitation I made arrangements to meet with this unknown gentleman, and from this meeting there evolved a research study on the psychological development of young radicals. In my comments here I will summarize certain observations on the development of students who become New Left leaders.

Vietnam Summer was a large and far-reaching group dedicated to organizing new constituencies to oppose American involvement in Southeast Asia. Those who conceived of the project, as well as those who actually led it, defined themselves as radicals, as members of the New Left, or the Movement for Social Change. They were strongly opposed to the war in Vietnam, but many were equally or more interested in other major changes in American policies, both domestic and international.

My study itself was not focused upon Vietnam Summer, but rather upon a relatively small group of young men and women who constituted the political staff of the National Office of Vietnam Summer in Cambridge, Massachusetts. This group consisted of approximately a dozen young men and women who had come up through the movement, New Leftists with a deep commitment to community organizing and peace work as a part of a broader program of social change. In their early or mid-twenties, they were committed radicals, most of whom had already devoted several years to full-time work in the movement.

My procedure was simply to interview these young men and women, catching them between appointments in the National Headquarters of Vietnam Summer. The first interview focused largely on their political activities and ideas as these had emerged in adolescence and after. The second interview was an exploration of the early family environment in which the individual had grown up. Third and subsequent interviews were an effort to establish connections between early life and tradition on the one hand, and current political views and activities on the other. In all, I interviewed intensively seventeen individuals in the National Office of Vietnam Summer. I decided to limit this report to observations on "committed" radicals, which I have defined to mean individuals who (a) consider themselves "radicals" and part of the movement, and (b) have spent at least one year during which their primary work involved community organizing, civil rights work, New Left coordinating work, or peace work. Eleven of those I interviewed met these criteria. One or two of them had combined a primary orientation to movement work with college or graduate school, but most had spent longer periods in full-time work with the New Left, the average time being two or three years. In addition, I had previously interviewed three individuals in connection with other studies who met these criteria; these three were remarkably similar psychologically to the Vietnam Summer leaders, and I have included them in this discussion. There were fourteen, then, in the group on whom these observations are based.

The age of those interviewed ranged from nineteen to twenty-seven, with a mean age of twenty-three. All of the radicals were white; three were women. Two came from lower-middle-class families, two from upper-class families, and the remainder from upper-middle-class families. Most frequently their fathers were businessmen, teachers, or professionals. Seven came from Protestant backgrounds, five from Jewish backgrounds, and two from Catholic families. Three came from clearly "radical" families, with parents who had been active in left-wing movements during the 1930's; the parents of most of the remainder were Democrats, often of a "Stevensonian" persuasion. All of the interviewees had at least begun college, and the colleges they had attended were generally academically excellent, highly selective liberal arts colleges or private universities. Socioeconomically, these young radicals came from relatively privileged and advantaged sectors of American society. Only two of the fourteen had

ever been in psychotherapy: one in weekly therapy for two periods of
several months, the other in psychoanalysis for about two years.

Given the smallness of the group on whom my observations were
made, a number of their special characteristics should be underlined. They
were clearly not "representative" of all New Leftists; nor could I, from the
information gathered during the summer, judge in any systematic way
how they might differ from other young radicals who might have been
interviewed in other contexts. Indeed, I am still not clear how one would
go about finding a "representative" group of young radicals.

For each of the individuals I interviewed I had an average of approximately five hours of interview material, plus, usually, an equal amount of
time in which I observed the individual in his work, in meetings, at national conferences, and so on. While the amount of information at my
disposal is extremely limited as compared to that which could be garnered
from an intensive psychotherapeutic relationship, the unusual openness,
candor, and introspectiveness of this group made me feel that, in most
instances, I was able to distinguish fact from self-justifying myth, and that
I was able to obtain a relatively accurate picture of each person.

I will turn in a moment to consider some of the more consistent psychological themes in the development of these young radicals. But before
I do so, I should note the incompleteness of this partial account. By focusing solely on the psychological themes that were found in these radicals, I
omit other issues of great importance. In particular, I will not consider
here the formative effect upon these young radicals of their average of two
or three years' experience in New Left organizing work, nor will I be able
to touch upon the equally important topic of the impact upon them of
social and historical forces that contributed to shaping their lives. It
should be understood, then, that in discussing psychological issues in radical development, I am arbitrarily separating one set of determinants of
radicalism and deliberately neglecting other group, experiential, and historical factors that have equal importance.

In the account that follows, I will underline themes which seem to me
distinctively important in the young radicals interviewed, attempting to
construct a picture of the "typical" psychological development of these
New Leftists. But this account should always be qualified by a continuing
awareness that, with this group even more than with most, the search for
consistencies neglects the most important consistency, namely, the intense
individuality of those I interviewed.

In discussions of the New Left two hypotheses are continually put forward. I will call these the Oedipal-rebellion hypothesis and the red-diaper-
baby hypothesis.

The Oedipal-rebellion hypothesis is clearly most widely held in the
general population and sometimes advanced even by scholarly observers

of the New Left. According to this thesis, especially as put forward by those least familiar with New Leftists, the position of today's young radicals reflects a violent rebellion against and hatred of all male, parental, and societal authority. The radical, according to this view, is "displacing" the conflicts of his family onto society and the world, "acting out" intrapsychic conflicts in his external behavior.

A more sophisticated version of the Oedipal-rebellion hypothesis was, on occasion, put forward by those close to the New Left. According to this sympathetic view, radicals tend to come from families in which they have experienced, perhaps to an unusual degree, the ultimate barrenness, flatness, and emptiness of American middle-class life. While not necessarily "rebels" against their families, these young radicals are seen as in strong reaction to the family milieu from which they come. Specifically, sympathy toward parents and even pity is said to be combined with a major effort to avoid parents' lives, lives seen as empty, spiritually impoverished, and often "quietly desperate."

A second, sharply contrasting hypothesis was often put forward by individuals active in New Left work. This thesis could be called the red-diaper-baby hypothesis, a phrase used within the Vietnam Summer office to characterize those workers who came from families with a radical or left-wing tradition. According to this hypothesis, present-day radicals come largely from politically radical families where, from the time of early childhood, they have been exposed to radical ideas about social reform, political action, and society. The development of the radical as a person, then, is portrayed as smooth, continuous, and uninterrupted, as a simple assimilation of parental values of dissent and indignation at modern American society, coupled with a determination to work toward correcting these injustices. In support of this hypothesis several highly publicized figures, such as Bettina Aptheker, the radical daughter of well-known Communist parents, are frequently cited.

In fact, however, neither the Oedipal-rebellion nor the red-diaper-baby hypothesis proved particularly relevant to the actual lives of those I interviewed. Both theories of radicalism overlook the actual complexity of human development, and each posits the possibility of either a total break with the past or a total acceptance of it, which rarely if ever occurs in life.

The Schism in the Paternal Image

The diversity of the actual patterns of relationship with parents found among the young radicals interviewed cannot be exaggerated. On the one hand, there were a few individuals, particularly those from left-wing backgrounds, who described idyllic relationships with their parents; close, understanding support and mutual sympathy were the rule throughout childhood and continued, with only occasional interruption, during adolescence into the present. At the other extreme was a smaller number whose development had been marked by violent rebellion against parents, rebellion which they invariably connected explicitly to their current involvement in radical politics. But perhaps the most striking general feature of these young radicals was their great current understanding of their parents, their relative detachment, compassion, and ability to view their parents "in the round" as complex differentiated human beings. And perhaps related to this current sympathy for parents was a portrait of early family relationships and a family atmosphere most often characterized by considerable parental warmth, sympathy, understanding, and idealism. Put into an oversimplified formula, these young radicals more often came from "happy homes" than not.

In addition, a number of more specific themes recurred frequently among those interviewed. A great variety of anecdotes, early recollections and later events suggest an unusually strong tie between these young men and their mothers, in the first years of life. Such a close maternal tie is, of course, not unusual among young Americans, but in many of these individuals it seems to have been particularly intense, and to have evolved into an unusual sensitivity and responsiveness to the mother's wishes.

Another common characteristic of the mothers of these young radicals was their eagerness for intellectual achievement from their sons. The pattern is well described by one interviewee who mentioned his mother's semijoking attitude when he returned home with a grade of 98: "Where are the other two points?" Most often the fathers seconded the maternal emphasis on intellectual attainment, and the sons complied by doing extremely well in academic work and showing considerable intellectual giftedness, if not precosity. Whatever the specific way in which maternal interest in intellectual achievement was transmitted, one of its corollaries in later life seems to have been the frequent identification of intellectuality with conformity to maternal pressures.

More central to the over-all development of these radical activists, however, was their intense and highly ambivalent involvement with their fathers. The term "ambivalent" somewhat understates the issue, for ambivalence toward fathers and mothers is routine, expectable, and unremarkable in the development of youth. With these young New Leftists, however, ambivalence toward their fathers was greater than that found in most young men and women; the image of the father, as seen through interviews, was radically split into two contradictory parts. On the one hand, the father was frequently portrayed as highly ethical, intellectually strong, principled, honest, and politically idealistic. But on the other hand, the same father in other contexts was sometimes seen as a drunken, humiliated, unsuccessful, weak, acquiescent, or otherwise inadequate person. This schism in the paternal image was found in almost all of those interviewed; it seems of great importance in the development of these young men and women.

Examples may help clarify the complexities of relationships to the father. One individual remembered very positively his long walks with his father during early childhood. Then the two would discuss social and political issues, and, in this context, he saw his father as effective, competent, and highly idealistic. But in other contexts the same interviewee emphasized his father's being dominated and tyrannized over by his mother, as being unnecessarily acquiescent and passive, and as being strikingly ineffectual in his work, which the mother effectively dominated. Another interviewee discussed at length his early hatred of his father and his later violent and successful rebellion against him. But when asked about the sources of his political beliefs, he cited first his father's "honesty" in recognizing the "fundamental illegitimacy" of the business system in which the father was extremely successful, and went on to suggest his strong identification with his father and his father's youthful questioning and rebellious attitude. Still another interviewee considered his father very much of a "failure," given his father's considerable basic talents, and had tried very hard not to follow in his father's footsteps, but, at the same time, he had strongly identified with his father's values of enterprise and constructive work, which had been more successfully actualized in his father's brothers and friends.

Further examples could be adduced, but the pattern is clear. In these young radicals there seemed to be an unusual and often quite conscious split in the image of the father, involving the simultaneous picture of him, his tradition, and the older generation as idealistic, honest, highly principled, and admirable but, on the other hand, as also weak, humiliated, ineffectual, and so on. The effort to repair this schism, to identify with the idealistic and effective father but to avoid having the father's weakness, ineffectuality, or passivity, seemed crucial in the later development of these New Leftists.

Within this basic context of an intensely ambivalent relationship to the father there was a continuum of family relationships, and especially paternal relationships, along which most activists could be placed. At one end of this continuum were those few from relatively "radical" political backgrounds, who convincingly described a family milieu of unusual warmth, demonstrativeness, openness, and congeniality. At the other end of the continuum was an equally small number of New Leftists who described early family environments of violent conflict or extraordinary isolation among family members.

In both types of families psychological development had special characteristics. For example, some young radicals described families which seemed extraordinary in their devotion to the independence of their children and their dedication to the highest moral principles, but their own developments suggested that such families may, in a subtle way, be particularly difficult for a capable son to cope with. Despite the strength they can give a growing child, they provide him as an adolescent with little to rebel against, and the attainment of independence and adulthood may become paradoxically synonymous with passive compliance to family wishes. It is as if the children of such families have been given so much that they can afford to demand more of themselves and of life when they reach adulthood.

At the other end of the continuum those families that gave their children a great deal to rebel against always seemed to have provided something to emulate as well. For example, one son engaged from early life in furious battles with his father, which clearly won his father's grudging respect; thereafter there existed an unstated but strong bond between father and son, perhaps because each saw in the other a fighter like himself. In other cases the father's domestic ineffectuality was partly offset by his intellectual effectiveness, his high principles, or his more effective past. In still another instance, while the son repudiated his father's actual humiliating failure, he identified strongly with his father's, and his father's father's values. For such young radicals overt repudiation was frequently coupled with identification, and, by the time they were interviewed, most were able to acknowledge not only the negative but the positive lessons they had learned from their fathers.

These complex father-son relationships suggest that neither the red-diaper-baby nor the Oedipal-rebellion hypothesis is adequate, although neither is totally incorrect. Like most stereotypes, they indicate one small part of the truth, while omitting the crux of the matter. The vast majority of those interviewed were in some respects *both* red-diaper-babies and Oedipal rebels. Their development involved a simultaneous identification with one aspect of the father, particularly with the father's principles, goals, and ideals, and an equally frequent rejection of another aspect of the father, particularly the father's ineffectuality, inactivity, subservience, or apparent failure.

Given the very real differences in the family situations of each of those interviewed, it was obvious that no one characterization could suffice to describe the relationship of the radical's parents to each other. Again, there was a full range from open parental hostility, occasionally verging on divorce, to a more common pattern of intense, close mutuality and sharing between the parents. Yet above and beyond these differences, virtually all of these families shared a common focus on morality, defined not as the narrow restraint of impulses, but as a higher ethical orientation toward personal relationships within the family and without.

Almost without exception, then, these young radicals came from families with *principled parents*. As children they were almost invariably disciplined by "psychological methods." Yet this term does not do justice to the role of principle in their families. Somehow their parents communicated, often without ever saying it outright, that human behavior was to be judged primarily in terms of its conformity with general ethical principles, that right conduct was to be deduced from general maxims concerning human relationships, and that what mattered most in the evaluation of individual worth was the ability to act in conformity with such principles. In some of these families the principles were specifically religious, as with the more than half of the interviewees who grew up in families with active religious affiliations. For a smaller number the principles were primarily ethical and cultural, particularly among young radicals from secular Jewish families with a strong ethical identification with Judaism. And in a few instances the principles were primarily philosophical and political, rather than religious or cultural. But for virtually all of these young radicals, the atmosphere created within their early families was one in which ethical principles occupied the highest positions, and in which human events and human conduct were automatically judged in accordance with these principles. This familial orientation to principle was an important continuity in the lives of these young radicals.

The Early Sense of Specialness

The preadolescent experience of these young radicals again varied enormously from individual to individual, depending on family, social, and historical circumstance. What distinguished virtually all of them was a feeling, from an early age, of being somehow different, separate, apart, and exceptional, a self-characterization which they viewed ambivalently and which continued to be important throughout their later development. The sources of this sense of specialness were varied, but they united around a few crucial themes. For one, these young radicals frequently came from families whose style, ethnicity, or ideology separated them from the surrounding community, a separation which contributed to an early sense of "alienness" from others in their environment. The sense of specialness was often intensified further by early intellectual excellence, a capacity which usually placed them in the intellectual "elites" of their grade schools and secondary schools. Moreover, many of the interviewees were leaders from an early age, especially in the defense of unpopular positions. One, for example, recalled leading a disastrously unsuccessful charge of the bullied children in his school against the bullies. Despite the catastrophic failure of this early revolutionary effort (the bullies triumphed as usual) he consciously related this act to his continuing interest in organizing the oppressed. Another interviewee recalled having been beaten up in grade school because of his parents' political views; still another, whose family represented a minority group in their neighborhood, was ostracized and bullied because of his minority-group status.

Another frequent source of an early sense of specialness was the apparently precocious political, social, and historical consciousness of these radicals as children. For several, the first memory was that of the end of World War II; another's earliest recollection involved a political figure who was mobbed by a hostile crowd; still another recalled his early bewilderment at his own favored social position in the community.

A more explicit political and social consciousness seemed generally to have developed during the early grades of school. Many reported holding unpopular views and defending them vigorously, usually with the support of their parents. In some instances these students were the "leaders of the opposition" around such issues as grade-school drills for atomic attack, local elections, or Presidential campaigns. Even when asked, they could rarely recall ever supporting a majority position in school. They were always supporters of the Democratic candidate in a strongly Republican area, advocates of peace in a bellicose community, or defenders of the underdog.

My emphasis on a sense of specialness, on early intellectual ability and moral precosity, should not be taken to suggest that these were unusually studious, withdrawn, or joyless children. The opposite seems to have been the case. Many were good sand-lot athletes; they had good friends and playmates, and they were the kinds of children who were routinely elected president of their grade-school classrooms. With few exceptions they described themselves as sociable and outgoing children, as "making friends easily," and as moving readily in the social world of school and family. The over-all picture, then, is one of a relatively happy and successful childhood, of general effectiveness in school, and of a globally pleasant recollection of the preadolescent years.

Turmoil-filled Adolescence

With the beginning of adolescence itself, usually at about the age of thirteen, a drastic reversal in outer behavior, paralleled by intrapsychic changes and conflicts, frequently occurred. The preadolescent pattern of outgoing activity was transformed, often in a few months, to a new style of seclusiveness, a feeling of social awkwardness, and a sense of moral inferiority, coupled with intense intellectual concerns and at times extreme religiosity. The outgoing happy child was transformed, as it were, overnight, into the shy, awkward, and tormented early adolescent.

Although such abrupt changes in behavior and inner life during adolescence are described as typical by European commentators on adolescence, they are in fact relatively infrequent in the development of young

Americans. The more typical pattern for American youth involves turning away from the family toward the peer group, immersion into its activities, and the use of one's age mates as a buffer against one's own impulses and one's ties to one's family. In a sense, then, many of the young radicals studied might be said to have experienced a more "European" adolescence than their typical American contemporaries. Certainly the asceticism, guilt, and defensive intellectualization of these young men and women fit, almost too perfectly, the classical description of early adolescence of upper-middle-class European youth.

The focal and generally quite conscious issue during this period was the emergence of sexuality. Again and again, those interviewed explicitly related their early adolescent conflicts to feelings about sex, about their own erotic fantasies about the opposite sex, and about the changes in their bodies. How much of this was fully conscious at the time we cannot be sure, but at the time of interview the relationship was presented as direct and unequivocal. The actual symptoms of inner turmoil varied considerably from individual to individual. One interviewee began at this point to elaborate a private fantasy kingdom, complete with aristocracies, masses, and revolutions, which at times became more important to him than his other activities. Others reported extraordinary self-consciousness and shyness, especially toward the opposite sex with whom they had once felt easy, relaxed, and carefree. Other interviewees became intensely and scrupulously religious in early adolescence, becoming highly involved in church or temple activities and, in one case, elaborating a private set of obsessional religious rituals. A strong propensity toward asceticism, toward rigorous self-discipline, and toward an effort to "deny the flesh" was related by several to guilt over masturbation and sexual fantasies. And most of those interviewed reported that at this time of their lives they had become intensely concerned with abstract philosophical and moral questions, and had spent much of their time in voracious reading, journal keeping, and theorizing.

In early adolescence, too, feelings of loneliness, solitude, and isolation came markedly to the fore. Several interviewees began adolescent diaries which they kept for many years, prefacing them with such thoughts as, "Since I have no one to talk to, I will have to talk to myself." Turning toward themselves rather than toward the peer group, these young radicals began a habit of self-analysis whose results were evident in the insight with which, years later, they could discuss their lives. Yet a journal is rarely an adequate companion, and feelings of painful loneliness were common. Sometimes, because of an explicit feeling that they were especially filled with evil thoughts, and often because they felt "different" from their contemporaries, they were forced back on their own resources. In time, necessity became a virtue for some; they learned to occupy themselves, and not only to tolerate loneliness but to need solitude.

Some time after this drastic reversal of behavior and the development

of asceticism and intellectualization, many of the interviewees also entered
into a period of violent rebellion against their parents, usually focused
around parental "unfairness" and "injustice." The particular issues at stake
in these midadolescent rebellions were not in themselves unusual; they
centered largely around the individual's view that his parents attempted to
restrict him excessively, did not allow him sufficient freedom, attempted to
control his life, to plan his future, and so on. But the intensity of the
rebellion seemed, in many instances, unusual, as did the feeling of moral
outrage and betrayal that accompanied it. Again, the issue of principle is
important. In at least some of these families, parental preaching was not
practiced when the chips were down. In particular, these adolescents felt
outrageously betrayed when the same parents who had consistently encouraged them to be independent, free-thinking and autonomous now in-
tervened in adolescence to attempt to direct their lives.

For a minority of those interviewed, the turmoil of early adolescence
eventuated in the development of psychological symptoms during late adolescence. Many of these symptoms, had they come to the attention of a
psychiatrist at the time, would have been considered relatively ominous.
They included, for example, the previously mentioned elaboration of a
fantasy world more real and engrossing than the actual world, the emergence of elaborately obsessional fears of sexual intimacy, an abortive suicide gesture, and the development of a rather paranoid view of the world.
Most of those interviewed, however, developed no overt symptoms but
described themselves as often unhappy, subjectively quite isolated, and
inwardly frustrated and unfulfilled despite outer success. These feelings or
symptoms culminated for many in late adolescence or early adulthood, in
the sense that they had reached the "end of the line."

Yet to discuss merely the turmoil, the frequent unhappiness, and, in a
few cases, the psychological symptoms of adolescence would be to overlook the continuing psychological strength shown by these young radicals.
Whatever their inner turmoil, whatever their private misery, and despite
symptoms that would have incapacitated others, these particular young
men and women "functioned" extremely well. Indeed, those with the most
intense conflicts or the most apparently crippling symptoms often seemed
to have been the most outwardly successful. The early adolescent period
of seclusiveness and withdrawal was gradually overcome; relationships
with the opposite sex were generally established, painfully and slowly, but
surely; and the preadolescent pattern of leadership coupled with intellectual achievement was generally resumed. In describing their college careers, some of those interviewed described themselves initially as "typical
college students." But further inquiry usually revealed that they had been
outstanding students, editors of college publications, or had held positions
of leadership in campus organizations with a social or political orientation.

The End of the Line

As they initially talked about their entry into movement activities, those interviewed described a singularly gradual, undramatic, and uneventful development. There were no conversions in this group. Instead, interviewees spoke of a slow process of increasing political involvement, each step of which seemed at the time necessary and inevitable, and which led slowly and imperceptibly to an emerging sense of self as a radical. These young activists almost uniformly found it impossible to identify any one period or issue around which they came to think of themselves as radicals. Nor could they select any particular experience as decisive to their political careers.

Yet seen in the context of their over-all psychological development, the slow, gradual movement toward increasing involvement in the New Left seemed related to a growing sense of discontent and inner frustration (despite outward success or the possibility of it) to an often conscious search for alternatives to their current activities and life styles—in short, to a subtle feeling that they had "reached the end of the line." This sense of increasing frustration did not stem from failure or rejection. What one interviewee called "the Establishment options" were clearly open to all of these young radicals. They were successful, well-organized students, often leaders of their contemporaries, always intelligent and capable; their superficial problem was that of a surfeit of options. But subjectively, none of these options seemed particularly interesting to them nor, in many cases, were they experienced as psychologically available at all.

Most often during the college years but sometimes before and sometimes after, these young radicals seemed to have reached a point where the Establishment options became psychologically exhausted, and it was generally at about the same time that they began to turn, gradually and unreflectively, toward increasing commitment to the Movement for Social Change. One interviewee, headed toward the career which his parents desired him to enter, began to do extremely poorly in his required courses and, out of the ensuing crisis, moved gradually into radical activities. Another, after a valiant effort at more conventional political involvement, felt an increasing sense of self-defeating frustration, became seriously ill for several weeks (a fact to which he attributed psychological meaning), and then turned toward involvement in more radical political activities.

In the development of a sense of having reached the end of the line, central issues are specialness, guilt, and self-doubt. Almost all of those interviewed retained a feeling of possessing special talents and abilities coupled with an unusually high sense of personal principle. For these young men and women, more than for most of their contemporaries, it was important to be doing things that were consistent with principle—to be people who not merely "had principles" but whose lives embodied and implemented their principles. The increasing sense of the inadequacy of the Establishment options was connected to a growing conviction that these options were ethically inadequate, as was the life trajectory that headed one toward them. In discussing their growing feelings of self-dissatisfaction, their feelings that they were "wasting life," that what they had been doing was in some way "self-destructive," the issue of principle and the profound guilt and shame that arose from failing to follow its dictates, were crucial.

But it would be wrong to overdramatize the "crisis" from which most of these young radicals moved toward a commitment to the New Left. To be sure, almost all of those interviewed felt a quiet but increasingly compelling sense that their lives were not adequate, that they were in some sense marking time; many had periods of dejection, discouragement, and depression when the world seemed flat, tasteless, and stale. But beyond this communality there were also enormous differences.

For most, no episode or decision could be found which adequately summarized their growing sense of failure, made more paradoxical and difficult to discuss by their continuing outward "success" and effectiveness. Indeed, for a vast majority, the process of radicalization only made psychological sense to them in retrospect. At the time they were not making self-conscious decisions, but only doing what seemed most "natural."

In the gradual evolution of a commitment to the movement, then, many factors were fused, with varying weights, depending on the individual and his circumstances. Perhaps the childhood sense of specialness made it more psychologically possible for these young men and women to turn toward movement which represents a special minority of young Americans; certainly the role of principle, and specifically the frustrations and guilts of an unprincipled life, played a crucial role for all. But beyond this the sense of reaching the end of the line also reflected different psychological issues for each person. What they shared was merely the growing explicit awareness that their present lives were inadequate.

The Growing Sense of Rightness

The brief years that have passed since the first development of a radical commitment have brought many different fates to those interviewed— organizing work in the slums, interruptions and resumption of college careers and graduate studies, participation in civil rights work in the South, teaching the children of migrant workers, developing groups of Southern white students who support civil rights, disappointments, defeats, and, occasionally, a rare success. But whatever their activities in the ensuing years, the central psychological theme of these years has been a growing sense of rightness, in both meanings of this ambiguous term. On the one hand, these young radicals reflect a growing feeling that what they are doing is psychologically "right" for them—in accordance with their needs, responsive to their talents, and consistent with their innermost fantasies. At the same time, "rightness" means a growing sense of moral rightness (not to be confused with fanaticism or self-righteousness)—a conviction that what they are doing (though frustrating, difficult, and filled with hardship and triviality) is for them unquestionably in accord with their own highest principles.

This confluence of psychological and ethical needs helped give to the activities and apparent "choices" of these young radicals a peculiar quality of automaticity and naturalness. For example, one individual reported seeing a group of civil rights picketers and joining them. He did not stop to think why but recalled only that this act seemed natural and inevitable in view of his religious upbringing, which had taught him to "bear witness" to his beliefs. When I noted that most individuals of his religion would not have borne witness in this way, he agreed but insisted that at the time it had "just seemed a natural thing to do."

Again and again, young radicals used similar phrases to characterize what from the outside would seem a decision or a choice. Psychologically, the perceived rightness of movement work virtually removed the need to choose. Such a sense of not choosing but acting "naturally" bespeaks a powerful fusion of conscious and unconscious motives in the service of the developing identity of a radical; specifically, it suggests that for these highly principled young men and women, a new harmony is being established between will and conscience, between ego and super ego, between self and principle.

Growing commitment to radical activities rarely involved any major change in the individual's values and principles. For such young men and women as these, who were generally brought up to believe that all men are equal, that prejudice, hatred, and discrimination are wrong, that suffering should be alleviated, that peace, justice, and equality are admirable values, and that violence should be minimized, the values of the New Left are not at all alien, and becoming a radical does not require accepting them, but only resolving to act on them.

In this light the argument that certain kinds of experience such as civil rights work in the South have a "radicalizing effect" on the *values* of the participants is basically incorrect. In so far as these young radicals are representative, their values and principles remain unchanged. What does change, however, is the perception of American reality. Movement work helps bring home to young radicals the extent to which their own values, by and large the values of our society, are simply ignored in large parts of this country, as in many of our dealings with other nations. What also changes is the awareness of how difficult it is to persuade others to implement the values they profess. And, finally, movement work clearly leads to an increased understanding of the tactics and strategies which might be effective in producing the social changes necessary to harmonize American practice with American principle.

As involvement in radical activism grew, the "hang-ups" of earlier adolescence disappeared or became minimal. Obsessional symptoms vanished, leaving in their wake only an unusual capacity for single-minded dedication to a task. The leaden depressions of the past became the realistic discouragements of the present. The fantasy world of knights and peasants was transmuted into the actual world of attempting to create a New Left in America. Those who came from a radical tradition became increasingly able to accept its full burden without being overwhelmed by it; those in manifestly violent rebellion against their fathers became more able to perceive as well the positive components in their identifications with them. So, too, the negative pole of the sense of specialness, the fear of being especially wrong, especially guilty, or especially unworthy, was transvalued into a more positive sense of working in a special movement.

In the continuing development of these young radicals, what is impressive is the highly integrative, "synthetic," and personally satisfying nature of the evolving identity. As individuals, the young radicals I interviewed possessed many of the characteristics of high levels of psychological integration, flexibility, and "adaptive" functioning. They had been able to establish continuity with some aspects of their parental tradition, while repudiating without excessive conflict other aspects of this tradition. Earlier symptoms had largely disappeared, and their aggravated conflicts with their parents had now become both milder and less important. Parents were increasingly seen as complex individuals in their own right. As a group these were young men and women with a capacity for commitment, for work, for love, and for play. They had learned to tolerate frustration, arduous work, and even defeat. Indeed, in the short run, at least, "winning" was no longer necessary for them.

What is important is the continuing effort to create new tactics, institutional forms, and intellectual formulations that can help transform the modern world. For these particular young radicals, then, the "identity" of a radical has so far been a highly integrative and satisfying one; they are exemplars of one unusual but nonetheless successful form of personal development.

Yet merely to emphasize the high degree of adaptation, psychological synthesis, and resolution of past conflict in these young radicals is not enough. The conflicts of the past are still often visible in the inner and outer tensions of their present lives. In each one there is invariably some small or large unresolved conflict—the reaction against the self-abasement of a father, a heightened identification with the ambitions of a mother, or the only partially successful effort to overcome the sense of superiority, which is one side of specialness. To call this a conflict-free group would be an overstatement; it would be more exact to say that these young radicals have been unusually able to find or create lives and a sense of themselves which enable them to live out their inner strengths, minimize their inner weaknesses, and reconcile their ambivalences.

Furthermore, from a clinical perspective, there was much in these young radicals that does not conform to our view of "typical" development after adolescence. These young men and women, while they had unusually strong commitments, had unusually few specific plans; their statements about their own futures were invariably vague and hedged about with conditions: "If this were to happen, I would do that." "Unless such and such occurs, I will probably do this." Despite my frequent use of the term "identity" to characterize their emerging sense of self and role, identity formation in these young men and women was far less complete than for most of their contemporaries. They did not view themselves as "finished" with their own development; they exposed themselves to new experiences in often deliberate efforts to create the conditions for personal change; they had not "settled down" (nor did they plan to) like most of their age mates. And when asked how they visualized themselves twenty years from now, they invariably responded with, "It all depends, . . ." and turned to a discussion of the social and political future of America and the world. From a diagnostic perspective, then, one might view these young radicals as suffering from a "protracted adolescence," still immersed during their mid-twenties in an "unresolved identity crisis."

Yet before such judgments, with their pejorative connotations, are sealed, we should recall the special involvement of these young men and women with social and historical changes which have yet to occur. "Leaders" in a movement without leaders, "revolutionaries" who believe their revolution will take a generation or more to achieve, and, perhaps, most important, highly identified as people with the historical process they seek to affect, they have linked their emerging identities to an emerging movement for social change which may never occur. Given this fusion of inner identity with an ongoing historical process, it follows that their development *must* be more unfinished than that of their peers, who have joined their selfhoods to more conventional and circumscribed tasks. Thus it may be that the radical always "stretches" his development over a longer period than his adjusted contemporaries, and that his identity can be achieved, if ever, only with the sociopolitical transformations he seeks.

Drug Users: Heads and Seekers

To the general public, one of the most alarming aspects of the youthful opposition has been the increasingly widespread use of hallucinogenic drugs. In 1967 and 1968, I was involved in a series of efforts to bring more light and less heat to the subject of drug abuse. My research involved intensive work with students who were heavily involved in drug use, but who contradicted almost all of the popular stereotypes about the "marijuana addict" or the "acid head." Furthermore, I have always opposed that view of drug use—or, for that matter, of any social phenomenon— which sees it solely as the result of the depravity (or the "problems") of the individual and neglects the overarching social and historical context in which it occurs. And finally, the "problem" of drug use among students seems to me hardly separable from the even greater problem of the American system of drug control, which I consider irrational, arbitrary, counterproductive, and savage.

In this essay, written in 1968, I tried to consider both the variety of student drug users and the relationship of drug use to changing pressures and values in American society—specifically to the emergence of what I called a "counterculture" of experience among college students. My estimates of the incidence of drug use are now far too low: in the intervening three years, drug use has spread from the most "intellectual" colleges out through large portions of the remainder of American secondary and higher education. But this basic typology of drug users still seems to me useful, while the motivations behind different kinds of drug use still seem to me roughly those I described here. Most important of all is my insistence that the fact that drugs are used and the way they are used —whether self-destructively or creatively—depends not only upon the psychology of the individual, but upon the social and political climate.

STUDENTS who use drugs are usually treated by the mass media as an alien war upon the student body of America. A spate of articles in popular magazines, specials on television, discussions in state legislatures, and hearings by Congressmen have helped create an image of the young drug user that equates "drug abuse" with moral leprosy and quite possibly with membership in the Mafia. Few subjects arouse feelings as intense and irrational as does the topic of student drug use; in few areas is there greater tendency to distort, to perceive facts selectively, and to view with alarm. Few topics are treated with so much heat and so little light.

Despite growing public agitation, however, we have remarkably little factual information about drugs on campus. Most colleges have not conducted surveys of drug use—or if they have, they have preferred not to publicize the results. Most students who use drugs do not volunteer themselves as psychological research subjects, for the mere possession of marijuana is a felony under federal law. As a result, what is known about the sociology and psychology of student drug users comes largely from that small minority of students who are sufficiently disturbed to seek out professional help. Surrounded with illegality and the taint of moral depravity, drug use on campus remains a largely unexplored area.

Yet, enough information is now available from scattered studies to permit preliminary extrapolation to a coherent picture of the student drug abuser. In the discussion that follows, I will not be concerned with the psychopharmacology or physical effects of drug use. Rather I will speculate about the meaning of this phenomenon in a variety of overlapping contexts—psychological, social, educational, and historical.

To begin to understand youthful drug use, we must start from a series of more specific questions. Who uses drugs? How do we define "drug use"? What are some of the psychological factors involved in drug use? How can we explain the fact that drug use is very common in certain kinds of colleges, but virtually nonexistent in others? If, as widely claimed, student drug use is related in some way to the characteristics of modern American society, what is the nature of the relationship?

Rates and Places

The term "drug" covers a multitude of substances that affect human physiology and functioning. Virtually every American is a routine user of prescribed and unprescribed psychoactive drugs like aspirin, alcohol, sleeping pills, or stimulants, whose primary intended effect is to alter mood, feeling, or psychological states. Indeed, at the present time more than 70 per cent of all prescriptions written by doctors in the United States are for psychoactive compounds—for example, tranquilizers, painkillers, and antidepressants. If we include—as we must—ethyl alcohol, caffeine, and nicotine among drugs, then the American who has never "used" drugs is a statistical freak.

Although drug use itself is not novel in American society, what is novel is the use by middle-class college students of new types of drugs for the sole purpose of altering mood and state of consciousness. Most student drug use involves the hallucinogens—a family of nonaddictive drugs that includes not only marijuana (cannabis) but other hallucinogenic, psychedelic, or psychotomimetic drugs like LSD, DMT, STP, psilocybin, and mescaline (peyote). Some of these drugs have been widely used since the beginning of recorded history; others are recent discoveries. What is new, then, is their use by a growing segment of American college youth. To be sure, most definitions of "drug abuse" lump together distinct individuals for whom drug use and experimentation have very different meanings. But for a start, let us accept the prevailing definition of "drug user" as anyone who has *ever* tried any one of the hallucinogens, and examine the pattern of use that results from accepting this definition.

Student drug use, defined as use of the hallucinogens, is rapidly increasing. But the widely publicized estimates that one in seven, one in four, or one in two of the 7 million college students in America can be considered drug abusers are vastly exaggerated. Even at those few colleges where drug use is most prevalent, surveys arrive at estimates of between 5 and 75 per cent of the student body who have "ever used" any of the hallucinogens. These studies, furthermore, tend to have been conducted at select colleges like California at Berkeley, Wisconsin at Madison, Michigan at Ann Arbor, Harvard, Stanford, Yale, Cal Tech, Princeton, Antioch, Swarthmore, Wesleyan (Connecticut), Goddard, and Reed. Approximately 3 per cent of American college students attend these institutions. Among the remaining 97 per cent, it already seems clear that drug use is far rarer, and in many instances nonexistent. A recent Gallup Poll arrives at an estimate of 5 to 6 per cent of college youth who have "ever tried" any hallucinogenic drug. Thus, while student drug use constitutes an important phenomenon, it probably touches directly less than one in ten of the young Americans who attend institutions of higher education.

The public impression of astronomically high rates of drug use in American college youth stems in part from the great visibility of the colleges where drug use is most common. Students of college cultures have found it useful to categorize colleges according to the relative presence or absence of what they term an intellectual climate. The correlation between intellectual climate and rates of drug use is very close; that is, the highest rates are found at small, progressive, liberal arts colleges with a nonvocational orientation, a high faculty-student ratio, high student intellectual caliber as measured by college boards, close student-faculty relationships, and a great value placed on the academic independence, intellectual interests, and personal freedom of students. At perhaps a dozen or so such colleges it seems likely that the proportion of students who have ever tried marijuana or some other hallucinogen exceeds 50 per cent. But there are more than 2,200 other colleges in the country.

Farther down the list, with regard to both intellectual climate and drug use, are the private university colleges, like Harvard, Stanford, Yale, and Chicago, and the major state universities, like Michigan, Wisconsin, and California, with a tradition (at least within their Colleges of Arts and Sciences) of intellectual excellence and academic freedom. Included on this list, as well, should be the major technological institutions like Cal Tech and M.I.T., notable for the extremely high ability of students they recruit. At such colleges student drug-use rates of between 10 and 50 per cent will be found at present.* Still farther down on the list are other state universities with a lesser reputation for academic excellence and intellectual or personal freedom. Here one thinks of colleges like Ohio State and the University of Oregon. At such institutions rates of drug use probably vary between 5 and 20 per cent. At the bottom of the list in terms of both student drug use and intellectual climate are those colleges that together enroll the majority of American students—upgraded state teachers colleges, junior colleges, community colleges, normal schools, the smaller religious and denominational colleges, and most Catholic colleges and universities. On such campuses student drug use rarely exceeds 5 per cent. These are the colleges most notable for their vocational and practical orientation, the absence of primary student intellectual interests, and the presence of strong anti-intellectual student subcultures centered around technical training and/or social activities like sports and fraternities.

Nor are drug users randomly distributed *within* any one institution. At large universities that include a number of separate schools, drug use is concentrated in the College of Arts and Sciences, the Graduate School, and in the Schools of Drama, Music, Art, and Architecture. Rates of drug use are notably lower in such schools as Business Administration, Engineering, Agronomy, and Education. Furthermore, within any school or faculty drug users are most likely to be found in the most intellectual, humanistic, and "introspective" fields (for example, music, literature, drama, the arts, and psychology); they are likely to be less common in practical, applied, extroverted, and "harder" areas like engineering or economics. Indeed, there is evidence from one liberal arts college that students who use drugs are characterized by *higher* grades than those who do not. The demographic evidence suggests a strong relationship between intellectuality and drug use within the college population.

These inferences, however, are open to two different interpretations. On the one hand, we might conclude that colleges with an intellectual climate recruit students with special personal characteristics that make them more prone to experiment with drugs. The institution, according to this view, merely acts as a magnet for young men and women who are

---

* Regional differences are also important: drug use is higher on the West Coast than on the East Coast. Also, proximity to a metropolitan center probably increases drug use, other things being equal.

likely to smoke pot no matter where they go to college. On the other hand, it could be argued that the climate and culture of some colleges actively push students toward drug use regardless of their personal characteristics. If a student attends a college where drugs are readily available and "everyone" is using them, he is more likely to do so himself. Similarly, certain college pressures (for example, relentless pressure for grades) or certain administrative practices (for example, respect for student autonomy) may also increase the likelihood of student drug use. In practice, both these interpretations seem correct: some colleges attract large numbers of potential drug users and then expose them to a climate in which using drugs becomes even more probable. To understand this interaction, we must consider types of drug users, motivations for drug use, and some of the pressures on college students today.

Tasters, Seekers, and Heads

A "drug abuser" is often defined as anyone who has ever experimented with any of the hallucinogens—who has ever inhaled marijuana, ever ingested any other hallucinogenic drug—or, in some instances, who has ever taken a barbiturate to get to sleep or an amphetamine (Benzedrine, Dexedrine) before an examination. If we limit ourselves to the hallucinogens, however, we usually find that up to half of the students listed as users turn out to have used drugs no more than three times, and to have no plans to continue. To call such students drug abusers or even users is misleading. It is like applying the epithet "alcoholic" or "drinker" to the college girl who once tasted a sip of beer but didn't like it, or labeling as a "smoker" the adult who at the age of twelve smoked a cigarette behind the barn but was sick and never smoked again. Probably the single largest group called drug abusers are in reality *tasters*. Such individuals, though often included in comments on drug abuse, have no place in a discussion of why students use drugs, since these particular students no longer use them.

If we eliminate the tasters from the ranks of student drug users, we are left with a contingent of probably less than 5 per cent of the college population. These students have used drugs (usually marijuana) a number of times, and they tell us that they "plan" to continue their experimentation. But even within this group of continuing users there are important distinctions to be made. The largest single group of actual drug users are students who have used drugs a relatively small number of times (for example, have smoked pot less than fifteen times) and who do not use them regularly (for example, not every day or weekend). Such a pattern of use generally indicates that, despite willingness to continue drug experimentation, the individual has in no way organized his life around it. For these occasional users drug use is generally a part of a more general pattern of experimentation and search for relevance both within and without the college experience—it is one aspect of a more encompassing effort to find meaning in life. Such students can be termed *seekers*, in that they seek in drug use some way of intensifying experience, expanding awareness, breaking out of deadness and flatness, or overcoming depression.

Finally, there is a relatively small but highly visible group of students who have made drug use a central focus of college life. Such students use drugs often and regularly—for example, every weekend—and they often experiment with a variety of different drugs. For such young men and women drug use is not just an intermittent assist in the pursuit of meaning, but a part of a more general "turned-on" ideology and a membership card to one of the collegiate versions of the hippie subculture. Such students are generally called *heads* (pot heads or acid heads) by their contemporaries; and they are by far the most knowledgeable about the effects, side effects, interactions, and meanings of the drugs available to students today.

But even among heads, drug use does not invariably constitute the deeply psychopathological and self-destructive phenomenon it is sometimes said invariably to be. Many such students have sufficient strength of character (and perhaps of physiology) to endure regular experimentation with marijuana (and even with more powerful hallucinogens or amphetamines) without suffering any enduring personal disorganization. Most students who use marijuana routinely do *not* experience the ominous personal deterioration, the "bad trips," or the loss of motivation that is sometimes thought to accompany even casual drug experimentation. To be sure, one of the intended effects of drug use is to produce a *transient* alteration of experience and consciousness; and to those who view this alteration from the outside, it may appear deplorable. Yet a majority of students who have used the hallucinogens report that the experience was enlightening, enjoyable, or meaningful. Most students who use marijuana regularly, and many of those who use the more powerful hallucinogens, never appear in clinics or consulting rooms (much less psychiatric hospitals). They "recover" from the drug experience, not obviously the worse for the wear, sometimes proclaiming loudly that they have gained a profound and valuable (if usually ineffable) insight into their own natures or that of the world. Judged by such criteria of mental health as the ability to work, to love, and to play, such individuals do not seem especially less "mentally healthy" than before their drug experiences.

A tiny but highly publicized group of heads, however, suffers serious ill effects from even single experiences with the hallucinogens. Students with serious pre-existing psychopathology are most vulnerable. And these same students seem most likely to experiment with drugs under conditions that even experienced drug users consider adverse—intense depression, personal isolation, and unpleasant surroundings. In extremely rare instances marijuana has been said to produce panic states or transient psychotic reactions, and similar reactions to LSD have been reported more often. Perhaps more important than the highly dramatic but usually reversible drug psychosis is the danger of lapsing into some relatively enduring form of personal disorganization—most commonly, a life style that involves a virtually total and apparently self-destructive immersion in a drug-using hippie subculture.

Yet even here short-term changes and long-range effects need to be distinguished. There are clearly some individuals who "regress" into a drug-using subculture for a period of months and even years, but who eventually re-emerge into a productive relationship with their fellow man and with society itself. "Dropping out" into the hippie world seems to be defined, for growing numbers of students, as a way of testing the psychological and social limits of the existing society, often as a preparation for returning to the world of action and commitment. To be sure, most Americans believe that there are better ways of testing the relationship of self to society than by entering the hippie subculture for two years. But our evaluation of the "ominous" implications of student drug use must be tempered by an awareness that many of those who drop out into the drug-using world eventually slide back into the mainstream. One of the disadvantages of the opprobrium that attends drug use is that labeling drug users "felons" or irredeemable "addicts" may in fact make it virtually impossible for them to return to a productive role in society.

The Question of Motives

Drug use is no different from any other form of human behavior, in that a great variety of distinct motives can co-operate to produce it. The particular weight of each of these motives and the way they are combined differs in each individual. Furthermore, drug use is affected not only by motives and forces *within* the individual, but by what is happening *outside* of him in his interpersonal environment, and in the wider social and political world. Thus, any effort to delineate types of motivations that enter into drug use is bound to be an oversimplification. For example, there are many individuals who share common characteristics with drug users but who do not use drugs, because drugs are not available on their particular campus. Similarly, there are individuals who have little in common with other drug users, but who nonetheless use drugs.

With these important qualifications, at least two of the more common patterns of motivation in student drug users can be defined. Consider first the seekers. Occasional but continuing drug users are rarely part of the hippie subculture, but such students do tend to have certain common characteristics. They are generally better-than-average students; they are intellectual and antivocational in their approach to their educations; and they are likely to be uncertain as to their future career plans. Sociologically, they tend to come from upper-middle-class professional and business families. Psychologically, such students are usually intense, introspective, and genuinely involved in their academic work, from which they hope to find "solutions" to the problems of life and society. (Often, however, they are disappointed in this hope.) As individuals, they usually have a great capacity for hard work. They are rarely "lazy" or indolent; and, when called upon, they can be orderly, regular, and highly organized. They also find it relatively easy to separate ideas from feelings, a fact that helps explain their high grades. They are strongly opposed to the war in Southeast Asia, do not express anger readily, and are often extremely idealistic.

But despite considerable academic success and the prospects of a good graduate school (possibly with a Woodrow Wilson Fellowship thrown in), such students are less seekers after grades or professional expertise than seekers after truth. They are extremely open to the contradictory crosscurrents of American culture; they read widely, be it in the theater of the absurd, modern existentialist literature, or the writings of the New Left. They are not in any systematic way alienated from American society, but they have not really made their minds up whether it is worth joining, either. Often, their own life styles and the exertions required to do well in a demanding college make such students feel "out of touch" with themselves. Although to an outside observer they usually appear more thoughtful and "in touch" than their classmates in the School of Engineering or Business Administration, they do not consider themselves to be sentient at all. On the contrary, they are continually struggling to experience the world more intensely, to make themselves capable of greater intimacy and love, to find some "rock bottom," some "gut level," from which they can sally forth to social and interpersonal commitments. Such students characteristically make enormously high demands upon themselves, upon experience, and upon life; contrasted with their demands, their current experience often seems barren, flat, and dull.

Marijuana and the more powerful hallucinogens fit very neatly with the search for experience for such students. On the one hand, they promise a new kind of experience to a young man or woman who is highly experimental. On the other hand, they promise intensity, heightened sentience, intensified artistic perceptiveness, and perhaps even self-understanding. Self-understanding is, of course, a prime goal for such individuals; for they are far more inclined to blame themselves than others for the inadequacies of their lives, and they often deliberately seek through self-analysis to change their personalities.

In students of this type, beginning or increasing drug use is often associated with feelings of flatness, boredom, stagnation, and depression. It is surprising how often drug users mention a major loss, depression, or feeling of emptiness in the period preceding intensified drug use. The loss may be a breakup with a girl friend, the realization that one's parents are even more fallible than one had previously known, the blow to intellectual self-esteem that almost invariably accompanies the first midterm grades in the freshman year at a selective college, or the growing sense of confusion and purposelessness that follows abandoning previously cherished vocational goals or religious values. Under such circumstances, if there is pot around, the likelihood of trying it (and continuing to use it) is increased.

The head is in many respects different from the seeker. Drug use occupies a more central place in the head's life and is almost always accompanied by disengagement from ordinary social expectations, by intense and often morbid self-exploration, and by a "turned-on" ideology profoundly hostile to the careerist, materialistic, and success-oriented goals of middle-class American society. Almost invariably, then, the head is a member of a drug-using subculture in which he finds an identity that enables him to drop temporarily out of the Establishment America from which he comes and toward which he was headed. For most young men and women, of course, membership in the hippie subculture lasts a summer, a term, a year, or possibly longer, but is followed by a gradual re-entry into the system. One study of drug-using college dropouts finds that they stay in the hippie world an average of a year and a half. After this most return to their families in the suburbs (average parental income: $15,000 a year) and usually to the highly academic colleges from which they dropped out. Only those with unmistakable artistic talent and those with major psychiatric problems (or both) are likely to remain longer.

Unlike most seekers, heads are genuinely alienated from American society. Their defining characteristic is their generalized rejection of prevalent American values, which they criticize largely on cultural and humanistic grounds. American society is trashy, cheap, and commercial; it "dehumanizes" its members; its values of success, materialism, monetary accomplishment, and achievement undercut more important spiritual values. Such students rarely stay involved for long in the political and social causes that agitate many of their activist classmates. For alienated students the basic societal problem is not so much political as aesthetic. Rejecting middle-class values, heads repudiate as well those conventional values and rules that deem experimentation with drugs illicit. For heads the goal is to find a way out of the "air-conditioned nightmare" of American society. What matters is the interior world, and, in the exploration of that world, drugs play a major role.

A second characteristic of many heads is a more or less intense feeling of estrangement from their own experience. Such students are highly aware of the masks, façades, and defenses people erect to protect themselves; they are critical of the social games and role-playing they see around them. They object to these games not only in others, but even more strongly in themselves. As a result, they feel compelled to root out any "defense" that might prevent awareness of inner life; self-deception, lack of self-awareness, or "phoniness" are cardinal sins. They have, moreover, a conscious ethic of love, expressed in a continual struggle for "meaningful relationships"—direct, honest, and open encounters with others. This ethic is sincerely felt, but it is often difficult for the alienated to achieve in practice. Thus, perhaps the deepest guilts in such individuals spring from their internal impediments to genuineness, directness, and open communication with others. As one student said, "For me, sin equals hang-up."

Despite their efforts to make contact with their "real selves" and to have "meaningful relationships" with others, alienated students often feel unusually separated from both self and others. They experience themselves as separated from others by a gray opaque filter, by invisible screens and curtains, by protective shells and crusts that prevent them from the fullness of experience. They recriminate themselves for their lack of expressiveness, spontaneity, and contact. One such student described human relations as being like people trying to touch each other through airtight space suits. Another talked of a wax that was poured over his experience, preventing him from rapport with the world. Possessed of an unusually strong desire for intense experience, but also unusually full of feelings of estrangement, such students find drugs that promise to heighten experience a tempting way out of the shell.

A third frequent characteristic of alienated students is a fantasy of fusion and merger, which contrasts sharply with their current feelings of estrangement. Many have a semiconscious concept of almost mystical union with nature, with their own inner lives, or with other people—of communication that requires no words, of the kind of oneness with nature, people, or the universe that has always characterized intense religious experience. For a student with unusual impatience with the boundaries that separate the self from the not-self, the powerful hallucinogens are especially attractive, for they can profoundly alter the boundaries of body and self. This change in boundaries is by no means always pleasant, and one of the most common sources of panic during drug experiences is the feeling of being "trapped" in an isolated, barricaded subjectivity. But at other times the hallucinogens *do* produce feelings of being in unusually direct contact, even fusion, with others.

On several grounds, then, the alienated student is strongly attracted by drugs and by the hippie world. Arguments against drug use based on traditional American values carry little weight for him; on the contrary, he takes great pleasure in violating these "middle-class" norms. His feelings of estrangement from his own experience lead him to attempt to break through the boundaries, shells, walls, filters, and barriers that separate him from the world. And his fantasy of fusion disposes him to seek out chemical instruments to increase his "oneness" with others. For a student who is young, alienated, and anticonventional, drug use is primarily a way of searching for meaning via the chemical intensification of personal experience.

In a broader developmental context, too, immersion in the drug-using hippie subculture is generally a part of a phase of disengagement from American society. Confronted with a society whose rules and values he profoundly distrusts, the head seeks in the counterculture of hippiedom a respite, a moratorium, or an escape from pressures and demands he does not want to confront. Yet merely to note the important element of withdrawal in the hippie's use of drugs may be to ignore the more important developmental meaning of drug use for the hippie. However ill-advised society may consider his choice of methods, the hippie is often unconsciously searching for a way to engage himself with himself and with others. And however regressive or self-destructive it may appear to some for a young man to drop out of American society, the hippie subculture often proves a rest-and-recovery area, or even a staging area, from which unusually sensitive, talented, and/or disturbed individuals take stock of themselves, explore their inner lives and their relationships with a small group of other people, and sometimes *return* to the established society. It seems likely that most hippies will follow this path.

There are, however, a few heads for whom drug use is both a symptom of and a trigger for serious psychopathology. In some cases drug use clearly accelerates a downhill course upon which the individual is already embarked; in other cases an overwhelmingly bad trip may topple a student whose previous equilibrium was fragile. Thus, drug use may really be a contributing factor to a picture of psychopathology. Indeed, some of those who are most compulsively drawn to chronic drug use are the same people who can least tolerate it. Already confused and precarious, they are unable to bear the induced alterations of consciousness produced by the hallucinogens and may move steadily or suddenly downhill.

The Pressure for Academic Performance

Some of the association between type of college and rate of drug use clearly results from the fact that highly "intellectual" colleges selectively attract students with a particular outlook and psychology. This process of attraction is complex. Admission policies that preferentially admit applicants with "serious intellectual interests" promote the process of selective recruitment. But even at colleges that admit almost all applicants, the power of the college image alone suffices to channel into relatively few colleges a great many students with psychological characteristics that incline them to experiment with drugs. The image of the intellectual college acts as a magnet for students like the seeker and the head. For "intellectual" or "alienated" high school students, certain colleges promise an in-gathering of kindred spirits. Conversely, the less intellectual, unalienated, unintrospective, and nonexperimental student is generally attracted to less "intellectual" colleges.

But psychological factors will take us only part way to understanding student drug use. Knowing what college a student attends is often a more accurate index of whether he has used drugs than is exploring his conscious and unconscious motives. The probability of drug use is a product of an interaction of individual psychology, institutional climate, and broader social setting. To understand what helps create a climate of opinion that is favorable to drug experimentation, we must examine the pressures that impinge upon students at intellectual colleges.

It is noteworthy that colleges where drug use is most common are usually "high-pressure" colleges. Typically, a great majority of undergraduates are preparing themselves for professional careers that require advanced graduate training: usually more than 75 per cent of graduates plan to continue their educations after the B.A. Furthermore, the magnetism of the college image and the fine screen of the admissions office almost always yield entering freshmen who have extremely high test scores and records of outstanding academic achievement in secondary school. To be sure, many of the most "intellectual" colleges make systematic efforts to mitigate these pressures by down-playing grades, by work-study programs, and so on. But despite the efforts of the college, students themselves are likely to *feel* pressured, both by their own desire to excel intellectually, and by the entrance requirements of graduate schools. And the congregation within such "intellectual" colleges of large numbers of intellectually able, competitive students helps generate an atmosphere that makes intense intellectual interests, outstanding academic performance, and approval by faculty, scholarship boards, etc., an important standard of personal worth and community recognition.

As a result, the more intellectual colleges are noteworthy for their *lack* of emphasis on the traditional American college pastimes of fun, fraternities, and football. "Play" and social life are generally downgraded. Students and faculty members agree that the purpose of college is to get a liberal education, not to improve one's social skills, not to make influential friends for later life, and not to enjoy oneself in a frivolous way. Intellectual commitment and cognitive talent are highly rewarded, while these colleges frown on "collegiate" pranks and "childish" displays of adolescent high spirits. What is valued at such colleges (and they increasingly set the tone for American higher education at large) is the ability to delay, postpone, and defer immediate gratification in the interest of acquiring a liberal education. "Serious" interests—be they intellectual, artistic, or political—are enjoined by a united student-faculty culture.

Such "elite" colleges present relatively few countervailing pressures to become more relaxed, joyous, interpersonally skilled, feeling, courageous, or physically expressive. Throughout the "intellectual" sector of American higher education, the most intense pressures are highly cognitive, narrowly academic, and often quantitative. The tangible rewards of American higher education—scholarships, admission to "good" graduate schools, remunerative fellowships, and community acclaim—go for a rather narrow kind of cognitive functioning that leads to writing good final examinations, constructing good term papers, being good at multiple-choice tests, and excelling on Graduate Record Examinations. Most of the students who attend these colleges are headed toward a professional world that requires the same kind of abstractive intelligence. Thus, it is the outstanding graduates of such colleges who go on to equally outstanding graduate schools, and eventually to outstanding appointments in outstanding hospitals, scientific laboratories, business corporations, and university faculties.

Over the past two decades the movement toward "intellectuality" in American colleges has been steady and marked. Throughout American higher education, cognitive, intellectual, and preprofessional outlooks are on the rise, while such traditional American student pastimes as panty raids, popularity contests, campus politics, and fraternity rushing are on a steady decline. The highly intellectual preprofessional student has less time and less motivation for the college pranks of his parents' generation. To survive and prosper in tomorrow's technological world, he must work terribly hard in college in order to be "really good in his field." He must perform well academically, and without "mistakes" that would lower his grade average. He must postpone a whole gamut of emotional satisfactions until he is older. A bad course, a bad year, or even taking a year off may mean not getting into graduate school or—worse—getting drafted.

There is much to be said for these pressures for intellectual performance, just as there is much that is admirable about those who possess narrowly academic skills. Today's college students at selective institutions are an unusually serious, well-informed, honest, and morally concerned group. While they scorn the round of fun and frivolity that dominated the lives of previous college generations, they in fact care deeply about each other, and a growing number are intensely concerned with the social and political future of their world. Yet, in describing the self-generated and educationally generated pressures upon them, I have used the word "performance" advisedly. "Performance" suggests alien activity, acting on a stage in order to impress others, a role played for the benefit of the audience. And to growing numbers of such students, intellectual performance is increasingly seen as a kind of role-playing of the worst sort. Indeed, one source of the growing demand for "relevance" and "student power" is this widely shared feeling that much academic and intellectual activity is somehow "alien" to the "real" interests and concerns of the student.

And it is indeed true that although the systematic quest for cognitive competence and academic performance occupies most of the time and effort of the preprofessional student at today's selective colleges, this quest does little to inform students about life's purposes and joys. One of the peculiar characteristics of academic performance is that even when performance is impeccable, most of the other "really important" questions remain unanswered: What is life all about? What really matters? What do I stand for? Why do I bother? How much do I stand for? What is relevant, meaningful, and important? What is meaningless, valueless, and false? For many students, then, the pursuit of academic competence must be supplemented by a more private, less academic, noncurricular quest for the meaning of life. When large numbers of students perceive their academic efforts as irrelevant to the really important "existential" and "ultimate" questions, then the way is open for a more private search for meaning, significance, and relevance. Together, they have begun to create an informal shared culture that counters and complements the academic professionalism of elite American colleges.

The Experiential Counterculture

The "better" American colleges rarely attempt to provide students with neatly packaged answers to their existential questions. To be sure, the most demanding colleges make systematic efforts to provoke undergraduates to challenge previous beliefs and to abandon unexamined dogmas. But they expect students to arrive at individual solutions to the riddles of life, all the while occupying themselves with getting good grades and getting ahead in the academic world. The college's message is often highly paradoxical: "Ruthlessly discard previous convictions and values; don't look to us for answers; most of your questions are sophomoric, in any case."

To the most sophisticated undergraduates, the traditional avenues to significance seem irrelevant, exhausted, insincere, or superficial. Traditional religious faith and the great political ideologies arouse relatively little interest among today's determinedly anti-ideological undergraduates. Nor does success within the "American way of life" constitute an answer to life's riddles for most students. There was a day when the quest for campus popularity seemed to many undergraduates but a reflection of a broader life philosophy of making friends, influencing people, and developing social skills. But today "popularity" has become a dirty word. Nor does "getting ahead in the world" provide an answer for intellectual students, most of whom start out already ahead in the world—the children of well-educated and well-situated middle-class parents. For these students, the old American dream of giving one's children "a better chance" makes little sense: they find it pointless to struggle for greater affluence when they already have more than enough. They are more worried about how to live with what they already have.

As the traditional avenues to meaning have dried up, and as academic performance itself seems increasingly irrelevant to the major existential concerns of students, a new informal student subculture has begun to emerge. Although not opposed to the life of the mind, this subculture is antiacademic. Although students who participate in it are publicly headed for professional careers, they privately focus on experience in the present rather than on long-range goals. Theirs is an informal *experiential counterculture*, which complements the formal culture of the academically oriented college. Central to this counterculture is a focus on the present—on today, on the here and now. At one level intellectual college students are required to defer enjoyment for a distant future in their academic and preprofessional work. But, informally, they emphasize immediate pleasure and experience. While society at large expects from them a reverence for the traditions of the past and a respect for traditional institutions, they stress in their own subcultures activity and receptivity in the present. Such future-oriented qualities as control, planning, waiting, saving, and postponing are little honored in the student subculture; nor are past-oriented qualities like revering, recalling, remembering, and respecting much emphasized. In contrast, the experiential subculture stresses genuineness, adventure, spontaneity, sentience, and experimentation. Since the past is seen as irrelevant (or "exhausted"), and since the future seems profoundly uncertain, the real meaning of life must be found within present experience—even as one worries about the Graduate Record Examinations.

The experiential counterculture has many variants, at least some of which are visible on almost every major American campus. One variant is what is sometimes called "student existentialism." At the more sophisticated campuses this outlook is manifest in an intense interest in existential writers, in the theater of the absurd, and in philosophers and psychologists who stress "existential" concepts. But even at less sophisticated colleges a similar focus is apparent in student emphasis on simple human commitments as contrasted with absolute values, in a "situation ethic" that questions the possibility of traditional long-range value commitments, and by a pervasively high estimation of sincerity, authenticity, and directness. Student existentialism is humanistic rather than religious, and its most immediate goals are love, immediacy, empathy, "encounter" with one's fellow man. Thus, in the counterculture what matters most is interpersonal honesty, "really being yourself," and a special kind of open and disinterested genuineness. What is most *un*acceptable is fraudulence, exploitation, "role-playing," artificiality, hypocrisy, and "playing games."

Along with the focus on the present and on "existential" values goes a very great tolerance for experimentation. Youth is increasingly defined (by youth itself) as a time for exploration, trial and error, and for deliberate efforts to enlarge, change, or expand personality. Experimentation in the interest of deliberate self-change is seen as essential to pursuit of meaning. Convinced that meaning is not found but created, members of the counterculture consider their own personalities the prime vehicles for the creation of significance. And since significance emerges from the self, it is only by transforming the self that significance can be achieved. In a kind of deliberate, self-conscious, and intentional identity-formation, apparently unconnected activities and experiences find their rationale. Self-exploration, psychotherapy, sexual experimentation, travel, "encounter groups," a reverence for nature, and "sensitivity training" are tools in the pursuit of meaning—along with drug use. Participation in this counterculture thus provides a powerful support for efforts to explore oneself, to intensify relationships with other people, to change the quality and content of consciousness. It provides a sanctioning context for drug use as one of the pathways of changing the self so as to create meaning in the world.

Drugs as a Commentary on Society

It is widely feared that student drug use is a commentary upon American society. Words like degeneracy, addiction, thrill-seeking, and irresponsibility are eventually introduced into most popular discussions of student drug use. So, too, student drug use is said to be related to the excessive permissiveness of parents, to the laxness of adult standards, to breaches in law enforcement, to disrespect for law and order, and to an impending breakdown of our social fabric.

Although these particular interpretations of the social implications of drug use are incorrect, drug use *is* importantly influenced by social, political, and historical factors. Those students who lust after significance or reject the prevalent values of American society are in fact reacting to and within a societal context. The sense of being locked off and enclosed in an impermeable shell is related not only to individual psychological states like depression, but to broader cultural phenomena. And the fact that a considerable number of the most able students have become convinced that significance and relevant experience are largely to be found within their own skulls is indirectly related to their perception of the other possibilities for fulfillment in the social and political world. In a variety of ways, then, student drug use is a commentary on American society, although a different kind of commentary than most discussions of youthful "thrill-seeking" would lead us to believe.

To single out a small number of social changes as especially relevant to understanding student drug use is to be arbitrary. A variety of factors, including rapid social change, the unprecedented possibilities for total destruction in the modern world, the prevalence of violence both domestic and international, the high degree of specialization and bureaucratization of American life, and a host of others are relevant to creating the context of values and expectations within which drug use has become increasingly legitimate. But of all the factors that could be discussed, three seem particularly relevant: first, the effect of modern communications and transportation in producing an overwhelming inundation of experience, which I will term *stimulus flooding;* second, the effect of *automatic affluence* in changing the values and outlooks of the young; third, the importance of recent social and historical events in producing a kind of *social and political disenchantment* that leads many students to seek salvation through withdrawal and inner life rather than through engagement and societal involvement.

Stimulus flooding and psychological numbing. Every society subjects its members to pressures and demands that they simply take for granted. Such pressures are woven into the fabric of social existence, are assumed to be a natural part of life, and become the object of automatic accommodation. These accommodations are rarely examined, yet they may profoundly alter the quality of human experience. Such is the case with the quantity, variety, and intensity of external stimulation, imagery and excitation to which most Americans are subjected. As Robert J. Lifton has pointed out, modern man in advanced societies is subjected to a flood of unpredictable stimulation of the most varied kinds; by newspapers, television, radio, and rapid travel, he continually exposes himself to novel and unanticipatable experience. This stimulus inundation, in turn, produces a self-protective reaction which, following Lifton, we can term psychic numbing.

Most individuals in most societies have at some point in their lives had the experience of being so overcome by external stimulation and internal feelings that they gradually find themselves growing numb and unfeeling. Medical students commonly report that after their first, often intense reactions to the cadaver, they simply "stop feeling anything" with regard to the object of their dissection. And we have all had the experience of listening to so much good music, seeing so many fine paintings, being so overwhelmed by excellent cooking, that we find ourselves simply unable to respond further. Similarly, at moments of extreme psychic pain and anguish, most individuals "go numb," no longer perceiving the full implications of a catastrophic situation or no longer experiencing the full range of their own feelings. This lowered responsiveness, this psychological numbing, seems causally related to the variety, persistence, and intensity of stimulation and emotion.

Most Americans have had the experience of returning to urban life from a calm and pastoral setting. Initially, we respond by being virtually deluged with the clamor of people, sights, sounds, images, and colors that demand our attention and response. The beauty and the ugliness of the landscape continually strike us; each of the millions of faces in our great cities has written on it the tragicomic record of a unique life history; each sound evokes a resonant chord within us. Such periods, however, tend to be transient and fleeting; and they usually give way to a sense of numbness, of nonresponsiveness, and of profound inattention to the very stimuli that earlier evoked so much in us. We settle in; we do not notice any more.

This psychological numbing operates at a great variety of levels for modern man. Our experience, from childhood onward, with the constantly flickering images and sounds of television, films, radio, newspapers, paperbacks, neon signs, advertisements, and sound trucks, numbs us to the sights and sounds of our civilization. Our continual exposure to a vast variety of ideologies, value systems, philosophies, political creeds, superstitions, religions, and faiths numbs us to the unique claims to validity and the special spiritual and intellectual values of each one: we move among values and ideologies as in a two-dimensional landscape. Similarly, the availability to us in novels, films, television, theater, and opera of moments of high passion, tragedy, joy, exaltation, and sadness often ends by numbing us to our own feelings and the feelings of others.

Modern men thus confront the difficult problem of keeping "stimulation" from without to a manageable level, while also protecting themselves against being overwhelmed by their own inner responses to the stimuli from the outer world. Defenses or barriers against both external and internal stimulation are, of course, essential in order for us to preserve our intactness and integrity as personalities. From earliest childhood, children develop thresholds of responsiveness and barriers against stimulation in order to protect themselves against being overwhelmed by inner or outer excitement. Similarly, in adulthood, comparable barriers, thresholds, and defenses are necessary, especially when we find ourselves in situations of intense stimulation.

A problem arises, however, if the barriers we erect to protect ourselves from the clamors of the inner and outer world prove harder and less permeable than we had originally wanted. In at least a minority of Americans the normal capacity to defend oneself against undue stimulation and inner excitation is exaggerated and automatized, so that it not only protects but walls off the individual from inner and outer experience. In such individuals there develops an acute sense of being trapped in their own shells, unable to break through their defenses to make "contact" with experience or with other people, a sense of being excessively armored, separated from their own activities as by an invisible screen, estranged from their own feelings and from potentially emotion-arousing experiences in the world. Most of us have had some inkling of this feeling of inner deadness and outer flatness, especially in times of great fatigue, letdown, or depression. The world seems cold and two-dimensional; food and life have lost their savor; our activities are merely "going through the motions," our experiences lack vividness, three-dimensionality, and intensity. Above all, we feel trapped or shut in our own subjectivity.

The continual flooding of stimulation to which modern men are subjected is thus related not only to the psychological conditions and institutional pressures that help create the feelings of numbness, but, indirectly, to the nature of perception and experience in an advanced technological society. One problem every modern American faces is how to avoid becoming entrapped in the protective shell he must construct to defend himself against being overwhelmed by stimulation. And the use of drugs, especially in the context of the experiential counterculture, becomes more attractive to youth precisely because the drugs preferred by students often have the effect of dissipating, blurring, or breaking down the boundaries of individual selfhood and personality.

Automatic affluence. No society in world history has ever provided its citizens with the automatic abundance that our society provides to a majority of Americans. In over ten years of interviewing students from middle-class and upper-middle-class backgrounds, I have yet to find one who was worried about finding a job and have met relatively few who were worried about finding a *good* job. Whatever their levels of aspiration, today's advantaged youth rarely think in terms of getting ahead in the world, acquiring increasing status, or struggling to "succeed." These goals, both relevant and important to their parents (products of the 1920's and the Great Depression), are largely irrelevant to today's youth. Like youth in every era, they turn from the successes of the past to the problems of the present and future. Thus, paradoxically, although they live in a society more affluent than any before it, they are far more outraged at poverty, injustice, inequality, exploitation, and cruelty than were their parents, who lived in a more impoverished society. Indeed, one of the central demands of today's politically active youth is that everyone have the benefits which they themselves have always taken for granted.

One of the undeniable benefits of affluence is that it brings increased opportunities for enjoyment and leisure and removes the need to devote oneself to a life of unrelenting toil in order to prosper. Affluence permits a de-emphasis of hard work, self-control, and renunciation, and makes possible the development of new cultures of leisure. As work, success, and achievement decline in relative importance, new values begin to replace them, and new patterns of consumption begin to reflect these new values. As "getting ahead in the world" no longer suffices to define the meaning of life, today's advantaged students turn increasingly to explore *other* meanings of life.

Two rather different alternatives have so far been tried. The first is the solution of the political activist, who remains primarily concerned with the fact that his own affluence and freedom have not been extended to all. Within America, his concern is with the poor, the deprived, the excluded, and the disadvantaged. Abroad, he focuses on the many failures of American foreign policy, failures that in his eyes involve a catastrophic gap between the values of a democratic society and the foreign policies that purportedly implement them. The activist would have us support rather than oppose movements of national liberation, and use our affluence not in military engagements but in programs of assistance to the developing nations. The activist is most likely to accept the traditional values of American society, especially those emphasizing justice, equality, opportunity, and freedom, and to insist that these values be more thoroughly practiced.

The second response to the question "What lies beyond affluence?" while not incompatible with the first, looks in a different area for an answer. This second response turns to a more fundamental critique of the premises and assumptions upon which technological America has been based. Instead of equality, it champions diversity; instead of pressing for the extension of affluence, it questions the meaning of affluence. Associated with a long tradition of romantic criticism of industrial and post-industrial society, this response points to the price of affluence—dehumanization, professionalization, bureaucracy, a loss of power over society, the absence of a sense of small scale, and the erosion of traditional community. For the romantic critic of American society, fulfillment, awareness and personal wholeness are more important than abundance and achievement. The life of the affluent middle class in America is seen as empty, spiritually impoverished, driven, and neurotic; the vaguely defined alternative involves expressiveness, self-knowledge, intense involvement with a small group of others, the fulfillment of nonmaterial artistic, spiritual, and psychological needs. "Self-actualization" is the goal; "Let each man do his thing" is the motto.

Automatic affluence, then, inevitably means that many of those who experience abundance as routine attempt to create goals beyond affluence.

In so far as the individual's main effort is to extend affluence, he is relatively immune to the appeals of the experiential, drug-using world, for his energies are oriented toward changing the world rather than himself. But in so far as his primary focus is antitechnological—upon self-fulfillment, personal change, and spiritual or humanistic fulfillment—this focus is highly consistent with the use of drugs. For drug use among college students is closely related to the effort to change oneself, to become more creative, to be more expressive, more emotionally open, and more genuinely in contact with the world. And the use of drugs is associated with a questioning or rejection of the traditional success ethic of American life, and with a search for new styles of living more oriented to leisure, to intimate personal relationships, and to spiritual expression. Thus, affluence indirectly produces a mood among some of its recipients that makes them receptive to drug use and other forms of personal experimentation.

Sociopolitical disenchantment. In juxtaposing two answers to the quest for meaning beyond abundance, I have implied a certain tension between them. It is not accidental that full-time and committed political activists are rarely intensive drug users; it is also important that the full-time denizens of the drug-using hippie subculture are rarely capable of sustained political activity. Sustained engagement in an effort to change the world is rarely compatible with the kind of self-absorption and inwardness that results from intensive and regular drug use; conversely, however strongly the committed drug user may feel about the inequities of American society, his primary efforts are usually directed toward self-change, rather than changing the world around him. Although some individuals alternate at different times in their lives between activism and alienation, it is very difficult to be an active social reformer and a head at the same time.

This argument suggests that disenchantment with the possibilities of meaningful social action is related to the development of an outlook conducive to drug use. To trace student drug use directly to such factors as racial injustices or the war in Vietnam would, of course, be a major oversimplification. But disenchantment with meaningful and honorable political activity creates a general climate of opinion that *is,* in turn, favorable to drug use. Specifically, the change in student attitudes toward political life and social reform since the assassination of President Kennedy seems importantly connected to the rise of drug use.

The influence of Kennedy upon the attitudes of youth is often exaggerated or stated in an oversimplified way. Many of the young, of course, disliked Kennedy, as did many of their parents. Furthermore, most of those who admired Kennedy personally had no intention whatsoever of entering public life. Kennedy's impact on the attitudes of youth was indirect: he and the group around him symbolized the conviction that it was possible for young, idealistic, and intelligent men and women to enter the political world and to "make a difference." Such Kennedy ventures as the Peace Corps further provided an outlet—and more importantly a symbol —for the idealistic energies of activist youth. Although Kennedy himself in fact rarely listened to the advice of students, such symbolic Kennedy acts as pots of coffee for peace marchers in front of the White House indicated at least an awareness of the opinion of the political young.

The image of political life conveyed by the Johnson Administration, especially from 1966 to late 1968, was vastly different. Not only have older views of politics as a form of horse trading, "compromising," and "wheeling and dealing" been reinstated, but large numbers of American college students have come to associate political involvement with gross immorality and even with genocide. In this context such revelations as that of covert C.I.A. funding of liberal student organizations like the National Students Association have the effect of convincing many intelligent and idealistic youth that politics—and, by extension, efforts to work to change the system from within—are dishonorable or pointless occupations.

The demise of the Civil Rights Movement and the collapse of the War on Poverty has also helped change the climate of opinion about political reform. In the early 1960's, the Civil Rights Movement was the chief catalyst for the rising tide of student political involvement. Sit-ins, Freedom Rides, the work of SNCC and other groups in the Deep South helped convince students that their efforts at social change would be honored, recognized, and responded to by the society at large. Students in the early 1960's saw themselves not so much in opposition to the policies of the nation as in the vanguard of these policies; and the passage of major civil rights legislation in 1964, followed by the promise of a major War on Poverty, gave support to this conviction. Thus there arose a hope that "American society would crash through" in remedying its own inequities. This hope had a widespread impact, not only upon that small minority of students who were actively involved in civil rights work, but upon others who were indirectly encouraged to plan careers of responsible social involvement.

But the events of subsequent years have altered this initial hope. The "white backlash" has made legislators extremely reluctant to assist the Negro revolution. The war in Vietnam drained funds away from domestic programs just when federal assistance was needed most. The student Civil Rights Movement for its part discovered that legal reforms only exposed more clearly the depth of the problems of black Americans, and pointed toward still more far-reaching psychological, social and economic changes that were more difficult to legislate from Washington. The War on Poverty collapsed into a small skirmish. Equally important, the rising militancy of black radicals pushed white students out of organizations like SNCC and CORE with the demand "Go home and organize your own people." Lacking national support, and "rejected" by their former black allies, white activists have increasingly despaired of working within the system, have become more radical, and are talking more militantly about "changing the system."

The changing image of political involvement has had two effects. On the one hand, it has contributed to the "radicalization" of those individuals who have remained activists: especially now among such students, disaffection with the established system is at a high that has not been reached in this country since the 1930's. But equally important, the revitalized image of the political process as dishonest, reprehensible, immoral, and unresponsive to both the ideals of America and the rights of the deprived has created a climate in which it is more and more possible to argue that salvation—if it can be found at all—must be found within the self or some countercommunity, rather than within the wider society. Given this belief, the individual in search of meaningful engagement with the world must either create new political institutions (as stressed by the rhetoric of the New Left) or else abandon political struggle altogether in a search for meaning within small groups of other disaffected people. It is in these latter groups that drug use is most common. If the world outside is corrupt, dehumanized, violent, and immoral, the world within—the almost infinitely malleable world of perception, sensation, communication, and consciousness—seems more controllable, more immediate, less corrupting, and ofttimes more pleasant. To be sure, there is a price to be paid for exclusive involvement in the interior world, but, for many young Americans, there simply seems to be no alternative.

Political and historical events do not have a direct, one-to-one relationship with drug use: the war in Vietnam does not *cause* students to smoke marijuana or experiment with LSD. But the political climate of the past few years has created a negative view of the possibility of meaningful involvement within the established institutions of the society, at the same time that it has convinced many students that society is in desperate need of reform. This climate of opinion in turn contributes to the assumption that if meaning, excitement, and dignity are to be found in the world, they must be found within one's own cranium. Drug use can indeed be a kind of cop-out, not from perversity or laziness, but simply because there seems to be no other alternative. Student drug use is indeed a commentary upon American society, but it is above all an indirect criticism of our society's inability to offer the young exciting, honorable, and effective ways of using their intelligence and idealism to reform our society.

Idealists: The Perils of Principle

No disagreement more sharply divides sympathizers from opponents of student activism than the issue of moral idealism versus moral nihilism. To the sympathizer it is the idealism of the youthful activist vis-à-vis a corrupt society that commands greatest respect and support; to the opponent it is the nihilism of the activist (masked by a cynical appeal to ideals) that most repels him. Student activism tends to evoke a moralistic response in those who observe it, while the alleged morality or immorality of the activist arouses more passion than any other aspect of campus unrest.

In this essay, written in 1969, I draw both upon Lawrence Kohlberg's bold and innovating research on moral development, and upon studies of student activists done by Jeanne Block, Norma Haan, and Brewster Smith in the San Francisco area in the 1960's. In essence, I argue that both idealists and nihilists are found in disproportionate numbers within the student movement, but that the idealists far outweigh the nihilists.

But the major importance of this essay, I think, is that it goes on to try to connect the emergence of the youthful opposition with major changes in the social and historical world within which young people today are growing up. Kohlberg's work provides perhaps the clearest example of developmental levels that seem to be most often attained under particularly contemporary conditions, and during the stage of "youth." And his work further suggests that those who have attained these "higher" developmental levels also tend to behave in distinctive ways—e.g., that they are less inclined to yield to conformist pressures and more inclined to protest in the name of their ideals. Speculatively, I try to suggest some of the historical factors that may be spurring the development of more advanced moral reasoning on a mass scale.

What is most important about this kind of research and about this line of thinking is that it tries to establish a bridge between psychological development and historical change—to connect the extent and type of human development to social, technological, and cultural changes that may stimulate such development. It is from such work, I think, that we can best understand the psychological and developmental component in the emergence of new social groupings, and thus perhaps move toward a better understanding of the psychology of historical change.

TO discuss student activism today without immediately becoming involved in moral issues seems almost impossible. In the rhetoric of politicians as in empirical research, judgments of moral praise or condemnation enter into (and frequently dominate) reactions to student protest. Political tracts, novels, research studies, biographies, and autobiographies that deal with student activism today generally emphasize the conflict between youth's personal morality (or immorality) and the immoral (or moral) practices of the surrounding world. Even the most thoughtful and scholarly analyses of contemporary student dissenters usually place them near one of two poles: "amoral and neurotic rebels" or "fine young idealists who may save us all." Whether we like it or not, the phenomenon of youthful protest seems to stimulate intense moral concerns in the beholder.

In the comments that follow, I will discuss data and interpretations concerning the moral development of politically active young men and women at a particular stage of life that coincides roughly with college and graduate school age. I will call this stage of life "youth." By speaking of "youth" instead of late adolescence, I mean to suggest that the experience of those whom we awkwardly term "late adolescents and young adults" is in many respects different from the experience of younger adolescents but, at the same time, that it differs profoundly from that of adults. In other writings I have argued that one of the characteristics of postindustrial societies is that they are beginning to sanction a previously unrecognized stage of development that intervenes between the end of adolescence proper and the beginning of adulthood. Not everyone passes through this stage: traditionally, most young men and women have had little real adolescence at all; and those few who have experienced adolescence as a developmental stage have usually entered adulthood immediately thereafter. But today, for a rapidly growing minority of young Americans—mostly college students, graduate students, members of the New Left, hippies, or in some cases military recruits—a previously unlabeled stage of development is opening up. This stage is defined sociologically by postadolescent disengagement from the adult society, developmentally by continuing opportunities for psychological growth, and psychologically by a concern with the relationship of self and society. It is this stage of life which I term the stage of youth.

In considering youthful activism and moral development, it is necessary to underline that moral development is not only an essential sector of development in its own right, but also a battleground upon which conflicts whose origins lie elsewhere are fought out. It is in fact arbitrary to isolate moral development from identity development, from ego development, from psychosexual development, from the development of intimacy, from new relationships with parents and peers, and from intellectual development. Nonetheless, moral development during youth has been more carefully studied than any other sector. In the work of Erikson, Lawrence Kohlberg, William Perry, and Smith, Block, and Haan, we have accumulating evidence about the relationship between moral development and the often disruptive, idealistic, moralistic and anticonventional behaviors of modern youth.

Moral Development and Sociopolitical Activism

The early psychoanalytic account of superego development, though it still provides an essential underpinning for any study of the psychology of morality, clearly omits or neglects many of the dynamic and structural complexities of moral development in later life. In so far as the classical psychoanalytic account stresses only the formation of the superego through the introjection of the same-sex parent at the conclusion of the Oedipus complex, it leaves out many subsequent changes in the superego and in morally determined behavior. Recently, psychoanalysts and others have shown greater interest in these changes. For example, it is now commonly recognized that during normal adolescence there can occur a "rebellion against the superego," by which the individual rejects not only his parents but that part of his own superego which is based upon unreflective internalization of their standards. Other students of adolescence have emphasized the increasing integration of the superego and ego, which can occur during this stage, and the greater elaboration of self-accepted moral principles, which form part of the ego ideal.

Psychoanalysis has largely dealt with the genetic and dynamic aspects of superego development. Jean Piaget's account of moral development, in contrast, emphasizes changes in the logic or structure of moral reasoning throughout childhood. And more recently, Lawrence Kohlberg, in a series of brilliant studies, has modified and extended Piaget's work by developing a comprehensive account of developmental changes in the structure of moral reasoning. Kohlberg finds that moral reasoning develops through three general stages. The earliest is the *preconventional* stage, which involves relatively egocentric concepts òf right and wrong as that which one can do without getting caught, or that which leads to the greatest personal gratification. The preconventional stage is followed, usually during later childhood, by a stage of *conventional* morality, during which good and evil are first identified with the concept of a "good boy" or "good girl" and then with the standards of the community, i.e., with law and order. The individual in the conventional stage may not *act* according to his perceptions of what is right and wrong; but he does not question the fact that morality is objective, immutable, and derives from external agencies like parental edicts, community standards, or divine laws.

Kohlberg also identifies a third and final stage of moral development that is *postconventional*—what Erikson has called the "ethical" stage. This stage involves reasoning more abstract than that found in earlier stages, and it may lead the individual into conflict with conventional standards. The first of two subphases within the postconventional stage basically involves the concept of right and wrong as resulting from a *social contract*— as the result of an agreement entered into by the members of the society for their common good—and therefore subject to emendation, alteration, or revocation. Conventional moral thinking views moral imperatives as absolute or given by the nature of the universe: social contract reasoning sees rules as "merely" convenient and therefore amendable.

Kohlberg identifies the highest postconventional phase as that in which the individual becomes devoted to *personal principles* that may transcend not only conventional morality but even the social contract. In this stage, certain general principles are now seen as personally binding though not necessarily "objectively" true. Such principles are apt to be stated in a very high level of generality: e.g., the concept of justice, the golden rule, the sanctity of life, the categorical imperative, the promotion of human development. The individual at this stage may find himself in conflict with existing concepts of law and order, or even with the notion of an amendable social contract. He may, for example, consider even democratically arrived-at laws unacceptable because they lead to consequences or enjoin behaviors that violate his own personal principles.

With the development of moral reasoning (as with all other sectors of development), precise ages cannot be attached to the attainment of specific stages. But Kohlberg's research indicates that those who attain postconventional levels generally do so during later adolescence and in the years of youth. *Figure 1* extrapolates from Kohlberg's research to give a rough indication of the timing of moral development, categorized according to his three general stages. The subjects on which this figure is based are middle-class American urban males; thus, at the age of sixteen they are probably college-bound; at twenty they are likely to be in college; and at twenty-four many are in graduate school. It is clear from Kohlberg's data that the highest (postconventional) phases are *never reached* by most men and women in American society, who remain at the conventional stage. Even at age twenty-four only 10 per cent of this middle-class urban male population have reached the personal principles phase, while another 26 per cent are at the social-contract phase.

Finally, *Figure 1* indicates that between the ages of sixteen and twenty the number of individuals in the preconventional stage increases. Kohlberg accounts for this increase by the phenomenon of "moral regression" as a routine developmental occurrence in many college students. Longitudinal studies conducted by Kramer have documented the occurrence of

Figure 1. Level of Moral Reasoning and Age*

Subjects: Middle-class Urban American Males

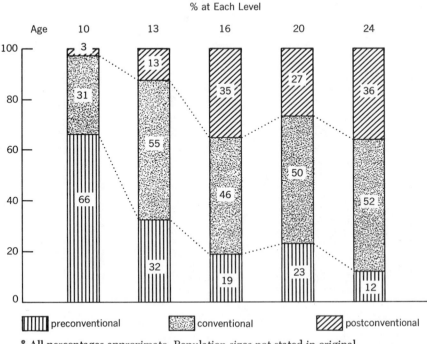

% at Each Level

preconventional   conventional   postconventional

* All percentages approximate. Population sizes not stated in original.

such regression in a number of late adolescent and youthful subjects. In what Kohlberg has termed the Raskolnikoff Syndrome, the individual moving toward postconventional morality regresses to the earlier, preconventional (egocentric) stage in an apparent effort to free himself from irrational and ego-dystonic guilt. Interestingly, Kramer finds that such young "Raskolnikoffs" eventually return to the developmental track at approximately the point where they dropped off.

The structure of moral reasoning is of course not all of moral development; conceivably an individual may reason one way, yet act in another. But several studies have demonstrated that the way a person reasons morally is closely related to his actual behavior under conditions of moral stress. *Figure 2* presents some central findings about moral reasoning and behavior in situations of moral conflict. The Milgram experiment is presented as an experiment in negative reinforcement. The subject is asked to administer high levels of electric shock to another experimental subject (actually a stooge). The stooge protests violently at the shock and eventually warns the subject that his heart condition makes the experiment dan-

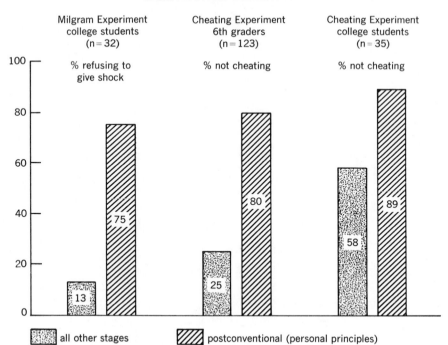

Figure 2. Level of Moral Reasoning and Behavior
in Moral Stress Conditions

gerous. The great majority of college students and the noncollege population, when encouraged by the experimenter to continue to administer
shock, do so despite the victim's protests. But Kohlberg finds that 75 per
cent of the subjects at the stage of personal principles—the highest stage
—refuse to continue shocking the victim, as compared to only 13 per cent
of subjects at all earlier stages. In another experiment, studying cheating
behavior in sixth graders, only 25 per cent of the conventional sixth graders did not cheat, while 80 per cent of the postconventionals did not cheat.
In a study of college students the corresponding figures were 58 per cent
and 89 per cent. There is strong evidence, then, that the level of moral
reasoning is associated with the actual morality of behavior.

Figure 3 portrays the relationship between level of moral development
and participation in student protest activities. This figure is based upon
research done by Brewster Smith, Jeanne Block, and Norma Haan at the
University of California at Berkeley. The subjects are male and female
college students at Berkeley and at San Francisco State College. They are
here divided into two groups: (1) the protesters, who have engaged in sit-
ins, peace marches, picketing, and various forms of disruption or direct

action over such issues as student freedom of speech, the war in Vietnam, or alleged racism in the university or in society; (2) all nonprotesting students, including political inactivists, apolitical fraternity and sorority members, and students who engage in social-service activities but do not take part in protests.

The findings of the Berkeley research are complex, but as summarized in *Figure 3*, they indicate a marked difference in the level of moral development of protesters and nonprotesters in this college population. A clear majority (56 per cent) of all protesters are at postconventional levels of morality, whereas only 12 per cent of nonprotesters have reached this level. The nonprotesters are overwhelmingly (85 per cent) in the conventional stage—that is, they define morality as adherence to law and order, or as involving some concept of being a "good boy" or "good girl." Only 36 per cent of protesters are at the conventional stage. Interestingly, the proportion of protesters at the preconventional stage is also disproportionately large—10 per cent of protesters as against 3 per cent of nonprotesters. Kohlberg's writings suggest that such individuals may be in a state of

Figure 3. Level of Moral Reasoning and
Sociopolitical Protest

Subjects: Students at U.C. (Berkeley) and S.F. State

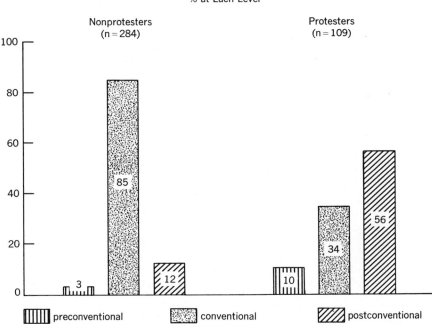

% at Each Level

moral regression (Raskolnikoffs), perhaps epitomized by certain variants of the hippie subculture.

The complexity of these data, however, is emphasized when we analyze them in a different way. Unlike *Figure 3*, *Figure 4* distinguishes between the behavior of those at different levels of moral development, not between the moral development of those who behave in different ways. The behavior here studied was being arrested as a result of the Free Speech Movement sit-in in Sproul Hall at Berkeley in 1964. This analysis indicates that the proportion of preconventionals involved was about the same as the proportion of postconventionals, although in absolute numbers there were many fewer preconventionals in Sproul Hall. These findings make clear that level of moral development and sociopolitical activism are not correlated in a linear manner. They suggest that any protest will, depending on the issues involved, enlist supporters from several different levels of moral development.

This conclusion is supported by an unpublished study of Kohlberg's on the participants in the Harvard College sit-in in the spring of 1969. Kohlberg predicted that at Harvard, unlike Berkeley, the students at the post-conventional level would *not* be overrepresented amongst those who sat

*Figure 4. Level of Moral Reasoning and Participation in FSM Sit-in (Berkeley, 1964) ***

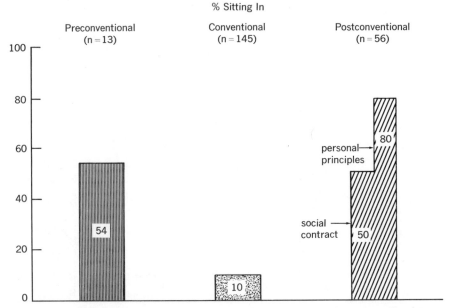

* Not all subjects who sat in were studied. Therefore, extrapolations to all subjects sitting in should be made cautiously.

in. He based this prediction on an analysis of the issues in the Harvard sit-in, which did not seem to him to involve a comparable appeal to abstract principles. His findings confirmed this prediction. These studies, then, do not indicate that high levels of moral development lead *automatically* to participation in all protests, sit-ins, confrontations, and disruptions. Rather they indicate that those who have reached higher levels of moral development are more likely to act in the service of their principles—protesting when their principles are at issue; refusing, also for reasons of principle, to take part in other protests and forms of activism.

Social Catalysts for Moral Development

I have so far presented research findings on the relationship between moral reasoning and sociopolitical activism. On the basis of such findings we would predict that an increase in the proportion of the student population at postconventional levels would also increase the likelihood of principled student sociopolictal activism. I will now argue, more speculatively, that modern social and historical conditions are providing new catalysts and facilitations for high levels of moral development, and that these new developmental attainments constitute *one* partial explanation of sociopolitical activism.

Kohlberg does not address himself specifically to the psychological or social catalysts of moral development. But his data makes clear that moral development is by no means guaranteed by aging, maturation, or socialization. Physical maturation may make possible the development of post-conventional morality, but it obviously does not ensure it. And the pressures of socialization may in many instances militate *against* the development of a principled morality that can place the individual in conflict with his socializing environment—for example, with college administrators, with political parties, with the police, or with the present American Selective Service System. If neither maturation nor socialization guarantee moral development, how can we explain it?

Haan, Smith, and Block have provided us with a first account of some of the psychological antecedents of various levels of moral reasoning in late adolescence and youth. They report, for example, that students at the highest moral stage of personal principles "had a history of preparedness within politically liberal families who frankly experienced and examined conflict, and with parents who exercised their own rights as people, rather than the power and control that society automatically ascribes to them." Their data—too complex to be summarized here—clearly indicates that family milieu during the preadolescent years plays an important role in facilitating or obstructing later moral development.

Here, however, I will not discuss the impact of these early experiences, but will consider the effects of more general social, historical, and political factors on adolescent and postadolescent changes in moral reasoning. That is, I will not consider why some individuals arrive in adolescence or youth already predisposed to develop to the postconventional or "ethical" stages in moral development, but will discuss in a speculative way why postconventional (ethical) moral reasoning may characterize a growing proportion of today's college generation in America and in the other advanced nations.

Disengagement from adult society. A prolonged period of disengagement from the institutions of adult society seems to facilitate moral development. Conversely, immediate entry into the labor force and early marriage with responsibilities for maintaining a family tend to constrain or obstruct moral development. Kohlberg's data, reported in *Figure 5*, showing higher modal levels of moral development in middle-class (college-bound or college) students than in lower-class (noncollege) youth, is consistent with this hypothesis. For, in so far as an individual during or immediately after puberty or adolescence takes a job, marries, and has

*Figure 5.   Level of Moral Reasoning and Social Class**

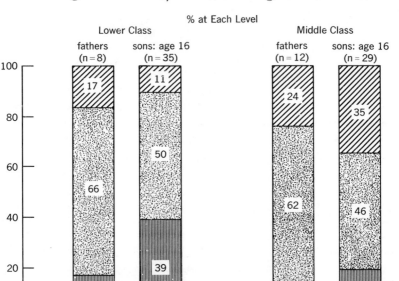

* All figures approximate. Percentages tabulated are of usage of moral reasoning at each level, averaged across subjects.

children, the opportunity for confronting and challenging conventional morality seems to lessen. The risks of unconventionality become greater; the price for departure from conventional morality, and especially for that moral regression which Kohlberg finds a frequent if usually temporary part of moral development, becomes too high for most individuals to pay.

Confrontation with alternate moral viewpoints. William Perry, in his pioneering studies of ethical and intellectual development during the college years, suggests that one prime catalyst for intellectual and moral development is confrontation with relativistic points of view in professors and fellow students. Such confrontations stimulate the student to abandon simple dualistic thinking about right and wrong, good and bad, truth and falsehood. He tends to move first toward a relativistic concept of morality and truth, and later, toward making personal commitments *within* a relativistic universe.

From a different perspective, Robert Redfield, in his discussion of the effects of the transition from peasant to urban societies, underlines the importance of culture contact in producing more high-level and synthetic ideologies. The peasant, confronted in the city with others who hold conflicting moral viewpoints, may be compelled to re-examine his own, and to seek a postconventional moral system that stands above and reconciles traditional moral pieties. Kohlberg's findings, reported in *Figure 6*, that postconventional levels are almost never attained by age sixteen in peasant societies, that they are more often attained by urban middle-class students in developing societies, and that they are most often attained in urban middle-class American society, support this line of reasoning. Put differently, an individual is more likely to move beyond a conventional moral system when he is personally confronted with alternative moral values, and especially when these are concretely epitomized in the people, the institutions, and the cultures among which he lives.

Discovery of corruption. A third catalyst for moral development, as for moral regression, is the discovery of corruption, hypocrisy, and duplicity in the world, especially in those from whom one originally learned the concepts of conventional morality. For example, disillusionment with parents—in particular, the discovery of moral turpitude (or, in Erikson's terms, lack of fidelity) in the parents' lives—may play a critical role in pushing the individual to reject the morality he learned from them. Obviously not all young men and women react identically to such discoveries. Some may accept them without regression: they will push the individual to higher stages of moral development. This advance seems especially likely if the discovery of corruption in the world is accompanied by growing awareness of one's own potential for corruption. Other youths, how-

Figure 6.   Level of Moral Reasoning and Type of Society*

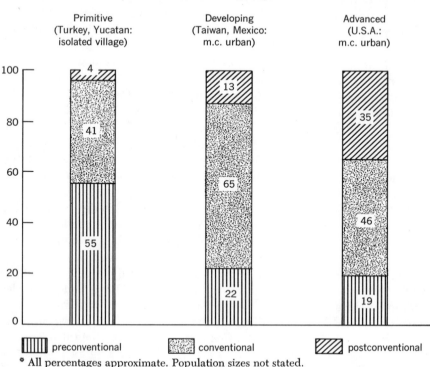

% at Each Level at Age 16

| Primitive (Turkey, Yucatan: isolated village) | Developing (Taiwan, Mexico: m.c. urban) | Advanced (U.S.A.: m.c. urban) |

[IIIII] preconventional   [::::] conventional   [////] postconventional

* All percentages approximate. Population sizes not stated.

ever, will react with at least a temporary regression to moral cynicism, in which they behaviorally flout and intellectually reject what they consider to be "hypocritical" conventional values.

Historical Pressures toward Moral Development

In the extension of higher education, the cross-cultural implosion, and the pervasive reductionism of our age, we have created important new catalysts, for better and for worse, for higher levels of ethicality, as for more marked moral regressions.

The extension of higher education.   Our own era has witnessed an historically unprecedented influx of students to colleges and universities. To cite but one statistic, during the time of the Russian student movement in the middle of the nineteenth century, there were never more than 8,000 university students in all of Imperial Russia. Today in America there are 8 million (about 1,000 times as many); while in Western Germany, France, and England there are by rough count 1.25 million. In most advanced nations of the world the proportion of young people who attend colleges and universities is increasing logarithmically; furthermore, this increase has largely occurred in the last two decades. The growing affluence of the highly industrialized nations permits them to keep millions of the young out of the labor force; the increasing need for high-level training in technological societies requires them to offer a university education to these millions.

Higher education does not, of course, inevitably entail moral growth. But one consequence of the prolongation and extension of higher education is that a massive group of young men and women have been disengaged for an increasingly protracted period from the institutions of the adult society, in particular from occupation and marriage. Freed of responsibilities of work, marriage, and parenthood, at least some find themselves in university atmospheres that deliberately challenge and undermine their pre-existing beliefs and conventional assumptions. Thus, the extension of youth via prolonged education on a mass scale probably tends to stimulate the development of postconventional moral thinking.

Culture contact and the cross-cultural implosion.   The individual who attends a liberal arts college or university is very likely to confront in his daily experience both peers and professors who preach and practice a different morality from the one he was brought up to take for granted. Many universities deliberately confront students with contrasting cultures that give allegiance to alien moral concepts, and deliberately provoke students to question the unexamined assumptions of their own childhoods and adolescences. They thus push the individual away from what Perry calls "dualistic" thinking, away from an unthinking acceptance of conventional moral "truths," and toward a more individuated moral position, at once more personal and more abstract.

But it should also be recalled that outside the university, as within it, we live in an age of extraordinary culture contact and conflict. The electronic revolution, coupled with the revolution in transportation, enables us to confront alien values within our living room or to immerse ourselves physically in alien cultures after a flight of a few hours. The days when one could live in parochial isolation, surrounded only by conventional morality, are fast disappearing. Conflicts of ideologies, of world views, of value systems, of philosophical beliefs, of aesthetic orientations, and of political styles confront every thoughtful man and woman, wherever he or she lives. If such confrontations stimulate moral development, then we live in an era in which technology and world history themselves provide new facilitation for moral growth. We are all today a little like Redfield's peasants who move to the city, living in a world where conflicting cultures and moral viewpoints rub against us at every turn. The urbanizing and homogenizing process has become worldwide: we live in an era of cross-cultural implosion. My argument here is that this cross-cultural implosion helps stimulate moral development.

Cynicism and reductionism. Universities often undertake to expose the student to the gap between preaching and practice in society, in admired individuals, and even in the student himself. Whatever their many conformist pressures, universities in America and abroad also have another side: they have often been focal points of criticism of the surrounding society—institutional consciences that may collectively remind the surrounding society of its failure to live up to its ideals. To attend a university may systematically expose the student to the actual corruption that exists in the world, in representatives of the *status quo,* and even in himself.

But this exposure to corruption is today by no means confined to the university itself: ours is, in general, an age of skepticism with regard to traditional moral pieties and platitudes. Hypocrisy and corruption are constantly exposed at a cultural as well as at an individual level. The debunking of traditional models and values is a favorite contemporary pastime; duplicity, dishonesty, compromise, and deceit are widely reported. Many of our most powerful intellectual systems are highly developed in their capacity to debunk, reduce, and explain away the ideologies, values, and convictions of others. The sociology of knowledge, psychoanalysis, Marxism, philosophical analysis, cultural relativism, and a variety of other idea systems can all be readily used (or misused) for this purpose. Thus, even if the individual does not discover corruption in his own parents or immediate world, he is still hard put to avoid confrontation with the corruption that exists in the wider society. In an age of debunking, conventional morality tends to suffer: individuals are pushed to higher levels of moral development or to moral regression. The data suggests that student protesters are disproportionately drawn from just these two groups: primarily the morally advanced, but secondarily, the morally regressed.

Ethicality and Zealotry

We may interpret world-wide student protest as *partly* a result of the fact that societies like our own are stimulating more individuals than ever before to higher levels of moral development. One aspect of the student movement must therefore be seen as a result of a psychological advance, and not as a result of psychopathology or psychological retardation.

But how should we judge the development of a morality based on a commitment to ethical principles that are maintained even when they conflict with conventional moral wisdom? Is it really an advance? In evaluat-

ing the meaning of the highest levels of moral development, we are immediately confronted with a paradox. On the one hand, Kohlberg identifies
such ethical reasoning with admirable men like Socrates, Gandhi, Lincoln,
and Martin Luther King—men for whom devotion to the highest personal
principles was paramount over all other considerations, and who as a result were moral leaders of their time. Yet on the other hand, especially
during the past two Cold War decades, we have been taught to view
abstract personal principles with considerable mistrust—as a part of ideology not in the Eriksonian sense but in a highly pejorative sense. Such
principles, it has been argued, are intimately—perhaps inevitably—related to the development of moral self-righteousness, zealotry, dogmatism,
fanaticism, and insensitivity. In pursuit of his own personal principles, a
man will ride rough-shod over others who do not share these principles,
will disregard human feelings, or will even destroy human life. During the
period when the "end of ideology" was being announced on all sides,
when instrumental and consensus politics was being extolled, we learned
to identify abstract personal principles with dogmatic and destructive
moral zealotry. How are we to combine these two perspectives? Do we see
in Brewster Smith's findings confirmation of the view that student activists
are dangerous moral zealots? Or do we adhere to Kohlberg's implication
that such individuals are more likely moral heroes than despots?

The answer lies, I think, in recalling my earlier observation that the
separation of the moral sector of human development from other sectors is
analytic and arbitrary. Anna Freud has taught us to think in terms of an
ideal "balance" between what she terms "developmental lines" (sectors of
development). Yet she has also shown that such balance is never found in
practice, and that in any specific individual we always find retardations or
accelerations of development within different sectors. Following Anna
Freud's thinking suggests that whether the highest stages of moral reasoning lead to destructive zealotry or real ethicality depends upon the extent
to which moral development is *matched by development in other sectors*.
The critical related sectors of development, I submit, are those which involve compassion, love, or empathic identification with others.

Most moral zealots, bigots, and dogmatists are probably best described, in Kohlberg's terms, as conventionalists, while others are perhaps
permanent regressees to the Raskolnikoff Syndrome. But there are at least
a few whom we know from personal experience or from history who seem
truly postconventional in moral reasoning but whose genuine adherence to
the highest moral values is *not* matched by compassion, sympathy, capacity for love, and empathy. In such individuals the danger of hurting men
to advance mankind, of injuring people in order to fulfill one's own moral
principles, is all too real. We see this danger realized in the pre-Nazi German Youth Movement, where postconventional morality often went hand

in hand with virulent anti-Semitism. Pascal put it well when he noted that "Evil is never done so thoroughly or so well as when it is done with a good conscience."

Thus, neatly to identify high levels of moral reasoning with any one kind of action, much less with human virtue, mental health, maturity, and so on is a serious mistake. What we might term "moral precocity" in youth —high moral development not attended by comparable development in other sectors of life—is often dangerous. The danger lies not in high levels of moral development in themselves, but in the retardation of other sectors of development. What is dangerous is *any* level of moral development, be it postconventional, conventional, or preconventional, in the absence of a developed capacity for compassion, empathy, and love for one's fellow man.

No one phrase will adequately characterize the other developmental accomplishments that are essential to humanize the highest levels of moral reasoning. But the history of revolutions that have failed through the very ardor of their search for moral purity suggests that the combination of abstract personal principles with a humorless and *loveless asceticism* is especially likely to be dangerous. There are of course many kinds of asceticism, some of them mature, self-accepted, and benign. But there are other asceticisms that are based upon inhibition of the capacity to love, upon failure in the development of interpersonal mutuality, and upon absence of empathy. Often these qualities are combined with ascetic self-denial based more upon unconscious fear and inhibition than upon self-accepted personal values. Lewis Feuer's recent critique of student movements identifies all student protesting activity with the excesses of those student movements where high principles have been combined with asceticism, e.g., the prewar German Youth Movement. But if we examine the current American student movement, we find less ground for concern: however highly principled many of today's dissenting students may be, they are scarcely an ascetic lot.

In the end, then, we reach the paradoxical conclusion that morality is necessary but not sufficient; even the highest levels of moral reasoning do not alone guarantee truly virtuous behavior. Kohlberg's research, of course, shows that men who reason at an advanced level tend to act morally as well. And the Berkeley research suggests optimism about the high level of moral development of many or most student activists. Yet what is true for most is not true for all; and historically many crimes have been committed in the name of the highest principles, sincerely held. In the end the findings of developmental psychology in the context of youthful political activism may merely return us to ancient truisms—mercy without justice is sentimental and effusive, while justice without mercy is cold and inhuman.

Radicals Revisited: Some Second Thoughts

In late 1969, I was asked to discuss the current state of knowledge about student radicals, commenting upon my own earlier work in the light of a plethora of empirical studies which had since been published. As of the end of 1970, there had been 100 empirical studies of student activists, radicals, and dissenters, and the results were both repetitive and consistent.

In this essay I summarize the state of research as of late 1969, pointing not only to the stable generalizations, but to the many problems that remain unanswered. Some of the issues I raise are substantive; others are methodological. In general, this essay is an effort not only to review the current state of understanding of the psychology of student activism, but informally to suggest an agenda for further research.

The student movement has clearly changed during the last decade, and many argue that more "pathological" types are being recruited to it. This may be true, but I am personally not convinced that the increasing justification and use of violence by the Left is necessarily the result of the recruitment of "new types" into the movement. Rather, the move toward violent tactics seems equally understandable as a reaction to the constant frustration that confronts the radical, who may end by covertly identifying himself with the very violence he is dedicated to oppose. Even open advocacy or practice of terrorism, then, need not be the result of personal psychopathology: it may equally well be—and is, in the few "terrorists" I know—the result of a political map of society that deems the America of 1970 identical to the Germany of 1940 and Nixon equivalent to Hitler. I believe this political map is incorrect; but given this map, it requires no further assumption of psychopathology in order to understand why terrorism was advocated as a tactic by a handful of radicals in 1970.

In considering the theoretical implications of research on activism, I argue that it casts into doubt the prevailing theories of socialization, acculturation, and integration as the dominant functions of education. I argue that we are witnessing a phenomenon I call "youthful desocialization," and suggest that the process of accommodating oneself

*to one's society needs to be distinguished from (and may be at odds with)
the process of education, internal development, individuation, and growth.
Whatever the immediate relevance of research on student radicals in
refuting popular conceptions of them as bums, animals, and rotten apples,
the long-range theoretical importance of this research lies in its potential
for enriching our understanding of human development as it is affected by
the unique characteristics of postindustrial society.*

IN the summer of 1967, I studied a small group of antiwar radical
student leaders. The study, clinical and exploratory, was published in
May, 1968. Even by that time the radical scene had changed so drastically
that many of my comments were already outdated. Now still more needs
to be said about the changes since then, about how they alter earlier generalizations about the psychosocial origins of student radicalism, and
about the lessons to be learned from recent studies of youthful activists.

I should state at the outset that I continue to see student activism as an
essentially constructive force in American life. I am far more worried
about police riots and American military violence than I am about student
violence, and I consider the radicalism of a minority of today's college
students a largely appropriate, reasonable, and measured response to blat-
ant injustices in our foreign policies, our domestic policies and practices,
and our university structure and policies. I do deplore (as a tendency)
that special self-righteousness of a minority of today's student radicals, the
nobility of whose purposes is not matched by an equal awareness of their
own ambivalence or potential for corruption, a lack that sometimes allows them to treat their opponents as less than human—as pigs, for example. But, in any case, the study of the psychology of radicals should
never be equated with the study of the causes of radicalism, much less
with its merits.

There was clearly something about the Civil Rights Movement—its
style, its mood, the character of its members and its target—that won the
sympathy of American liberals. (Many Southerners, of course, found the
tactics and goals of the movement nihilistic, communistic, violent, or, at
the very least, provocative.) The tactic of militant nonviolence—whether
adopted as a Gandhian first principle or as a useful tactic—seemed an
altogether worthy and admirable principle. To be sure, the sit-in was essentially disruptive and confrontational. To the restaurant owner whose
floor was covered by demonstrating civil rights workers, a sit-in seemed a
violation of his property rights and an obstruction of his business. But to
the greater part of the liberal American public the disruptive and obstruc-
tive element in these tactics seemed justified, a relatively mild way of expressing opposition to unjust and discriminatory policies.

But as the student movement has journeyed from the South to the

North, from the ghetto to the campus, new reactions have come to prevail. There is a new tendency to try to separate the "good guys," who remain nonviolent, constructive, and idealistic from the "bad guys," who are nihilistic, violent, destructive, and anarchistic. This distinction pervades political rhetoric and has found its way into scholarly publications as well. In several recent discussions, for example, I have been asked to contrast the "constructive and idealistic" young radicals I studied two years ago with the "nihilistic and violent" radicals who have purportedly replaced them today.

I believe there has been a change toward militancy, anger, and dogmatism in the white student movement, but that it has been greatly exaggerated. At least part of the distance between sitting in at a Southern segregationist lunch counter (thereby preventing its owner from doing business) and occupying a Northern college administration building (thereby "bringing the machine to a halt") is a difference in target, not tactics. In both cases individuals use their bodies to obstruct, disrupt, or prevent the orderly conduct of business as usual. To be sure, there are other differences, too; but the one central difference is in our attitude toward Southern segregationists and Northern college presidents. Part of the distance the student movement has traveled is the distance from Selma to Morningside Heights, from Bull Connor to Nathan Pusey.

Yet the mood, temper, and rhetoric of the student movement *has* drastically changed. In place of a nonviolent willingness to endure the punishments decreed by law for violations of local ordinances, we instead see an often angry and militant demand for amnesty. (It should be recalled, of course, that in the early days of the Civil Rights Movement a demand for amnesty would have been quixotic: civil rights workers had no choice but to accept the punishment that was inflicted upon them. Today, in contrast, *de facto* amnesty is often a real possibility, in practice if not in principle.)

More important, the often religiously Christian or Gandhian nonviolent mood of the Civil Rights Movement has been replaced by a more defiant, more angry, more politically revolutionary stance among today's student radicals. The influence of Mao Tse-tung, mediated through the Progressive Labor Party and Worker-Student Alliance, is only one of many new influences. The writings of Fanon, Debray, and other apostles of armed revolution have had their effect; the models of revolutionary leaders like Castro, Guevara, and Ho Chi-Minh have become more important; and Marxist and neo-Marxist concepts increasingly dominate the political rhetoric of radicals. In addition, the rising militancy of portions of the black community has had its impact upon white students, now effectively excluded even from campus alliances with blacks. There often ensues something analogous to a game of chicken: black militants and white radicals vie with each other to up the ante, each demonstrating to the other that they are more truly revolutionary.

How do we account for this shift in mood, tone, and rhetoric in the student movement? Is the New Left recruiting new members who are more violent, more uncontrolled, more nihilistic, and more destructive than the "gentle" civil rights workers of the past? Has there been an influx of what within the student movement are called "crazies"? Or is essentially the same group (in personality terms) reacting differently because of a different political situation? Can we distinguish in any useful way within the student movement between the "nihilistic" and "idealistic" activists?

At this point, anyone who, like myself, is essentially a clinician must remind himself of what we all know but frequently forget: the essential ambivalence of human nature. Even the most cursory reading of the history of the Russian revolutionary student movement shows that some of its most able and devoted leaders began as populist idealists of the highest principle but moved on to become members of the terrorist, or "nihilist," movement, forever thereafter named after them. It seems unlikely that their basic characters, ideals, and personalities changed in any fundamental way. Instead, we must posit "learning from experience," situational reactions to harassment, defeat, and czarist repression which led to the surfacing of aspects of personality that were previously controlled, suppressed, or repressed. Introspection should further convince us that ambivalence is not confined to student activists, nor indeed to students; psychologists and educators, among others, exhibit the same mixture of feelings. The point is obvious: the same person, depending on circumstances, is invariably both an idealist and a nihilist.

Some people, though, are more nihilistic or idealistic than others, and recent research has pointed to the existence, within the student movement, of two distinct personality types, which can be loosely associated with the nihilistic-idealistic distinction. Robert Liebert, a New York psychoanalyst, after intensive interviewing of a large group of white and black participants and nonparticipants in the Columbia "liberation" of 1968, found that students in the occupied buildings fell along a continuum of idealistic and constructive to nihilistic and destructive. He hypothesized that there were different developmental patterns in each group and noted their different style and approach to political action. But he found that the "great majority" of students in the buildings at Columbia were idealists and argued plausibly that most nihilists in his sense are never admitted to college (or at least not to Columbia). So while the distinction between nihilists and idealists can be made, the empirical conclusion nevertheless emphasizes the predominance of idealists even among the purportedly obscene, destructive, and nihilistic students involved in the Columbia disruption.

Similar conclusions emerge from far-reaching research conducted at the University of California at Berkeley and San Francisco State College by Brewster Smith, Jeanne Block, and Norma Haan. Their research is especially conclusive in its analysis of the relationship between moral development and participation in student protest activities. It supports what many commentators have also suggested—namely, that moral issues are at the heart of student revolt. (See "Idealists: The Perils of Principle," pp. 297–300, for a summary of this research.)

Jeanne Block makes an important distinction between what she terms "parental continuity" and "parental discontinuity" groups among activists and protesters. The parental continuity group was extremely critical of American society, but its members evidenced strong continuity with their parents and their parents' values. The parental discontinuity group was critical of *both* American society *and* their parents. Contrasting these two groups, both active politically, Block found that they differed in a variety of respects: members of the discontinuity group (the "rebellion" group) adopted more of a hippie life style, seemed more profoundly alienated from American society, and were less conventionally "responsible" in their other activities. Members of the continuity group (the "chips off the old block") were less expressive, less irresponsible, and less affected by personal conflicts.

These studies thus suggest the viability of a rough distinction between nihilistic and idealistic radical activism. Indeed, research on the relation between moral development and activism points to what may be a bipolar grouping within the activist camp. For Smith and his colleagues find that both extremes—the postconventionals and the preconventionals—are overrepresented in the protesting group. But again there is the question of ambivalence. For even the preconventional (egocentric) student is, we know from other evidence, likely to be in a temporary and usually partial state of regression to earlier concepts of morality, all as a part of a long-range trajectory toward postconventional ethical thinking. Which potential is activated in him—preconventional or postconventional, egocentric or ethical—depends much upon the fate of his causes and the company he keeps. In short, if the distinction between nihilists and idealists among today's student radicals holds water, it is with the essential qualification that everyone is always a little of both.

Two years ago, in discussing the personality development of radicals, I contrasted two hypotheses. The first, the Oedipal-rebellion hypothesis, rests on the notion of strong Oedipally-based rebellion against the father "acted out" symbolically during late adolescence and youth in attacks on authority figures like college presidents, generals, the Establishment, and government policies and leaders. The second hypothesis, the red-diaper-baby theory, posits that today's student radicals are the children of yesterday's radicals.

In the last two years the Oedipal-rebellion thesis has received widespread publicity. Lewis Feuer, in his brilliant but tendentious book *The Conflict of Generations,* makes Oedipal rebellion the basis for his explanation of the psychodynamics of student radicalism. Bruno Bettelheim has offered Oedipal rebellion, among other explanations, as one of the causes of student revolt. Ben Rubenstein and Morton Levitt have analyzed the psychodynamics of the student movement in terms of "totem and taboo." And Joseph Alsop, in a recent article in *Newsweek,* lumped me together with Feuer and Bettelheim as one of those who "takes seriously" the Oedipal rebellion hypothesis.

I take it seriously enough to argue that it is incorrect. So, too, it should be noted, does virtually every other investigator who has done empirical research on the subject. Seymour Martin Lipset, the Harvard sociologist, hardly a hero of or apologist for today's student radicals, concludes a recent summary of research on student activism by noting that the central finding on politically active left-wing students, not only in America but elsewhere in the world, is that they come from liberal and politically active families. This is hardly evidence of Oedipal rebellion. Despite the great variety of personality types and motivations that enter into radicalism, empirical studies find continuity with parental values to be the rule and discontinuity the exception. Within any group of activist protesters it is possible, as the new research shows, to distinguish two subgroups, one of which consists of chips off the old block, the other of rebels. But even then the evidence suggests that the chips off the old block are more numerous and that unequivocal rebellion against the same-sex parent is more likely to lead to a withdrawn posture of dissent, to a hippie quietism.

Yet in considering relationships with parents, as with the whole question of generational continuity, one must again recall the central fact of ambivalence in human development. Even in working with students who present themselves as unqualifiedly hating their parents, we frequently find that beneath hatred, defiance, and rebellion lie love and dependency, all the more intense because they have been so strongly repudiated. Similarly, Adorno *et al.*'s *The Authoritarian Personality* and a series of later studies have shown that many individuals who portray their parents as virtually perfect turn out to possess at a less conscious level a contrasting and opposite view of harsh, tyrannical, and hated parents. It would be contrary to everything we know about human development and generational relations were we not to find mixed feelings about parents in any group. What is impressive, then, in the studies of student radicals is the *relative* predominance of positive feelings, positive identification, and basic value continuity.

Another thesis commonly advanced, especially in popular discussions of today's student radicalism, is that today's student activists behave as they do because of the Spockian permissiveness of their upbringing. "Permissiveness" is used as a bad word, and the explanation usually goes on to note that students have not learned self-restraint, have never experienced the force or coercion they desperately needed in order to develop inner controls, and have no respect for limits, older people, etc. This view has been advanced not only by such critics of the student movement as Bruno Bettelheim, but also, a number of years ago (in modified form), by Richard Flacks, a founder of SDS and now a distinguished researcher on student activism. Flacks found that the parents of activists, compared with those of nonactivists, would be less distressed were their children to drop out of college or to live (unmarried) with a member of the opposite sex; he also found that activist students less often reported that their parents were strict. In his initial writings he interpreted this as evidence of parental permissiveness, one factor in what he termed the "deviant socialization" of student radicals.

Three recent studies, however, discredit the permissiveness hypothesis. One, an unpublished Ph.D. thesis by Lamar Thomas, a student of Flacks, compares the children of politically active parents of both the Right and the Left. It finds generally higher levels of political activity among the children of left-wing parents, but *no* relationship in either group between activism and permissiveness. A second study, by Block, Haan, and Smith, concludes (on the basis of data on almost 1,000 students) that permissiveness is not a determining variable of activism. And William Cowdry at Yale found no relationship between permissiveness and anti-war activism among college seniors.

But even if permissiveness is not the issue, recent studies suggest that methods of discipline and family values *are* important. In my study in 1967, my radical subjects emphasized the subtle yet pervasive power of parental principle in their upbringing. They had been brought up in families with a moral atmosphere that was largely implicit but nonetheless powerful. The methods of discipline used in these families generally avoided physical punishment, direct coercion, even ostracism. Instead, reasoning and the transmission of high expectations were the favored methods of inculcating family values. Parental expectations were communicated by the promotion of independence, by the assumption that the child would accept responsibility and control himself, and by the use of such indirect (but powerful) sanctions as the expression of disappointment in the child when he misbehaved.

Empirical research has, in general, confirmed these findings. Flacks's study, which involved intensive interviewing of the parents of activists and nonactivists, found important distinctions in the value emphases of activist and nonactivist families. In activist families he found a greater emphasis on the importance of ideas (intellectualism), on the expression of feelings (romanticism), and on serving others (humanitarianism)—

and a lesser emphasis on strict control of impulse (low moralism). Approaching the same questions differently, the Smith research group found, in general, that the socialization experiences reported by protesters emphasized training for independence by parents who themselves had strong independent interests not involving their children. These studies are consistent with the hypothesis that the dominant socialization pattern for today's student activists involves not permissiveness but a highly principled family culture, which is transmitted to children through the use of reasoning and persuasion and the encouragement of independence in thought and action.

As for the critical question of social versus psychological determinants of political attitude and behavior, most researchers have found consistent demographic and socioeconomic correlates of political activism. In general, these point to a relationship between activism and high socioeconomic status, high parental education, and high parental involvement in professional and, in particular, "helping" vocations. (Flacks finds that higher levels of education characterize even the grandparents of activists.)

But as Lipset points out, many sociodemographic characteristics have known psychological concomitants. The use of reasoning and persuasion in bringing up children, for example, is more common in upper-middle-class than in working-class families. Similarly, religion has been shown to be associated with activism: a disproportionate number of students from Jewish families are involved in radical protest activities. The theoretical problem these findings raise can be seen in an example. Suppose we find that the mothers of political activists show a distinctive concern for the nurture of their children. We still do not know how to interpret this finding. Does it indicate a causal relationship between maternal nurturance and filial activism? Or does it merely reflect the accidental fact that more radicals, being Jewish, have nurturant Jewish mothers? According to the second interpretation, radicalism might be "caused" by other factors directly connected with Jewishness (for example, familiarity with or enjoyment of the position of an out-group member). Or it might be related to still other factors indirectly connected with Jewishness (for example, great stress on acting in the service of one's beliefs). Without further studies that control for these factors, we do not know whether psychological or sociological variables are more important.

Several recent studies permit us to approach this question, however, at least in a preliminary way. Flacks's research controlled for type of college attended, area of residence, and class in college. It thus provided at least an informal control on socioeconomic status, and the fact that Flacks found distinctive differences between the families of activists and non-activists is consistent with the view that "family culture" variables are critical in political activism. Haan and Block, moreover, have recently responded directly to Lipset's challenge by reanalyzing their data with religion controlled. Analyzing family socialization variables independently for two groups, Jews and non-Jews, they found that within each of these groups the same socialization variables continued to be associated with political activism. And Cowdry, studying a highly homogeneous Yale College senior class, found many socialization variables but no social, religious, or demographic factors associated with activism.

Still, the issue cannot be settled with only the evidence at hand. In all probability several interacting factors are involved. On the one hand, it seems clear that *if* children are brought up in upper-middle-class professional families with humanitarian, expressive, and intellectual values, and *if* the techniques of discipline emphasize independence and reasoning, and *if* the parents are themselves politically liberal and politically active, then the chances of the child's being an activist are greatly increased, regardless of factors like religion. But it is also clear that these conditions are fulfilled most often in Jewish families. And there may be still other factors associated with social class and religion that independently promote activism; for example, being in a Jewish minority group that has preserved its culture in the face of opposing community pressures for centuries may in some way prepare or permit the individual to take controversial positions as a student.

Another question left unanswered by most research on student activism is whether we have been studying the determinants of radical beliefs, of action in general, or of the interaction between a particular set of radical beliefs and a particular type of radical action. The typical study of student activists selects for intensive investigation a group defined by *behavioral* criteria: were they or were they not arrested for disruption at Dartmouth in 1969? Did they or did they not take part in Mississippi Summer? Such "activists" then are typically compared with a "control group"—usually a random sample of the college population. The extremely consistent differences routinely found in such research provide the current portrait of the activist.

But how should the differences be interpreted? Do they reflect radical *beliefs?* If so, then occupying a building or participating in an antiwar protest presumably reflects the intensity of the beliefs: we suppose there is a direct connection between the strength of one's beliefs and the probability of acting on them. But it is equally possible that by contrasting activists defined by behavioral criteria with others in the college population, we are studying something besides beliefs—namely, a tendency to take action in the name of one's convictions. This factor of "consistency" between beliefs and behavior may, in fact, turn out to have determinants other than those of beliefs alone.

In his recent research on this issue, Cowdry, then a Yale College senior, studied a random sample of the Yale class of 1968. He was initially interested in examining how attitudes toward the war in Vietnam were related to plans concerning military service. But in the course of his study, a strongly worded antiwar resolution was distributed with wide publicity to the entire senior class. Since two-thirds of the class said they opposed the war but only one-third signed the resolution, Cowdry was able to compare two groups with equally strong antiwar sentiments: the group that signed the resolution and the one that did not. His findings support the view that *with* antiwar attitudes held constant, the determinants of beliefs are different from the determinants of action (signing the resolution). Indeed, his study suggests that many of the characteristics of activists reported in previous studies may be related not as much to having radical beliefs as to behavior-belief "consistency." For the two groups that were "consistent" (the antiwar signers and the prowar nonsigners) were in many respects more like each other than either group was like the "inconsistent" group (the antiwar nonsigners). One question raised by this finding is whether the observed characteristics of behaviorally defined activists—especially the socialization variables associated with activism—have any necessary relation to left-wing (as opposed to right-wing) views, or whether they are concomitants of taking action consistent with one's beliefs—regardless of where these beliefs fall on the political spectrum.

One further finding of interest emerged from Cowdry's study. He found that antiwar beliefs were associated with a set of characteristic self-descriptions: the antiwar students described themselves as more expressive, more aesthetic, more idealistic than did the prowar students. At the same time, Cowdry found that virtually these same characterizations were applied to their fathers by "consistent" students (antiwar signers), but *not* by "inconsistents" (antiwar nonsigners). This suggests that the student most likely to hold radical beliefs *and* act on them is identified with a humanitarian, idealistic, and expressive father. Conversely, the student most likely to hold radical beliefs but not act upon them is one who sees *himself* as humanitarian, idealistic, and expressive but has developed this self-characterization in rebellion against his father.

Several points, based on the voluminous body of research on student radicals, can be made:

1. Student radicals are an elite group, and not the "rabble of rejects" they have been termed. There is an impressive uniformity in the finding of a great variety of studies conducted by different researchers using different methods with different populations: Free Speech Movement students at Berkeley, activists at San Francisco State, Mississippi Summer volunteers, Columbia radicals, Michigan State and Penn State SDS members,

Dartmouth College arrestees, and so on. These similarities can be summarized, perhaps oversimplified, in a sentence: The activist group is, compared to the student population from which it is drawn, an "elite" group in virtually every respect.

2. Moral issues are central to student radicalism. The most impressive differences found between activists and nonactivists have been in the area of moral development. There are many other statistically significant differences, but the moral differences observed are so overwhelming that they suggest that Smith and his co-workers are close to the heart of the matter. To be sure, the determinants of levels of moral development are themselves extremely complex and not perfectly correlated with activism. Nevertheless, recent research strongly indicates that a central factor in radical political activism is level of moral development.

3. There are several routes to radicalism. With regard to male radicals, for example, at least two pathways to radical beliefs can be distinguished. The first is the pathway of identification. Both father and son are described as expressive, humanitarian, and idealistic. The son identifies with his father, although the son is usually more radical. Such sons are very likely to be radicals in action as well as beliefs. They generally fall into the "idealistic radical" group. There is, however, clearly a second pathway to radical beliefs, though less often to radical actions: the pathway of rejection of identification. Such students describe themselves as expressive, idealistic, and humanitarian but describe their fathers as distinctively *not* any of these things. They are rather less likely to be politically active, more likely to adopt an apolitical or "hippie" style of dissent, and, if they become involved in political action, more likely to fall within the "nihilist" group.

4. A great many students with vehemently radical beliefs do not implement their beliefs in action. Most psychological research has so far emphasized the enduring states and characteristics of those who act. But for every activist there are many others who share his beliefs but do not act. In our democratic society it is commonly asserted that citizens with strong political convictions should be willing to express them and work to implement them. If we assume that "consistency" between beliefs and action is desirable, we need to know better what produces it, regardless of political convictions. As yet, little is known about the psychological and social processes by which individuals are activated, by which a community is politicized, and by which potential activists find and activate each other. Nor do we know anything about short-term and long-term consequences to the individual of implementing—or not implementing—his beliefs.

5. Psychological explanations alone are not adequate to understand today's student radicals. Student radicalism has developed within a social, cultural, and, above all, a political context. High levels of moral develop-

ment, for example, did not begin with the Civil Rights Movement; nor can we interpret the recent changes in mood, tone, rhetoric, ideology, and style of the student movement primarily in terms of the changing personality composition of radical groups. More to the point, we must study the evolution and rationale of the student movement itself. For example, even such minimal goals of student activists as an end to the war in Vietnam, a major attack on racism and poverty, and a "restructuring" of the university have not been attained. Given this fact, it probably does not take complex psychological explanations to explain the rise in militancy, anger, and dogmatism that we see.

6. Most important, the study of student radicalism exposes the ideological bias and theoretical inadequacy of many of the concepts by which we have attempted to understand the relationship of men to politics and society. Until recently the most widely used concepts have focused largely upon processes that lead to stasis and stability in society and politics. The study of socialization has focused upon how children adapt their personalities to the social roles, norms, and institutions of their society. The study of acculturation has emphasized how values and symbol systems are internalized so that they become part of the individual. And into many such analyses there has crept a covertly evaluative element: viable societies are assumed to be those which "effectively socialize" the young into their available roles; valid cultures are those which inspire the greatest consensus and loyalty to their symbols and values. The evaluative weight of the concepts of "socialization" and "acculturation" becomes apparent when we reverse the terms: "desocialization" connotes misanthropy, anomia, and possibly psychiatric illness, while "disacculturation" connotes a collapse of values into barbarity or nihilism.

The study of student radicals indicates that these connotations are often incorrect, and that the study of socialization and acculturation must be complemented by the study of desocialization and disacculturation as the psychological correlates and, to some extent, the causes of social and political change. Indeed, some purportedly "socializing" environments (like liberal arts colleges and universities) do anything but neatly "socialize" or "integrate" all their charges into available social roles, existing social institutions, traditional values, and conventional symbol systems. On the contrary, we witness today, both in America and in other nations, a phenomenon that can be called *youthful desocialization*. Traditional roles, institutions, values, and symbols are critically scrutinized and often rejected, while new roles, institutions, values, and symbols more adequate to the modern world are desperately sought.

Research on student activism points to the enormous complexity of youthful desocialization. On the one hand, this research finds underlying value continuity between most activists and their families. But on the other hand, it also reveals discontinuity, innovation, and change: rejection by the children of liberal parents of many liberal assumptions in favor of more radical political beliefs, the emergence of new political tactics, efforts to find new political procedures, roles, institutions, and methods for change. Youthful desocialization, then, is always *partial*, but it may still be far-reaching and politically decisive. The tumult, controversy, and criticism that pervades higher education today, then, should remind us that if we are to understand change, innovation, reform, and revolution, we cannot do so solely with concepts designed to explain stability and equilibrium. In addition, we must attempt to understand the forces that lead intelligent, talented, and idealistic men and women (both young and old) to refuse, challenge, or revitalize the conventional wisdom.

III. The Two Revolutions

IN recent years I have returned repeatedly to the interpretive and theoretical questions raised by the rise of an oppositional youth culture. The very fact that no social theory anticipated or forecast the emergence of a youthful opposition suggests that something has been profoundly wrong with the way we have understood the modern world. Just as an experimental failure that refutes the hypothesis it tests is often the most fruitful experiment from the point of view of scientific theory, so the failure of liberal and radical theories to anticipate the emergence of a massive movement of dissenting youth in the industrialized nations constitutes a major challenge to critical social theory.

The essays that follow in no way constitute a comprehensive theory: they only provide some building blocks upon which a theory of the youthful opposition may some day be developed. Each of these essays addresses itself, in a different way, to the historical meaning and social significance of the adversary youth culture. And each insists that we will not understand this new culture without understanding what is genuinely new in our historical world. Both sympathizers and deprecators of the youthful opposition tend to underline its similarities with youth movements in the past—they point, for example, to the ubiquity of generational conflict throughout history, or they trace the new opposition to the emergence of youth as a "revolutionary class," with a common relationship to the means of production. It may be that history occasionally repeats itself, but I think this is rare, especially now, when so few of the basic historical assumptions of previous eras remain valid. My stress in these essays is therefore on the novelty of the modern situation, and on the absence of any historical guide that might enable us to anticipate the future.

These essays presuppose that we live in revolutionary times, and that the unexpected emergence of an oppositional youth culture is both a reaction against and an expression of the unprecedented revolutions of our time.

Youth, Change, and Violence

This essay, written in 1967, grew out of the study of the antiwar radical leaders of Vietnam Summer 1967: it is a companion piece to "Radicals: Renewal of the Tradition." That essay dealt primarily with the psychological development of a group of young radicals; this one deals with the social and cultural context within which these young radicals and the movement with which they were identified both developed.

After underlining what I take to be the common characteristics of what I here call "postmodern" youth, I stress two factors in an effort to explain these characteristics. First, I return to the issue of accelerating social change, emphasizing how rapid value change creates internal value contradictions in parents, contradictions that are recognized and reacted against by their children. Similarly, rapid social change serves to undermine what I call the "institutionalized hypocrisies" which, in more static times, help rationalize the universal gap between creed and deed. But even more important than accelerating social change, I argue, is the ubiquitous contemporary issue of violence, symbolized and partly caused by the threat of thermonuclear warfare. The issue of violence today colors and shapes our most private fears and fantasies, in much the same way that the issue of sex affected our Victorian forebears. Not only is the issue of violence central, but the struggle against violence is critical to the understanding of modern youth. And the danger of that struggle (a danger that later became apparent in the romance with violence among a handful of radical youth) is that those who struggle against violence will ultimately become identified with the very object of their struggle.

WE often feel that today's youth are somehow "different." There is something about today's world that seems to give the young a special restlessness, an increased impatience with the "hypocrisies" of the past, and yet an open gentleness and a searching honesty more intense than that of youth in the past. Much of what we see in today's students and nonstudents is of course familiar: to be young is in one sense always the same. But it is also new and different, as each generation confronts its unique historical position and role.

Yet we find it hard to define the difference. Partly the difficulty derives from the elusive nature of youth itself. Still, this generation seems even more elusive than most—and that, too, may be one of the differences. Partly the problem stems from the sheer variety and number of "youth" in a society where youth is often protracted into the mid-twenties. No one characterization can be adequate to the dropouts and stay-ins, hawks and doves, up-tights and cools, radicals and conservatives, heads and seekers that constitute American youth. But although we understand that the young are as various as the old in our complex society, the sense that they are different persists.

In giving today's American youth this special quality and mood, two movements have played a major role: the New Left and the hippies. Both groups are spontaneous creations of the young; both are in strong reaction to what Paul Goodman called the "Organized System"; both seek alternatives to the institutions of middle-class life. Radicals and hippies are also different from each other in numerous ways, from psychodynamics to ideology. The hippie has dropped out of a society he considers irredeemable: his attention is riveted on interior change and the expansion of personal consciousness. The radical has not given up on this society: his efforts are aimed at changing and redeeming it. Furthermore, both "movements" together comprise but a few per cent of their contemporaries. But although neither hippies nor New Leftists are representative of their generation, together they are helping to give this generation its distinctive mood. By examining the style of these young men and women, we come closer to understanding what makes their generation "different."

The Style of Postmodern Youth

Today's youth is the first generation to grow up with "modern" parents; it is the first "postmodern" generation. This fact alone distinguishes it from previous generations and helps create a mood born out of modernity, affluence, rapid social change, and violence. Despite the many pitfalls in the way of any effort to delineate a postmodern style, the effort seems worth making. For not only in America but in other nations, new styles of dissent and unrest have begun to appear, suggesting the slow emergence of a youthful style that is a reflection of and reaction to the history of the past two decades.

In emphasizing style rather than ideology, program, or characteristics, I mean to suggest that the communalities in postmodern youth groups are to be found in the *way* they approach the world, rather than in their actual behavior, ideologies, or goals. Indeed, the focus on process rather than program is itself a prime characteristic of the postmodern style, reflecting a world where flux is more obvious than fixed purpose. Postmodern youth, at least in America, is very much in process, unfinished in its development, psychologically open to an historically unpredictable future. In such a world, where ideologies come and go, and where revolutionary change is the rule, a style, a *way* of doing things, is more possible to identify than any fixed goals or constancies of behavior.

Fluidity, flux, movement. Postmodern youth displays a special personal and psychological openness, flexibility, and unfinishedness. Although many of today's youth have achieved a sense of inner identity, the term "identity" suggests a fixity, stability, and "closure" that many of them are not willing to accept: with these young men and women it is not always possible to speak of the "normal resolution" of identity issues. Our earlier fear of the ominous psychiatric implications of "prolonged adolescence" must now be qualified by an awareness that in postmodern youth many adolescent concerns and qualities persist long past the time when (according to the standards in earlier eras) they should have ended. Increasingly, postmodern youth are tied to social and historical changes that have not occurred, and that may never occur. Thus, psychological "closure," shutting doors and burning bridges, becomes impossible. The concepts of the personal future and the "life work" are ever more hazily defined; the effort to change oneself, redefine oneself, or reform oneself does not cease with the arrival of adulthood.

This fluidity and openness extends through all areas of life. Both hippie and New Left movements are nondogmatic, nonideological, and to a large extent hostile to doctrine and formula. In the New Left the focus is on "tactics"; amongst hippies, on simple, direct acts of love and communication. In neither group does one find clear-cut long-range plans, life patterns laid out in advance. The vision of the personal and collective future is blurred and vague: later adulthood is left deliberately open. In neither group is psychological development considered complete; in both groups, identity, like history, is fluid and indeterminate. In one sense, of course, identity development takes place; but, in another sense, identity is always undergoing transformations that parallel the transformations of the historical world.

Generational identification. Postmodern youth views itself primarily as part of a generation rather than an organization; it identifies with its contemporaries as a group, rather than with elders; and it does not have clearly defined leaders and heroes. Its deepest collective identification is to its own group or "movement"—a term that, in its ambiguous meanings, points not only to the fluidity and openness of postmodern youth, but to its physical mobility and the absence of traditional patterns of leadership and emulation. Among young radicals, for example, the absence of heroes or older leaders is impressive: even those five years older are sometimes viewed with mild amusement or suspicion. And although postmodern youth is often widely read in the "literature" of the New Left or that of consciousness-expansion, no one person or set of people is central to its intellectual beliefs. Although postmodern youth lives together in groups, these groups are without clear leaders.

Identification with a generational movement, rather than a cross-generational organization or a nongenerational ideology, distinguishes postmodern youth from its parents and from the "previous" generation. In addition, it also creates "generational" distinctions involving five years and less. Within the New Left clear lines are drawn between the "old New Left" (approximate age, thirty), the New Left (between twenty-two and twenty-eight), and the "new New Left" or "young kids" (under twenty-two). Generations, then, are separated by a very brief span; and the individual's own phase of youthful usefulness—for example, as an organizer—is limited to a relatively few years. Generations come and go quickly; whatever is to be accomplished must therefore be done soon.

Generational consciousness also entails a feeling of psychological disconnection from previous generations, their life situations, and their ideologies. Among young radicals there is a strong feeling that the older ideologies are exhausted or irrelevant, expressed in detached amusement at the doctrinaire disputes of the "old Left" and impatience with "old liberals." Among hippies the irrelevance of the parental past is even greater: if there is any source of insight, it is the timeless tradition of the East, not the values of the previous generation in American society. But in both groups the central values are those created in the present by the "movement" itself.

Personalism. Both groups are highly personalistic in their styles of relationship. Among hippies personalism usually entails privatism, a withdrawal from efforts to be involved in or to change the wider social world; among young radicals personalism is joined with efforts to change the world. But despite this difference, both groups care most deeply about the creation of intimate, loving, open, and trusting relationships between small groups of people. Writers who condemn the depersonalization of the modern world, who insist on "I-thou" relationships, or who expose the elements of anger, control, and sadism in nonreciprocal relationships, find a ready audience in postmodern youth. The ultimate measure of man's life is the quality of his personal relationships; the greatest sin is to be unable to relate to others in a direct, face-to-face, one-to-one relationship.

The obverse of personalism is the discomfort created by any nonpersonal, "objectified," professionalized, and, above all, exploitative relationship. Manipulation, power relationships, superordination, control, and domination are at violent odds with the I-thou mystique. Failure to treat others as fully human, inability to enter into personal relationships with them, is viewed with dismay in others and with guilt in oneself. Even with opponents the goal is to establish intimate confrontations in which the issues can be discussed openly. When opponents refuse to "meet with" young radicals, this produces anger and frequently demonstrations. The reaction of the Harvard Students for a Democratic Society when Secretary McNamara did not meet with them to discuss American foreign policies is a case in point. Equally important, perhaps the most profound source of personal guilt among postmodern youth is the "hang-ups" that make intimacy and love difficult.

Nonasceticism.   Postmodern youth is nonascetic, expressive, and sexually free. The sexual openness of the hippie world has been much discussed and criticized in the mass media. One finds a similar sexual and expressive freedom among many young radicals, although it is less provocatively demonstrative. It is of continuing importance to these young men and women to overcome and move beyond inhibition and Puritanism to a greater physical expressiveness, sexual freedom, capacity for intimacy, and ability to enjoy life.

In the era of the Pill, then, responsible sexual expression becomes increasingly possible outside of marriage, at the same time that sexuality becomes less laden with guilt, fear, and prohibition. As asceticism disappears, so does promiscuity: the personalism of postmodern youth requires that sexual expression must occur in the context of "meaningful" human relationships, of intimacy, and of mutuality. Marriage is increasingly seen as an institution for having children, but sexual relationships are viewed as the natural concomitant of close relationships between the sexes. What is important is not sexual activity itself, but the context in which it occurs. Sex is right and natural between people who are "good to each other," but sexual exploitation—failure to treat one's partner as a person—is strongly disapproved.

Inclusiveness.   The search for personal and organizational inclusiveness is still another characteristic of postmodern youth. These young men and women attempt to include both within their personalities and within their movements every opposite, every possibility, and every person, no matter how apparently alien. Psychologically, inclusiveness involves an effort to be open to every aspect of one's feelings, impulses, and fantasies, to synthesize and integrate rather than repress and dissociate, not to reject or exclude any part of one's personality or potential. Interpersonally, inclusiveness means a capacity for involvement with, identification with, and collaboration with those who are superficially alien: the peasant in

Vietnam, the poor in America, the nonwhite, the deprived, and the deformed. Indeed, so great is the pressure to include the alien, especially among hippies, that the apparently alien is often treated more favorably than the superficially similar: thus, the respect afforded to people and ideas that are distant and strange is sometimes not equally afforded those who are similar, be they one's parents or their middle-class values. One way of explaining the reaction of postmodern youth to the war in Vietnam is via the concept of inclusiveness: these young men and women react to events in Southeast Asia much as if they occurred in Newton, Massachusetts, Evanston, Illinois, Harlem, or Berkeley, California: they make little distinction in their reactions to their fellow Americans and those overseas.

One corollary of inclusiveness is intense internationalism. What matters to hippies or young radicals is not where a person comes from, but what kind of relationship is possible with him. The nationality of ideas matters little: Zen Buddhism, American pragmatism, French existentialism, Indian mysticism, or Yugoslav communism are accorded equal hearings. Interracialism is another corollary of inclusiveness: racial barriers are minimized or nonexistent, and the ultimate expressions of unity between the races, sexual relationships and marriage, are considered basically natural and normal, whatever the social problems they currently entail. In postmodern youth, then, identity and ideology are no longer parochial or national; increasingly, the reference group is the world, and the artificial subspeciation of the human species is broken down.

Antitechnologism. Postmodern youth has grave reservations about many of the technological aspects of the contemporary world. The depersonalization of life, commercialism, careerism, and familism, the bureaucratization and complex organization of advanced nations—all seem intolerable to these young men and women, who seek to create new forms of association and action to oppose the technologism of our day. Bigness, impersonality, stratification, and hierarchy are rejected, as is any involvement with the furtherance of technological values. In reaction to these values, postmodern youth seeks simplicity, naturalness, personhood, and even voluntary poverty.

But a revolt against technologism is only possible, of course, in a technological society; and to be effective it must inevitably exploit technology to overcome technologism. Thus in postmodern youth, the fruits of technology—synthetic hallucinogens in the hippie subculture, modern technology of communication among young radicals—and the affluence made possible by technological society are a precondition for a postmodern style. The demonstrative poverty of the hippie would be meaningless in a society where poverty is routine; for the radical to work for subsistence wages as a matter of choice is to *have* a choice not available in most parts of the world. Furthermore, to "organize" against the pernicious aspects of the technological era requires skill in the use of modern technologies of organization: the long-distance telephone, the use of the mass media, high-speed travel, the mimeograph machine, and so on. In the end, then, it is not the material but the spiritual consequences of technology that postmodern youth opposes: indeed, in the developing nations, those who exhibit a postmodern style may be in the vanguard of movements toward modernization. What *is* adamantly rejected is the contamination of life with the values of technological organization and production. It seems probable that a comparable rejection of the psychological consequences of current technology, coupled with the simultaneous ability to exploit that technology, characterizes all dissenting groups in all epochs.

Participation. Postmodern youth is committed to a search for new forms of groups, of organizations, and of action where decision-making is collective and arguments are resolved by "talking them out," where self-examination, interpersonal criticism, and group decision-making are fused. The objective is to create new styles of life and new types of organization that humanize rather than dehumanize, that activate and strengthen the participants rather than undermine or weaken them. And the primary vehicle for such participation is the small, face-to-face primary group of peers.

The search for new participatory forms of organization and action can hardly be deemed successful as yet, especially in the New Left, where effectiveness in the wider social and political scene remains to be demonstrated. There are inherent differences between the often taskless, face-to-face group that is the basic form of organization for both hippies and radicals and the task-oriented organization—differences that make it difficult to achieve social effectiveness based solely on small primary groups. But there may yet evolve from the hippie "tribes," small Digger communities and primary groups of the New Left, new forms of association in which self-criticism, awareness of group interaction, and the accomplishment of social and political goals go hand in hand. The effort to create groups in which individuals grow from their participation in the group extends far beyond the New Left and the hippie world; the same search is seen in the widespread enthusiasm for "sensitivity training" groups and even in the increasing use of groups as a therapeutic instrument. Nor is this solely an American search: one sees a similar focus, for example, in the Communist nations, with their emphasis on small groups that engage in the "struggle" of mutual criticism and self-criticism.

The search for effectiveness combined with participation has also led to the evolution of "new" styles of social and political action. The newness of such forms of political action as parades and demonstrations is open to some question; perhaps what is most new is the *style* in which old forms of social action are carried out. The most consistent effort is to force one's opponent into a personal confrontation with one's own point of view. Sit-ins, Freedom Rides, insistence upon discussions, silent and nonviolent demonstrations—all have a prime objective to "get through to" the other side, to force reflection, to bear witness to one's own principles, and to impress upon others the validity of these same principles. There is much that is old and familiar about this, although few of today's young radicals or hippies are ideologically committed to Gandhian views of nonviolence. Yet the underlying purpose of many of the emerging forms of social and political action, whether they be "human be-ins," "love-ins," peace marches, or "teach-ins," has a new motive—hope that by expressing one's own principles, by "demonstrating" one's convictions, one can, through sheer moral force, win over one's opponents and lure them as well into participating with one's own values.

Antiacademicism. Among postmodern youth one finds a virtually unanimous rejection of the "merely academic." This rejection is one manifestation of a wider insistence on the relevance, applicability, and personal meaningfulness of knowledge. It would be wrong simply to label this trend "anti-intellectual," for many new radicals and not a few hippies are themselves highly intellectual people. What is demanded is that intelligence be engaged with the world, just as action should be informed by knowledge. In the New Left, at least among leaders, there is enormous respect for knowledge and information and great impatience with those who act without understanding. Even among hippies, where the importance of knowledge and information is less stressed, it would be wrong simply to identify the rejection of the academic world and its values with a total rejection of intellect, knowledge, and wisdom.

To postmodern youth, then, most of what is taught in schools, colleges, and universities is largely irrelevant to living life in the last third of the twentieth century. Many academics are seen as direct or accidental apologists for the "Organized System" in the United States. Much of what they teach is considered simply unconnected to the experience of postmodern youth. New ways of learning are sought: ways that combine action with reflection upon action, ways that fuse engagement in the world with understanding of it. In an era of rapid change, the accrued wisdom of the past is cast into question, and youth seeks not only new knowledge, but new ways of learning and knowing.

Nonviolence. Finally, postmodern youth of all persuasions meets on the ground of nonviolence. For hippies, the avoidance of and calming of violence is a central objective, symbolized by gifts of flowers to policemen and the slogan "Make love, not war." And although nonviolence as a philosophical principle has lost most of its power in the New Left, nonviolence as a psychological orientation is a crucial—perhaps *the* crucial—issue. The nonviolence of postmodern youth should not be confused with pacificism: these are not necessarily young men and women who believe in turning the other cheek or who are systematically opposed to fighting for what they believe in. But the basic style of both radicals and hippies is profoundly opposed to warfare, destruction, and exploitation of man by man, and to violence, whether on an interpersonal or an international scale. Even among those who do not consider nonviolence a good in itself, a psychological inoculation against violence, even a fear of it, is a unifying theme.

The Credibility Gap: Principle and Practice

In creating the style of today's youth, the massive and violent social changes of the past two decades have played a central role. Such social changes are not only distantly perceived by those who are growing up but are immediately interwoven into the texture of their daily lives as they develop. The social changes of the postwar era affect the young in a variety of ways: in particular, they contribute to a special sensitivity to the discrepancy between principle and practice. For, during this era of rapid social change, the values most deeply embedded in the parental generation and expressed in their behavior in time of crisis are frequently very different from the more "modern" principles, ideals, and values that this generation has professed and attempted to practice in bringing up its children. Filial perception of the discrepancy between practice and principle may help explain the very widespread sensitivity among postmodern youth to the "hypocrisy" of the previous generation.

The grandparents of today's twenty-year-olds were generally born at the end of the nineteenth century and brought up during the pre-World War I years. Heirs of a Victorian tradition as yet unaffected by the value revolutions of the twentieth century, they reared their own children, the parents of today's youth, in families that emphasized respect, the control of impulse, obedience to authority, and the traditional "inner-directed" values of hard work, deferred gratification, and self-restraint. Their children, born around the time of the First World War, were thus socialized in families that remained largely Victorian in outlook.

During their lifetimes, however, these parents (and in particular the most intelligent and advantaged among them) were exposed to a great variety of new values that often changed their nominal faiths. During their youths in the 1920's and 1930's, major changes in American behavior and American values took place. For example, the "emancipation of women" in the 1920's, marked by the achievement of suffrage for women, coincided with the last major change in actual sexual behavior in America: during this period, women began to become the equal partners of men, who no longer sought premarital sexual experience solely with women of a lower class. More important, the 1920's and the 1930's were an era when older Victorian values were challenged, attacked, and all but discredited, especially in educated middle-class families. Young men and women who went to college during this period (as did most of the parents of those who can be termed "postmodern" today) were influenced outside their families by a variety of "progressive," "liberal," and even psychoanalytic ideas that contrasted sharply with the values of their childhood families. Moreover, during the 1930's, many of the parents of today's upper-middle-class youth were exposed to or involved with the ideals of the New Deal, and sometimes to more radical interpretations of man, society, and history. Finally, in the 1940's and 1950's, when it came time to rear their own children, the parents of today's elite youth were strongly influenced by "permissive" views of child-rearing that again contrasted sharply with the techniques by which they themselves had been raised. Thus, many middle-class parents moved during their lifetime from the Victorian ethos in which they had been socialized to the less moralistic, more humanitarian, and more "expressive" values of their own adulthoods.

But major changes in values, when they occur in adult life, are likely to be far from complete. To have grown up in a family where unquestioning obedience to parents was expected, but to rear one's own children in an atmosphere of "democratic" permissiveness and self-determination—and never to revert to the practices of one's own childhood—requires a change of values more total and comprehensive than most adults can achieve. Furthermore, behavior that springs from values acquired in adulthood often appears somewhat forced, artificial, or insincere to the sensitive observer. Children, clearly the most sensitive observers of their own parents, are likely to sense a discrepancy between their parents' avowed and consciously held values and their "basic instincts" with regard to child-rearing. Furthermore, the parental tendency to "revert to form" is greatest in times of family crisis, which are, of course, the times that have the greatest effect upon children. No matter how "genuinely" parents held their "new" values, many of them inevitably found themselves falling back on the lessons of their own childhoods when the chips were down.

In a time of rapid social change, then, a special *credibility gap* is likely to open between the generations. Children are likely to perceive a considerable discrepancy between what their parents avow as their values and the actual assumptions from which parental behavior springs. In many middle-class teen-agers today, for example, the focal issue of adolescent rebellion against parents often seems to be just this discrepancy: the children argue that their parents' endorsement of independence and self-determination for their children is "hypocritical" in that it does not correspond with the real behavior of the parents when their children actually seek independence. Similar perceptions of parental "hypocrisy" occur around racial matters; for example, there are many parents who in principle support racial and religious equality but become violently upset when their children date someone from another race or religion. Around political activity similar issues arise; for example, many of the parents of today's youth espouse in principle the cause of political freedom but are not involved themselves in politics and oppose their children's involvement lest they "jeopardize their record" or "ruin their later career."

Of course, no society ever fully lives up to its own professed ideals. In every society there is a gap between creedal values and actual practices, and in every society the recognition of this gap constitutes a powerful motor for social change. But in most societies, especially when social change is slow and institutions are powerful and unchanging, there occurs what can be termed *institutionalization of hypocrisy*. Children and adolescents routinely learn when it is "reasonable" to expect that the values people profess will be implemented in their behavior, and when it is not reasonable. There develops an elaborate system of exegesis and commentary upon the society's creedal values, excluding certain people or situations from the full weight of these values, or "demonstrating" that apparent inconsistencies are not really inconsistencies at all. Thus, in almost all societies a "sincere" man who "honestly" believes one set of values is frequently allowed to ignore them completely, for example, in the practice of his business, in his interpersonal relationships, in dealings with foreigners, in relationships to his children, and so on—all because these areas have been officially defined as exempt from the application of his creedal values.

In a time of rapid social change and value change, however, the institutionalization of hypocrisy seems to break down. "New" values have been in existence for so brief a period that the exemptions to them have not yet been defined, the situations to be excluded have not yet been determined, and the universal gap between principle and practice appears in all its nakedness. Thus, the mere fact of a discrepancy between creedal values and practice is not at all unusual. But what is special about the present situation of rapid value change is, first, that parents themselves tend to have two conflicting sets of values, one related to the experience of their early childhood, the other to the ideologies and principles acquired in adulthood; and second, that no stable institutions or rules for defining hypocrisy out of existence have yet been fully evolved. In such a situation, children see the emperor's nakedness with unusual clarity, recognizing the value conflict within their parents and perceiving clearly the hypocritical gap between creed and behavior.

This argument suggests that postmodern youth may not be confronted with an "objective" gap between parental preaching and practice any greater than that of most generations. But it is confronted with an unusual internal ambivalence within the parental generation over the values that parents successfully inculcated in their children, and it is "deprived" of a system of social interpretation that rationalizes the discrepancy between creed and deed. It seems likely, then, that today's youth may simply be able to perceive the universal gulf between principle and practice more clearly than previous generations have done.

This points to one of the central characteristics of postmodern youth: it insists on taking seriously a great variety of political, personal, and social principles that "no one in his right mind" ever before thought of attempting to extend to such situations as dealings with strangers, relations between the races, or international politics. For example, peaceable openness has long been a creedal virtue in our society, but it has never been extended to foreigners, particularly with dark skins. Similarly, equality has long been preached, but the "American dilemma" has been resolved by a series of institutionalized hypocrisies that exempted Negroes from the application of this principle. Love has always been a central value in Christian society, but really to love one's enemies—to be generous to policemen, customers, criminals, servants, and foreigners—has been considered folly.

These speculations on the credibility gap between the generations in a time of rapid change may help explain two crucial facts about postmodern youth: first, it frequently comes from highly principled families with whose principles it continues to agree; second, it has the outrageous temerity to insist that individuals and societies live by the values they preach. And these speculations may also explain the frequent feeling of those who have worked intensively with student radicals or hippies that, apart from the "impracticality" of some of their views, these sometimes seem to be the only clear-eyed and sane people in a society and a world where most of us are still systematically blind to the traditional gap between personal principle and practice, national creed and policy, a gap that we may no longer be able to afford.

Violence: Sadism and Cataclysm

Those who are today in their early twenties were born near the end of World War II, the most violent and barbarous war in world history. The lasting imprint of that war can be summarized in the names of three towns: Auschwitz, Hiroshima, and Nuremberg. *Auschwitz* points to the possibility of a "civilized" nation embarking on a systematized, well-organized, and scientific plan of exterminating an entire people. *Hiroshima* demonstrates how "clean," easy, and impersonal cataclysm can be to those who perpetrate it, and how demonic, sadistic, and brutal to those who experience it. And *Nuremberg* summarizes the principle that men have an accountability above obedience to national policy, a responsibility to conscience more primary, even, than fidelity to national law. These three lessons are the matrix for the growth of postmodern youth.

The terror of violence that has hung over all men and women since the Second World War has especially shaped the outlooks of today's youth. In the first memories of a group of young radicals, for example, one finds the following recollections: a dim recall of the end of World War II; childhood terror of the atomic bomb; witnessing the aftermath of a violent riot in the United States; being frightened by a picture of a tank riding over rubble; being violently jealous at the birth of a younger brother; taking part in "gruesome" fights in the schoolyard. Such memories mean many things, but in them, violence-in-the-world finds echo and counterpart in the violence of inner feelings. The term "violence" suggests both of these possibilities: the *psychological* violence of sadism, exploitation, and aggression, and the *historical* violence of war, cataclysm, and holocaust. In the lives of most of this generation the threats of inner and outer violence are fused, each activating, exciting, and potentiating the other. To summarize a complex thesis into a few words: *the issue of violence is to this generation what the issue of sex was to the Victorian world.*

Stated differently, what is most deeply repressed, rejected, feared, controlled, and projected onto others by the postmodern generation is no longer its own sexuality. Sex, for most of this generation, is much freer, more open, less guilt- and anxiety-ridden. But violence, whether in one's self or in others, has assumed new prominence as the prime source of inner and outer terror. That this should be so in the modern world is readily understandable. Over all of us hangs the continual threat of a technological violence more meaningless, absurd, total, and unpremeditated than any ever imagined before. Individual life always resonates with historical change; history is not merely the backdrop for development, but its ground. To be grounded in the history of the past two decades is to have stood upon, to have experienced both directly and vicariously, violent upheaval, violent world-wide revolution, and the unrelenting possibility of world-wide destruction. To have been alive and aware in America during the past decade has been to be exposed to the assassination of a President and the televised murder of his murderer, to the well-publicized slaughter of Americans by their fellow countrymen, and to the recent violence in our cities. To have been a middle-class child in the past two decades is to have watched daily the violence of television, both as it reports the bloodshed and turmoil of the American and non-American world, and as it skillfully elaborates and externalizes in repetitive dramas the potential for violence within each of us.

It therefore requires no assumption of an increase in biological aggression to account for the salience of the issue of violence for postmodern youth. The capacity for rage, spite, and aggression is part of our endowment as human beings: it is a constant potential of human nature. But during the past two decades—indeed, starting before the Second World War—we have witnessed violence and imagined violence on a scale more frightening than ever before. Like the angry child who fears that his rage will itself destroy those around him, we have become vastly more sensitive to and fearful of our inner angers, for we live in a world where even the mildest irritation, multipled a billionfold by modern technology, might destroy all civilization. The fact of violent upheaval and the possibility of cataclysm has been literally brought into our living rooms during the past twenty years; it has been interwoven with the development of a whole generation.

It should not surprise us, then, that the issue of violence is a focal concern for those of contemporary youth with the greatest historical consciousness. The hippie slogan "Make love, not war" expresses their sentiment, although in a form that the "realist" of previous generations might deem sentimental or romantic. Although few young radicals would agree with the wording of this statement, the underlying sentiment corresponds to their basic psychological orientation. For them, as for many others of their generation, the primary task is to develop new psychological, political, and international controls on violence. Indeed, many of the dilemmas of today's young radicals seem related to their extraordinarily zealous efforts to avoid any action or relationship in which inner or outer violence might be evoked. Distaste for violence animates the profound revulsion many of today's youth feel toward the war in Southeast Asia, just as it underlies a similar revulsion against the exploitation or control of man by man. The same psychological nonviolence is related to young radicals' avoidance of traditional leadership lest it lead to domination, to their emphasis on person-to-person participation and "confrontation," and even to their unwillingness to "play the media" in an attempt to gain political effectiveness. Even the search for forms of mass political action that avoid physical violence—a preference severely tested and somewhat undermined by the events of recent months—points to a considerable distaste for the direct expression of aggression.

I do not mean to suggest that postmodern youth contains a disproportionate number of tight-lipped pacifists or rage-filled deniers of their own inner angers. On the contrary, among today's youth, exuberance, passionateness, and zest are the rule rather than the exception. Nor are hippies and young radicals incapable of anger, rage, and resentment—especially when their principles are violated. But for many of these young men and women, the experiences of early life and the experience of the postwar world are joined in a special sensitivity to the issue of violence, whether in themselves or in others. This confluence of psychological and historical forces helps explain the intensity of their search for new forms of social organization and political action that avoid manipulation, domination, and control, just as it contributes to their widespread opposition to warfare of all kinds.

Yet the position of the psychologically nonviolent youth in a violent world is difficult and paradoxical. On the one hand, he seeks to minimize violence, but on the other, his efforts often elicit violence from others. At the same time that he attempts to work to actualize his vision of a peaceful world, he must confront more directly and continually than do his peers the fact that the world is neither peaceful nor just. The frustration and discouragement of his work repetitively reawaken his anger, which must forever be rechanneled into peaceful paths. Since he continually confronts destructiveness and exploitation in the world, his own inevitable potential for destructiveness and exploitiveness inevitably arouses in him great guilt. The young men and women who make up the New Left in America, like other postmodern youth, have far less difficulty in living with their sexual natures than did their parents; but what they continue to find difficult to live with, what they still repress, avoid, and counteract is their own potential for violence. It remains to be seen whether, in the movement toward "resistance" and disruption of today's young radicals, their psychological nonviolence will continue to be reflected in their actions.

In pointing to the psychological dimension of the issue of violence, I do not mean to attribute causal primacy either to the experiences of early life or to their residues in adulthood. My thesis is rather that for those of this generation with the greatest historical awareness, the psychological and historical possibilities of violence have come to potentiate each other. To repeat: witnessing the acting out of violence on a scale more gigantic than ever before or imaginatively participating in the possibility of worldwide holocaust activates the fear of one's own violence; heightened awareness of one's inner potential for rage, anger, or destructiveness increases sensitivity to the possibility of violence in the world.

This same process of historical potentiation of inner violence has occurred, I believe, throughout the modern world and brings with it not only the intensified efforts to curb violence we see in this small segment of postmodern youth, but other more frightening possibilities. Postmodern youth, to an unusual degree, remains open to and aware of its own angers and aggressions, and this awareness creates in the young a sufficient understanding of inner violence to enable them to control it in themselves and oppose it in others. Most men and women, young or old, possess less insight: their inner sadism is projected onto others whom they thereafter loathe or abjectly serve; or, more disastrously, historically heightened inner violence is translated into outer aggression and murderousness, sanctioned by self-righteousness.

Thus, if the issue of violence plagues postmodern youth, it is not because these young men and women are more deeply rage-filled than most. On the contrary, it is because such young men and women have confronted this issue more squarely in themselves and in the world than have any but a handful of their fellows. If they have not yet found solutions, they have at least faced an issue so dangerous that most of us find it too painful even to acknowledge, and they have done so, most remarkably, without identifying with what they oppose. Their still-incomplete lives pose for us all the question on which our survival as individuals and as a world depends: can we create formulations and forms to control historical and psychological violence before their fusion destroys us all?

You Have to Grow Up
in Scarsdale

*In this essay, written in 1969, I argue that in the youthful opposition we
are witnessing the overlap of two distinct "revolutions," each with a
different historical origin. The first revolution is the now-traditional but
once radical demand for inclusion, citizenship, or "universalism"—the
demand that all men be granted the freedoms, goods, and privileges that
were once the prerogative of a tiny aristocracy or a small upper*
bourgeoisie. *The second revolution is built upon the first: it is the
revolution of those who take the freedoms, goods, and privileges of the
first revolution for granted, seeing them largely as facts of life. Such
people, mostly young, seek some new fulfillment beyond material
abundance, some psychological liberation beyond political freedom. They
are sensitive not only to the direct oppressions of political tyranny and
economic scarcity, but to the more subtle oppressions of psychological
repression, group pressures, and social expectation. Basically, they are
struggling to define the postscarcity world, to answer the question "What
lies beyond affluence?"*

*In arguing that the second revolution becomes possible only because of
the success of the first, I differ with many social theorists who, like myself,
remain in basic sympathy with the youthful opposition. For one, I believe
that the emergence of a youthful opposition results from massive social
changes that are in many cases benign and beneficial—e.g., the rise of a
dozen societies in the world where men and women no longer need worry
about starvation or material security; the extension within these societies
of considerable political freedom and social security; an economic system
so "automatically" productive that men may rail against the "consumer
society" without being considered insane. Thus, I do not agree with those
radicals who see the emergence of the youthful opposition as the simple
consequence of oppression, repression, or the degradation of the quality of
life in the liberal industrial states.*

*Secondly, I differ from those theorists of the counterculture who
interpret it as involving a total break with the past. I, in contrast, see not*

*only a rejection of much that is corrupt, immoral, and unjust in the existing
society, but also an affirmation of values deeply imbedded within Western
societies. Whatever its lapses from democratic practice, the youthful
opposition has emphasized equality, justice, and individual participation
in politics. Indeed, the issues around which the oppositional youth culture
has been able to organize and act most effectively have always been
impeccably traditional issues like opposition to racism, the search for
peace, or the demand for fuller participation in the democratc process.*

*Even what I call the second revolution—the quest for a world beyond
materialism, the rejection of careerism and vocationalism, and the
emphasis on genuineness, relatedness, community, and love—can hardly
be counted a total break with Western culture. On the contrary, each of
these values has roots in the traditions of American and other Western
societies; each involves an effort to live out the dreams and private
fantasies of previous generations. What originally appeared as the
ideology of the antibourgeois Bohemian and romantic world becomes,
with the advent of mass affluence, a possible guideline for the actual
conduct of life. The ideals of the second revolution can scarcely be
considered a radical break with Western history.*

*In stressing these continuities with the past, I do not mean to deny
the revolutionary potential of the youthful opposition. Nor am I qualifying
my insistence that the contemporary world is genuinely without precedent,
and that the emergence of a new youthful opposition springs from
uniquely modern conditions. But I am arguing that this "revolution," like
all revolutions, builds upon the past, reordering its priorities and values
and seeking to fulfill its promises. At both an historical and psychological
level, it remains true, as Erik Erikson has argued, that every effort to
break with the past is also an effort to actualize what was latent in the
previous generation.*

WE long ago learned to expect students in underdeveloped countries
to lead unruly demonstrations against the *status quo*. What is new, unexpected, and upsetting to many is that an apparently similar mood is
sweeping across America, France, Germany, Italy, and even Eastern European nations like Czechoslovakia and Poland. Furthermore, the revolts
occur not at the most backward universities, but at the most distinguished, liberal, and enlightened—Berkeley, the Sorbonne, Tokyo, Columbia, the Free University of Berlin, Rome, and now Harvard.

This development has taken almost everyone by surprise. The American public is clearly puzzled, frightened, and often outraged by the behavior of its most privileged youth. The scholarly world, including many who
have devoted their lives to the study of student protest, has been caught
off guard as well. For many years American analysts of student move-

ments have been busy demonstrating that "it can't happen here." Student political activity abroad has been seen as a reaction to modernization, industrialization, and the demise of traditional or tribal societies. In an already modern, industrialized, detribalized, and "stable" nation like America, it was argued, student protests are naturally absent.

Another explanation has tied student protests abroad to bad living conditions in some universities and to the unemployability of their graduates. Student revolts, it was argued, spring partly from the misery of student life in countries like India and Indonesia. Students who must live in penury and squalor naturally turn against their universities and societies. And if, as in many developing nations, hundreds of thousands of university graduates can find no work commensurate with their skills, the chances for student militancy are further increased.

These arguments helped explain the "silent generation" of the nineteen fifties and the absence of protest, during that period, in American universities, where students were often "indulged" with good living conditions, close student-faculty contact, and considerable freedom of speech. And they helped explain why "superemployable" American college graduates, especially the much-sought-after ones from colleges like Columbia and Harvard, seemed so contented with their lot.

But such arguments do not help us understand today's noisy, angry, and militant students in the advanced countries. Nor do they explain why students who enjoy the greatest advantages—those at the leading universities—are often found in the revolts. As a result, several new interpretations of student protest are currently being put forward, interpretations that ultimately form part of what Richard Poirier has termed "the war against the young."

Many reactions to student unrest, of course, spring primarily from fear, anger, confusion, or envy, rather than from theoretical analysis. Governor Wallace's attacks on student "anarchists" and other "pinheaded intellectuals," for example, were hardly coherent explanations of protest. Many of the bills aimed at punishing student protesters being proposed in Congress and state legislatures reflect similar feelings of anger and outrage. Similarly, the presumption that student unrest *must* be part of an international conspiracy is based on emotion rather than fact. Even George F. Kennan's recent discussion of the American student Left is essentially a moral condemnation of "revolting students," rather than an effort to explain their behavior.

Oedipal Rebels or Neo-Luddites?

If we turn to more thoughtful analyses of the current student mood, we find two general theories gaining widespread acceptance. The first, articulately expressed by Lewis S. Feuer, in his recent book on student movements, *The Conflict of Generations,* might be termed the Oedipal-rebellion interpretation. The second, cogently stated by Zbigniew Brzezinski, may be called the theory of historical irrelevance.

The explanation of Oedipal rebellion sees the underlying force in all student revolts as blind, unconscious Oedipal hatred of fathers and the older generation. Feuer, for example, finds in all student movements an inevitable tendency toward violence and a combination of "regicide, parricide, and suicide." A decline in respect for the authority of the older generation is needed to trigger a student movement, but the force behind it comes from "obscure" and "unconscious" forces in the child's early life, including both intense death wishes against his father and the enormous guilt and self-hatred that such wishes inspired in the child.

The idealism of student movements is thus, in many respects, only a "front" for the latent unconscious destructiveness and self-destructiveness of underlying motivations. Even the expressed desire of these movements to help the poor and exploited is explained psychoanalytically by Feuer: empathy for the disadvantaged is traced to "traumatic" encounters with parental bigotry in the students' childhoods, when their parents forbade them to play with children of other races or lower social classes. The identification of today's New Left with blacks is thus interpreted as an unconscious effort to "abreact and undo this original trauma."

There are two basic problems with the Oedipal-rebellion theory, however. First, although it uses psychoanalytic terms, it is bad psychoanalysis. The real psychoanalytic account insists that the Oedipus complex is universal in all normally developing children. To point to this complex in explaining student rebellion is, therefore, like pointing to the fact that all children learn to walk. Since both characteristics are said to be universal, neither helps us understand why, at some historical moments, students are restive and rebellious, while at others they are not. Second, the theory does not help us explain why some students (especially those from middle-class, affluent, and idealistic families) are most inclined to rebel, while others (especially those from working-class and deprived families) are less so.

In order really to explain anything, the Oedipal-rebellion hypothesis would have to be modified to point to an unusually severe Oedipus complex, involving especially *intense* and unresolved unconscious feelings of father-hatred in student rebels. But much is now known about the lives and backgrounds of these rebels—at least those in the United States—and this evidence does not support even the modified theory. On the contrary, it indicates that most student protesters are relatively *close* to their parents, that the values they profess are usually the ones they learned at the family dinner table, and that their parents tend to be educated, liberal or left-wing, and politically active.

Furthermore, psychological studies of student radicals indicate that they are no more neurotic, suicidal, enraged, or disturbed than are nonradicals. Indeed, most studies find them to be rather more integrated, self-accepting, and "advanced," in a psychological sense, than their politically inactive contemporaries. In general, research on American student rebels supports a "generational solidarity" (or chip-off-the-old-block) theory, rather than one of Oedipal rebellion.

The second theory of student revolts now being advanced asserts that they are a reaction against "historical irrelevance." Rebellion springs from the unconscious awareness of some students that society has left them and their values behind. According to this view, the ultimate causes of student dissent are sociological rather than psychological. They lie in fundamental changes in the nature of the advanced societies—especially, in the change from industrial to postindustrial society. The student revolution is seen not as a true revolution, but as a counterrevolution—what Daniel Bell has called "the guttering last gasp of a romanticism soured by rancor and impotence."

This theory assumes that we are moving rapidly into a new age in which technology will dominate, an age whose real rulers will be men like computer experts, systems analysts, and technobureaucrats. Students who are attached to outmoded and obsolescent values like humanism and romanticism unconsciously feel they have no place in this postindustrial world. When they rebel they are like the Luddites of the past—workers who smashed machines to protest the inevitable Industrial Revolution. Today's student revolt reflects what Brzezinski terms "an unconscious realization that they [the rebels] are themselves becoming historically obsolete"; it is nothing but the "death rattle of the historical irrelevants."

This theory is also inadequate. It assumes that the shape of the future is already technologically determined, and that protesting students unconsciously "know" that it will offer them no real reward, honor, or power. But the idea that the future can be accurately predicted is open to fundamental objection. Every past attempt at prophecy has turned out to be grievously incorrect. Extrapolations from the past, while sometimes useful in the short run, are usually fundamentally wrong in the long run, especially when they attempt to predict the quality of human life, the nature of political and social organization, international relations or the shape of future culture.

The future is, of course, made by men. Technology is not an inevitable master of man and history but merely provides the possibility of applying scientific knowledge to specific problems. Men may identify with it or refuse to, use it or be used by it for good or evil, apply it humanely or destructively. Thus, there is no real evidence that student protest will emerge as the "death rattle of the historical irrelevants." It could equally well be the "first spark of a new historical era." No one today can be sure of the outcome, and people who feel certain that the future will bring the obsolescence and death of those whom they dislike are often merely expressing their fond hope.

The fact that today's students invoke "old" humanistic and romantic ideas in no way proves that student protests are a "last gasp" of a dying order. Quite the contrary: *all* revolutions draw upon older values and visions. Many of the ideals of the French Revolution, for example, originated in Periclean Athens. Revolutions do not occur because new ideas suddenly develop, but because a new generation begins to take *old* ideas seriously—not merely as interesting theoretical views, but as the basis for political action and social change. Until recently the humanistic vision of human fulfillment and the romantic vision of an expressive, imaginative, and passionate life were taken seriously only by small aristocratic or Bohemian groups. The fact that they are today taken as real goals by millions of students in many nations does not mean that these students are "counterrevolutionaries," but merely that their ideas follow the pattern of every major revolution.

Indeed, today's student rebels are rarely opposed to technology per se. On the contrary, they take the high technology of their societies completely for granted and concern themselves with it very little. What they *are* opposed to is, in essence, the worship of technology, the tendency to treat people as "inputs" or "outputs" of a technological system, the subordination of human needs to technological programs. The essential conflict between the minority of students who make up the student revolt and the existing order is a conflict over the future direction of technological society, not a counterrevolutionary protest against technology.

In short, both the Oedipal-rebellion and the historical-irrelevance theories are what students would call "put-downs." If we accept either, we are encouraged not to listen to protests, or to explain them away, or to reject them as either the "acting out" of destructive Oedipal feelings or the blind reaction of an obsolescent group to the awareness of its obsolescence. But if, as I have argued, neither of these theories is adequate to explain the current "wave" of student protest here and abroad, how can we understand it?

The Extension of Development

One factor often cited to explain student unrest is the large number of people in the world under thirty—today the critical dividing line between generations. But this explanation alone, like the theories just discussed, is not adequate, for in all historical eras the vast portion of the population has always been under thirty. Indeed, in primitive societies most people die before they reach that age. If chronological youth alone were enough to insure rebellion, the advanced societies—where a greater proportion of the population reaches old age than ever before in history—should be the *least* revolutionary, and primitive societies the *most*. This is not the case.

More relevant factors are the relationship of those under thirty to the established institutions of society (that is, whether they are engaged in them or not); and the opportunities that society provides for their continuing intellectual, ethical, and emotional development. In both cases the present situation in the advanced nations is without precedent.

Philippe Aries, in his remarkable book *Centuries of Childhood,* points out that until the end of the Middle Ages, no separate stage of childhood was recognized in Western societies. Infancy ended at approximately six or seven, whereupon most children were integrated into adult life, treated as small men and women, and expected to work as junior partners of the adult world. Only later was childhood recognized as a separate stage of life, and our own century is the first to "guarantee" it by requiring universal primary education.

The recognition of adolescence as a stage of life is of even more recent origin, the product of the nineteenth and twentieth centuries. Only as industrial societies became prosperous enough to defer adult work until after puberty could they create institutions—like widespread secondary-school education—that would extend adolescence to virtually all young people. Recognition of adolescence also arose from the vocational and psychological requirements of these societies, which needed much higher levels of training and psychological development than could be guaranteed through primary education alone. There is, in general, an intimate relationship between the way a society defines the stages of life and its economic, political, and social characteristics.

Today, in more developed nations, we are beginning to witness the recognition of still another stage of life. Like childhood and adolescence, it was initially granted only to a small minority but is now being rapidly extended to an ever-larger group. I will call this the stage of "youth," and by that I mean both a further phase of disengagement from society and the period of psychological development that intervenes between adolescence and adulthood. This stage, which continues into the twenties and sometimes into the thirties, provides opportunities for intellectual, emotional and moral development that were never afforded to any other large group in history. In the student revolts we are seeing one result of this advance.

I call the extension of youth development an advance advisedly. Attendance at a college or university is a major part of this extension, and there is growing evidence that this is, other things being equal, a good thing for the student. Put in an oversimplified phrase, it tends to free him—to free him from swallowing, unexamined, the assumptions of the past, to free him from the superstitions of his childhood, to free him to express his feelings more openly, and to free him from irrational bondage to authority.

I do not mean to suggest, of course, that all college graduates are free and liberated spirits, unencumbered by irrationality, superstition, authoritarianism, or blind adherence to tradition. But these findings do indicate that our colleges, far from cranking out only machinelike robots who will provide skilled manpower for the economy, are also producing an increasing number of highly critical citizens—young men and women who have the opportunity, the leisure, the affluence, and the educational resources to continue their development beyond the point where most people in the past were required to stop it.

So, one part of what we are seeing on campuses throughout the world is not a reflection of how bad higher education is, but rather of its extraordinary accomplishments. Even the moral righteousness of the student rebels, a quality both endearing and infuriating to their elders, must be judged at least partially a consequence of the privilege of an extended youth; for a prolonged development, we know, encourages the individual to elaborate a more personal, less purely conventional sense of ethics.

What the advanced nations have done is to create their own critics on a mass basis—that is, to create an ever-larger group of young people who take the highest values of their societies as their own, who internalize these values and identify them with their own best selves, and who are willing to struggle to implement them. At the same time, the extension of youth has lessened the personal risks of dissent: these young people have been freed from the requirements of work, gainful employment, and even marriage, which permits them to criticize their society from a protected position of disengagement.

But the mere prolongation of development need not automatically lead to unrest. To be sure, we have granted to millions the opportunity to examine their societies, to compare them with their values, and to come to a reasoned judgment of the existing order. But why should their judgment today be so unenthusiastic?

What protesting students throughout the world share is a mood more than an ideology or a program, a mood that says the existing system—the power structure—is hypocritical, unworthy of respect, outmoded, and in urgent need of reform. In addition, students everywhere speak of repression, manipulation, and authoritarianism. (This is paradoxical, considering the apparently great freedoms given them in many nations. In America, for example, those who complain most loudly about being suffocated by the subtle tyranny of the Establishment usually attend the institutions where student freedom is greatest.) Around this general mood, specific complaints arrange themselves as symptoms of what students often call the "exhaustion of the existing society."

The Two Revolutions

To understand this phenomenon, we must recognize that since the Second World War some societies have indeed begun to move past the industrial era into a new world that is postindustrial, technological, postmodern, posthistoric, or, in Brzezinski's term, "technetronic." In Western Europe, the United States, Canada, and Japan, the first contours of this new society are already apparent. And, in many other less-developed countries, middle-class professionals (whose children become activists) often live in postindustrial enclaves within preindustrial societies. Whatever we call the postindustrial world, it has demonstrated that, for the first time, man can produce more than enough to meet his material needs.

This accomplishment is admittedly blemished by enormous problems of economic distribution in the advanced nations, and it is in terrifying contrast to the overwhelming poverty of the Third World. Nevertheless, it is clear that what might be called "the problem of production" *can*, in principle, be solved. If all members of American society, for example, do not have enough material goods, it is because the system of distribution is flawed. The same is true, or will soon be true, in many other nations that are approaching advanced states of industrialization. Characteristically, these nations, along with the most technological, are those where student unrest has recently been most prominent.

The transition from industrial to postindustrial society brings with it a major shift in social emphases and values. Industrializing and industrial societies tend to be oriented toward solving the problems of production. An industrial ethic—sometimes Protestant, sometimes socialist, sometimes communist—tends to emphasize psychological qualities like self-discipline, delay of gratification, achievement-orientation, and a strong emphasis on economic success and productivity. The social, political, and economic institutions of these societies tend to be organized in a way that is consistent with the goal of increasing production. And industrial societies tend to apply relatively uniform standards, to reward achievement rather than status acquired by birth, and to emphasize emotional neutrality ("coolness") and rationality in work and public life.

The emergence of postindustrial societies, however, means that growing numbers of the young are brought up in family environments where abundance, relative economic security, political freedom, and affluence are simply facts of life, not goals to be striven for. To such people the psychological imperatives, social institutions, and cultural values of the industrial ethic seem largely outdated and irrelevant to their own lives.

Once it has been demonstrated that a society *can* produce enough for all its members, at least some of the young turn to other goals: for example, trying to make sure that society *does* produce enough and distributes it fairly, or searching for ways to live meaningfully with the goods and the leisure they *already* have. The problem is that our society has, in some realms, exceeded its earlier targets. Lacking new ones, it has become exhausted by its success.

When the values of industrial society become devitalized, the elite sectors of youth—the most affluent, intelligent, privileged, and so on—come to feel that they live in institutions whose demands lack moral authority or, in the current jargon, "credibility." Today the moral imperative and urgency behind production, acquisition, materialism, and abundance has been lost.

Furthermore, with the lack of moral legitimacy felt in the system, the least request for loyalty, restraint, or conformity by its representatives— for example, by college presidents and deans—can easily be seen as a moral outrage, an authoritarian repression, a manipulative effort to "co-opt" students into joining the Establishment and an exercise in "illegitimate authority" that must be resisted. From this conception springs at least part of the students' vague sense of oppression. And, indeed, perhaps their peculiar feeling of suffocation arises ultimately from living in societies without vital ethical claims.

Given such a situation, it does not take a clear-cut issue to trigger a major protest. I doubt, for example, that college and university administrators are in fact *more* hypocritical and dishonest than they were in the past. American intervention in Vietnam, while many of us find it unjust and cruel, is not inherently *more* outrageous than other similar imperialistic interventions by America and other nations within the last century. And the position of blacks in this country, although disastrously and unjustifiably disadvantaged, is, in some economic and legal respects, better than ever before. Similarly, the conditions for students in America have never been as good, especially, as I have noted, at those elite colleges where student protests are most common.

But this is *precisely* the point: it is *because* so many of the *other* problems of American society seem to have been resolved, or to be resolvable in principle, that students now react with new indignation to old problems, turn to new goals, and propose radical reforms.

What we are witnessing on the campuses of the world is a fusion of *two revolutions,* with distinct historical origins. One is a continuation of the old and familiar revolution of the industrial society, the liberal-democratic-egalitarian revolution that started in America and France at the turn of the eighteenth century and spread to virtually every nation in the world. (Not completed in any of them, its contemporary American form is, above all, to be found in the increased militancy of blacks.) The other is the new revolution, the postindustrial one, which seeks to define new goals relevant to the twentieth and twenty-first centuries.

In its social and political aspects the first revolution has been one of universalization, to use the sociologist's awkward term. It has involved the progressive extension to more and more people of economic, political, and social rights, privileges, and opportunities originally available only to the aristocracy, then to the middle class, and now in America to the relatively affluent white working class. It is, in many respects, a *quantitative* revolution. That is, it concerns itself less with the quality of life than with the amount of political freedom, the quantity and distribution of goods, or the amount and level of injustice.

As the United States approaches the targets of the first revolution, on which this society was built, to be poor shifts from being an unfortunate fact of life to being an outrage. And, for the many who have never experienced poverty, discrimination, exploitation, or oppression, even to *witness* the existence of these evils in the lives of others suddenly becomes intolerable. In our own time the impatience to complete the first revolution has grown apace, and we find less willingness to compromise, wait, and forgive among the young, especially among those who now take the values of the old revolution for granted—seeing them not as goals, but as *rights*.

A subtle change has thus occurred. What used to be utopian ideals— like equality, abundance, and freedom from discrimination—have now become demands, inalienable rights upon which one can insist without brooking any compromise. It is noteworthy that in today's student confrontations no one requests anything. Students present their "demands."

So, on the one hand, we see a growing impatience to complete the first revolution. But, on the other, there is a newer revolution concerned with newer issues, a revolution that is less social, economic, or political than psychological, historical, and cultural. It is less concerned with the quantities of things than with their qualities, and it judges the virtually complete liberal revolution and finds it still wanting.

"You have to have grown up in Scarsdale to know how bad things really are," said one radical student. This comment would probably sound arrogant, heartless, and insensitive to a poor black, much less to a citizen of the Third World. But he meant something important by it. He meant that *even* in the Scarsdales of America, with their affluence, their upper-middle-class security and abundance, their well-fed, well-heeled children and their excellent schools, something is wrong. Economic affluence does not guarantee a feeling of personal fulfillment; political freedom does not always yield an inner sense of liberation and cultural freedom; social justice and equality may leave one with a feeling that something else is missing in life. "No to the consumer society!" shouted the bourgeois students of the Sorbonne during May and June of 1968—a cry that understandably alienated French workers, for whom affluence and the consumer society are still central goals.

What, then, are the targets of the new revolution? As is often noted, students themselves don't know. They speak vaguely of "a society that has never existed," of "new values," of a "more humane world," of "liberation" in some psychological, cultural, and historical sense. Their rhetoric is largely negative; they are stronger in opposition than in proposals for reform; their diagnoses often seem accurate, but their prescriptions are vague; and they are far more articulate in urging the immediate completion of the first revolution than in defining the goals of the second. Thus, we can only indirectly discern trends that point to the still-undefined targets of the new revolution.

Goals of the New Revolution

First, there is a revulsion against the notion of quantity, particularly economic quantity and materialism, and a turn toward concepts of quality. One of the most delightful slogans of the French student revolt was "Long live the passionate revolution of creative intelligence!" In a sense, the achievement of abundance may allow millions of contemporary men and women to examine, as only a few artists and madmen have examined in the past, the quality, joyfulness, and zestfulness of experience. The "expansion of consciousness"; the stress on the expressive, the aesthetic, and the creative; the emphasis on imagination, direct perception, and fantasy—all are part of the effort to enhance the quality of this experience.

Another goal of the new revolution involves a revolt against uniformity, equalization, standardization, and homogenization—not against technology itself, but against the "technologization of man." At times, this revolt approaches anarchic quaintness, but it has a positive core as well—the demand that individuals be appreciated, not because of their similarities or despite their differences, but because they *are* different, diverse, unique, and noninterchangeable. This attitude is evident in many areas: the insistence upon a cultivation of personal idiosyncrasy, mannerism, and unique aptitude. Intellectually, it is expressed in the rejection of the melting-pot and consensus-politics views of American life in favor of a post-homogeneous America in which cultural diversity and conflict are underlined rather than denied.

The new revolution also involves a continuing struggle against psychological or institutional closure or rigidity in any form, even the rigidity of a definite adult role. Positively, it extols the virtues of openness, motion, and continuing human development. What Robert J. Lifton has termed the "protean style" is clearly in evidence. There is emerging a concept of a lifetime of personal change, of an adulthood of continuing self-transformation, of an adaptability and an openness to the revolutionary modern world that will enable the individual to remain "with it"—psychologically youthful and on top of the present.

Another characteristic is the revolt against centralized power and the complementary demand for participation. What is demanded is not merely the consent of the governed, but the involvement of the governed. "Participatory democracy" summarizes this aspiration, but it extends far beyond the phrase and the rudimentary social forms that have sprung up around it. It extends to the demand for relevance in education—that is, for a chance for the student to participate in his own educational experience in a way that involves all of his faculties: emotional and moral as well as intellectual. The demand for "student power" (or, in Europe, "codetermination") is an aspect of the same theme: at Nanterre, Columbia, Frankfurt, and Harvard, students increasingly seek to participate in making the policies of their universities.

This demand for participation is also embodied in the new ethic of "meaningful human relationships," in which individuals confront each other without masks, pretenses, and games. They "relate" to each other as unique and irreplaceable human beings and develop new forms of relationships from which all participants will grow.

In distinguishing between the old and the new revolutions, and in attempting to define the targets of the new, I am, of course, making distinctions that students themselves rarely make. In any one situation the two revolutions are joined and fused, if not confused. For example, the Harvard students' demand for "restructuring the university" is essentially the second revolution's demand for participation; but their demand for an end to university "exploitation" of the surrounding community is tied to the more traditional goals of the first revolution. In most radical groups there is a range of opinion that starts with the issues of the first (racism, imperialism, exploitation, war) and runs to the concerns of the second (experiential education, new life styles, meaningful participation, consciousness expansion, relatedness, encounter, and community). The first revolution is personified by Maoist-oriented Progressive Labor Party factions within the student Left, while the second is represented by hippies, the "acid Left," and the Yippies. In any individual, and in all student movements, these revolutions coexist in uneasy and often abrasive tension.

Furthermore, one of the central problems for student movements today is the absence of any theory of society that does justice to the new world in which we of the most industrialized nations live. In their search for rational critiques of present societies, students turn to theories like Marxism that are intricately bound up with the old revolution.

Such theories make the ending of economic exploitation, the achievement of social justice, the abolition of racial discrimination, and the development of political participation and freedom central, but they rarely deal adequately with the issues of the second revolution. Students inevitably try to adapt the rhetoric of the first to the problems of the second, using concepts that are often blatantly inadequate to today's world.

Even the concept of "revolution" itself is so heavily laden with images of political, economic, and social upheaval that it hardly seems to characterize the equally radical, but more social, psychological and cultural transformations involved in the new revolution. One student, recognizing this, called the changes occurring in his California student group "too radical to be called a revolution." Students are thus often misled by their borrowed vocabulary, but most adults are even more confused, and many are quickly led to the mistaken conclusion that today's student revolt is nothing more than a repetition of Communism's in the past.

Failure to distinguish between the old and new revolutions also makes it impossible to consider the critical question of how compatible they are with each other. Does it make sense—or is it morally right—for today's affluent American students to seek imagination, self-actualization, individuality, openness, and relevance when most of the world and many in America live in deprivation, oppression, and misery?

The fact that the first revolution is "completed" in Scarsdale does not mean that it is (or soon will be) in Harlem or Appalachia—to say nothing of Bogotá or Calcutta. For many children of the second revolution, the meaning of life may be found in completing the first—that is, in extending to others the "rights" they have always taken for granted.

For others the second revolution will not wait; the question "What lies beyond affluence?" demands an answer now. Thus, although we may deem it self-indulgent to pursue the goals of the new revolution in a world where so much misery exists, the fact is that in the advanced nations it is upon us, and we must at least learn to recognize it.

Finally, beneath my analysis lies an assumption I had best make explicit. Many student critics argue that their societies have failed miserably. My argument, a more historical one perhaps, suggests that our problem is not only that industrial societies have failed to keep all their promises, but that they have succeeded in some ways beyond all expectations. Abundance was once a distant dream, to be postponed to a hereafter of milk and honey; today most Americans are affluent. Universal mass education was once a utopian goal; today in America almost the entire population completes high school, and almost half enters colleges and universities.

The notion that individuals might be free, en masse, to continue their psychological, intellectual, moral, and cognitive development through their teens and into their twenties would have been laughed out of court in any century other than our own; today that opportunity is open to millions of young Americans. Student unrest is a reflection not only of the failures, but of the extraordinary successes of the liberal-industrial revolution. It therefore occurs in the nations and in the colleges where, according to traditional standards, conditions are best.

But for many of today's students who have never experienced anything but affluence, political freedom, and social equality, the old vision is dead or dying. It may inspire bitterness and outrage when it is not achieved, but it no longer animates or guides. In place of it, students (and many who are not students) are searching for a new vision, a new set of values, a new set of targets appropriate to the postindustrial era—a myth, an ideology, or a set of goals that will concern itself with the quality of life and answer the question "Beyond freedom and affluence, what?"

What characterizes student unrest in the developed nations is this peculiar mixture of the old and the new, the urgent need to fulfill the promises of the past and, at the same time, to define the possibilities of the future.

What's Bugging the Students?

*Like dozens of other organizations, the American Council on Education
prepared a report on campus unrest. In the course of its deliberations, it
commissioned papers on the discontents of each of the "constituencies" of
the university. I was asked to comment on "what's bugging the students,"
to provide recommendations for "preventing or resolving conflicts," and,
incidentally, to avoid any protracted discussion of the causes of student
discontent.*

*I accepted the commission but, in the essay that follows, devoted some
time to a critique of the request—e.g., the notion that one could
generically speak of "the students," the assumption that all conflicts should
be "prevented or resolved," the hope that one could discuss the discontents
of students without also discussing the causes of these discontents.*

*The crux of this essay, however, is an effort to apply the thesis of the
previous essay—the thesis of the two revolutions—to a taxonomy of
modern American students. In effect, I argue here that in 1969 the most
meaningful way of looking at the diversity among American students is
by examining their relationship to the first and second revolutions. I
distinguish between three groups: (1) those who are "solidly in," in that
they take for granted the benefits and privileges of the affluent society and
thus are in the vanguard of the second revolution; (2) those who are
"tenuously in," a silent majority of students who have had a taste of
affluence but who do not yet feel secure in its benefits; and (3) those who
are "excluded," in that they are still struggling to be granted the minimal
rights of the first revolution.*

*One object of this typology is to dispel the popular view that "the
students" all hold identical views. Ironically, this misconception pervades
not only popular and political rhetoric, but intellectual controversy as
well. Apologists and critics alike often speak of the oppositional young as
if they were the young, forgetting that in January, 1970, the majority of
American college students agreed that Mr. Nixon was doing a good job
as President. Furthermore, even among those students who are in
opposition, there is an enormous diversity not readily captured by such
concepts as counterculture, new culture, or consciousness III—or, for that*

matter, by my own concept of "postmodern youth." To understand the youthful opposition, one must understand its internal tensions and contradictions, the many forces and ideologies vying for its control, and the variety of human types recruited to it. Much of the fate of the new opposition will depend on the outcome of its own internal struggles.

ANYONE who agrees, in any brief span, to analyze "what's bugging the students" and to provide "recommendations for resolving conflict" should be suspect. Suspicion should heighten if the charge to the writer suggests that recommendations are needed for "preventing or resolving conflicts among members of the campus constituencies or between them and the members of other constituencies (students, faculty, administrators and presidents, trustees)." For the charge takes for granted some of the assumptions that are today most questioned by dissenting students; for example, that conflict on campus should necessarily be prevented or resolved, that some inclusive or definitive statement can be made about the students, that it is appropriate for someone who is not a student to attempt to summarize the complaints of students.

By way of disclaimer, let me first note that I am not convinced all campus conflicts should be prevented or resolved. On the contrary, I believe conflict is an inevitable precursor, concomitant, and consequence of change—whether constructive or destructive. Under many circumstances, I believe one should deliberately create conflict: e.g., psychological conflict within those whose behavior belies their professed values; social conflict between those who condone or ignore injustice and those who wish to correct it. Furthermore, the most expedient way to prevent or resolve conflict may be to eliminate or silence those who create it. None of this is to say that conflict, whether psychological or social, is inevitably desirable; it simply notes that the value of conflict cannot be judged apart from its contexts, objects, and results.

Second, the question "What's bugging the students?" suggests, at the very least, that psychological factors may be central in understanding the discontents of today's students. We more characteristically speak of being "bugged" by personal hang-ups than by social injustice, warfare, racism, or hypocrisy. Yet I must conclude that what bugs student activists is not only their intrapsychic problems, but even more the nature of American society, the world, and their colleges. Psychological factors play a major role in sensitizing some students to issues that do not concern others, but intrapsychic factors alone are not *causes* of student tension.

Finally, the concept of "the students" bears close examination. We have rightly learned not to speak loosely about "the Negroes," "women," or "the Russians," recognizing that the generic label obscures the great variety within such groups. But, for some reason, we have not yet extended this same caution to the students. I will argue that different things bug different students.

Although almost every conceivable cause of conflict has already been discussed and documented, often at great length, it is impossible to make recommendations for resolving conflict without identifying its causes, albeit in a sketchy and telegraphic way.

Two Social Revolutions

First, I believe that what are euphemistically called "campus tensions" result in considerable part from social and historical changes and political and administrative policies that do not originate primarily in colleges and universities. Much of the turbulence in highly industrialized societies stems from the two highly explosive social revolutions that are simultaneously under way. The first is the ancient process of "inclusion" in the industrial society—what Ralf Dahrendorf has termed "the extension of citizenship." The first revolution involves the demand that American society include as full citizens many persons who have traditionally been excluded from the mainstreams of social, economic, and political life: those who are not white, adult, middle-class, Protestant, Anglo-Saxon, and male. Thus, from blacks, young people, women, Jews and Catholics, a variety of ethnic groups, and working- and lower-class individuals we hear ever more strident demands to be counted in as full members of society, granted full legal rights and equal psychocultural esteem. Because the rhetoric of American society is a rhetoric of democracy and full citizenship, and because of the high levels of material abundance, social security, and formal political freedom in our society, the demand for inclusion is today becoming more clamorous and insistent.

But overlapping, and to some extent opposing, this first trend are the less articulate but strongly felt demands of those who form part of a second revolution. This revolution, less sociopolitical than psychocultural, occurs chiefly in the children of those who have made it in the existing system: children of intellectuals, professionals, high-level government administrators, market researchers, and the cosmopolitan upper middle class of America, France, West Germany, Japan, and so on. For such men and women—most of them young—the promises of the first revolution seem already fulfilled: citizenship is attained; inclusion is assured. The new questions that arise for such young men and women concern the meaning and quality of life in a postindustrial setting. Their first provisional answers emphasize qualitative transformation: a rejection of the human, bureaucratic, and ecological price paid to attain high levels of industrialization; a search for fulfillment and more intense experience; and an effort to achieve new forms of intimacy, awareness, and community.

This contrast between the two revolutions provides the framework for much of my analysis of current tensions on the campus. It requires distinguishing the psychohistorical position of those who are so solidly *in* the existing society that they take its accomplishments for granted, the position of those who are still effectively excluded from society, and the position of those whose place in society is still so precarious that their major efforts go to secure stronger footholds. It requires a contrast between those who are "solidly in" the system on one hand and those who are "tenuously in" or "excluded" on the other.

I do not assume, however, a community of interest between all who share the same or contiguous sociohistorical positions. There are enormous differences between those who are tenuously in and those who are excluded. The tenuously in (the great majority of the "silent Americans") feel threatened from two directions: by those who are solidly in (the "experts" who allegedly control everything) and by the excluded (who appear to threaten the status and values of those who are tenuously in). But no matter how explosive socially may be the demands of those who are still effectively excluded from the rewards and esteem of full citizenship in society, these demands are essentially traditional and pose no revolutionary threat to the prevailing social and value system (although, indeed, they challenge existing political alignments). In contrast, the inarticulate aspirations of those who are solidly in the society but have begun to question its values and worth seem ultimately more revolutionary, though less politically explosive.

A second factor behind today's student unrest is the prolongation of psychological development—specifically, of adolescence. Its extent is apparent in the crudest social indicators. Since the turn of the century, the average amount of education received by each student group has increased by approximately one year per decade. Also, the average age for the onset of puberty has decreased by approximately one-fifth of a year per decade. Finally, the average student of any given age today appears to score approximately one standard deviation above the average student of the same age a generation ago on most standardized measures of intellectual performance. A student in the middle of his class today would probably have stood in approximately the top 15 per cent a generation ago; put differently, he is approximately one grade ahead, at any given age, of his parents when they were that age.

Translated into individual terms, this means that the average sixteen-year-old of today, compared with the sixteen-year-old of 1920, would probably have reached puberty one year earlier, have received approximately five years more education, and be performing intellectually at the same level as a seventeen- or eighteen-year-old in 1920. Today's high school and college students are about a year more mature physiologically and a year more developed intellectually than their parents were at the same age, but on the other hand, they must defer adult responsibilities, rights, and prerogatives five years longer.

These changes have revolutionary implications for higher education. There are more than 7 million full- and part-time students involved, an increase of well over 100 per cent in the last fifteen years. The better students are even better prepared than they were a generation ago, and upgraded secondary education (at least in white, suburban, middle-class areas) has meant an increase not only in achievement levels, but also in levels of sophistication, cosmopolitanism, moral reasoning, and intellectual comprehension; this is especially marked among the most privileged white young Americans.

There is incomplete but growing evidence that these changes have resulted not only in a quantitative increase in the knowledge of the average student, but also in qualitative changes in the reasoning capacity and moral development of many young men and women. These qualitative psychological changes entail greater autonomy, individuation, and interpersonal maturity; they frequently involve a relativistic or postrelativistic outlook on knowledge, and a highly principled style of moral reasoning. To oversimplify, today's students are more likely to challenge, to question, and to think for themselves than were students of earlier generations.

A third factor in student discontent is what Kingman Brewster, Jr., calls the "involuntary" nature of university attendance for many students. The present Selective Service System makes college education virtually a sure-fire way to avoid the draft, while dropping out of college is an excellent way to assure induction. Furthermore, this same system imposes upon morally sensitive students the guilt of being spared military service, at least for a time, solely by virtue of family background, previous education, or intellectual endowment—factors for which the individual himself has little or no responsibility.

But, as Brewster has noted, the draft merely aggravates pressures that existed and will continue to exist, even were it to be abolished or become more equitable. The indiscriminate use of college degrees as passports for occupational entry, the strong social pressure upon middle-class children to attend and complete college and often graduate or professional school as well, and the opprobrium heaped upon students who discontinue or interrupt advanced education, all mean that colleges abound with students who have no particular reason to be there and who would quite consciously prefer to do something else somewhere else.

As one consequence, these involuntary students put pressures on their colleges to serve a variety of needs that colleges are not well equipped to meet. A student who is pressured to attend and fearful of leaving college, but who would rather be involved in a worthy program of social reform or political action, inevitably presses the university to allow him to undertake this program for academic credit. The student who finds academic learning irrelevant is likely to demand relevance, even though it may involve kinds of experience which college cannot well offer. In brief, colleges are essentially rather limited institutions, and their captive audiences today create unbearable pressures upon them to be all things to all men, including a variety of men (and women) who would much prefer to be elsewhere.

A final factor—perhaps the most important—that profoundly affects the campuses today and provides the immediate target of much activist protest is the emergence of major contradictions in American society. Some of these contradictions, like racism, have long existed but have only recently been fully exposed; others are the product of changes in American society, economy, and international position. It has become clear, for example, that industrialization was achieved at no small price in terms of human regimentation and ecological despoliation. It has become more obvious to white Americans that the legacy of slavery has never fully been overcome but is still translated into psychological and structural forms of racism that effectively exclude blacks from full citizenship. It has become more patent that there is a contradiction between America's traditionally democratic and peaceful view of herself internationally and her increasingly imperial role in the modern world. Some may argue that the extent of repression, hypocrisy, injustice, or cruelty within society has increased; in my view, it has, in general, decreased. Yet the level of *awareness* of injustice has clearly increased, and the sense of living in an unjust, irrational, hypocritical, and cruel world is undoubtedly growing, especially among the thoughtful young.

These factors affect students unevenly and, in many cases, do not consciously affect them at all. In particular, the emerging contradictions of society are noted and deplored by only a minority of today's more than 7 million college students. With the vast influx into community colleges, two-year colleges, upgraded state teachers colleges, and a variety of other public and private institutions, millions of students today are attending college who would not have done so a generation ago. As new kinds of students enter higher education, the level of those who attend the most selective colleges rises steadily. An educational system that once was explicitly elite has now become increasingly democratic, enrolling almost half the secondary-school graduates. One consequence, inevitably, is that as the social composition of higher education becomes more diversified, any generalization about the students becomes increasingly more difficult.

The Varieties of Students

There are many useful ways of classifying students, but I will discuss three broad groups, classified largely according to social background and position vis-à-vis the existing society. The popular imagination, fed by the mass media, is attracted by oversimplified images of students. A decade ago it was still the tail end of the "silent generation"; today, it is the "now generation," the "angry generation," and so on. These images often reflect real trends and are socially important in themselves, since it is the image of students, not the facts about students, that tends to determine public and legislative action. Yet any discussion of students must begin by noting that in the academic year 1968–69, *most* of this country's 2,500 colleges did not have a group of Students for a Democratic Society, *most* colleges experienced no protest over anything more serious than dining-hall regulations or parietal hours, and *most* students, as of 18 December 1969, believed that Richard M. Nixon was doing a good job as President. Indeed, data from the American Council on Education's Office of Research suggests that during the present academic year, *most* freshmen arrive even less sympathetic to student radicalism than in the past. Seymour Martin Lipset has pointed out that, until the last year or so, students appeared to be fully as hawkish as the general public on the war in Vietnam. At most colleges student activists and radicals spend much time deploring the apathy of the majority of their classmates, who persist in being interested in dates, football, and getting ahead in the world. Similarly, despite much discussion and some reality behind talk of the generation gap, recent studies suggest that this gap is nowhere nearly as wide as it is made to appear, that most students say they admire their parents, get along well with them, and agree with a great many of their basic values. This is as true of student radicals, most of whom come from left-wing families, as it is of student conservatives, most of whom come from conservative families.

The media, of course, has a vested interest in dramatic and sensational "news": thus, pot parties are staged at Northwestern, motorcyclists are induced by television cameramen to roar across the campus of the University of California at Berkeley, while a focus upon the most volatile campuses gives an impression of constant student uproar, dissent, violence, and disruption. Selective editing invariably exaggerates the extent of violence, and selective aiming of the camera in the first place confirms the popular stereotype of the bearded, nihilistic, anarchistic, acid-head revolutionary.

Such images are important in themselves as well as for what they tell us about American society. Their prevalence determines public reaction to students; many policies are guided by such stereotypes, even when the author consciously knows better. The widespread mood of public indignation against students, long-hairs, intellectuals, and other "subversives" cannot be understood without appreciating the power of the stereotype of students. And the widespread currency of this stereotype points to fear of the young, to the extent that activists and hippie youth constitute a psychological challenge to the existing system, and the degree to which the students are joining and, perhaps, even replacing blacks as the objects upon whom adults project their own fears and repressed desires. Students, too, are affected by the stereotype, accepting its basic correctness and often feeling out of it because they are neither militant nor angry nor present-oriented.

Although the prevailing stereotype of the students is inaccurate, it is important to note its kernel of truth and to account for its prevalence. For one, the stereotype is far more accurate when applied to the most selective, liberal, and "progressive" institutions of higher education than when applied to the vast majority. A recent ACE study shows that the second best way to predict whether or not a campus will have protests over United States policy in Vietnam is to calculate the proportion of National Merit Scholarship winners in the freshman class. (The best way is to calculate the percentage who mark "none" for religion.) A casual survey of the institutions that have had the most publicized confrontations during the past two years demonstrates that the list is a roster of the most distinguished colleges and universities. If we were to eliminate the Ivy League, Berkeley, the Universities of Wisconsin and Michigan, Cal Tech and MIT, and a dozen or so private, "high-quality," and "progressive" liberal arts colleges from the current portrait of student dissent, that portrait would virtually dissolve. Yet these colleges together enroll well under 5 per cent of the college students in the United States.

The widespread impression of revolution on campus springs partly from the fact that the most visible, selective, and prestigious institutions, which by and large recruit students of the highest intelligence and the greatest independence, are the same colleges where student protest is growing. These institutions have traditionally trained a disproportionate number of the leaders of business, government, and university life. They are the pacesetters of higher education, the colleges that other colleges emulate in their struggle for status and visibility. Students at these colleges, furthermore, often constitute models for students at institutions of lesser status, who emulate the dress, slang, and political outlooks of those at the pacesetters. Trends begin in institutions like Berkeley, Antioch, or Harvard, spread throughout other institutions, and simultaneously into the secondary schools that send students to the elite colleges. In some cases—for example, white bucks and pink shirts in the fifties—by the time the chain of dispersion has been completed at the lowest level, those in the pacesetting institutions have abandoned the fashions they began.

We may now consider the dissatisfaction of three rather different groups, noted earlier. The discussion here deals with types, not individuals, and, therefore, it applies exactly to no one person.

The Excluded

The first thing to be noted about the excluded is that they are, by and large, excluded from colleges as well as from the existing society, and until recently were especially excluded from colleges of the highest visibility, prestige, and selectivity. In 1968, only 6 per cent of all American college students were black, while 3 per cent were members of other nonwhite minorities. In 1969, the percentage remained the same, although there was some shift toward the high-status colleges. The proportion of blacks that completes graduate and professional schools is even smaller. Furthermore, many blacks in college attend all-Negro institutions whose academic offerings and institutional climate have been pungently described by Riesman and Jencks. Even the massive efforts to recruit black students into the high-prestige institutions have had extremely uneven effects today; at very few elite institutions are blacks represented in numbers proportionate to their percentage of the national population. The same is largely true of chicanos, American Indians, and members of other excluded minority groups. Underrepresented in the university population as a whole, they still attend the colleges of the lowest institutional quality. Although race and color enormously aggravate the educational problems of black, Indian, and Mexican-American students, low social class and poverty in general, even in the absence of color, have a similar effect not only upon structural exclusion from the mainstreams of society, but also upon university or college attendance.

If any one theme runs through the demands of the excluded, particularly black students, it is for an end to exclusion and for full citizenship, with respect and esteem, in the university and society. Despite the angry and at times revolutionary rhetoric of many black students, and despite the adoption by a few small groups like the Black Panthers of a quasi-Marxist analysis, the position of black students is essentially that of the individual outside the system who demands immediate and full admission.

The vehemence and form of black students' demands spring partly from the oppression and exclusion that have taken not only political, economic, and institutional forms, but also psychological and cultural forms. Perhaps the most degrading consequence of racism is that its victims come to believe in their own inferiority. One of the most bitter consequences of American history as generally taught has been to deprive blacks of any sense of an honorable past. And one result of many well-intentioned and, at times, insightful analyses of "Negro personality" and "Negro culture" has been to confirm blacks in their fear that their psyches were inadequate, while their "culture of poverty" was really, in Oscar Lewis's words, a "poverty of culture."

Inclusion, for black and other so-called Third World students, comes to be defined not only in terms of admissions policies, scholarships, and so on, but also in social-psychological terms. Demands for special programs, control over black studies appointments, separate residential facilities, and the like are centrally impelled by the desire to right the balance of self-esteem and respect. Nevertheless, black students as a group, especially those from working- and lower-class backgrounds, remain highly motivated by a desire to enter the system and to share in its benefits. As compared to white students at the same colleges, they tend to be more vocational in their educational goals, more skill-oriented in their definition of curriculum, less experiential in their educational and curricular demands. At colleges that recruit large numbers of relatively alienated, cosmopolitan middle-class white students (for example, the State University of New York at Old Westbury), black students object strongly to the experiential outlook of white students, which they contemptuously describe as "grooving on the grass."

Black students, indeed, present a major short-run challenge to the structure of higher education. The ACE's Office of Research has shown that demonstrations by black students tend to occur once a "critical mass" of about fifty black students has congregated on a campus. When this happens one can almost routinely expect demands for increased black admissions, special black-studies programs, special and sometimes separate residential facilities, and so on. These demands are rarely impossible to meet, but doing so, especially in public institutions, may have severe political consequences both in faculty backlash and legislative reactions. Yet, in a more fundamental social concept, black students do not, in my opinion, constitute a basic threat to American society or colleges and their prevailing values. The attack on careerism and materialism found among affluent white students is rarely as intense among blacks. To oversimplify: black students today reject the university and the college only because it deprives them of esteem, dignity, and a sense of their own value, even as it may exclude them and their brothers from admission. But they less often challenge the fundamental assumptions of higher education, the mode of teaching and learning prevalent at universities, or the traditional work-oriented values of American society.

The Tenuously In

Higher education has always been an avenue of upward mobility in American society and has become increasingly so since the passage of the Morrill Act establishing land-grant colleges. More than half the country's students define their college education primarily as a means of acquiring the skills and credentials essential for success *in* the existing society. Their approach to higher education is thus vocational, in contrast to the liberal arts emphasis on understanding the world, gaining insight into oneself, and finding one's identity. If there is a "silent majority" in higher education, it is in the vocational group.

A vocational approach to higher education is not, of course, perfectly correlated with any one socioeconomic background or psychohistorical position. Excluded blacks, for example, tend to be highly vocational in their view of higher education. Yet as a group, the white "vocationalists" in colleges and universities tend to have a number of common characteristics. They are, by and large, the first in their families to attend college, and they generally come from lower-middle-class and, increasingly, working-class families. They attend community colleges, junior colleges, and those upgraded teachers colleges that Alden Dunham aptly calls "colleges of the forgotten Americans." Often the women in this group are preparing to be teachers, while the men may be interested in teaching (especially at the secondary school level), engineering, business administration, agronomy, and related fields.

Within this group there is, of course, enormous variation. Politically, the vocational group includes most students who believe ardently in law and order, believe in the wisdom and morality of American policies in Southeast Asia, and regard the speed of racial integration as excessive. But most often students in this category exhibit that political apathy so frustrating to the minorities of activists and hippies who attend the same colleges. Relatively uninformed about the world, conservative (usually without being reactionary), but essentially nonpolitical in outlook, these students constitute a more or less unpoliticized mass upon which the stability (or inertia) of most college student bodies rests.

The life styles of vocational students also vary extensively. Many attend commuter colleges, and their life style is still primarily determined by their parents and high school friends. Others in residential colleges accept older collegiate patterns focusing upon fraternity life, dating, and the fun-and-football syndrome. Still others view college in primarily social terms, defining social skill and "contacts" as the prerequisite for occupational advancement in modern society.

Although few of these students are politicized, it is from this group that the greatest danger of a student counterreaction against left-wing student activism exists. As the research of Brewster Smith and his colleagues at the University of California and San Francisco State suggests, politically conservative and inactive students tend to be at a different level of moral development than political activists: inactives define right and wrong largely according to conventional community standards and the requirements of law and order. Student activists, who tend to be more "advanced" in moral reasoning, evoke a mystified response from most of their apolitical classmates who, like the general public, confuse the principled reasoning of the activist with hedonism and egocentricity. Thus, the apolitical vocationalist is likely to perceive the activist as an opportunist and, in times of crisis, to focus upon him the full force of moral indignation. Furthermore, campus conflicts, disruptions, building occupations, and protest marches are seen by the vocationalist as willful distractions from the main business of college, which is acquiring vocational skills and getting a good education. Thus, the demands of activists and radical or hippie students for more experiential education, for greater student participation, for student voice in curricular planning, and even faculty appointments are interpreted as subversions of the primary purpose of education and, in addition, as disrespectful violations of the authority of the faculty "who really know."

The dominant motivation of most vocational students, then, is not to challenge the system, but to enter it without much questioning the price of admission. The discontents of such students are largely focused on immediate and personal issues. Often this focus is realistic, for their family backgrounds deprive them of the unquestioned affluence upon which upper-middle-class, second-generation students can fall back, while their lower social status and less adequate secondary school educations mean that a college degree, indeed, may be for them prerequisite to a good job and upward social mobility. In current campus conflicts, the tenuously-in students have remained largely invisible. They rarely join with activists in attacking the war in Vietnam, allegedly racist policies, militarism, or even the hegemony of the faculty and administration. In fact, they rarely even attend the colleges and universities where activists are found in large proportions.

If the recent spate of campus disruptions continues, however, the resentment of vocational students will probably grow apace, just as the resentment of their lower-middle-class and working-class parents is growing. The universities and colleges they attend are competing—generally unsuccessfully—with the elite institutions; the resulting institutional inferiority complexes extend to many vocational students, convincing them that their degrees are really not as "valuable" as those from the prestige institutions. Thus, a variant of the traditional American resentment against experts, intellectuals, and East Coast snobs is often found among such students and could be readily mobilized, at least for brief periods. Already the conservative coalitions that spring up to oppose radical students—even on many elite campuses—at times of campus crisis contain a disproportionate number of vocationalists.

Interstudent conflict is, of course, unlikely at colleges that draw very few vocationalists or nonvocationalists; it is likely only at colleges where the two groups are equally balanced. At most progressive private liberal arts colleges there are so few vocationalists that they are virtually silenced, and their resentment expresses itself indirectly, for example, through transferring or dropping out. And at most upgraded state teachers colleges, there are so few nonvocationalists (and, specifically, so few radicals or hippies among them) that they must usually resign themselves to chronic complaining about the apathy of their fellows. But at large, usually public institutions that draw big groups of *both* vocationalists and nonvocationalists, possibilities for interstudent conflict will be great in the years to come.

Just as intellectuals in the elite colleges and universities have generally lavished sympathy upon the excluded but withheld it from the tenuously in, a too-common failing of intellectual students and their intellectual professors and administrators is simply to condemn out of hand the apathetic or careerist students. Yet these students also have real and legitimate discontents. They see their values eroded, undermined, and mocked by more intellectual students; they must absorb the undeserved anger that many adults direct toward *all* students; and—most important—they often find their goal of learning technical skills and instrumental abilities blocked by activist-inspired experiential courses that not only fail to turn them on, but also leave them with little substantial and usable knowledge.

In the future, then, we may witness a growing polarization within the student group as a whole, with the lines between vocationalists and nonvocationalists more sharply drawn. The student silent majority may find at least an intermittent voice, with the result that the existing polarization between hawks and doves among the general public, administrators, and faculty may find a counterpart among students themselves. Put differently, the divisions and angers growing throughout society will be felt increasingly within the student population; and there may arise a more vocal student constituency that believes—with considerable justification—that its interests are neglected because of a too-exclusive preoccupation with the clamorous demands of minority groups on the one hand and the insistent pressures of intellectuals and activists on the other. As those who attend college approach a majority the traditional resentment of the less-educated for the college-educated may be increasingly transformed into a new resentment by the vocationalists against the intellectuals *among* college students.

The Solidly In

The solidly in receive the overwhelming bulk of attention, approbation, and censure in any discussion of American higher education. These are students who define their educational goals in nonvocational terms:

they are interested in exploring the world, bringing critical judgment to bear upon its problems, finding their identities, or defining new life styles.

Socially and economically, such students (called "forerunners" by *Fortune*) are drawn from the children of college graduates who are now professionals, executives, teachers, social workers, lawyers, and the like—that is, from families where economic affluence and social status were virtually guaranteed facts of life from birth onward. Such students are more often graduates of the academically high-powered secondary schools, have a more intellectual orientation to college, get better grades, and attend the prestige colleges. Remunerative, secure, and even politically powerful positions in society are open to them. What is in question is whether they *want* such positions.

A liberal arts, nonvocational, intellectual, or identity-seeking outlook is, of course, not identical with dissent. On the contrary, most nonvocational students, whatever their criticisms of the existing society, hope that somehow it will prove capable of reform, and that they will be able to enter it as active participants. Such students, however, usually maintain a critical, skeptical distance from the system and see their educations not as a form of socialization or skill training, but as a chance to explore both themselves and the world around them. Most do not finally reject the system, but neither do they embrace it. They have not made up their minds yet.

But it is from *among* students in this category that most active dissenters are recruited, and also from among this group that "sympathizers," willing to join with activists around specific issues or experiment with hippie life styles, are largely drawn. The *Fortune* poll (see table) estimates that approximately 20 per cent of the forerunners (about 700,000 students) are potential supporters of the New Left, when "support" is construed as disenchantment with American society. This group of 700,-000 overlaps another group of about the same size that identifies with the less political counterculture that the hippies have come to symbolize. From the nonvocational group, then, are drawn not only most political activists, but also most drug experimenters and advocates of encounter groups, meditation, astrology, *I Ching*, communes, and the plethora of styles, values, fads, and fashions that together define dissenting college students.

The two groups within the solidly-in category that most concern the general public are those I shall call *activists* and *hippies*—recognizing the inadequacy of the labels and the overlap of the groups. Several dozen research studies have yielded strikingly consistent results about the student activist. Compared to his classmates in the same college, the activist is characterized by his intellectual viewpoint; his high socioeconomic status; the likelihood that his parents will be politically active and left-of-

*Selected Differences between "Practical-Minded" (Vocational)
and "Forerunner" Students**

	Percentages	
Beliefs	Vocationals (58 per cent)	Forerunners (42 per cent)
No favored Presidential candidate in 1968	25	50
United States is a "sick" society	32	50
"Dove" on war in Vietnam	45	69
Draft resistance is justified under some circumstances	36	67
Civil disobedience is justified under some circumstances	32	66
The police were not justified at Chicago in 1968	40	60
Too little is being done for black people	38	71
Would not enjoy being in business	26	46
Containing the Communists is worth fighting for	59	28
There should be more emphasis on law and order	78	39
There should be more respect for authority	73	41
Accept the prohibition on marijuana	69	37
Desire more emphasis on technological improvement	75	56
Factors influencing career choice:		
Family	48	25
Money	58	21
Job prestige	33	13

SOURCE: "What They Believe: A Fortune/Yankelovich Survey," *Fortune*, January, 1969; reprinted by permission; © 1968 Time Inc.
* Groups identified by self-defined "purpose of college education."

center professionals, intellectuals, teachers, artists, or ministers; and his nonreligious outlook. Similarly, the likelihood of protests themselves can be relatively well predicted simply on the basis of the characteristics of the student body as a whole. The more students who fit this description, the more probable are protests over Vietnam, racism, and student power. Research studies of political activists also emphasize the relative solidarity between them and their families and fail to support the popular view that student political activism in general is a form of rebellion against parental values.

With regard to the hippie, however, the evidence is different. Like the activist, he comes from a family with relatively high socioeconomic status and is likely to be the son of college-educated parents. But his parents are less often politically active, less often in the helping professions, and more often in marketing, public relations, advertising, or entertainment. He is more likely to define himself as a critic not only of society's practices, but also of his parents' values and life style. In such students the element of rebellion or rejection of parental values is indeed strong.

The discontents of the nonvocational group are more sharply articulated and more often expressed in social and political terms. Three issues above all have concerned these students and have constituted the direct focus of virtually every campus protest, confrontation, or disruption. The two primary issues are the war in Vietnam and racism in America, especially as the college or university itself seems implicated. One study of seventy-four campus protests in the academic year 1968–69 found that protests in 1969 involved one or both these issues. But increasingly in the last year, the issue of student participation in decisions about college life has begun to appear as the third major focus of student discontent.

This is not the place for a discussion of the war in Vietnam, of psychological and structural racism, or of student involvement in college decision making. The point is that for dissenting students each of these issues involves a sincerely held moral conviction, from which dissent grows. For example, the fear of being drafted and killed in Vietnam, however real, is rarely the basic cause for student objection to the war. The objection is primarily a moral one; for many students this includes objection to a Selective Service System that allows most students *not* to be drafted. Similarly, opposition by white students to racism is less often based on direct experience with blacks than upon moral considerations (one of many factors that anger black students in dealing with whites). Finally, the advocacy of student power reflects the moral indignation of the student who feels himself to be a *part* of a university community in whose governance he has no voice.

Many observers have argued that the underlying causes of campus tensions lie outside the campus and that, consequently, little can be done on campus to alleviate these tensions. This view is, in my opinion, partly correct, but it should not be taken to mean that student protests are merely a "displacement" of concerns that might better be directed elsewhere. For most student protests are directed against college policies that appear to involve collusion with immoral forces in the society at large. To call these protests merely symptomatic is to ignore the fact that colleges and universities have, indeed, been highly involved in the war in Vietnam, and that many or most have, to greater or lesser degree, acquiesced in the prevalent structural racism of American society. It is not accurate, then, to dismiss the student tension as nothing but a reflection of war and racism *outside* the campus, when what many protesting students explicitly object to is the influence of war and racism on the campus. The prevailing thrust of protest has been in the direction of the disengagement of colleges and universities from the "immoral" policies and practices to which activists object.

But there is another sense in which the dissent of the nonvocational college student indeed reflects a major crisis in American (and Western) culture. The old motivations that still sustain the vocationalist are no longer adequate for the forerunner. Upward mobility, career success, prestige, money, family togetherness—these goals no longer serve to animate a growing minority of students. When this happens two routes are open. The first is to extend to others the rights and opportunities taken for granted by the affluent, secure, and politically free white student; this leads to socio-political activism, to a concern with the deprived at home and abroad. The second route is the cultural revolution of the experiential counterculture, with its search for significance and transcendence in the here-and-now. This route leads to the commune, to drugs, to meditation, and to the anti-scientific outlook of some students. As more and more students enter college from families that are solidly in the system, we can expect increasing experimentation with both these routes, each influenced by the changing social and political scene.

One factor that will influence the choice of routes is the organization and strength of the student political movement. As of January, 1970, it seems fair to say that the New Left, as it was constituted between 1962 and 1969, has ceased to exist. SDS has become a set of explicitly Leninist-Maoist factions, divided over tactics and details of analysis, but sharing a dogmatically revolutionary position. The splitting and "ideologization" of SDS means that most students attracted to the older style of the New Left now have no organization. Many are repelled by the schisms, doctrines, or tactics of SDS factions, but they are equally skeptical about the coalition politics of liberal Left groups.

"Internal emigration."   Furthermore, the public backlash against student activism; the ascendency of political figures like Ronald Reagan, John Mitchell, and Spiro Agnew; the trial of the Chicago Seven; and the widespread fear and, to some extent, fact of repression of political dissent served, as of January, 1970, to turn an increasing number of students away from political action and toward more private forms of dissent. The first half of the academic year 1969–70 has seen an extraordinary proliferation of the nonpolitical counterculture among dissenting students and the rise of many groups, communes, cults, and sects dedicated to the transformation of consciousness, new modes of experiencing, and unalienated relationships. This could presage a wider trend: a tendency to deal with the contradictions of American society not by active social and political involvement, but rather by withdrawal and "internal emigration."

A second factor relevant to the future of student dissent is the administrative response to student protests and—even more important—the general mood, climate, and policies of colleges and universities. The small body of research on institutional characteristics and student unrest reaches the apparently paradoxical conclusion that unrest is greatest at those institutions that are the most liberal, permissive, and flexible. This finding, of course, results from the fact that the most protest-prone students attend the most liberal institutions. More detailed studies of the relationship between protests and specific institutional policies vis-à-vis student participation, the surrounding community, recruitment of minority students, university-military contracts, and so on are urgently needed. So, too, are comparative studies of the effects of institutional response to student protest and disruption.

My own experience suggests, first, that responsive administrators and faculty members can often prevent destructive conflicts by prompt and reasonable responses to student complaints, grievances, requests, and demands—or, even better, by anticipating these grievances before they become focused into demands; second, that slow and nonpunitive response to actual confrontations and disruptions, including efforts to respond to student grievances and to avoid police intervention, often serves to de-escalate student protest and at the same time to facilitate needed institutional change; and third, that external control or limitations on the capacity of a college to define its own solutions to its own internal tensions almost always aggravates these tensions.

But whatever happens to the student movement or on the campuses, I doubt that it will basically lessen the level of discontent. To some extent student tensions can be channeled into more or less productive routes, but even channeling is likely to backfire. What is happening on American campuses is also happening in the universities of most economically advanced nations, and it will continue in one form or another.

Recommendations

In general, I believe that the grievances which students have brought to our attention are real and in urgent need of correction. But I also believe that American colleges and universities have been (and, I hope, will continue to be) among the most vulnerable and least oppressive institutions in society. Their principal contribution has been to provide sanctuary (and even stipend) for a great variety of deviants, creators, misfits, innovators, crackpots, and geniuses who have found their way into the student bodies, faculties, and presidencies. I see the greatest danger to higher education today not as arising directly from students, but rather indirectly from the backlash of a public increasingly disenchanted with the "products" of higher education. Colleges and universities are highly vulnerable in the long run because they cannot be self-sustaining: they depend on outside funding that can easily be cut off. And I view the greatest danger to this country, within the universities and outside, as the increasing polarization of the tenuously in and the unstable alliance of the solidly in and the excluded. If this polarization grows, I fear that the tenuously in will triumph. It therefore seems to me critical, not only ethically but also politically, to attempt to understand and to respond to the grievances of those who believe their interests have been neglected.

I make the following recommendations:

1. The rage of the excluded, like the disaffection of a portion of the solidly in, can be changed only by major changes in national policies. These should include (a) an end to the war in Vietnam and a change in foreign policy so that any other such war becomes impossible; (b) a reallocation of national resources to end structural racism and to begin to eliminate poverty; (c) a commitment to provide assistance to the impoverished nations of the world; (d) a sustained national effort to preserve a livable environment; and (e) an intensive examination of the adequacy of the existing political, social, and economic institutions of American society in light of the needs of the last third of the twentieth century. Were this country to move toward these objectives, campus tension would still persist, but it would be less enraged, less disaffected, more constructive.

2. American higher education must learn to tolerate and, at times, encourage conflict, rather than avoid it. Tolerating conflict may require developing new institutional mechanisms for its on-campus expression; it will certainly require from faculty members, administrators, and the public a more relaxed and less panicked attitude toward confrontations, demands, and even disruptions. Contrary to some opinions, neither Western civilization nor American higher education will crumble because a college yields to student demands or fails to call the police. Contrary to other opinions, students are often wrong or inadequately informed; at times they violate the rules of the college so basically that they must be separated from it. Campus conflicts, at present, generate more agitation than they deserve; we must grow used to them.

3. American colleges must become more voluntary and open to "traffic" in and out. At present, only a third of those who enter four-year colleges graduate from the same colleges four years later; the uninterrupted undergraduate career is a myth. Socially approved channels for interrupting, discontinuing, and resuming higher education must now be created. A more equitable Selective Service System, embodying early service and abolishing student deferments, must be developed. Students who do not want what college offers should be encouraged to leave and seek valuable and relevant experience elsewhere.

4. Colleges and universities should not attempt to provide all things for all men. There are many experiences, desires, goals, and achievements that are humanly and socially worthy and important but have no place in a college or university. Specifically, preparation for military service, psychotherapy, active involvement in social change, and so on may all be worthy

objectives, but they should be implemented outside the college and not within its formal structure. The pressure for "relevance" and "experience" from students should be acquiesced to only when consistent with the institutions' educational goals and resources.

5. Colleges and universities should maintain and increase their autonomy and independence. Specifically, this means that institutions of higher education must retain the capacity to respond in their own manner to their own tensions, free from outside interference or pressure. Direct or indirect pressures from externally appointed or elected boards of governance, state legislatures, and so on must be minimized. To merit this autonomy, colleges and universities must resist the pressure from students and faculty to become political agencies for social change through community-action programs. At the same time, they must refuse to become agents or executors of government or military policies, should not undertake secret defense contracts, and should not be involved in teaching or research whose primary purpose (or most likely intended consequence) is the destruction of human life or the impairment of human development.

6. Students should be maximally involved in the governance of each college and university. The precise meaning of "maximal involvement" must vary from institution to institution, depending on its traditions and the nature of its faculty and student body. But minimally, participation should involve student representation on major faculty committees and policy-making bodies, student representation on boards of trustees, and the systemic gathering of student opinion concerning faculty teaching ability. Actual student participation in decisions concerning faculty appointments, promotion, and tenure, while presenting many problems, deserves to be tried in some colleges on an experimental basis.

7. American colleges must deliberately seek a "mix" of student types. Present enlistment, recruitment, and selection processes tend to make student bodies at each college homogeneous. In the long run, this promises to create an educationally reinforced characterological split in the American public. An atmosphere of diversity, openness, and respect must be fostered within each college, whereby the rights and outlooks of students with distinct orientations to higher education are preserved.

8. The needs, grievances, and tensions of that majority of college students that views education in vocational terms should be heeded. Programs of genuine worth, use, and relevance to such students should be continued and strengthened. In the rush to respond to the urgent demands of the excluded and the activists, the educational needs of less vocal, more respectful, and less militant students must not be slighted. Indeed, there are many nonvocational students who would prosper more in college were they to work elsewhere until they can return with a more instrumental definition of educational goals.

9. Student political involvement should be supported. If presently un-

convinced students are to be shown that American institutions can create meaningful social change, it must be because students can share in producing such change. To make this possible, the voting age should be lowered to eighteen, and residence requirements should be altered to ensure college students and others of their age group the vote. Students should be encouraged in the expression of opinions and in mounting actions directed at off-campus issues. At the same time, a mood that makes political involvement mandatory should be avoided, and the right of students to be "apathetic" should be respected.

Vulnerabilities of the Counterculture

Theodore Roszak's The Making of a Counter Culture *was the first of several recent books that tried to define, rationalize, and justify the youthful opposition. Roszak's book is probably best understood as an effort to provide a theoretical basis for the counterculture, rather than as an effort to describe it accurately. The same is largely true of subsequent books—for example, Charles Reich's* The Greening of America *or, to a lesser extent, Philip Slater's excellent work* The Pursuit of Loneliness. *Given the diffuse, diverse, disorganized, and unstructured nature of the youthful opposition, it is probably inevitable that those who write about it should impose on it their own vision of what it should be at best—or, if they are critical, of what it could become at worst.*

A request in 1969 to review Roszak's book gave me an opportunity to express some of my own ambivalence about the romanticism of Roszak's particular interpretation of the counterculture and of the counterculture itself. There are fine lines between criticizing the dominant culture, mocking it, parodying it, and being co-opted by it. The turn away from politics, the atavistic mood visible in the counterculture, is understandable given the frustrations of political life. But the idealization of the shaman and move to the commune seem to me to risk an unwitting repetition of traditional American privatism, which sees salvation as a purely individual matter and denies the public origins of private woes. The search for individual awareness, sentience, and consciousness is important as a part of the second revolution; so, too, the effort to create new forms of communal life and collective action outside of the traditional political arena can be creative and constructive.

But an uncritical turn toward culture and consciousness runs the risk of simply dropping out of the struggle for social change altogether. Even today, I believe that the greatest danger for the youthful opposition (and for the country at large) is not the danger of the youthful romance with violence, guerrilla warfare, and terrorism, but the much greater danger of a kind of unwitting cop-out/drop-out that would substitute macrobiotics for politics and altered states of consciousness for social change. If all of those who have fundamental criticisms of existing American life abandon politics, this leaves the public arena in the hands of others who generally have less noble, less humane visions of the meanings and purpose of human life and community. For this reason, it is important constantly to underline the enormous vulnerability of the counterculture to seduction, encapsulation, and co-optation by the very culture it nominally opposes.

IN case anyone still doubted it, what happened at Harvard and Woodstock proved it. Something new is happening among the young. At Harvard, after the police dragged off the student occupiers of University Hall, the student body voted to strike, thus dispelling the myth that radicals have no real support among their "sane, responsible" classmates. At Woodstock, 300,000 or more students (and nonstudents) filled the wet air with the heady sound of folk and rock, the sweet smell of pot, and earnest talk of love, peace, and "our generation."

But what does it mean? Is it only the modern equivalent of goldfish swallowing, or is it the murderous rebellion of a generation of young Oedipuses? Is it happening because the young are obsolete, or because they are the wave of the future? Are they serious or frivolous? Are they nihilistic barbarians assaulting the gates of civilization, or are they our gentle redeemers?

Theodore Roszak, in *The Making of a Counter Culture*, argues that the revolt of the young is serious, important, and redemptive. Roszak teaches history at California State at Hayward and knows whereof he speaks. Not much over thirty himself, he is *for* the counterculture but not quite *in* it, and he has written an important analysis of the revolt of the affluent young. What is new about the young today, he argues, is that they are forming "a culture so radically disaffiliated from the mainstream assumptions of our society that it scarcely looks to many as a culture at all." Although this counterculture today involves only a minority of the young, Roszak describes them as "young centaurs" who may yet save us all.

Much of Roszak's book is devoted to a careful analysis of the writers who anticipated the counterculture: Herbert Marcuse and Norman Brown, Allen Ginsberg and Alan Watts, Timothy Leary and Paul Goodman. On a few points Roszak is critical of them; for example, he warns against Timothy Leary's advocacy of drugs as a chemical route to instant transcendence, and against the debasement of the counterculture into light shows and rock festivals. But on most points he agrees with them. In Roszak's view American technocracy is coercive, it destroys men's souls as it despoils their landscape, and despite its façade of democracy and freedom it savagely manipulates its citizens. Roszak interprets the rise of the counterculture as above all a reaction against the subtly but powerfully repressive world view upon which technocratic society is built.

The Making of a Counter Culture is less a description of the counter culture than an effort to give it a coherent intellectual rationale. Roszak's special demon is what he calls "objective consciousness"—a "scientific" way of experiencing the world that involves a sharp separation between objective and subjective knowledge, an alienated detachment from other people, and the mechanization of knowledge and experience. Beneath the inhumanities, neglects, and injustices of modern American society, Roszak locates the core problem in the way men experience themselves, each other, and the world.

Against this technocratic world view, Roszak commends his alternative of "visionary imagination." His real culture hero is the shaman, the medicine man of primitive societies. The shaman is "adept in cultivating those exotic states of awareness in which a submerged aspect of his personality seems to free itself from his surface consciousness to rove among the hidden powers of the universe." From the shaman's vision "there flows a symbiotic relationship between man and non-man in which there is a dignity, a gracefulness, an intelligence that powerfully challenges our own strenuous project of conquering and counterfeiting nature." Roszak's solution, then, is to counter "objective consciousness" with its romantic opposite—the subjective, the symbiotic, and the organic.

There are two difficulties with this analysis. The first is that Roszak interprets the rise of the counterculture as a revolution of the repressed against the system that represses them. But, in fact, the revolt of the young occurs not among the most oppressed or repressed, nor among those on whose shoulders the "organizational harness" of technocracy falls most heavily. The counterculture is largely a subculture of white, upper-middle-class youth. In contrast to them, young men and women who are trying hard to get into the system (or to make sure they stay in) don't have the time or energy for subjectivity, symbiosis, and the organic—much less for shamanism. Most blacks, chicanos, and working-class youths, like the sons and daughters of the lower middle class, view the counterculture with mistrust and hatred. The youth revolt recruits only that minority of the young who are so solidly *in* technocratic society that they can afford to demand something more of life than security, affluence, and the prospect of political power.

The counterculture arises, then, not because the young today are more repressed, but because some of them are so *little* repressed that they can raise their sights. Historically, the Byronic romanticism characteristic of Roszak's counterculture has arisen only among the privileged classes of prosperous societies. People who *really* live in organic, tribal, symbiotic, and shamanistic cultures generally can't wait to escape into the world of affluence, science, and technology. It is only after technology has triumphed, and only for those whose lives are glutted with the goodies it provides, that some of the young can begin to look nostalgically back at the delights of shamanism.

While Roszak is right in noting the oppositional self-definition of the counterculture, he fails to notice that the same counterculture that rejects careerism, materialism, and science is built upon, implicitly accepts, and often caricatures much of the rest of American society. Specifically, the counterculture takes for granted the technology, the institutions, and the economy necessary to provide its own material base—a high standard of living, psychochemistry, cars, films, electronics, an enormously prolonged education, and so on.

The second difficulty with Roszak's subjective solution is that he defines the core problem in American society as a problem of consciousness and therefore finds his basic solution in expanding consciousness so as to include everything embodied by the shaman. However radical this idea may be philosophically, it is essentially antipolitical. Indeed, if I were President Nixon, eager to cool youthful protest, I would urge my young radical opponents to accept Roszak's view that "objective consciousness" is the core problem, and that a return to shamanism is the way out. Most young people would probably be too sensible to believe me. But those who did—the hard core—would be likely to take off for the mountains to cultivate their visionary imagination, to develop unalienated ways of relating to each other, and to have symbiotic encounters with nature. Some of their activities might even turn out to be commercially exploitable. Record companies could make money from their protest songs, advertisers could use their psychedelic art, and fashion designers could make shamanistic dress the new vogue once mini-skirts and bell-bottoms have passed. Most convenient of all, the dissenting young would concentrate themselves in camps isolated in the mountains or in youth ghettos around college campuses. They could easily be kept there with a small police force, a few trained dogs, and a little tear gas.

Furthermore, the definition of the problem as a kind of "false consciousness" and a search for a solution in a different kind of consciousness run the risk of simply caricaturing a deep privatism in American culture that seeks salvation solely in inner life or personal relationships. The counterculture may replace the barbecue pit with the hippie pad, family togetherness with the encounter group, and the suburban coffee hour with the commune, but the focus is still on the private world instead of on the social and political scene. Roszak doesn't want this to happen, but his recommendation makes it more likely, because the energies devoted to cultivating the "visionary imagination" will be diverted away from stopping the war in Vietnam, making our cities livable, ending racism, eliminating poverty, and helping the Third World.

Roszak identifies many aspects of the counterculture brilliantly, but he fails to see how deeply it is itself implicated in technocracy, and that as long as it remains totally defined by opposition, it must remain a thin, small, and vulnerable subculture. In a technological age it is not enough to refuse technology, because those who command its enormous powers (the powers of "objective consciousness") will always retain the upper hand. Technocracy cannot simply be rejected; it must be humanized. "Objective consciousness" cannot simply be refused; it must be incorporated into a world view that also includes the visionary imagination. If American technocracy is the thesis, Roszak admirably defines the antithesis. We still await the synthesis.

Scenarios of Confrontation

The Harvard disruption in 1969 made clear that no American university was immune from student protest. In 1970, a request to review three books about the occupation of Harvard's University Hall gave me an opportunity to examine some of the scenarios of confrontation on American campuses.

The three scenarios I discuss here are, of course, oversimplified constructs: in the end, there are as many scenarios as there are confrontations. But there are similarities as well among them: e.g., the conviction before the confrontation that there will be no confrontation on this campus, and the belief after the confrontation that nothing like this has ever happened before on an American campus. No one likes to believe that his disruption is virtually identical to dozens of others. Yet as one studies the literally hundreds of campus incidents, clear patterns begin to emerge, and defining these patterns is one focus of this essay.

Apart from attempting to define three major scenarios of a campus protest, I argue that although the ultimate causes of campus unrest clearly lie off the campus, what happens once a given protest begins depends very much upon the people who are on the campus. Radical rhetoric to the contrary notwithstanding, there is no evidence that campus conditions have anything much to do with the presence or intensity of student discontent. But campus conditions, and above all the behavior of the university faculty and administration, profoundly affect the course of student protest, determining whether protests end in massive disruption and violence, or whether they produce constructive changes without violence. What may start out on two campuses as "the same issue"—e.g., student discontent over the continuing presence of ROTC—may end up with very different outcomes, depending on the responses of administrators, local police, faculty, trustees, alumni, and students.

There are many reasons—some of which I mention in this essay—for believing that student dissent will not vanish, even if the immediate issues upon which it is focused were resolved. Nor do I believe that campus unrest constitutes a "problem" to be solved if possible by eliminating student discontent. What can be done, however, is to help students organize their actions so as to have maximum effect on the issues with which they are concerned. The question, then, is not how student protest *can be cooled, but how it can be made effective, and—after the deaths of students in 1969 and 1970—how innocent lives can be protected.*

TO ask how it could have happened at *Harvard* reveals a basic misunderstanding of "campus unrest" and of modern society. Yet the assumption that student protest results from there being something wrong with students or colleges dies hard. After 1964, that assumption drove faculty members away from Berkeley toward what they thought would be the quieter groves of Academe at places like Harvard and Columbia. The same assumption led Archibald Cox, the Harvard law professor who headed the Fact-Finding Commission on the Columbia disturbances, to predict that it wouldn't happen at Harvard because of Harvard's close faculty-student relationships, residential houses, and tradition of undergraduate teaching.

Yet it has long been clear that campus unrest is not "caused" by some flaw in the student body. The experience of Michigan State is illustrative. Several years ago, in its campaign for national prominence, Michigan State decided to go after National Merit Scholarship winners. Special scholarships and a hard sell produced almost as many Merit scholars as Harvard, the frontrunner, had. Most of these students were enrolled in special honors programs that provided close student-faculty contact. All things considered, it seemed like a fine idea.

But these students unexpectedly transformed what had been a vast, somnolent, nonpolitical campus into a college with an underground newspaper, an active SDS chapter, visible cultural alienation, a drug culture, and extreme political disaffection—all led by the much-sought-after National Merit scholars. They and their friends even picketed state legislators in nearby Lansing, thus destroying the myth that all the radicals were in far-off Ann Arbor.

Dozens of research studies have since confirmed the lesson of Michigan State: a "good" student body, as defined by high aptitude scores, intellectual motivation, and plans to complete college and graduate school, makes student unrest more likely.* One study of several hundred American colleges and universities showed that about 90 per cent of all protests involving the war in Southeast Asia could have been predicted simply by knowing the characteristics of the student body. Students who mark "none" for religion, who have high IQ's, who are intellectually oriented and politically liberal, and who come from educated professional families are likely to "cause trouble," especially if you put a lot of them on one campus. In short, Harvard.

Conversely, the best way *not* to have student protests is to congregate

---

* This account applies to white students. The frequency of protests involving black students (at predominantly white colleges) is directly related to their numbers: protests become probable once a "critical mass" of about fifty black students is reached.

in a small college a homogeneous group of extremely pious, dumb, conservative students who view higher education as vocational training and come from politically inactive working-class or lower-middle-class families. Most of America's 7 million students are closer to this profile than to the Harvard profile. Predictably, therefore, most of America's 2,500 "institutions of higher education" did *not* strike after Cambodia, Kent State, and Jackson State.

Studies of the psychological characteristics of "protest-prone" students merely amplify the Harvard profile. Compared with their inactive classmates, protesters turn out to be more independent, more freethinking, less conventional. The vulgar theories of student neuroticism, Oedipal rebellion, boredom, paranoia, hedonism, or family permissiveness as causes of protest all prove to be wrong. But the cliché about student activists being "idealistic" is empirically correct; differences in "level of moral reasoning" distinguish protesters from nonprotesters more decisively than any other variable, with the protesters being greatly more "principled" and less "conventional."

But none of this supports the claim that the social-psychological characteristics of the student body "cause" student protest. On the contrary, student characteristics merely create a state of readiness or unreadiness, a tinder box that may be wet or dry. Yet once this conclusion became clear, those who stopped blaming students for campus unrest usually moved on to blame their colleges. Thus Governor Reagan, when not threatening a "blood bath" of student nihilists, tends to lay the blame for campus troubles at the door of an indifferent, aloof, spineless, and lazy faculty.

Most liberal educators also agree that improving campus conditions should help to quiet the restless natives. In essence, the most common recommendations urge using industrial psychology on students: give them better "channels of communication," appoint them to more committees, try work-study programs, and above all "involve them more." In offering these recommendations, no one pays much attention to the experience of Antioch, where for decades students have been involved to the eyeballs in work-study, governance, and even faculty appointments, yet where alienation, radicalism, and protest nonetheless flourish.

Furthermore, there is not a shred of evidence that academic problems are causal or that curricular and governance reforms make any difference to unrest. As a group, activists are no less satisfied with the *academic* side of their education than anyone else. Since protesters are generally better students than nonprotesters, they already get more of the faculty contact that is supposed to solve their discontents. And many of the proposed solutions for campus unrest seem more likely to stir it up. In the present political climate, closer faculty-student relationships, smaller seminars, or anything else that encourages students to think independently or act on their convictions is likely to produce protest. Educational reforms that challenge students to think for themselves are desirable on other grounds, but to advertise them as a means of "cooling student protest" is to advertise gasoline as a fire extinguisher.

All of this seems fairly obvious. But it has not stopped commentators from being continually surprised when "some of our finest students" keep cropping up in occupied buildings or when "some of our most distinguished universities" keep having student troubles. This surprise suggests an inability to hear what students are actually saying. Students do not protest, strike, or occupy buildings because they want to be on faculty committees or in order to cozy up to their professors. In virtually every major disturbance on any American campus in the past five years, they have explicitly objected to the university's collusion with the war in Southeast Asia and/or its insensitivity to or collaboration with the prevalent racism of American society. To maintain that youthful unrest is "symptomatic" of something other than the sorry state of the nation is to reveal a motivated deafness to what students have been shouting at the top of their lungs.

In setting off campus turmoil, the issues matter, and if we are to talk about "causes" we must first talk about a long list of these issues: war, racism, injustice, poverty, repression, imperialism, hypocrisy, pollution, manipulation, and the involvement, indifference, or collusion of American higher education with such evils. To be sure, the issues also exist on many quiescent campuses. So social-psychological and institutional factors play a role. But this role is not to "cause" unrest, but to open the eyes and ears of students to real issues.

Once a protest is launched, however, the situation changes, and the local scenery becomes crucial. What happens then depends mostly on the personalities of the participants: e.g., on the tactics and goals of radical student groups, on faculty involvement, on the administration, and on the trustees or regents. There are three general scenarios of "campus unrest."

Scenario I is the Responsive (or Co-optive) Scenario, epitomized by Brewster at Yale or Perkins at Cornell. At Yale in the fall of 1969, for example, a small group of SDSers and friends occupied a building to protest the firing of a black woman working in a college dining hall. The lady in question was immediately rehired, and the occupying students were suspended but, having vacated the building, were reinstated with a warning. The whole affair blew over without causing much fuss except for a series of lively faculty debates on the appropriateness of the penalty.

Or again, Yale students went on strike before the May Day Rally in New Haven to support a fair trial for the New Haven Black Panthers. President Brewster immediately announced his personal "skepticism" that black revolutionaries could obtain justice in the courts, the Yale College faculty sanctioned the strike, and the university opened its doors wide to tens of thousands of uninvited demonstrators. No one got hurt, and Brewster, with an assist from Spiro Agnew, emerged a campus hero.

This scenario takes strong leadership, political savvy, and moral courage to carry off. The danger is, of course, that the president, as at Cornell, may not be able to bring the faculty and trustees along with him. The scenario is therefore especially dangerous where there are large faculties of business administration, engineering, and agronomy, or a conservative board of regents. In that case, the president is finished, and a new president committed to Scenario III will soon be found. Thus we now have Hayakawa at San Francisco State.

Scenario II is the Sit-It-Out Scenario, exemplified by the University of Chicago. Through two occupations of the administration building, Chancellor Levi simply waited out the occupiers, transferring university functions to other buildings when possible, appointing investigating commissions to study the controversial issues, and loudly announcing that Daley's legions would *not* be called in.

Meanwhile back at the building, another characteristic scenario unfolds. Deprived of the threat of a bust, the occupiers begin to recognize that only a few among them are committed revolutionaries. A split develops between the short-haired political radicals and the long-haired "new life style" radicals. The former have the advantage of discipline, ideology, and experience, but the latter are more numerous. Furthermore, within a few days the Liberation School in the building proves more boring than the classes outside, the food in the building gets worse than the food in the college dining halls, and even the thick carpet on the president's floor is revealed as harder than the dormitory mattresses. Students start going to classes, eating in the dining halls, and sleeping in their rooms—all the while "occupying" the building. Soon the investigating commission brings in a report proposing some fairly reasonable compromise, which unifies the rest of the campus behind the administration and further splits the occupiers. Within a few days the occupiers emerge from the building to face disciplinary proceedings that end up by expelling their "ringleaders."

The trouble with Scenario II is that the president has to ward off enormous pressures from all sides while the building is occupied. On the one hand, he has to suppress *ad hoc* faculty negotiating committees and prevent open warfare between excited faculty hawks and doves. On the other hand, he must placate trustees, alumni, and police officials who demand an immediate bust. He also has to retain his cool while occupiers Xerox his mail, spray-paint revolutionary slogans on his office walls, and upend his office furniture. Scenario II thus requires a president with iron control over his own feelings, over his trustees, over the faculty, and over most of the students. Few men can maintain this control through more than one or two major confrontations.

Scenario III is the most familiar: the Bust Scenario of Berkeley-Columbia-Harvard. Here the president becomes convinced that unless the occupiers of the building are immediately expelled, the University, Higher Learning, and ultimately Western Civilization will crumble. The manifest issues of the protest are seen as "contrived," mere "pretenses for student violence"—a view reinforced by cynical radicals like Mark Rudd but not shared by most of the occupiers. The predictable bust follows, with predictably bloody heads, predictable police brutality, and today the predictable danger that a student or two may get killed.

The classic postbust scenario involves a student strike, the granting of most student demands, the polarization of the faculty, and the resignation or early retirement of the president. There ensues much brave talk about "restructuring," which leads to new faculty-student committees and sometimes to some minor improvements in college life.

Three recent books about Harvard describe a variant of Scenario III. But since all deal primarily with the question "How could it have happened at *Harvard?*" all will be of primary interest to Harvard alumni. *The Harvard Strike* was written by four on-the-spot reporters for the Harvard radio station, WHRB. Their account is detailed, mildly euphoric, and predictably critical of President Pusey; their style owes much to *Time* magazine. The book will take its rightful place on the lengthening shelf of comparable accounts of similar events elsewhere.

Steven Kelman, Harvard 1970 and the author of *Push Comes to Shove*, spent much of his time at Harvard trying to organize the Harvard chapter of the Young Peoples' Socialist League (YPSL). Kelman is an "hereditary Socialist" who dislikes SDS and drugs, but really cares about Norman Thomas, socialism, and the working classes. His account is mostly an exposé of the dirty linen of cultural revolutionaries and political revolutionaries in Harvard SDS. He provides much useful documentation for anyone interested in exploring further the irrationality and manipulativeness of some radical students.

Kelman's basic accusation against YPSL's opponents in SDS is that they are undemocratic, manipulative, and self-righteous to the point of snobbery and elitism, besides which they were considered much more newsworthy than YPSL by the Harvard *Crimson*. Much of what Kelman says is clearly valid: the infatuation of upper-class Progressive Labor Party members with the "proletariat" is based on scant understanding of "hard hats" and teamsters; the new life-style "revolution" of the children of the intelligentsia is often antidemocratic and antipolitical in its cultural elitism. And Kelman's question to a classmate, "If grass is so great, how come you're so unhappy?" is a really good question.

But for all the validity in his criticisms, Kelman emerges as not a whit less self-righteous than his opponents in SDS. He never really wonders why his brand of old-line socialism failed to excite much enthusiasm among his Harvard classmates, and he never really asks why the "cultural revolution" drew so many of his classmates to it. Instead of explaining, he condemns. Furthermore, Kelman's angry book is written almost entirely to those on his left; but if we are to believe his account, they have long refused to pay any attention to what he says. Alas, his book will mostly be read by those far to his right, and it will be used (much against his wishes) to provide further ammunition for the Reagans, Mitchells, and Agnews in their politically profitable war against the alienated and radical young.

If, after reading Kelman, one still believed that youth had a monopoly on virtue, Zorza's book, *The Right to Say "We,"* should dispel the illusion for good. Zorza is a young Englishman filled with the excessive self-regard that studying in Cambridge, Massachusetts, confers upon some students. He shares with Kelman and the WHRB reporters the conviction that what happened at Harvard has planetary significance. And he further believes that transcendental discoveries were made in or near the Harvard Yard in April, 1969. Zorza's book is of interest largely as a specimen of the phenomenology of one Harvard sophomore in the late 1960's. He alternates between fantasies of the power and the glory that will accrue to him and his classmates because of their Harvard education, fantasies of a genteel cultural revolution, fantasies of being a "student leader," and fantasies that his generation has discovered for the first time in history such qualities as human relatedness.

Because each of these books is primarily concerned with how it could happen at *Harvard,* we learn little from them about campus unrest in general or even about radicalization in particular. As the WHRB report indicates, President Pusey was admittedly distant and somewhat devious in his attempts to maintain ROTC despite faculty disaccreditation. And by choosing the Bust Scenario, Pusey unwittingly assured the departure of ROTC, delivered students to a strike, split the faculty, and hastened his own retirement. But recent campus history makes clear that human warmth, administrative candor, and political genius are as scarce in most college presidents' offices as in the White House. Harvard SDS in 1969 was doubtless undemocratic, manipulative, snobbish, and elitist, as Kelman claims—but then these have always been said to be the characteristics of Harvard men. And Zorza's belief that his is the first generation ever to discover the meaning of community—well, it takes us nowhere.

In any case, understanding exactly what happened at Harvard in April, 1969, does not help much in explaining the world-wide revolt of the educated young. We already knew that the likelihood of protests at places like Harvard was extraordinarily high. These books merely help us to understand how what could have been an isolated protest was escalated into a police bust and a student strike.

For broader understanding we must look beyond Harvard and beyond the United States. Ultimately, the causes of campus unrest are no less complex than the societies that spawn unrest. But they lie in the interaction of real issues and a student generation uniquely prepared to perceive and respond to these issues. The real problems of industrially advanced countries are thus one "cause": enormous warfare expenditures; persistent inequality, poverty, and racism; the despoliation of the environment; a manipulated consumer society. Some of the issues are new: no nation in modern history has so brutally devastated a third-rate power as America has devastated Indochina; never before have universities assumed such importance as the research-development-training centers of a society. But many of the other issues are old: inequality, racism, hypocrisy, and poverty have been around a long time, and in even more virulent forms than today.

Thus issues are necessary but not sufficient. By themselves, they are like trees falling silently in the forest with no one to notice them. The second "cause" is therefore the new youthful audience, hypersensitive to issues that most men and women in previous generations chose to ignore. An essential part of the dynamic of advanced industrial societies is the creation of new groups of young men and women who view traditional truths with skepticism, established institutions with wariness, and decreed policies with mistrust. These young can be, as Kelman accuses and Zorza illustrates, naïve, manipulative, ahistorical, spiteful, and neurotically driven. Their "countercultures" are often shallow, thin, and transparently parasitic on the dominant society.

But the oppositional young are extraordinarily attuned to the real problems and vulnerabilities of the technocratic society. And every indicator points to a continuation and spread of their critical disengagement. Their experiments in life styles, counterinstitutions, countercultures, and unalienated consciousness are beginning to define a new reaction against the technocratic order that dominates all the most powerful nations of the world. The opposition of the young provides no "solutions" to the problems it pinpoints; campus unrest is the antithesis, not the "answer," to the issues that inspire it. But if there are ever to be solutions and answers, they must bring together the technological wizardry and productivity of industrialized societies with the oppositional mentality of youth. That synthesis might really lessen campus unrest, even at Harvard.

The Unholy Alliance

*In September, 1970, Michael Lerner and I worked briefly for the staff of
the Scranton Commission, which was preparing the Report of the
President's Commission on Campus Unrest. Out of that collaboration
between Lerner, a political scientist, and me grew a joint interest in the
accuracy of the political rhetoric that surrounded the issue of campus
unrest during the 1970 Congressional campaign. We were impressed by
the underlying similarity between the polemics of the mindless Right and
the mindless Left; more important, we were convinced that what we call
the "extremist" attacks on the university bore almost no relationship to the
known facts about higher education and campus unrest. This article
(1970) is our effort to underline the similarities between the two attacks
on the university, and to counter polemics with facts.*

*The article was considered "outrageously counterrevolutionary" by
some of our more radical friends, while we received dozens of letters from
right-wing correspondents accusing us of being Communist toadies and
apologists for student violence. Whatever the political limitations of this
piece—and we agree there are several—it provides a summary of studies
about the relationship between campus characteristics and campus unrest,
together with an argument, addressed primarily to our friends on the
Left, that American higher education, far from being the prime target for
radicals, should be viewed as an ambivalent ally in the struggle for social
change. Here our views are parallel to those of many radicals like Herbert
Marcuse, Noam Chomsky, Robert Paul Wolff, Eugene Genovese, and
Barrington Moore. For, despite the innumerable failings and compromises
of American higher education, the university is one of the few places
where truly critical thinking about American society sometimes takes
place. For that reason alone, if for no other, higher education is worth
defending.*

AMERICAN higher education is taking a beating from political extremists of both the right and the left wing, and the beating is having its
intended effect. Polls show that Americans are fed up with campus unrest,
which they consider the nation's number-two problem. In the 1970 Con-

gressional campaign, many politicians considered attacking "violent students" and "lax faculty members" an excellent way to win votes.

The most highly publicized attacks on the universities have come from the right wing. The administration's acrimonious alliterator has barnstormed the country, blaming campus disorders on "the disgusting permissiveness of campus officials." Governor Ronald Reagan agrees: "The campus . . . has now become the arena for oppression by revolutionaries, vandals, arsonists and terrorists." And Martha Mitchell, the wife of the Attorney General, summed up the views of many rightists when she said, "The academic society is responsible for all our troubles in this country. These are the people that are destroying our country."

But the attack on higher education from the extreme Left is just as vehement. "American universities are absolutely central components of the social system of technological warfare-welfare capitalism," says an SDS pamphlet. According to the Free Speech Movement in Berkeley in 1964, the student is a mere "mercenary, paid off in grades, status and degrees, all of which can eventually be cashed in for hard currency on the job market. . . . Credits for courses are subtly transformed into credit cards, as the multiversity inculcates the values of acquisitive society." Said a radical Harvard student recently, "It isn't just one man . . . it's a lot of men who sit on the Corporation, who have certain interests. They may not think such nasty thoughts all the time, but they do things that are a lot nastier. And they don't come down to see us: they send their pigs down here to do it for them."

Behind their superficial differences in rhetoric, right- and left-wing extremists are in astonishing agreement about higher education. First, they agree that campus discipline is unjust and politically motivated—for the rightist, it is permissive; for the leftist, it is repressive. Second, they agree that universities systematically indoctrinate their students with abhorrent political ideas—for the rightist, with radical and revolutionary ideas; for the leftist, with the values of the welfare-warfare state. Third, they agree that American higher education has become "politicized"—for the rightist, into a launching pad for revolution; for the leftist, into a tool of the military-industrial Establishment. In short, the radical extremes are allied in blaming the campuses for unrest.

Many Americans reject these extreme charges against the campus. But they are aware that higher education has myriad failings: the multiversity is impersonal; educational quality is often poor; many campuses were inadequately prepared for disorders when they came. Thus, even though they reject the extremist attack, many people have been persuaded that the shortcomings of the campus *are* a crucial cause of campus disruption, and that campus reforms would lessen or perhaps eliminate the disorders that have swept higher education.

But this conclusion, however plausible it seems, is actually incorrect. We have examined hundreds of studies of student protesters, of the institutions where protest occurred, of the attitudes of students and faculty members toward protest issues, and of the consequences of protest. These studies support neither the extremist charges nor, more important, the more plausible view that campus reforms will significantly affect campus unrest.

Are Violent Protests Typical?

Consider first the widespread impression, created by the mass media and reinforced by certain politicians, that disruptive and violent disorders are typical of campus unrest.

In fact, the overwhelming proportion of campus protests in recent years has been peaceful, orderly, and within the bounds of dissent protected by the First Amendment of the Constitution. A study of campus protests in 1968–69 showed that more than three-fourths of America's 2,500 colleges and universities experienced either no protests at all or peaceful protests. Violent protests involving property damage or personal injury occurred on less than 7 per cent of all campuses. During the last academic year the American Council on Education found that incidents occurred on two-thirds of all campuses, but only about 9 per cent reported violent incidents. And last May, after Cambodia, Kent State, and Jackson State, only 4 per cent of 1,800 college presidents reported violent protests on their campuses. The evidence, then, is clear: violent and disorderly protests are the exception, not the rule, in American higher education.

Furthermore, the absolute number of protests on American campuses has not increased dramatically in the last six years. From a 1964–65 study of 849 colleges, we can estimate that there were about 3,700 campus protests per 1,000 colleges. A roughly comparable study conducted in 1969 –70 showed only a small rise to 3,860 protests per 1,000 colleges.

How, then, has the impression been created that an ever-larger proportion of campus protest involves illegality and disorder? What are the facts?

The number of campus protests concerned with social, political, and off-campus issues has increased sharply in recent years. In 1964–65, only 34 per cent of protests concerned off-campus issues. But in the last academic year, more than 80 per cent of all incidents involved issues like the war, racial policies, and ecology. A survey of college presidents showed that 57 per cent judged that Cambodia, Kent State, and Jackson State alone had a "significant impact" on their campuses.

Where violence has occurred it has become increasingly intense. On the one hand, there have been more incidents of burning, trashing, and bombing—although many of these have not been perpetrated by students. On the other hand, these incidents have led to greatly increased police and National Guard intervention, and to the unwarranted violence of civil authorities at Kent State and Jackson State. The percentage of campuses reporting students arrested increased from less than 5 per cent in 1968–69 to almost 12 per cent in 1969–70.

American students show diminishing confidence in the ability of established institutions to achieve social changes that students consider increasingly necessary. For example, in May, 1970, 75 per cent of American college students agreed that "basic changes in the system will be necessary" to improve the quality of life in America, while only 19 per cent believed this country "is currently on the right track." More important, 44 per cent maintained that "social progress" was more likely to occur through "radical pressure from outside the system" than through the "major institutions in our system—government, business, etc."

The year 1969 saw the rise of a new urban terrorism initiated by a tiny handful of young, mostly nonstudent extremists. The killing of a graduate student in the terrorist bombing of the mathematics building at the University of Wisconsin is the most dramatic symbol of the emergence of groups willing to use violence systematically. Even more disturbing is the attitude of a minority of students who condone terrorism.

Political rhetoric and selective reporting by the mass media thus conceal the real complexity of the situation on the campuses. Politicians and the media thrive on oversimplification, emphasizing the dramatic confrontations but not the far more common peaceful protests. The terrorist acts of an infinitesimal fraction of 1 per cent of young people are used to condemn the majority of students. Neglected in this oversimplification is the fact that the vast majority of American students, at the same time that they become more frustrated, more opposed to the war, and less confident in basic American institutions, have so far remained committed to peaceful dissent.

Most American students, then, like most of the American public, are caught in a pincer movement between the extreme Right and the extreme Left. On the one hand, rightist politicians tar all student protestors with the brush of terrorism. On the other hand, the handful of terrorists are equally eager to identify peaceful dissent with guerrilla warfare and to persuade Americans that there is no middle ground. Each extreme feeds on the other in what Clark Kerr, not noted for overstatement, has called an "unholy alliance against democracy." Without real student violence the extremists of the Right could not call for repression, and without the violent call to repression by the extreme Right, left-wing terrorists would find little support among their fellows.

In the middle are 99 per cent of American students, constantly told that they either *are* or *must be* violent. Erik Erikson long ago suggested that if you label a person with opprobrium long enough, he will eventually accept this "negative identity." Together, the extremists of the Right and the Left who dominate the headlines are helping to enforce an identity of violence upon students. At the same time, these extremists are succeeding in convincing other Americans either that peaceful dissent is unjustified, or that the only effective form of social action is violence.

But what *does* cause the unrest that clearly exists on American campuses? Most people would agree that even one violent protest on campus is one too many. The 500 to 600 that occurred last year were clearly too many. The question remains, then, whether the extremist analysis of the causes of dissent is accurate: are the universities permissive or repressive? Do they indoctrinate their students with abhorrent political ideas? Is the campus becoming politicized? And are these alleged failings the causes of campus unrest?

Is Discipline Permissive (or Repressive)?

One element in the current wave of disruption is the failure of college administrators to vigorously uphold the law. . . . To allow permissiveness in the enforcement of campus laws is to teach delinquency with respect to community laws. Administrators are being severely exploited by hard-core militants who know that the conscience of an administrator in an academic environment leads him to bend over backwards. . . .   GOVERNOR RONALD REAGAN

A University which orders a thousand club-swinging fascist cops against its students and praises their action, a University which directs plainclothesmen to viciously beat innocent spectators and praises their action, a University that permits mounted police to violate her grounds and to trample students and faculty outside her gates and praises their action, this University is not safe for Man.   "The Communes," Columbia University, after the police bust, 1968

Extremists of Right and Left agree that university discipline is both unjust and politically motivated. The argument that dominates the headlines from the Right is that the "permissiveness" of campus authorities and faculties is responsible for the "wave of violence" on the campuses. Left extremists agree that student violence is related to unjust discipline, but they see it as a response to the unjustified punishment of students and to police brutality. Leftists claim that police actions at Columbia and the Chicago Convention or the deaths at Kent and Jackson State demonstrate the "repressive" nature of the American system and the complicity of the universities with that system. In fact, of course, some extremists work to provoke police violence, just as the police have hired agents who incite students to violence. Each side then uses charges of "police brutality" or "student violence" to recruit new supporters.

But the facts suggest that neither critique of campus discipline is correct. Though exact figures are hard to come by, available evidence indicates that campus officials have not as a rule failed to punish students for violent, illegal protest. There are exceptions that make headlines: the black students who appeared with guns on the Cornell campus shocked the nation, even though they were later turned over to local authorities for prosecution. But media exploitation of these examples hides the basic trends. One study of twenty-eight colleges and universities showed that campus protests resulted in 950 suspensions or expulsions of students, along with another 800 reprimands. Another study found violent protests were followed by campus or civil-court discipline in more than 75 per cent of the colleges where they occurred. Considering that "violent protests" included protests in which fist fights broke out between demonstrators and counterdemonstrators, the finding that 75 per cent of these protests resulted in disciplinary action against students suggests a firm response.

Are student demonstrators being coddled by civil authorities? The number of students arrested increased from 4,000 in 1968–69 to 7,200 last year. If we study in detail some of the most publicized campus disorders, like Berkeley 1964, University of Chicago 1969, Columbia 1968, or Harvard 1969, in every case students were either convicted by the courts (almost 800 at Berkeley) or suspended and expelled by the university (123 at the University of Chicago).

As to the left-wing charge of the systematic repression of students, this, too, has little substance. Clearly, police have far too often reacted with illegal violence to campus disorders that profoundly threatened them on many levels, and for which they were usually ill-trained and ill-equipped. But this is scarcely the norm. The behavior of New Haven police during the May Day demonstrations is a case in point. Faced with rock-throwing demonstrators eager to provoke trouble, Chief Ahern's highly professional force responded with minimum violence and inflicted no serious injuries on anyone. Similar stories of police restraint could be told in countless other communities during the student demonstrations that followed the invasion of Cambodia and the deaths at Kent and Jackson State. Those two colleges provided the tragic and inexcusable exceptions. But 1.5 million students were involved in demonstrations during May, 1970, and the overwhelming majority met a restrained response from civil authorities.

Does Higher Education Indoctrinate Its Students?

[In] last year's lurch-ins, smash-ups, and lock-outs on so many distracted campuses . . . the real common denominator was the covert encouragement given the neo-Nazis by certain professors. It amounted to a surreptitious, lip-smacking "Go-ahead-and-bust-things-up-and-we'll-stand-behind-you" prodding . . . these mixed-up mentors encouraged their present hecklers to rebel for the sake of rebelling, to demonstrate for the sake of demonstrating, to flout authority for the sake of chaos.   MAX RAFFERTY

The faculty is engaged in the process of transmitting lies from one group to another, and the lies they tell, especially in the social sciences, are lies that help to perpetuate the *status quo*. . . . Or else they teach the wrong stuff. If you're in economics . . . they teach you how to do statistics so you can work for the Pentagon or for GM. Or, if you're in sociology, you don't learn how to criticize the society. . . . It's complete ideology we get from our professors. . . . That's why so few professors side with us.   MARK RUDD

The second charge heard from extremists is that college students are systematically indoctrinated—either to become violent radicals or complacent robots of the system. Rightists assail radical professors; leftists view the universities as centers of indoctrination for the military-industrial complex.

Clearly there are radical professors, and clearly universities do train students for careers in the American system. But once again the facts contradict the ominous cast that extremists try to lend to these realities. For example, one extensive study of the role of the faculty in campus unrest finds that faculty support or leadership of disruptive and violent protests was extremely rare. From this study we can infer that in less than 2 per cent of disruptive or violent protests were *any* faculty members involved as leaders. And in most such cases faculty leadership consisted of one or two men in a faculty community overwhelmingly opposed to their actions.

Faculty members do, however, frequently support nonviolent protest against the war or social injustice. One study showed 49 per cent of all protests involved at least one faculty member. Another study found that 15 per cent of a national sample of faculty members had supported the goals and tactics of the most recent campus protest, although faculty support was almost entirely restricted to nonviolent protests. Indeed, the most common role of faculty members has been to deter headstrong students from disruptive or violent action. Even most "radical" faculty members are as committed to nonviolence, or as opposed to counterproductive violence, as they are committed to basic social change.

Even if faculty members do not actually lead their students into violent protests, it could still be true, as rightists charge, that they indoctrinate their students with revolutionary or violent ideas. But this claim is also incorrect. The Carnegie Commission on Higher Education, in a recent comprehensive survey of American faculty members, found that 81 per cent of faculty members agree that "campus disruptions by militant students are a threat to academic freedom," while 79 per cent believe that "students who disrupt the functioning of the college should be expelled or suspended." Indeed, the typical American faculty member emerges from the Carnegie study as a man with political views like those of most other Americans with comparable education and background. He tends to oppose the war and racist practices. But predictably, as far as his own campus is concerned, he is generally conservative, defending institutional neutrality, and strongly opposed to disruption and violence.

The radical Left, in contrast, charges that higher education indoctrinates students with a military-industrial, racist-imperialist mentality. This charge also suffers before the facts. Studies of the effects of higher education show that it lessens rather than increases students' unquestioning acceptance of the *status quo*. When students who go to college are compared with youths of equal ability and motivation who do not, we find that the college students become less authoritarian, more open to new views, less dogmatic, and more inquiring and open-minded. In brief, if college inculcates anything, it is the necessary qualities of democratic man. Such studies show that higher education, far from processing students into robotlike acceptance of the military-industrial society, leads them to great independence, precisely because it provides that "intellectual stimulation" that Vice President Agnew reports he found so rewarding in his own college years.

The most decisive refutation of the leftist charge that the universities are centers for reactionary indoctrination is the growing liberalism of college students. Radicals who claim universities castrate their students intellectually find it impossible to explain why American students are taking an increasingly active role in attempting to redress the injustices of American society.

In short, the charge of indoctrination—Right or Left—does not stand well with the facts. What higher education *does* do, though doubtless not well enough, is to help promote a more questioning, open-minded, tolerant, and searching attitude in its students. But this is a consequence not of reactionary brainwashing or radical indoctrination, but of "intellectual stimulation" itself.

Is the University Politicized?

The rich and powerful private universities, the gigantic state universities (which pay no more attention to their state governments than an overgrown spoiled brat to a neurotically indulgent parent), and innumerable colleges which follow in their wake are taking the parents' and taxpayers' money and maintaining privileged sanctuaries within which irregular hostile forces wage psychological and urban guerrilla warfare against the United States. . . . The universities are killing themselves, killing America, killing civilization.

MEDFORD EVANS, Associate Editor, *American Opinion*

We began to understand the university system in a different way. No longer could we criticize it for being an ivory tower, because we began to see that the university itself was a key part of the machinery of violence that was being used in Vietnam. Our professors were using their so-called academic freedom to perfect methods of torture, methods of chemical and biological warfare. The Department of Defense was financing endless studies of how to defeat guerrillas and revolutionaries.   TOM HAYDEN

The third charge on which extremists basically agree is that the universities have been politicized—transformed either into revolutionary bases or tools of militarism. The traditional posture of the university has been "institutional neutrality." Extremists believe this posture has today been abandoned with disastrous results. Reactionaries say politicization has made the campuses into launching pads for revolution: even the involvement of students and faculty as private citizens in antiwar and antiracist politics is seen as an erosion of academic neutrality. Radical leftists in turn seize upon the issue of military research and training to demonstrate the "complicity" of the campuses with the military-industrial complex.

The facts fail to support either of these positions. To be sure, "institutional neutrality" is, in the broad sense, a "political" position. And the university is necessarily a part of the society that sustains it. But the evidence shows that extremely few American colleges or universities have taken institutional positions on anything except matters that directly affect their immediate self-interest.

Again and again members of campus communities have tried to make it clear (though not always successfully) that they speak as individuals, not as representatives of their colleges. This distinction between the actions of individual members of academic communities, acting as citizens, and the actions of their institutions is often lost on the public. In May, 1969, the sight of college presidents joining students in talks with Congressmen on the Vietnam War often created the impression that colleges as institutions had taken a position on the war. In fact, only 4 per cent had.

Surveys of faculty opinion make it clear that "politicization" of the university would be bitterly opposed by the overwhelming majority of faculty members. The Carnegie Commission survey of faculty opinion found that when it comes to protecting their own turf or allowing anyone else to speak for them on political issues, most faculty members are very conservative. Indeed, as a group, they are considerably more dedicated to academic freedom and institutional neutrality than are most members of the general public.

The extreme Left charge of politicization relies heavily on the fact that a few major universities have been dependent on secret research funds for their teaching and research operations. But, in 1966–1967, the federal government in fact contributed only 13 per cent of the direct instructional costs of higher education. If we include indirect costs, the federal share shrinks to 4 per cent—a remarkably tiny indicator of the university's complicity. It is true that the federal government provides the lion's share of research funds: about 87 per cent of 2 billion dollars in 1967. But this year only 1.89 per cent of federal research grants was classified. In short, out of the total university research budget, about 1.5 per cent is related to secret military work.

Some would say that even 1.5 per cent is too much, while others would deplore the dependence of a few institutions on military-research contracts. But whatever view one takes, the charge that American higher education is dominated by military-research money hardly stands up to examination. The Massachusetts Institute of Technology, generally cited as the classic instance of a military-research-dominated institution, is ending all classified defense research but does not plan to go out of business. In fact, most federal grants, like most business contributions, go to areas that are little involved in politics. Medical education, for example, is largely dependent on both public and private grants. But it takes a twisted logic to argue that federal support for training researchers to study cancer or control pollution is part of a reactionary plot linking universities to the war machine.

The more general leftist charge that the universities are unduly tied to political and corporate interests often starts from the fact that boards of regents and trustees are weighted with corporate executives. Their political views are usually more conservative than those of the campus communities they oversee. As Jerry Rubin sees it, "We learned the *inside* story. . . . The very same racists who controlled the business world controlled the university, too."

Yet it is ironic that leftists, who once bitterly assailed Senator Joseph McCarthy's tactic of "guilt by association," today use this same tainted brush against all trustees with business associations, arguing that their business contacts prove they are mere tools of the military-industrial complex. Trustees from the business world can be enlightened—witness the governing board of Yale; or they can be vindictive—witness many of the regents of the University of California. In our view, trustees and regents should represent a far wider range of views, ages, and interests than they generally do. But on principle it is perfectly proper that those who help finance higher education should have their representatives involved in overseeing institutions supported by alumni gifts and public taxes.

There are *dangers* of politicization of the university. But they are more subtle than the extremists of either the Right or the Left recognize. One danger is that there might develop on American campuses a climate of opinion so unanimous that active discussion of some issues would be effectively silenced. By and large this has not happened, but it is a danger against which academic communities must constantly guard. Another danger is that "string-attached" research, training, or action grants could lead universities into massive "complicity" with controversial political policies. Yet the over-all trend in recent years has been *away* from such "string-attached" grants. The greatest danger of politicization today, however, comes from a public rapidly being persuaded that the universities are centers of sedition and causes of unrest. Politically motivated efforts to "get rid of campus radicals," however profitable they might be to unscrupulous candidates, would indeed erode the fundamental principles of institutional neutrality and academic freedom.

The three major extremist charges against the university must all be labeled false. Improper discipline, indoctrination, and politicization are dangers that higher education must constantly resist. But the claim that American higher education has systematically employed disciplinary procedures in either a permissive or a repressive way is simply not supported by the facts. Nor have colleges and universities brainwashed their students into bomb-throwing revolutionaries, much less converted them into obedient robots for the military-industrial complex. As for politicization, the over-all trend in recent years has been toward increasing academic freedom and institutional neutrality. On all counts, then, the extremist allegations that point to the "failings" of the campus as the causes of campus unrest are simply not supported by an overview of the facts.

Does Educational Discontent Cause Protests?

Few Americans would completely agree with the extremist positions that we have outlined. But many conservatives, moderates, liberals, and radicals, in the very act of refuting the extremist charges, have uncritically assumed a causal link between the shortcomings of the campus and student unrest. Americans know there is much wrong with higher education; they know there is much student unrest. In the process of rejecting the specific content of extremist charges, they have unwittingly begun to accept the underlying assumption that campus unrest is the result of university shortcomings. But this alleged causal link simply does not stand up before the evidence.

Consider the common charge that unrest is caused by "the impersonality of the multiversity." There is no question that vast campuses with immense classes and little personal attention for students have grown up: one-quarter of our 7 million college students are today enrolled in campuses of more than 15,000 students. Since protests are both more common and bigger on these large campuses, it is easy to assume a connection between impersonality and protest.

But the connection is false. There is more of everything at larger institutions. Large campuses are also more likely to have chapters of Young Americans for Freedom (a right-wing group), literary magazines, science clubs, fraternities, and massive football rallies. The obvious explanation is that compared to small colleges, large universities have more students available for almost everything. Not surprisingly, they have more and bigger protests as well.

But suppose we compare large and small campuses in terms of the number of *protests per 10,000 students* that occur on them. We come to the paradoxical conclusion that there are *fewer* protests per 10,000 students at large institutions than at small ones. The statistic is partially artificial: protests are not like the number of cases of influenza, which should bear a perfect relationship to campus size. But this statistic does put in perspective the allegation that the "impersonality" of the multiversity *causes* campus unrest.

The second apparently plausible charge is that the educational deficiencies of colleges cause campus unrest. Students generally arrive at college with high expectations about both the educational experience and the social life that await them. They are invariably disappointed. Colleges with a rich social life are rarely as stimulating intellectually as students expect, and vice versa. Many students' hopes are dashed in their freshman year; as a result, some are genuinely dissatisfied with their college experience.

Surprisingly, however, 75 per cent of college seniors at all institutions (including the vast multiversities) consider higher education "basically sound," while only 4 per cent judge it "basically unsound." Another poll found that college students have a higher opinion of universities than of any other institution in American life. More important, research has shown no relationship between the student's educational dissatisfaction and his involvement in protests. A study of the Free Speech Movement at Berkeley in 1964 found that arrested students and their supporters were just as pleased with their education as their nonprotesting classmates. Another study compared SDS members and student-government leaders at Michigan State: both groups thought they were getting an equally fine education.

Furthermore, if protests result from discontent with education, we would expect those who get the worst education to protest most. But other studies show that student protesters tend to be more intellectually oriented and somewhat better students than nonprotesters. As a result, at any given college, protesters generally receive more personal attention (smaller classes, honors programs) and more intense intellectual stimulation. Furthermore, the colleges and universities where protests have been most common are not those that provide inferior education. The roster of colleges with large protests includes most of America's most distinguished institutions, where the quality of undergraduate education is highest.

One study demonstrates especially conclusively the absence of any relationship between college characteristics and the proportion of students involved in antiwar protests. The researchers first "held constant" the characteristics of incoming freshmen. Enabled by statistical techniques to assume that all of the colleges studied admitted identical students, they then examined the effects on protests of fifty-eight different objective characteristics of each college.

But once the characteristics of incoming freshmen were controlled for, the researchers found that only *one* of their fifty-eight measures of campus characteristics was related to the percentage of students in antiwar protests. That one measure was the presence on campus of many organized musical and artistic activities! And taking that campus characteristic into account increased the accuracy of their prediction about antiwar protests by only .54 per cent—hardly a notable increase.

Among the campus characteristics that did *not* have any connection with the per cent of students in antiwar protests were the type of college or university, the type of administrative control (public versus private), geographic region, the severity of administration policies about a variety of student activities, the verbal aggressiveness of students in the classroom, the cohesiveness (school spirit) of the campus, the regularity of student sleeping habits, the extent to which classroom activities were formally organized, the degree of student involvement in classroom discussions, and so on.

This study, like a similar study of protests over racial issues, shows that once we control for the kind of freshmen admitted, campus characteristics have a negligible effect on student involvement in protest. If this is true, then arguments that the campus itself is the cause of unrest are simply incorrect. And proposed solutions to the "problem of campus unrest" that urge campus reforms are building on a frail reed indeed.

The liberal critique of higher education starts from real shortcomings of American campuses. But the apparently plausible argument that these shortcomings—impersonality, poor education, and so on—are *causally* related to campus unrest turns out to be completely untrue. The mountain of studies on campus unrest indicates that the campus itself has virtually nothing to do with whether protests occur on it. For an explanation of campus unrest we must look elsewhere—on the one hand to the changing characteristics of the students entering American higher education, and on the other hand, to the issues about which they protest.

Protesting Students and Real Issues

Research on student protest and campus unrest indicates very clearly that the best way to predict the presence or size of protests on any given campus is to study the characteristics of incoming freshmen. In the previously mentioned study, researchers found that simply knowing the kinds of freshmen admitted to American colleges would have enabled them to predict with 81 per cent accuracy the per cent of students involved in antiwar protests. A freshman class that has a high per cent of freshmen who mark "none" for religion on questionnaires, many National Merit Scholarship winners, and many students who seek competence in a performing art tends to have large antiwar demonstrations. In all, thirty-three different characteristics of the freshman class were related significantly to antiwar protests. Comparable results were obtained in a study of protests over race-related issues.

This study confirms what dozens of other researchers have found: students who protest are different in a variety of ways from those who do not, and the main reason some campuses experience more and bigger protests than others is that these campuses admit more of the kinds of students who appear "protest-prone."

Aware of this conclusion, some Americans have begun to argue that the best way to "stamp out campus unrest" would be to deny college admission to students who are "protest-prone." Yet once we begin to study the implications of this policy, it turns out to be both illegal and disastrous in its results.

First, a policy of excluding the "protest-prone" would of course be illegal, unconstitutional, and quite contrary to the spirit of American democracy. Peaceful dissent and nonviolent protest—which constitute the overwhelming proportion of campus unrest—are not only legal but in the long run essential to the vitality of this nation. Under the First Amendment, the Constitution explicitly protects the right of free speech and dissent. Discriminatory admission policies aimed at excluding potential dissenters would be contrary to the hard-won freedoms of this nation. Any institution that adopted such a policy would violate the very law of the land that the policy was intended to protect.

Furthermore, the students to be kept out would include many of the best students in the country. Study after study has shown that students involved in protests tend to be above-average students who do well on aptitude tests, who are intellectually independent and inquiring. They place special stress on values like serving their fellow men, acquiring a good education, expressing their convictions and feelings directly, and solving the problems of their society.

"Protest-prone" students, then, tend to be young men and women that most American families take pride in, that American high schools consider their best products, and that colleges consider themselves lucky to attract. To keep them out of American higher education, colleges would have to give preference to students who do *poorly* on aptitude tests, who *lack* intellectual independence and curiosity, who have *little* interest in serving their fellow men, who do *not* wish to express their convictions and feelings, and who are *not* interested in solving the problems of their country. To bar potential protesters from college would thus deprive American society of the educated talents of young men and women whose ability and idealism it desperately needs if the problems of our society are to be solved.

But even if we considered it desirable to exclude protest-prone students from colleges, we have no way of doing so with any accuracy. It is fairly easy to predict the institutions that will have large protests against the war or alleged racial inequities. But it turns out to be very difficult to predict the individual students who will be actively involved in protests. Predictions of protests by institutions have an accuracy of up to 80 per cent. But predictions of individuals who will protest are only about 18 per cent accurate. Any net cast out for protest-prone students would therefore catch mostly students who would not become involved in protests at all.

Finally, to try to close the college gates to potential protesters would be extraordinarily counterproductive. It would produce precisely the kind of bitterness, rage, and turn toward violence that it attempts to prevent. No imaginable policy could be better calculated to turn moderate high school graduates into extremists, liberal students into arsonists and revolutionaries. Students locked out of American campuses on the dubious grounds that they *might* engage in protests, a small proportion of which *might* be disruptive or violent, would be rightly embittered and enraged. A policy intended to reduce disruption and violence would only produce and even justify it. In short, an effort to exclude students who might protest would be not only illegal, destructive to society, and impossible to achieve, but massively counterproductive.

We conclude that most political discussions of campus unrest bear almost no relationship to the known facts. They are a mixture of misinformation, innuendo, stereotyping, and falsification. The "disgusting permissiveness" of American campuses is not responsible for student unrest. Nor are the political characterizations of student protesters as bums, rotten apples, nihilists, and animals applicable to the vast majority of students who protest local practices and national policies.

American higher education, despite its many defects, has accomplished the extraordinary feat of educating nearly half of this nation's youth— something never before achieved in world history. And American students, despite their myriad shortcomings, have shown a concern with social justice, peace, and the quality of American life that commencement orators have been urging upon them for decades. The view that "campus unrest" is a national disaster to be solved by attacking higher education or protesting students is both inaccurate and unjust.

Research on campus unrest and student protesters agrees on one critical point: the major determinants of protest among students are their moral values and their perceptions of the world around them. Over the last generation we have carefully brought up our children to be committed to social justice, racial equality, and peace. But simply having high values and a special sensitivity to injustice and hypocrisy is not by itself enough to produce protest. In addition, students must see their values contradicted and their commitment to social change obstructed by the actual practices and policies of their society. Today our society is still deeply involved in a war that most Americans believe we never should have entered, still accepts widespread psychological and social racism, still does not provide many Americans with an adequate standard of living and health, still cannot restore the quality of the environment. These social facts, which contradict the values taught to young Americans in their homes, their schools, and their churches, must be considered as much the "causes" of campus unrest as the growing readiness of students to protest in the service of their ideals.

If the continuing deficiencies in American life are to be remedied—and most Americans agree they must be—then both higher education and college students desperately need public understanding and support, rather than politically motivated attacks. For although the shortcomings of higher education do not *cause* campus unrest, they do severely *limit* the capacity of our campuses to educate a generation adequately equipped to deal with the problems of the last third of the twentieth century.

Many criticisms of American higher education seem to us fully justified. The mammoth multiversities are indeed impersonal. Most young Americans do not receive the quality of education they deserve. American universities urgently need reforms in governance. More adequate preparations for campus disorders are called for. Greater emphasis must be placed on teaching and learning. Campus members must be more explicit about their responsibilities, and not simply about their rights. And American campuses must work to re-create a real sense of community. If American higher education is to educate well the many millions who will enter college in the next decades, it must change; and change will, in turn, require the understanding and support of the American public.

Nor should we forget the shortcomings of protesting students. For all of their intelligence, commitment, and idealism, they are at an age when thinking tends to be particularly ideological. Their intelligence and social concern in no way guarantees the wisdom of the policies they propose. Many naïvely believe that the personal ethics by which they are attempting to shape their individual lives can be projected without modification as guides for a national policy. Many lack awareness of the social, legal, economic, and political requirements of a technological nation of 200 million people. Many show great empathy for the downtrodden, oppressed, and poor, but astonishingly little empathy for working-class and middle-class Americans. Many pride themselves on being a post-Freudian generation but are bad psychologists, with little awareness of how painful it is for people to change the convictions and values on which they have built their lives. And many lack understanding of the enormous obstacles that must be overcome before the social changes they desire can be achieved.

In short, dissenting students are usually idealistic and intelligent, but not always wise. The very shortcomings of youth mean that today more than ever before they must be *educated*. The qualities youth inevitably lacks—experience, informed intelligence, and awareness of complexity, tolerance for others with different views, compassion for one's adversaries, and above all wisdom—are precisely the qualities that higher education at its best helps stimulate in the young. The unprecedented challenge to American colleges and universities is to help inform the idealism of dissenting students with understanding and wisdom.

It is for this reason that the crisis produced by the attacks of extremists against higher education is so grave. The first result of a triumph of extremists would be to cut off support from higher education. We already see this beginning to happen. Yet without support higher education cannot improve; and without vital colleges and universities the young cannot be educated to deal with the problems of the nation. Colleges must deal firmly with disruptive protest and pursue terrorism with severity. But firmness will be of no avail if support for higher education is choked off and if violent protest and its severest pathology, terrorism, are not recognized as the tragic symptoms of basic national problems.

Higher education must be reformed to serve society better, not destroyed as a scapegoat for underlying national problems. Students must be educated to be wise, humane, and effective, not attacked as anarchists and terrorists. And the extremist attacks on higher education must be seen for what they are—efforts to polarize the nation further, insults to the decency and intelligence of the American public, divisive calls to anarchy or repression.

Epilogue: Revolution or Counterrevolution?

This essay began as a lecture delivered in 1970 to the Carnegie Foundation for the Advancement of Teaching, and eventually grew into its present form. It is an effort to consider the general theoretical implications of the new opposition by contrasting what I term the revolutionary and the counterrevolutionary theories of youthful dissent. In asking about the general historical meaning of the counterculture, however, I ask a question that I cannot adequately answer. It is therefore precise to call the second half of this essay an agenda, for my sense of the inadequacy of existing theories of the youth revolt is accompanied only by a sense that much more work needs to be done before a more adequate theory can be constructed.

I am not sure whether it is disappointing or appropriate that a book of this kind ends not with a proclamation or a polished theory, but with a lengthy list of things that need to be done. It is probably a little of both. It is disappointing in that I wish that I could either find in the work of others the theoretical, descriptive, and political answers I seek, or else provide them myself. Yet it may also be fitting. For this book chronicles my own increasing awareness of the inadequacies of the structures of liberal thought, which I was brought up to take for granted, and my increasing sense of a need to re-evaluate and go beyond traditional liberalism. And this book also records my constant belief that the youthful revolt is more than a passing fad. It may therefore be appropriate to conclude this collection of essays by insisting that the new opposition points to new, fundamental, and unresolved contradictions in technological society, and to argue that the outcome of the challenge presented by the new opposition will not be determined for decades.

Finally, there is a sense in which this essay is a memorandum to myself, an effort to outline the areas in which I think it profitable to work in the future. For my current work is taking me away from the specific study of youthful dissent toward a more general consideration of youth as a stage of life, toward a theoretical interest in the relationship between

*psychological development and sociohistorical change, and toward an
effort to contribute to a critical social theory of contemporary society.
French students during the revolt of May, 1968 chanted, "Ce n'est qu'un
début." The surfacing of a new opposition, like the French student
revolt, is but a preface to the continuing social, political, and cultural
crisis of nations like our own.*

NO issue today divides the public or intellectual community so deeply
as does the "counterculture," the "new culture," "consciousness III"—what
I will call the new youthful opposition. Hawks and doves on the youth
question debate campus unrest with an intensity and heat generally re-
served only for the weightiest ideological matters. The mildest criticism
of the youthful romance with violence or the gentlest critique of radical
mindlessness evokes epithets like "reactionary," "counterrevolutionary," or,
worst of all, "liberal" from the passionate defenders of the youthful opposition. But conversely, hawks on the youth question feel that the expression of guarded optimism about the decency of students or the claim
that most young people act from idealistic motives makes the speaker a
sychopant, a Pied Piper, or an "apologist."

Merely to deride this debate would blind us to the real importance of
the issues raised. However fashionable it has become to laud or lambaste
the dissenting young, serious issues lie hidden behind the current polemics in little magazines. For the debate about the oppositional young
ultimately involves a debate about the nature of man and society, and
requires that we examine our basic assumptions about both. I suspect
that this debate, which crosscuts and confounds the traditional distinctions between conservatives and liberals, may well define the basic terms
of intellectual inquiry, controversy, and creativity during the decades
ahead.

The debate is important because no event is quite so interesting theoretically as an event that we were led to believe could not occur. A
scientific experiment that confirms a prediction is ultimately of far less
importance than an experiment that fails. For if our predictions are
merely confirmed, we are only re-enforced in our attachment to the ways
of thinking that led us to anticipate correctly what was going to happen.
But when prediction fails, we are obliged to re-examine the theories upon
which the prediction was based, so as to explain, at least in retrospect,
the events we failed to anticipate.

The emergence of a youthful opposition is an instance of an historical
event that was predicted by no one twenty years ago. Marxist theorists
either continued to cherish hopes of a working-class revolt in the capitalist nations, or else devoted their theoretical energies to explaining how
monopoly capitalism had successfully co-opted the potentially revolu-

tionary spirit of the working class. Even the most sophisticated neo-Marxists did not predict that those who apparently benefited most from capitalist societies would help lead a new attack upon them. In a comparable way, what I will group together as "liberal theories" not only failed to anticipate the emergence of the youthful revolt, but predicted that such a revolt would become progressively *less* likely as affluence and higher education spread. To understand the theoretical importance of the current debate over the meaning of the youthful opposition therefore requires us to examine in broad outline the widely shared theoretical assumptions of liberal thinkers in the 1950's and early 1960's.

The "Liberal" Analysis

Liberal theories of man have usually started from the malleability or plasticity of human nature. The cultural anthropologists' discovery of the enormous variety of human belief and behavior in primitive cultures led to the view that man was almost totally adaptable to his social environment. Even psychoanalysis, with its heavy initial emphasis upon innate biological factors in development, was modified so as to place far greater stress on environmental influences in shaping the child's personality, and to minimize the importance of innate developmental sequences.

Given this implicit or explicit assumption of human plasticity, psychology as a field concentrated upon the processes by which human beings are influenced, shaped, and molded. For example, among the most highly developed areas in social psychology are the study of attitude change and small-group behavior. Attitude-change studies stressed the way convictions, beliefs, and values could be changed through experimental manipulation. Small-group studies explored how groups influence their members. In general, psychologists attempted to discover the "laws" that governed the molding and alteration of men's feelings, beliefs, convictions, and behavior.

If liberal psychology emphasized human plasticity and the techniques by which human conviction and behavior can be molded and modified, liberal social theories stressed equilibrium, stability, and the mechanisms of social control. The basic model of human society was the model of the "social system," constantly seeking to reach "dynamic equilibrium." The major theoretical effort of liberal sociologists went into explaining precisely *how* this equilibrium, harmony, lack of conflict, or absence of revolution had been guaranteed.

Many of the most powerful liberal theories in politics and economics can also be understood as efforts to explain the mechanisms of social equilibrium. Political theorists emphasized the stabilizing effects of competing interest groups, each with "veto power" over the others. The importance of pluralistic tolerance, of "democratic consensus," and of "liberal personality" was extensively studied. Still others examined how social conflicts are routinized—channeled into institutional forms that minimize social disruption and encourage compromise and reconciliation. For their part, some economists have emphasized the "countervailing powers" that prevent the domination of the economy by any one set of monopolistic interests. Even Keynesianism can be seen as an effort to define the means whereby a stable economy might be guaranteed. Experts on labor relations scrutinized the way highly organized trade unions and the institutions of collective bargaining minimized class struggle, promoting peaceful "conflict resolution." In virtually all areas of scholarly endeavor, then, the major theoretical emphasis was upon explaining that stability which was considered the goal and norm of societal existence.

The liberal assumptions of human plasticity and sociopolitical equilibrium were joined explicitly in the theory of socialization and acculturation. Malleable man was said to be related to stable society through a series of special socializing institutions like the family and the education system, whose primary function was to "integrate" the individual into society. Specifically, families' and schools' chief job was to teach children the social roles and cultural values necessary for adult life in that society. Key societal norms, symbolic systems, values, and role models were said to be "internalized" during the socialization process, and their internalization resulted in adults who were "adjusted"—who "functioned" with the symbols, values, and roles expected by their society.

The family is seen as the primary socializing and acculturating institution. But with the advent of early and prolonged schooling, formal education has increasingly supplemented the family as an agency of socialization. In highly industrialized states, it was argued, prolonged education is inevitable, for the skills required to operate a complex industrial state take many years to learn. Similarly, each of the higher vocations, occupations, and professions has its own set of specialized norms and ethics, its own methods and techniques, its own body of knowledge. So even the far reaches of higher education—graduate and professional school—have generally been described in terms of "professional socialization." Indeed, a generation of studies of the impact of higher education on students has been almost exclusively organized around the single concept of socialization.

Liberal social theorists did not naïvely confuse stability with stasis. A society in a state of basic equilibrium might still be a society that was changing rapidly: the equilibrium could be "dynamic." Social change created social strains and psychological stresses; but if all went well, it did not finally upset the basic social equilibrium. Between social strain and social disequilibrium stood a series of "mechanisms of social control," ranging from the police force to the practice of psychotherapy, which served to reduce societal tension by resocializing or isolating deviant individuals and by encapsulating or co-opting deviant social movements. The ideal kind of social change was seen as incremental—slow, quantitative, gradual and nonrevolutionary. Indeed, some social changes like rising economic prosperity or increasing education were believed to increase the stability of the societies in which they occurred. Increasing prosperity meant that more human needs could be met by society, while prolonging education provided more individuals with a lengthier and more thorough socialization experience.

Nor were liberal social theorists ignorant of the fact that revolutions, social convulsions, and dramatic upheavals abound in history. But convulsive social upheavals were almost always seen as symptoms of a breakdown of the system of social control, and as regressive or destructive in their consequences. "Meaningful social change" was thought most likely to occur through "gradualism" and "piecemeal social reform." Nor have liberal theorists blinded themselves to the existence within every society of murderers, artists, radicals, racists, inventors, crackpots, and geniuses—i.e., of "unsocialized" or "deviant" men and women. But individual behavior that deviated markedly from the norm was seen as the result of aberrant or deviant socialization, generally during the years of early childhood.

In principle, there is no reason why functional failures—e.g., breakdown in mechanisms of social control—should be deemed undesirable. Nazi Germany abounded with mechanisms of social control, from the Gestapo on down. Had they failed from a functional point of view, we might well have deemed this failure ideal from a broader ethical or political point of view. Nor is there any logical reason why societal equilibrium should be maintained: it is conceivable in principle that sudden and dramatic revolutions might result in human betterment. Similarly, there is no *a priori* reason to equate individual "deviance" with sin or pathology. In fact, individual "deviants" are the wellsprings of art, philosophy, religion, and all constructive ideological innovation: one might applaud rather than deplore "deviance."

But in practice, liberal social theories have tended to identify functional "failures" with undesirable moral failures. The collapse of the French Revolution into Bonapartism or of the Russian Revolution into Stalinism was used to demonstrate the general undesirability of revolutions, and to confirm the implication that social change involving naked conflict was the undesirable result of a "breakdown" in the system of social control. Similarly, the study of psychological deviance has largely been a study of criminals, psychopaths, delinquents, or other "desocialized" or "unsocialized" individuals whose behavior resulted in patently undesirable consequences.

The internal logic of liberal theories thus pushes them toward psychological explanations of both individual deviance and social revolution. At an individual level, criminals, artists, and rebels are seen as the products of anomalies in childhood experience. Psychoanalytic theory was extensively adapted in order to explain—and to explain away—radicalism, innovation, creativity, homosexuality, delinquency, and so on in terms of their alleged childhood origins. But since, by definition, the deviant individual must be the product of deviant socialization, the sophisticated liberal never blamed the deviant himself for his deviance. Instead, he blamed the deviant's early environment—especially his family—and aimed his reformist efforts at changing the family circle that was said to produce deviance. Thus, for example, one characteristic liberal solution to racial tensions was to reform the "inadequate" Negro family, which allegedly bred so much suffering and crime. At a collective level, mass revolutionary movements like fascism, Nazism, or communism were often traced to the special conditions of childhood socialization in the nations where these movements prospered. Psychological "strains" transmitted to individuals through their families were thought to culminate in bizarre or irrational collective behavior: e.g., the authoritarian German family led indirectly to Nazism; early swaddling contributed to the totalitarian Russian character, and so on.

In looking to the future, liberal theorists naturally enough foresaw more of what their theories led them to view as normal, desirable, and inevitable: more industrial productivity, more technologization, more piecemeal reform, higher education, more stability, and more effective management. Admittedly, problems were anticipated—for example, the problem of avoiding political apathy when most major social and ideological problems had been solved. Most liberal writers urged that new ways must be found to involve the young in the political future of their nation, and most deplored the "privatism" of the "silent generation" of the 1950's. Other problems were also foreseen: the problems of mass culture, of the lonely crowd, of the use of leisure time, of the organization man, of rapid job obsolescence, and so on. But compared with the old problems of scarcity, economic depression, class warfare, and ideological conflict, these new problems seemed minor. It was persuasively argued by writers like Daniel Bell, Seymour Martin Lipset, and Edward Shils that the age of ideology was over, and that the remaining problems of Western civilization could be defined as largely instrumental—as problems of "how" and not of "what." As a result, it was believed that these problems would eventually yield to scientific knowledge, professional expertise, and technical know-how.

Theories like these attempted to explain—indeed they *did* explain—the relative domestic stability of the Western democracies in the 1950's, along with the general acceptance, acquiescence, or apathy of educated youth. But in retrospect, they were too airtight and too historically parochial. We can now see that they took a particular historical moment —one that today seems abnormal in its tranquillity—and constructed theories that elevated this particular moment into the natural state of affairs. And among other things, this liberal system of ideas—it would be fair to call it an ideology—effectively prevented us from anticipating, much less understanding, what was increasingly to happen among a growing minority of the young during the 1960's. Like Marxist theories, liberal theories demonstrated the *impossibility* of wide-scale dissent by the educated, privileged young in the highly industrialized democracies.

We cannot, however, simply deprecate the achievements, the usefulness, or the enduring power of the diverse points of view that share what I have called "liberal" assumptions. Men and women are indeed malleable in many ways, and readily influenced. Societies do often exhibit stability and employ powerful resources to preserve equilibrium. And men and women are indeed socialized to the society in which they live from the moment they draw their first breath. It is easy to caricature, criticize, and mock liberal social thought, but it will be the work of a generation to develop a view of the world that does a better job. In the meanwhile, we had best admit that we are all at least partly liberals in our theoretical bases, sometimes the more so as we insist on our radicalism.

Yet in its treatment of the relationship of youth to society, liberal social thought, like Marxism, predicted precisely the opposite of what has actually happened. And that fact alone should impel us to question and redefine the basic assumptions from which liberalism began. The emergence of a youthful opposition, then, demands new theories not only of youthfulness, but of human nature, of society, and of their relationship. Theoretically, this is perhaps the prime significance of the youthful revolt.

Two Current Theories

Given the failure of liberal theories to anticipate the growing disaffection of the affluent young, it was inevitable that other views would emerge. Most of these views are not worthy of serious consideration: they select some single factor like parental permissiveness, the war in Vietnam, the idealism of youth, faculty instigation, Communist conspiracy, or the Oedipus complex as satisfactory explanations of what is happening. But two new analyses of the youthful opposition are emerging that have theoretical depth, scope, and profundity: they properly attempt to understand the new opposition in terms of a broader theory of man and society. The first theory, which is an adaptation of liberal theories, asserts in essence that the youth movement in the industrialized nations is historically a counterrevolutionary movement, a reaction against the more basic forces involved in the growth of a new technological society. The second theory counters by claiming that the dissenting young are true revolutionaries, an historical vanguard that is defining a new and better society. It is worth examining each theory in greater detail.

Youth as a counterrevolutionary force. Consider first the "counterrevolutionary" theory of youth. The most thoughtful proponents of this view are men like Zbigniew Brzezinski, Lewis Feuer, and, in very different ways, Raymond Aron, Daniel Bell, Alvin Toffler, Bruno Bettelheim, and Herman Kahn. These thinkers differ on a great many key issues, and it does each an injustice to group them together without also underlining their differences. But they are usually in essential agreement on several major points.

First, they agree that we are in the midst of a major social transformation that is taking us out of an industrial society into the postindustrial, technological, postmodern, superindustrial, or, in Brzezinski's terms, "technetronic" society of the future. The new society will be highly rationalized. It will be characterized by high productivity, automation, increased leisure time, more individual choices, better social planning, greater opportunities for the expression of individual interests, rapid rates of social change, more rational administration, and the demand for enormously high levels of education among those who occupy positions of leadership. It will be a society of complex large-scale organizations, global communications, and a basically technical approach to the solution of human problems. In this society, power will lie increasingly not with those who possess economic capital, but with those who possess educational "capital." In the technetronic society, the "knowledge industry," centered above all in the professoriate and in the universities, will be the central industry of society and the central motor of historical change.

The second assumption common to the counterrevolutionary theory of youth is that periods of basic historical transition are inevitably marked by social disturbances. The introduction of factories in Europe and America in the nineteenth century was marked by growing class conflict and the Luddite Movement, which led displaced agricultural workers to try to destroy the factories that were depriving them of work. Today, the transition into the technetronic age is marked by an equally violent revulsion by those whose skills and values are made obsolete by the new social revolution.

Specifically, a postindustrial society imposes what Daniel Bell terms a heavy "organizational harness" upon the young: it requires them to study for many years, to acquire highly specialized technical skills, to stay in school, and to postpone gratification well into biological adulthood. Equally important, this new society renders obsolete a large number of traditional values, skills, and outlooks. A technetronic society above all needs skilled executives, systems analysts, computer programmers, trained administrators, and high-level scientists. Those who possess these skills are in the forefront of historical change: their talents are needed; their outlooks are valued. But those identified with "traditional" fields like the humanities and the social sciences find that their values and skills are becoming increasingly unnecessary, irrelevant, and obsolete; they are today's neo-Luddites. The ideals of romanticism, expressiveness, and traditional humanism may dominate the contemporary youth culture, but they do not dominate the social structure—the specific institutions that are changing our lives. One consequence, then, is what Bell terms the disjuncture between the culture—specifically the adversary culture of intellectuals and many students—and the dominant social structure of large-scale organization, technology, mass communications, and electronics.

The conclusion that the revolt of the young is essentially counterrevolutionary follows from the first two points. According to this theory, the humanistic young are rebelling because of their latent awareness of their own obsolescence. The "organizational harness" around their necks is too tight and heavy for them to endure. An ever-larger group of young men and women feel that they have no place in the modern world, for they lack salable skills, basic character styles, and value orientations that are adaptable to the emergent postindustrial society. They are, as Bruno Bettelheim puts it, "obsolete youth." They rebel in a blind, mindless, and generally destructive way against rationalism, intellect, technology, organization, discipline, hierarchy, and all of the requisites of a postindustrial society. Sensing their historical obsolescence, they lash out like the Luddites against the computers and managers that are consigning them into the "dustbin of history." It is predictable that they will end with bombing, terrorism, and anarchy, for the obsolete young are desperately pitting themselves against historical forces that they cannot stop. But students of engineering, business administration, and so on—students in the fields most rewarded in the technetronic society—do not protest or rebel; instead, it is the obsolescent humanist and social scientist who lead the counterculture.

Although theorists differ as to precisely *which* unconscious forces are expressed in student dissent, the logic of the counterrevolutionary argument makes a recourse to psychologism almost mandatory. For if the manifest issues of student unrest are seen as pseudo issues, disguises, and rationalizations, then we are forced into the realm of the not-conscious in our search to locate the "real" motives behind the youthful opposition. And in today's post-Freudian age, such explanations are likely to involve recourse to concepts like unconscious Oedipal feelings, adolescent rebellion, castration anxiety, and the "acting out" of feelings that originate in the early family.

As a result, the counterrevolutionary view of youth is associated with an interpretation of psychoanalysis that sees Oedipal urges as driving forces for student rebellion. To be sure, theorists do not agree about the exact nature of the Oedipal forces that are acted out. Some like Feuer see a simple re-enactment of the jealous child's hatred of his powerful father; others see a blind striking out against surrogates for a father who was not powerful *enough* to inoculate his son against excessive castration anxieties; another psychoanalyst has pointed to insufficient parental responsiveness as a causative factor in radicalism; early family permissiveness or failure to set limits has also been blamed. But whatever the precise irrational forces behind the youthful revolt are said to be, the counterrevolutionary theory, by denying the validity of the youth movement's own explanations of its acts, is forced to hypothesize unconscious motivations as the "real" motives behind the revolt.

A final conclusion follows from this argument: no matter how destructive the revolt of the young may be in the short run, that revolt is historically foredoomed to failure in the long run. The technetronic society, the postindustrial world, the superindustrial state—these forces are unstoppable. The liberal democratic state is being basically transformed, but the rantings and rampagings of the young, devoted to obsolescent ideas of self-expression, anarchism, romanticism, direct democracy, liberation, and the expansion of consciousness, cannot stop this transformation. The revolt of the young may indeed be, in Daniel Bell's phrase, the emergent "class conflict" of postindustrial society. But from Bell's analysis, it follows that students are a neo-Luddite, counterrevolutionary class, and that their counterrevolution will fail. Increasingly, power will be held by those who have more successfully acquired the capital dispensed by the knowledge industry. The counterculture is, in Brzezinski's words, the "death rattle" of the historically obsolete.

The counterrevolutionary theory of the youth revolt is a reformulation of liberal theory, modified to make room for the convulsions of the last decade. Within any social equilibrium theory, there must be room for the possibility that the system will temporarily get "out of balance." The assumption of thinkers like Brzezinski is that we have entered a period of imbalance that accompanies the transition from an industrial to a technetronic society. In this transitional period, traditional mechanisms of social control, older forms of integration between social structure and culture, and previous forms of socialization have ceased to function adequately. But in the future, it is assumed, equilibrium can once again be regained. Upon arrival in the technetronic society, the postindustrial society, or the world of the year 2000, the temporary storm squalls on the weatherfront between industrial and postindustrial society will have dissipated, and we will once again be in a state of relative social equilibrium. If we can only wait out the transition, maintaining and repairing our basic institutions, we can build a new equilibrium—one that will grind under the youthful opposition just as triumphant industrialism destroyed the Luddites. In the meanwhile we must fight to preserve decency, civilization, rationality, and higher education from the depredations of the mindless young.

Youth as a revolutionary force.   The second major theory holds that the dissenting young are historically a revolutionary force. This theory views the counterculture as a regenerative culture, and interprets those forces that oppose it as ultimately counterrevolutionary. This view is expressed in different forms in the works of Theodore Roszak and Charles Reich, in the writings of members of the counterculture like Tom Hayden and Abbie Hoffman, and, most convincingly of all, by Philip Slater. Let us consider the basic assumptions of the revolutionary view of the youth culture.

First, this theory also accepts the notion that industrialized societies are in a period of major cultural, institutional, and historical transition. But it alleges that the thrust of the liberal democratic state has exhausted itself. What is variously termed "corporate liberalism," the "establishment," or the "welfare-warfare state" is seen as fundamentally bankrupt. Admittedly, industrial states have produced unprecedented wealth. But they have not been able to distribute it equitably, nor have they found ways to include large minorities in the mainstream of society. Furthermore, their basic assumptions have led directly to disastrous "neoimperialistic" wars like the American involvement in Southeast Asia. Corporate liberalism has produced a highly manipulated society, in which "real" human needs and interests are neglected in the pursuit of political power, the merchandising of products, or the extension of overseas markets. Large-scale organizations have dehumanized their members, depriving men of participation in the decisions that affect their lives. The electronic revolution merely provides the rulers of the corporate state with more effective means of manipulating the populace. Corporate liberalism has today revealed its bankruptcy.

The second assumption of this theory is that the economic successes and moral failures of liberal industrial societies today make possible and necessary a new kind of consciousness, new values, new aspirations, and new life styles—in short, a new culture. The old industrial state was founded upon the assumption of scarcity. It was organized to reduce poverty, to increase production, to provide plenitude. But today it has largely succeeded in this goal, and as a result, a new generation has been born in affluence and freed from the repressed character structure of the scarcity culture. In an era of abundance, the niggardly, inhibited psychology of saving, scrupulosity, and repression is no longer necessary. Alienated relationships between people who view each other as commodities are no longer inevitable. The "objective consciousness" of the scientist or technician is becoming obsolete. In brief, the material successes and moral failures of corporate liberalism permit and require the emergence of a new and truly revolutionary generation with a new consciousness, a postscarcity outlook, and a new vision of the possibilities of human liberation.

It follows from this analysis that the new oppositional culture is not an atavistic and irrational reaction against the old culture but a logical outgrowth of it—an expression of its latent possibilities, a rational effort to remedy its failings, in some sense its logical fulfillment. If the central goal of the old culture was to overcome want and if that goal has been largely achieved, then the counterculture stands on the shoulders of the old culture, fulfilling, renewing, and expressing that culture's latent hopes. Far from being historical reactionaries, the counterculturists are the historical vanguard. Their alleged anarchism and anti-intellectualism are but efforts to express the desire for human liberation whose roots lie in the postponed dreams of the old culture. As the British philosopher Stuart Hampshire has recently suggested, the dissenting young are not against reason, but only against a constricted definition of reason as a quantitative calculus that ignores human values and needs.

The revolutionary theory of youth also entails a definite view of the psychology of young rebels and revolutionaries. It asks that we take them completely at their word when they state the reasons for their protests, disruptions, dropouts, or rejections. The dissenting young are seen as miraculously healthy products of the irrational, dangerous, and unjust world they inherited. Their motives are noble, idealistic, and pure, while their statements of their goals are to be taken at face value. They are not animated by their childhood pasts, but by a vision (which they may, however, find it difficult to articulate) of a freer, more peaceful, more liberated, and more just society. As for the Oedipus complex, to discuss the psychological motives of the members of the youthful opposition at all is seen as a typically "liberal" way of distracting attention from the real issues. Thus, even if the dissenting young behave in an undemocratic, dogmatic or violent way, one "understands" their behavior by discussing the undemocratic, dogmatic, and violent society to which they are objecting.

This view of the psychology of the youthful opposition follows logically from the assumption that the young are in the historical vanguard. For in general, historical vanguards must be endowed with ordinary wisdom and prescience, and with a special freedom from that gnawingly irrational attachment to the personal or historic past that plagues most nonvanguard groups. In the views of one theorist, "radical man" is the highest possible form of human development; another political theorist has argued that only rebellion can attest to human freedom, and that among today's young, only those who rebel are truly free. The argument that the youthful revolt arises from psychopathology is here encountered by its opposite—by the claim that the new opposition springs from the extraordinary insight, maturity, high consciousness, and "positive mental health" of its members.

Finally, as is by definition true of any historical vanguard, the triumph of this vanguard is seen as ultimately inevitable. With rising abundance, new recruits to the counterculture are being created daily. It is the old, then, who are obsolete, not the young. The locomotive of history, so to speak, has the youth movement sitting on the front bumper, scattering its opponents in a relentless rush into the future. Eventually the opponents of progressive change will be defeated or will die of old age—only then will the truly liberating potentials of the postscarcity era be actualized in society.

In many respects the theory of the youth movement as revolutionary is embryonic and incomplete. The counterrevolutionary theory builds upon the highly developed resources of liberal social thought. But the "revolutionary" view, rejecting both liberalism and Marxism, presents us more with a vision of what the counterculture might be at its best than with a complex or thorough social analysis. Only in the work of Philip Slater do we have the beginnings of a critical examination of liberal theory, a task so enormous that it is obviously beyond the capabilities of any one man, much less one book. Other writers who view the counterculture as revolutionary largely limit themselves to a vision that is more literary than descriptive and that makes little attempt to connect the emergence of the counterculture to the structural changes emphasized by writers like Bell, Brzezinski, or Kahn. In this sense, the revolutionary theory of the new opposition remains more of a promise than a fulfillment.

The Limits of Both Theories

My presentation of two polar theories obviously does scant justice to the complexity of the specific theorists who have seriously considered the counterculture. There is no unity, much less membership in a "school," either among those who oppose or among those who support the youthful opposition. Among its critics, for example, Feuer and Bettelheim concentrate upon the psychopathology that allegedly animates its members, while Brzezinski or Kahn focuses upon the structural or social conditions that make the youthful opposition obsolete. Similarly, there is an enormous difference between the romantic portrait of "consciousness III" presented by Reich and the more careful social-psychological analysis offered by Slater in his *The Pursuit of Loneliness*.

But no matter how oversimplified this account of the revolutionary and the counterrevolutionary theories, if either interpretation of youthful dissent were fundamentally adequate, this discussion could end. It therefore behooves us to examine each of these theories critically.

We should first acknowledge that each of these views has its highly persuasive points. Those who view the new opposition as historically counterrevolutionary are correct in underlining the increasing importance of technology, complex social organizations, and education in the most industrialized nations. They have pointed accurately to the new role of a highly educated and technologically trained elite. And they seem to help us explain why youthful dissenters are virtually absent among potential engineers, computer specialists, and business administrators, but disproportionately drawn from the ranks of social scientists and humanists.

Above all, however, the opponents of the youthful opposition are accurate in their criticism of that opposition. They rightly argue that the counterculture almost completely neglects the institutional side of modern life. Thus the call for liberation, for the expansion of consciousness, and for the expression of impulse has not been matched by the creation or even by the definition of institutions whereby these purposes could be achieved and sustained. Furthermore, in its cultural wing, the new opposition has often been callous to continuing injustice, oppression, and poverty in America and abroad. In its political wing, the counterculture has been vulnerable to despair, to apocalyptic but transient fantasies of instant revolution, to superficial Marxism, and to a romance with violence. Finally, the youthful opposition as a whole has never adequately confronted or understood its own derivative relationship to the dominant society. Perhaps as a result, it has too often been a caricature rather than a critique of the consumption-oriented, manipulative, technocratic, violent, electronic society that it nominally opposes. In pointing to the weakness of the counterculture, its critics seem to me largely correct.

Yet there is a deep plausibility, as well, in the theory that the youthful opposition is in historical terms a revolutionary movement. In particular, the "revolutionary" theorists accurately capture the growing feeling of frustration and the increasing sense of the exhaustion of the old order that obsess growing numbers of the educated young in industrialized nations. Furthermore, they correctly recognize the irony in the fact that the most prosperous and educated societies in world history have generated the most massive youthful opposition in world history. And in seeking to explain this unexpected opposition, the revolutionary theory understands well its relationship to the "systemic" failings of corporate liberalism—its failure to include large minorities in the general prosperity, its exploitative or destructive relationship to the developing nations, its use of advanced technology to manipulate the citizens in whose interest it allegedly governs, its neglect of basic human needs, values, and aspirations in a social calculus that sees men and women as merely "inputs" or "outputs" in complex organizations.

The strengths of each theory, however, are largely negative: in essence, each is at its best in pointing to the flaws of the culture or the social system defended by the other. But judged for its positive contribution, each theory tends to have parallel weaknesses: each disregards the facts at odds with its own central thesis. In order to do this, each operates at a different level of analysis: the counterrevolutionary theory at the level of social institutions, the revolutionary theory at the level of culture. As a consequence, each theory neglects precisely what the other theory correctly stresses.

The counterrevolutionary theory of the new opposition starts from an analysis of social institutions, modes of production, and the formal organization of human roles and relationships. Despite its emphasis upon the psychopathology of the new rebels, it is fundamentally a sociological theory of institutional changes and technological transformations. It stresses the importance of applied science, the growth of new educational institutions, and the power of the new elite that dominates the "knowledge industry." In defining the future, it emphasizes the further development of rational-bureaucratic institutions and the revolutionary impact of new electronic technology upon social organization, communication, and knowledge. But it tends to forget consciousness and culture, treating ideas, symbols, values, ideologies, aspirations, fantasies, and dreams largely as reflections of technological, economic, and social forces.

Theorists who argue that the new opposition is historically revolutionary operate at a quite different level of analysis. For them, the two key concepts are culture and consciousness. What matters most is feelings, aspirations, outlooks, ideologies, and world views. Charles Reich's recent analysis of three kinds of consciousness is explicit in asserting that institutions are secondary and in the last analysis unimportant. Most other revolutionary theorists also start from an analysis of a "new consciousness" to argue that the decisive revolution is a cultural revolution. How men view the world, how they organize their experience symbolically, what their values are—these are seen as historically determining. Institutional changes are said to follow changes in human aspirations and consciousness.

Daniel Bell has written of the disjuncture of social structure and culture in modern society. We need not accept his entire analysis to agree that this disjuncture is reflected in theories about youthful dissent. For on closer examination, they turn out to be talking about either social structure *or* culture, but rarely about both. The key weakness of the counterrevolutionary theory is its neglect of consciousness and culture, its assumption that social-structural, technological, and material factors will be decisive in determining the future. The parallel weakness of the revolutionary view of youthful dissent is its disregard of the way organized systems of production, technology, education, communication, and "social control" influence, shape, and may yet co-opt or destroy the youthful opposition. In fact, then, these two theories are not as contradictory as they seem: in many ways, they are simply talking about two different aspects of the modern world.

A second limitation of both theories is their assumption that the trends they define are historically inevitable. In this respect, both theories are eschatological as well as explanatory. The postindustrial, or technetronic, view assumes the future inevitability of a postindustrial, technetronic, technocratic society. Given this assumption, it follows logically that anyone who opposes the technetronic society is historically counterrevolutionary. Brzezinski, for example, writes in *Between Two Ages:*

The Luddites were threatened by economic obsolescence and reacted against it. Today the militant leaders of the [student] reaction, as well as their ideologues, frequently come from those branches of learning which are more sensitive to the threat of social irrelevance. Their political activism is thus only a reaction to the more basic fear that the times are against them, that a new world is emerging without either their assistance or their leadership.

Brzezinski's claim that the youth revolt constitutes a counterrevolutionary force clearly rests upon the assumption that the technetronic society is inevitable.

Exactly the same assumption of historical inevitability is made by supporters of the counterculture. Reich is very explicit about this in *The Greening of America:*

[The revolution] will originate with the individual and with culture, and it will change the political structure only as its final act. It will not require violence to succeed, and it cannot be successfully resisted by violence. It is now spreading with amazing rapidity. . . . It is both necessary and inevitable, and in time it will include not only youth, but all people in America.

Given Reich's assumption that history is on the side of the counterculture, it follows automatically that those who oppose it are actually counterrevolutionary.

But this claim that the future is in fact predetermined by blind historical forces is open to major question. In retrospect, most previous claims about the historical inevitability of this or that trend have turned out to have been mere expressions of the wishes of those who made these claims. It makes equal or better sense to believe that "history" is on the side neither of the technetronic revolution nor of the counterculture. In fact, we may deny that history is on anyone's side, arguing that history is simply made by human beings, acting individually and in concert, influenced by the institutions in which they live *and* by their consciousness and culture.

If we reject the assumption of historical inevitability, both the counterrevolutionary and the revolutionary theories must be understood in part as efforts to justify a set of special interests by attributing historical inevitability to them, and perhaps ultimately as exercises in the use of prophecy to convince others of the truth of the prophecy and thereby to make the prophecy self-fulfilling. Andrew Greeley has compared Charles Reich with the ancient Hebrew prophets. The similarities are vivid. Although the more academic prose of Brzezinski, Feuer, or Bettelheim does not lend itself so readily to comparisons with the Old Testament, the same prophetic tendencies are there as well. But in either case, the claim that God or His modern-day equivalents—history, technology, and culture—are on our side is best understood as a claim that men make to rally support and persist despite adversity.

What both theories fail to comprehend is the extent to which the emergence of a new youthful opposition requires us to embark upon a critical re-examination of concepts of man, society, and their interrelationship that we have heretofore taken largely for granted. This inability to come to grips with the theoretical challenge posed by the new opposition is seen clearly in each theory's attitude toward education. Neoliberals who view student dissent as largely counterrevolutionary are committed to a view of education as socialization. Given this view, it follows that a postindustrial society characterized by prolonged higher education should be a society where youthful dissent is rare. The eruption of widescale disaffection among the most educated products of the most industrialized societies thus requires neoliberal theories to posit wide-scale "deviant socialization," or else to argue that higher education is failing to "do its job." In fact, however, the extensive evidence concerning the backgrounds of young dissenters provides little support for the "deviant socialization" interpretation of the new opposition. And paradoxically, those institutions of higher education that liberals have traditionally seen as doing the "best job" seem to be the breeding grounds for the greatest disaffection.

Those who view youthful disaffection as a revolutionary phenomenon are faced with the same dilemma. They tend to see higher education as a way of "integrating" or "co-opting" youth into the existing society. It therefore comes as a surprise that higher education seems to promote disaffection and to be closely related to the emergence of a youthful counterculture. But those who view the youth movement as revolutionary have so far failed to offer any adequate explanation of why many young men and women in so many nations have escaped the net of socialization.

The fact that theorists of neither persuasion can explain the contemporary correlation between higher education and dissent indicates the need for a critical analysis of our prevailing assumptions concerning human malleability, social equilibrium, and socialization. To undertake this re-examination will be the task of many years; it will necessarily be the work of a generation, not of an individual. But it is impressive that, for all of the talk today about "radical thought" and the "New Left," the basic assumptions of liberalism have been subjected to so little fundamental criticism.

What follows is not an attempt to provide this critical reanalysis, or even to outline it. Rather, it is an agenda, or more precisely, some items on an agenda which, if accomplished, might move us toward a better understanding of the meaning of the new opposition and of contemporary society. This agenda is presented tentatively, and largely as an indication of the theoretical problems that have been opened up by a decade of dissent. Since it is easier to point out the flaws in the views of others than to propose unflawed alternatives to them, even these items for an agenda are bound to be anticlimactic. But not to run the risks of at least suggesting an agenda would be even worse.

In brief, the work I believe needs to be done falls into three broad categories. First, there must be a critical reanalysis and reformulation of the theoretical assumptions with which we attempt to understand man and society. Second, we must begin to come to terms with the characteristics of modern society and modern man in their own right, and not in terms of strained analogies to the past. Third, a revised theoretical framework and a better understanding of contemporary man in society should help define a new political agenda.

Plasticity, Equilibrium, and Socialization

The first assumption to be reanalyzed critically is the assumption of virtually limitless human malleability and influenceability. Without denying that men can adapt to most surroundings, that they often conform to the pressures of their peers, or that they internalize social norms and cultural concepts, we need to rediscover and emphasize those elements in "human nature" that make men less than totally plastic.

I believe that the most fruitful line of inquiry will involve an intensive study of the sequences and stages of human development, and especially of those developmental processes that remain more or less constant regardless of historical era or social context. We need to return to Freud's concept of human development as not simply a smooth process of internalizing societal expectations, but rather as the arduous work of mastering internal conflict, without which psychological growth could not occur. Equally relevant is the developmental psychology of Jean Piaget, who insists that the child's growth proceeds through psychologically necessary stages and sequences that cannot be short-circuited. In the developmental process as defined by both Freud and Piaget, the imprint of the social environment is assimilated and interpreted through the steadily changing internal structures of personality, which has its own laws and imperatives.

To trace the full implications of a developmental view of personality for a theory of man and society would be the topic of a lengthy work. Here it should suffice to note that a developmental approach clearly contradicts the almost exclusively environmental view of psychological change that has dominated liberal thought. Critically interpreted, the work of Freud and Piaget may help us understand man not merely as an adjusting and adapting animal, but as a creature whose growth has both important societal prerequisites and a dynamic of its own. We can then think of man as possessing a "human nature" that can be "violated" by social expectations; we may then be better able to see man as possessing innate potentials for autonomy and integration that may at times lead him into conflict with his society.

We will also need to explore in detail the ways in which these developmental potentials may be actualized or frustrated by any given social or historical context. Recent studies that demonstrate the existence of developmental potentials that are not actualized in most men and women under contemporary conditions point to sociohistorical influences upon adult personality of a kind that have not heretofore been studied. I have elsewhere argued (see "Prologue: Youth as a Stage of Life") that one important factor in the emergence of a new opposition is the unfolding, on a mass scale, of developmental potentials that in the past were actualized, if at all, only in a tiny minority of men and women.

A related task should involve a critical scrutiny of the large body of studies of attitude change, group pressures, and interpersonal influence. We will need to distinguish, for example, more sharply than we have done so far between attitudes and belief systems on the one hand and the cognitive frameworks or developmental levels within which any given attitude or belief is held. William James long ago contrasted the once-born and the twice-born: the once-born are those who unreflectively and "innocently" accept the convictions of their childhoods; the twice-born are those who may adhere to exactly the same convictions, but who do so in a different way after a protracted period of doubt, criticism, and examination of these beliefs. Viewed as attitudes, the beliefs of the once-born and the twice-born may be identical: but the mind-set, cognitive framework, or developmental level of the once- and twice-born are extremely different. In other words, we need to examine not only the beliefs men hold, but the *way* they hold them—the complexity, richness, and structure of their views of the world. Politically and socially, it may be more important that members of a given subculture possess a relativistic view of truth than that they are conservatives or liberals.

Finally, the role of conflict in human development needs to be re-examined. Liberal psychology has tended to minimize the catalytic importance of conflict in growth: conflict was seen as neurotic, undesirable, and productive of regression. But there is much current evidence that individuals who attain high levels of complexity in feeling, thinking, and judging do so *as a result of* conflict, not in its absence. Students of cognitive development, like observers of personality development, find that disequilibrium, tension, and imbalance tend to produce growth. If this is true, then the absence of psychological conflict or tension may be as pathological as the overabundance of conflict, and the liberal view of the ideal man as smoothly socialized and conflict-free may need to be discarded.

To add further items to this agenda for psychology would take us to still more technical topics. The point is that, in ways we have not yet understood, our theories of human nature, our psychological research, and our methodologies have all been influenced by the largely unstated assumptions of human plasticity and smooth accommodation to pressures of the social environment. We need not deny that men are in some ways plastic and influenceable in order to consider anew everything in man that makes him unmalleable, uninfluenceable, and resistant to socialization.

Turning to broader theories of society, a comparable critical reexamination of basic assumptions seems in order. Above all, the utility of the equilibrium model of society must be examined. Increasingly, critical sociologists have begun to suggest that a "conflict" model of society and of social change may be more suited to the facts of contemporary history than a theory of societal balance. Just as we should appreciate the catalytic role of conflict in human development, so the critical importance of conflict in social change must be acknowledged. Both human and social development, I believe, are best viewed as dialectic processes, involving force, counterforce, and potential resolution; thesis, antithesis, and potential synthesis. At a societal level, such a view would require us to start from change, struggle, revolution, and transformation as the basic and "natural" state of affairs rather than viewing them as unfortunate exceptions that require special explanation.

This view of society would put social change in the first chapter, not in the last chapter as one of the unexplained problems of our theory. It would see conflict between individuals, groups, and historical forces as a necessary and vital component of historical change, not as a result of a "failure" of the "mechanisms of social control." It would also entail that any given "resolution" of conflicting historical forces should in turn generate new antithetical forces which will oppose that resolution, thus continuing the dialectic of change. A sociology based on the theory of conflict would especially attempt to understand the processes by which new conflicts are generated out of apparent equilibrium, rather than focusing solely upon how equilibrium is maintained.

Such a view of society obviously moves us away from liberalism and toward Marxism. But Marxism, too, must be examined critically. Just as we today should reject the nineteenth-century biology and physics upon which Freud based his psychological determinism and many of his specific views of personality, so we need not continue to accept the nineteenth-century economism and millenialism of Marxist thought. Marx's view that the critical historical conflict was class conflict, although it reflected the facts of the mid-nineteenth century, may less clearly reflect the realities of the late twentieth century. And the nineteenth-century optimism which led Marx to believe that historical conflict would ulti-mately be progressively resolved, like his millenial view of the classless state as the end of historical conflict, seems today unwarranted. Finally, we must question whether the historical dialectic in fact "stopped" at the end point defined by Marx, or whether it continues today in ways that Marx could not have foreseen.

However we reinterpret Marx, one corollary of a dialectic view of social change is that the historical significance of a group, institution, social force, or ideology will inevitably change as historical conditions change. A group that is progressive during one historical era may become reactionary at a later period. Marx emphasized that during its struggle against feudalism, the *bourgeoisie* was a progressive force, although dur-ing the nineteenth century, the triumphant *bourgeoisie* had become re-actionary in its opposition of the demands of the revolutionary working class. Following the logic of a dialectic analysis would lead us to expect that the once-revolutionary proletariat might in its turn become defensive and opposed to progressive social change. And especially as the rate of historical change accelerates, the transformation of social groups from progressive to reactionary, from revolutionary to counterrevolutionary, may well occur during the lifetime of their members.

If we re-examine critically both the concept of malleable man and the concept of stable society, then we must also re-examine the concept of socialization as the key process whereby the individual is joined to society.

We need not deny that socialization occurs in order to point to other processes of equal or greater importance that connect the individual and society in more complex ways. For example, as Erik Erikson has noted, every society must accommodate itself to the developmental needs of the growing child. By attending more carefully to the in-born developmental schedules and potentials of the child, adolescent, youth, and adult, we may better understand the constraints upon society's capacity to "integrate" individuals of any given age. Just as it is not possible for the seven-year-old to comprehend hypothetico-deductive reasoning, so it may not be possible for the highly educated, relativistic youth to accept his society's norms and precepts without criticism. Instead of emphasizing only how society molds the individual to meet social needs, we must also consider how human needs and developmental processes set outer limits on what societies can reasonably expect of their members.

If we abandon the notion of society as a stable and homogeneous entity, then the process whereby individuals and their societies interrelate becomes vastly more complex. For if every society contains within it important internal conflicts, then growing children are exposed not to a stable, self-consistent set of social expectations and cultural values, but to social and cultural contradictions. Intrapsychic conflicts and social contradictions will thus be mutually related, although never in a simple one-to-one fashion. Furthermore, in times of rapid historical change, the societal conflicts to which one generation is exposed will differ from those of the previous generation; partly for this reason, individuals of different historical generations will typically differ from each other in basic personality.

The full agenda for the re-examination of our understanding of the relationship between men and societies will be lengthy. But as we examine our theoretical assumptions, it will not suffice simply to reject out of hand what I have termed "liberal" views. The goal must be more ambitious: it must be to analyze these views critically, preserving what is valid in them while complementing them with new understanding of the inherent logic of human development, of the central role of conflict in social change, and of the forces in man that militate against acquiescent acceptance of the existing social order.

Contradictions within the Knowledge Sector

The second, related theoretical task is to understand in detail the special characteristics of modern personality and modern society. Even if a critical analysis of the basic assumptions of liberal thought were completed, the substance of a more adequate account of what is unique about our own era would still be lacking. Here, once again, I can only indicate the general lines of thought that seem most likely to be worth pursuing.

If we start from a dialectical view of historical change, but admit that Marx's juxtaposition of a revolutionary proletariat and a reactionary *bourgeoisie* did not necessarily mark the last stage in the dialectic, then we must entertain seriously the possibility that the conflicts about which Marx wrote have been largely resolved and that new conflicts have today begun to emerge. I believe it is useful and accurate to consider the corporate liberal state as embodying to a large extent the synthesis of the class conflicts that preoccupied Marx. In this respect, liberal theorists were correct in arguing that earlier conflicts between capitalist entrepreneurs and exploited workers had been softened and essentially reconciled by the growth of powerful bureaucratic trade unions able to negotiate with large but publicly regulated corporations. The "welfare state" indeed mitigated many of the most vicious exploitations of unrestrained nineteenth-century capitalism. The "liberal consensus" of the mid-twentieth century tolerated a wide spectrum of political opinion and many forms of deviant behavior. Furthermore, if "ideology" is narrowly defined to mean Stalinism, fascism, and Nazism, then it was largely accurate to say that the age of ideology was dead.

In the period before and after the Second World War, then, the dominant class conflicts of the nineteenth and early twentieth centuries were increasingly resolved, reconciled, or synthesized in the liberal-democratic-capitalist or socialist states in Western Europe, America, and, after the war, Japan. These new industrial states proved themselves immensely productive economically and immensely inventive technologically. Older problems of mass poverty increasingly disappeared, while the proportion of workers involved in primary and secondary production dwindled to a decreasing minority. First in America, and then increasingly in Western Europe and Japan, the middle class grew to be the largest class, the working class became increasingly prosperous, and both classes became more and more committed to the preservation of the existing society. Especially during the years of the Cold War, a domestic equilibrium was reached in the liberal democracies, and this equilibrium provided the empirical ground upon which liberal social thought grew and by which it seemed confirmed. To be sure, like all historical syntheses, this one was far from complete: large minorities were excluded from the general prosperity; problems of poverty amidst affluence continued; subtle forms of imperialism replaced the earlier forms, and so on. Yet all things considered, the decades from 1945 to 1965 were remarkable for the absence of basic social conflict in all of the highly industrialized non-Communist nations.

The ascendency of the corporate liberal state, however, did not mark an end to social conflict or to the dialectic of history. The successes of the emergent technological society were purchased at an enormous moral and ecological price. Fulfilling the promises of liberalism was far from complete, and it became apparent that the liberal program itself would not suffice to fulfill them. Increases in national productivity were not enough to include in the mainstream of affluence those whose poverty was "structural" rather than merely economic. Racism persisted in America despite a century's public commitment to end it. Effective political power remained in the hands of a small minority of the population. It is therefore incorrect to say that the traditional economic, social, and political conflicts of industrial societies were totally "solved." It is more accurate to say that for the first time in history the day could be foreseen when with the techniques at hand they *might* be solved, but that liberal social thought and liberal reformism proved largely ineffective in solving them.

The inability of liberalism to complete its own agenda was one of the new contradictions that became apparent only with the advent of the corporate liberal society. The second contradiction was in some ways more profound, and even more directly related to the emergence of a youthful opposition. The liberal democratic states in America, Western Europe, and Japan provided a large proportion of the people with material goods, social security, cultural opportunities, and relative political freedom, all of which had been the goals of previous generations. There thus arose a new generation that took for granted the accomplishments of corporate liberalism, expressing neither gratitude nor admiration for these achievements. To this new generation, what were instead important were first of all the inabilities of a liberal society to fulfill its own promises; and second, the surfacing of a set of cultural and psychological goals that had previously been deferred in the liberal society. These newly surfaced aspirations had to do above all with the quality of life, the possibilities for self-expression, full human development, self-actualization, the expansion of consciousness, and the pursuit of empathy, sentience, and experience.

I have elsewhere tried to outline in more detail some of the emergent aspirations of the new youthful opposition. Here it should be enough to reiterate that the roots of this new opposition lie precisely in the successes of liberalism—e.g., its success in extending to most of the population the material and social benefits it had promised, but its inability to complete the process or to define goals beyond abundance. To the new generation, and specifically to the most affluent, educated, and secure members of this generation, the historical successes of the corporate liberal state were less important than its moral, ecological, psychological, and cultural failures.

To understand the new conflicts in corporate liberal society, I believe we must above all examine the role of the "knowledge sector." For the liberal-democratic and industrialized nations are increasingly dominated neither by capitalists nor by workers, but by a vast new "intelligentsia" of educated professionals who exert unprecedented influence on both public policy and private practice. In some ways their contemporary role is analogous to the traditional role of intellectuals, artists, and Bohemians in earlier historical eras. But because of their increasing numbers and influence, they occupy an altogether different place in technological societies. What they share is that the enterprises in which they are engaged depend upon extensions, manipulations, or applications of knowledge and ideas. The knowledge sector thus includes not only universities, scientific laboratories, research institutes, and the world of creative artists, but a much broader set of enterprises including corporate research and development, the communications industry, data analysis and data processing, the major higher professions, advertising, merchandising, administrative science, personnel management, entertainment, systems analysis, and so on. So defined, the knowledge sector is clearly that sector of contemporary industrialized societies that has grown most rapidly in size and power.

Neo-Marxist theorists have tended to see this knowledge sector as a "new working class" or "technical intelligentsia"—merely the handmaiden of the capitalist managers and politicians assumed to exercise real power. Theorists of the postindustrial state, in contrast, have emphasized the dominance of the knowledge sector in advanced societies, viewing academics as the key professionals and universities as the key institutions of the postindustrial society. Still others, operating in a more traditional liberal framework, have seen the knowledge sector as one of many "interest groups" competing in the process of defining social and political policy.

But in the end, none of these characterizations seems quite adequate to define the unique role of the knowledge sector in the technological societies. Only by remote analogy can workers in this sector be considered a true "working class," for only rarely are they the direct or indirect victims of capitalist exploitation. On the face of it, the argument of Bell, Brzezinski, and others that the knowledge sector constitutes the dominant sector of technological societies seems closer to the truth. But this view in turn tends to exaggerate the power of the academic profession and the indispensability of such institutions as universities to technological society. It is also tempting to accept the liberal analysis of the knowledge sector as merely one of many interest groups; but this view, too, fails to acknowledge the very special powers that today accrue to those who possess knowledge and the visible tokens of its possession: higher degrees, recognition in the knowledge community, access to the mass media, and so on.

Rather than define the knowledge sector as a new working class, as a ruling group, or as another interest group, we would do better to start by assuming that its relationship to the rest of society cannot be adequately understood in historical analogies. To try to define the relationship between the knowledge sector and the rest of society in terms of capitalist-worker analogies is like attempting to define the capitalist-worker relationship as a kind of lord-vassal relationship. Often exploited yet more often manipulating, immensely influential yet vastly vulnerable, an interest group but one that possesses unprecedented power, the role of the knowledge sector in modern society must be defined as unprecedented, new, and *sui generis*. Indeed, one of the major theoretical tasks ahead is the careful definition and explication of the relationship between this new sector and the remainder of society.

Spokesmen for the knowledge sector have tended to define this sector as relatively value-free and "objective" in its approach to human and social problems. The plausibility of this view rests upon the propensity of the knowledge sector to invoke "scientific" analyses of problems, to define rationality in quantitative terms, and to attempt to exclude "irrational" feelings or "sentimental" moral considerations from decision making. The main agents of the knowledge sector have usually presented themselves as neutral, cool, and technical servants of others, as less concerned with ultimate moral ends than with efficiency, accuracy, rationality, and the levelheaded consideration of the costs and benefits of alternative courses of action. One of the chief characteristics of the knowledge sector, even as it has moved toward increasing influence, has been to publicly proclaim its "neutrality"—its indifference to the major moral, psychological, and political questions of the day.

Yet in the last decade, it has become clear that the "value-free" self-definition of the knowledge sector masks an important ideology, an ideology increasingly recognized and challenged by the new opposition. This ideology can be termed "technism," that is, a set of pseudo-scientific assumptions about the nature and resolution of human and social problems. Most highly articulated in various forms of systems analysis, technism insists that the highest rationality involves measurement and consigns the incommensurable (feelings, values, "intangibles") to a lesser order of rationality and reality. Military policies are therefore judged in terms of quantitative indices like body counts, kilotonnage, sorties flown, mega-deaths, planes lost, or enemy dead per dollar. Education is seen as a complex form of human "processing," with freshmen as "inputs," graduates as "outputs," dropouts as "wastage," and efficiency measured in terms of "Ph.D. production" or "lifetime income increments." Technism further assumes that innovation is desirable, that growth is imperative, that whatever is technically possible should be done, and that large quantities are preferable to small ones. Drawing heavily upon the mystique of science, technism adds to true science a series of further assumptions that qualify it as an ideology, albeit one that prefers not to recognize itself or be recognized as such.

Paradoxically, however, it is from within the knowledge sector that today there also emerges the most astringent critique of technism. Institutions of higher education, once predicted to become the central institutions of postindustrial society, have indeed become the prime exemplars of a technist approach to problems of government, business, and social planning; but they have also become the prime generators of the antitechnist, romantic, expressive, moralistic, anarchic humanism of the new opposition. Rejecting technism, this opposition stresses all those factors in human life and social experience that do not fit the technist equations. If "value-free," objective technism is the dominant voice of the dominant knowledge sector, then expressive, subjective anarchism is the subversive voice. Theodore Roszak's eulogy of the counterculture is illustrative, for Roszak abhors above all what he calls "objective consciousness"—the technist consciousness of the scientist or program analyst. The new opposition can thus be seen as the ideological reflection of an emergent contradiction *within* the knowledge sector, as the new antithesis to the knowledge sector's technism, as embodying a counteremphasis upon people, upon "creative disorder," upon the nonquantifiable, the subjective, and the qualitative. Increasingly, this contradiction between objective technism and subjective anarchism defines the key ideological polarity of our time.

The intimate relationship between the knowledge sector and the new opposition is also apparent when we examine the social origins of the members of the opposition. For the core of the counterculture consists not of the children of the working class or of the lower middle class, but of the children of the knowledge sector. I have elsewhere insisted that the new opposition is not monolithic, and that we must distinguish its "political" from its "cultural" wing. Available evidence suggests that members of the political wing tend to be recruited disproportionately from among the children of professors, social workers, ministers, scientists, lawyers, and artists. These young men and women are the most concerned with institutional, social, and political change, and are also most likely to express solidarity with the basic values of their parents. Recruits to the cultural, expressive, aesthetic, or "hippie" wing of the counterculture, in contrast, tend to be drawn to a much greater degree from the families of media executives, entertainers, advertising men, merchandisers, scientific administrators, and personnel managers. These young men and women are more concerned with the expansion of consciousness, the development of alternative life styles, and the pursuit of communal ways of living. As a rule, they reject not only the conventional values and institutions of American society, but the values and life styles of their parents. The parents of the "politicals" are thus the more established members of the knowledge sector, while the parents of the "culturals" are the "newly arrived," whose membership in the knowledge sector is more tenuous and ambivalent. If we accept the analogy between knowledge in technological society and capital in industrial society, the parents of the political wing of the opposition are more often the holders of "old money," while the parents of the cultural wing are more often "*nouveaux riches.*"

A variety of factors within the knowledge sector clearly co-operate to generate its own opposition. Among these, for example, are the ambivalences of the parents of youthful dissenters toward the very knowledge sector in which they are employed. But no factor is of greater importance than the impact of higher education upon its recruits. Higher education bears a paradoxical relationship to the knowledge sector. On the one hand, higher education is essential for the maintenance and growth of the knowledge sector; but on the other hand, higher education provides many of the catalysts that push students to develop a critical consciousness which leads them to become part of the youthful opposition, and thus to oppose the dominant ideology of the knowledge sector.

To explore this paradox fully should again be the topic of a lengthy essay. Here I can only emphasize the obvious fact that technological societies require extremely high levels of knowledge and education of their members. "Knowledge societies" like our own must expose millions of young people to ideas, and in such a way as to encourage a critical analysis of these ideas. For only up to a point can higher education in a technological society be narrowly technical. By definition technical education attempts to teach the student a given body of knowledge, along with methods for applying that knowledge to the solution of problems. But when, as today, existing bodies of knowledge change rapidly, and when existing techniques for applying knowledge to the solution of problems become quickly obsolete, then a system of higher education that remains exclusively technical teaches obsolescence. To avoid this, higher education must encourage students to examine ideas critically, to take multiple points of view in looking at a particular problem, and to become familiar with contrasting ways of looking at the world. Higher education must therefore attempt to produce in students a "critical" approach to a particular area or subject matter.

But once a student has acquired the ability to approach one subject critically, it is hard to prevent him from applying the same critical orientation to other areas of life and society. Given the discovery that there are many distinct perspectives on "truth" in natural science, engineering, or literature, the student is likely to become a relativist in moral and ideological matters as well. Taught to challenge traditional beliefs in a narrow academic arena, at least some students will move quickly to challenge traditional moral codes in society. What can be thought of as a "critical consciousness"—a mind-set disposed to question, examine, probe, and challenge—tends to generalize from the area where it was first learned to other areas, and finally to all of life. The result is, increasingly, an across-the-board relativization of knowledge, a pervasive individualization of morality.

Precisely because a technological society cannot rely exclusively upon a narrowly technical system of higher education, it must foster a high degree of critical consciousness among its most educated products, and this critical consciousness is readily turned against the dominant assumptions and practices of the technological society. In a way not often acknowledged by educators but increasingly sensed by the general public, higher education today is "subversive" in that it is helping to create youths who challenge many of the basic assumptions of their society. Prolonged mass higher education is a major factor in "producing" millions of young dissenters from the social order that creates them.

This argument indicates that higher education is a key process whereby the contradictions of technological society are being generated. To be sure, higher education also has a socializing function, as pointed out by liberal theories, and for many of those who are exposed to it, socialization remains its primary result. Especially when higher education remains narrowly technical, and when students by previous inclination or present experience reject alternative views of the world and accept conventional definitions of morality, then education performs the function currently assigned it by most liberals and radicals, namely, the function of integrating the individual into society. But increasingly, higher education conspires with the mass media and the juxtaposition of cultures within modern societies to create millions of young men and women who are unwilling to accept the existing social order uncritically.

These notes on contemporary society are obviously incomplete, sketchy, and doubtless often wrong. They should indicate, however, my conviction that in analyzing contemporary technological societies, we do well to start from one of the central points emphasized by the "counter-revolutionary" theorists, namely the ascendancy of the knowledge sector. But an analysis of the meaning of this sector, I believe, leads not to the conclusion that it will inevitably triumph, but rather to the realization that the knowledge sector is riven through with basic contradictions, and that it is generating its own critics on a mass scale.

A New Politics

The connection between social theory and political action is exceedingly complex. No matter how refined, precise, and detailed a theory, it does not necessarily or automatically lead to a political agenda. Yet on the other hand, political action in the absence of social theory tends to be random, haphazard, trial-and-error, and empirical in the worst sense. Such is the case with much of what today passes as "radical politics": lacking any grounding in critical social theory, it tends to consist in *ad hoc* reactions of moral indignation, to lack any long-range direction, to fritter away the best energies of its members in internecine battles, or to adopt programs inspired by a pop-Marxist analysis of guerrilla warfare in some far-off ex-colonial nation.

The alternative is to try to think seriously about the basic issues and forces in contemporary industrialized societies. The arguments outlined above indicate my basic agreement with the counterrevolutionary theorists of youth that we are in a period of transition "between two ages," in Brzezinski's phrase, and that this transition is likely to be prolonged and difficult. This analysis also suggests, however, that the emergence of a new opposition is a sign of the surfacing of new contradictions within the dominant knowledge sector of technological society, and specifically, that youthful dissent is the expression of an historically revolutionary trend.

Several general political implications follow from this line of reasoning. For one, it follows that visions of immediate social or political revolution are based on a flawed social and historical analysis. The processes of sociohistorical change in which we are living are long-term, secular processes, which will take at least a generation to work themselves out. Those who have a serious interest in effecting meaningful social change must therefore be prepared to devote decades, and even a lifetime, to this enterprise; those whose energies flag after a week, a month, or a year will be of little help.

If we view the youthful opposition as reflecting emerging contradictions within the dominant knowledge sector of technological societies, then we would be wrong to ally ourselves politically with either the "value-free" technism that I have defined as thesis in this conflict, or with the subjective anarchism that I have defined as the antithesis. In the long run, what will be called for will be a synthesis of technism with anarchism, of "scientific objectivity" with the romantic expressiveness of the counterculture. It would therefore be a political mistake to embrace unreservedly the future of either the systems analyst or of the tribal communard. Instead we should work toward a future that could bring together the enormous power placed in man's hands by his technology and the vision of human liberation proclaimed by the counterculture. A politics that aligns itself with either the thesis or the antithesis will be a politics that settles for too little.

Another corollary of the views outlined here concerns the need to support a particular kind of higher education. Those who bitterly oppose the new opposition are already eager to limit higher education to technical education, eliminating or de-emphasizing its critical component. This strategy, if successful, could well reduce the numbers of those who possess that critical consciousness which seems vital for membership in the new opposition. It is therefore important for all who sympathize with the opposition to seek to extend higher education that is truly critical. The current radical attack upon higher education is, I think, misguided when it fails to discriminate between technical and critical education. Higher education in the broad sense not only has been but should continue to be the nursery for the new opposition. And the possibility that the new opposition might eventually generate enough political power to create major social changes depends in large part on the continuing creation, through education, of an ever-larger minority (and eventually even a majority) who share the basic orientations of that opposition. This process will take, at the very least, a generation. But it will not occur at all unless higher education as critical education is nurtured.

It also follows from these comments that those who today argue that the working class in the highly industrialized nations retains its revolutionary potential are incorrect. If we insist that the dialectic of social change did not cease with Marx's death, then it makes theoretical sense that groups like the working class, which once were revolutionary, might have become largely counterrevolutionary. Empirical evidence supports this proposition: the new "revolutionary class" appears to be a subsector of the knowledge sector, while the working class constitutes a conservative and at times a reactionary force. No political program today can or should neglect the real interests of the dwindling and often still exploited working class. But political programs based on the assumption that the working class in the industrialized nations can be exhorted to assume its "true" revolutionary role are built upon an historical mirage.

The proposition that social forces that begin as progressive generally end as reactionary obviously applies to the youthful opposition itself. As the youthful opposition ceases to be youthful, it must constantly guard against further evolution into a reactionary force. Already we can envision how this could occur: the collectivism of the counterculture could readily become an insistence upon the abrogation of individual rights; the tribalism of consciousness III could well portend a society of coercive group membership; the counterculture's opposition to technism could degenerate into a mindless hatred of reason, science, intellect, reflection, and accuracy. Today the youthful opposition is so weak politically that none of these dangers seems socially or politically important. But should the opposition gain in strength, its own reactionary potentials might well unfold.

In essence, then, a politics consistent with this agenda must be one that rejects both the "value-free" technism of corporate liberalism and the subjective anarchism of the counterculture, attempting instead the painful and slow work of creating a synthesis of the institutions of technological society with the culture of oppositional youth. That synthesis must ultimately entail the creation of a culture where the concept of liberation is not merely a facile slogan, but a commitment to the hard work of creating institutions within which genuine human relatedness may be attained. That synthesis must attempt to combine new-culture participation with old-culture competence, consciousness III enthusiasm with consciousness II professionalism—and all of this in ways that have hardly begun to be imagined, much less tried. It must involve an effort to turn modern technology around so that it facilitates man's liberation instead of encouraging his manipulation, so that it makes wars less possible rather than more likely, so that it helps men understand each other rather than oppose one another.

It is easy to call for a synthesis in general terms; it will be difficult to achieve it in practice. Nor do I believe that such a political synthesis is inevitable or even highly probable. We are indeed at an historical juncture, a turning point, a cultural and institutional crisis. And the youth revolt, the counterculture, the new opposition—these define one pole, one catalyst, one ingredient in that crisis. But history is not necessarily on the side of progress, synthesis, or the good. What happens in the next decades will depend not upon blind institutional and cultural forces, but upon the intelligence, good will, and hard work of countless individual men and women. It is possible today to begin to imagine a society far better than any society men have known—a society where technology serves man, where abundance makes possible higher levels of human development, where men and women attain new freedom not only from hunger, injustice, and tyranny, but from the inner coercions of greed, power-lust, and envy. The political agenda should be to move toward these goals, and to do so even in the absence of certainty that history is on our side.

Acknowledgments

THE accumulated personal and intellectual debts of more than a decade obviously cannot be adequately enumerated in a few pages. But some of my major gratitudes to others should be at least briefly acknowledged here.

Over the years, my research has been supported by a variety of sources, including the Laboratory for Human Relations at Harvard, the National Institute of Mental Health, the Foundations Fund for Research in Psychiatry, and, currently, the Ford Foundation. The most substantial assistance, however, has come from Mrs. Alice Treat Altvater, Mrs. Mary Damian Dixon, and Mrs. Sylvia Wishingrad Rifkin, who have skillfully typed countless drafts of each of these chapters, brewed endless cups of coffee, and improved the grammar, spelling, style, and substance of these essays.

Even more important has been the intellectual and personal stimulation that has come from working closely with a variety of extraordinary teachers, colleagues, and friends, including Henry A. Murray, David Riesman, Erik H. Erikson, Robert Jay Lifton, Robert Coles, Theodore Lidz, Stephen Fleck, John Demos, Richard Almond, Michael Lerner, and Mark Gerzon, among others. The Group for Psychohistorical Studies has provided a continuing assembly of personal and intellectual kinsmen struggling with comparable problems of method and theory. More recently, the Carnegie Commission on Higher Education has helped me complement my usual worm's-eye view of individual students with a more Olympian perspective on the problems of American higher education.

Central to work like mine has been the opportunity to conduct a continuing dialogue over the years with a great variety and number of students. These students remain nameless here, but it is no exaggeration to say that what I have learned about youth and dissent, I have learned from them. So, too, I think that whatever balance of judgment I have retained vis-à-vis youth comes largely from daily contact with young men and women who are neither saviors nor demons, but for the most part simply open, troubled, searching, generous, and thoughtful people.

Ellen Uviller Keniston has played an unusually large role in my work.

Not only has she provided the usual wifely tolerance and support for my efforts, but her perceptiveness, sensitivity, and intelligence have made her a valued if largely unacknowledged collaborator in almost everything I have done. I thank her especially.

These essays were originally published in the following places:

"Youth as a Stage of Life," *The American Scholar* (as "Youth: A 'New Stage' of Life"), Fall, 1970, 39:4, 631–54.

"The Decline of Utopia," *The American Scholar* (as "Alienation and the Decline of Utopia"), Spring, 1960, 29:1–40.

"The Speed-up of Change," *Daedalus* (as "Social Change and Youth in America"), Winter, 1962, 91:145–71.

"The Political Revival," *The American Scholar* (as "American Students and the 'Political Revival' "), Winter, 1963, 32:40–64.

"Faces in the Lecture Room," *The Contemporary University: U.S.A.*, Robert S. Morison, ed. Boston, Houghton Mifflin, 1966, 315–45, from the Daedalus Library, Vol. 6.

"The University as Critic," *Whose Goals for American Higher Education?* (as "Responsibility for Criticism and Social Change"), Charles G. Dobbins and Calvin B. T. Lee, eds. Washington, D.C., American Council on Education, 1968, 145–63.

"The Sources of Student Dissent," *The Journal of Social Issues*, July, 1967, 23: 108–37.

"The Alienated: Rejection of Conventional Adulthood," *The Self in Social Interaction* (as "Psychology of Alienated Students"), Chad Gordon and Kenneth Gergen, eds. New York, John Wiley & Sons, 1968, 1:405–15.

"Dropouts: Development through Discontinuity," *Psychiatry* (as "Psychosocial Issues in Talented College Dropouts"), with Stephen J. Hirsch, February, 1970, 33:1, 1–20.

"Radicals: Renewal of the Tradition," *Journal of American College Health Association* (as "Why Students Become Radicals"), December, 1968, 17:2, 107–18.

"Drug Users: Heads and Seekers," *The American Scholar* (as "Heads and Seekers: Drugs on Campus, Counter-Cultures and American Society"), Winter, 1968–69, 38:97–112.

"Idealists: The Perils of Principle," *American Journal of Orthopsychiatry* (as "Student Activism, Moral Development and Morality"), July, 1970, 40:4, 577–92.

"Radicals Revisited: Some Second Thoughts," *Change* (as "Notes on Young Radicals"), November–December, 1969, 25–33.

"Youth, Change and Violence," *The American Scholar*, Spring, 1968, 37:227–45.

"You Have to Grow Up in Scarsdale," *The New York Times Magazine* (as "You Have to Grow Up in Scarsdale to Know How Bad Things Really Are"), April 27, 1969.

"What's Bugging the Students?" *Educational Record,* Spring, 1970, 51:2, 116–29.

"Vulnerabilities of the Counterculture," *Life* magazine (as "Counter Culture: Cop-out . . . Or Wave of the Future?"), November 7, 1969.

"Scenarios of Confrontation," *The New York Review of Books* (as "Harvard on My Mind"), September 24, 1970.

"The Unholy Alliance," *The New York Times Magazine* (as "The Unholy Alliance against the Campus"), with Michael Lerner, November 8, 1970.

"Revolution or Counterrevolution?" *Social Policy*, July, 1971.